# Community Care Assessments:
# A Practical Legal Framework

*Second Edition*

Richard Gordon, QC
and
Nicola Mackintosh

**LAW & TAX**

© Richard Gordon (Chapters 1, 3 to 10 and 13) 1996
© Nicola Mackintosh (Chapters 2, 11, 12, 14, 15, Appendix 1 and selection
of Materials) 1996
© The authors  joint copyright on the Case Study  1996
ISBN 0752 00222 8

*Published by*
FT Law & Tax
21–27 Lamb's Conduit Street
London WC1N 3NJ

A Division of Pearson Professional Limited

*Associated offices*
Australia, Belgium, Canada, Hong Kong, India, Japan, Luxembourg,
Singapore, Spain, USA

First published 1993
Second edition 1996

A CIP catalogue record for this book is available from the British Library.

Printed in Great Britain by Hartnolls

# Contents

## Materials

## Materials 1: Statutory Material

## Materials 2: Relevant Orders, Directions and Regulations

## Materials 3: General Guidance

## Materials 4: Specific Guidance

**Materials 5: Executive Letters on Implementation**

## Appendices

### Appendices 1: Checklist and Guides

### Appendices 2: Judicial Review Case Study

# Foreword to the
# First Edition

The new regime for community care offers a range of opportunities and a range of pitfalls. Its fundamental characteristic is that it is a legal regime, containing within it a series of duties, discretions and judgment calls, but bounded and shaped by law. The growth and sophistication of modern public law, through the processes of judicial review, now mean that a statutory regime cannot be understood simply by reading the statute: the common law made by the judges can be called in to investigate the fairness and legal propriety of what local and central government do as they seek to implement legislation.

It would be a great pity if the presence of legal controls were to lead to defensive and opaque decision-making, and there is no reason why it should. Reasoned decisions conscientiously taken in conformity with the law will not only avoid the time- and resource-consuming ordeal of judicial review; they will be better and fairer decisions.

Richard Gordon's book is thus not primarily a battle plan for lawyers, though it will certainly enable lawyers to get a sound grasp of the legislation and to advise clients about their entitlements. It is a guide to sound decision-making. The principles of fairness and legality which the law attaches to decision-making powers, especially those which touch people's most basic needs, are not an obstacle course designed to trip the unwary. But they do require knowledge, information, advice and forethought, and none of these comes easily in relation to a scheme as innovative and as complex as that which came into force on 1 April 1993.

By enabling administrators and decision-makers to do their sensitive jobs within the law, then this book will primarily contribute to sound public administration and through it to responsive community care for some of the neediest people. But secondly, by furnishing lawyers with the information they need to assure respect for people's entitlement to fair and lawful decision-making, it will provide the back-up without which rights are fruitless and obligations hollow. Properly understood, the two functions are complementary, not antagonistic, and it is the strength of Richard Gordon's work on the legislation that it serves both functions equally. His own high standing as a specialist writer, adviser and advocate in the field of public law, and especially in the area of social services, makes this an authoritative and dependable book, an aid for the needy and a significant contribution to government within the law.

Stephen Sedley

# Preface

The second edition of this work has necessitated both by the increasing amount of Government Guidance in relation to community care and also by developing case law which has laid down important new principles.

Since the last edition the *Gloucestershire* cases have clarified the all-important relationship between lack of financial resources and the duty to make service provision where a statute lays down an absolute statutory duty. Recent decisions, albeit at first instance, have highlighted the significance of 'guidance' issued under the Local Authority Social Services Act 1970, and there have been decisions confirming the liberal trend to *locus standi* of pressure groups to bring judicial review in the field of community care assessment.

There has also been important new legislation including the Carers (Recognition and Services) Act 1995 which is included in this new edition. The Disability Discrimination Act 1995 has only tangential relevance to the community care structure and is therefore not included. However, issues may arise under that Act in relation to discriminatory provision of services.

Because of the fast-moving nature of the subject and its likely future development this new edition is co-authored. Responsibility for our respective contributions has been divided although we have read and approved each other's work. Chapters 2, 11, 12, 14 and 15 have been written by Nicola Mackintosh, and she has also selected the voluminous statutory and guidance material as well as revising the Practitioner Checklist included in the first edition. Richard Gordon QC has written and revised Chapters 1 and 3, 4, 5, 6, 7, 8, 9, 10 and 13. The Case Study has been produced jointly.

There are, for the first time, chapters on the increasingly important topics of hospital discharge, NHS and social services overlap and on charging for non-residential community care services. Additionally, this edition includes all up-to-date relevant Government Guidance and other legislative material. The revised chapters deal with all the new case law, much of which is unreported.

As with the first edition the aim has been to set out all salient features of the community care assessment and service provision regime in a form which neither simplifies nor renders it opaque. Every effort has been made to ensure that the book is helpful both to those representing the interests of service users and local authorities alike. Our hope is that a wider under-standing of the essential legal framework of community care will reduce lit-igation and increase the prospect of more effective service provision.

The law is stated as at 1 September 1996.

Richard Gordon QC                                    Nicola Mackintosh
39 Essex Street                                          *TV Edwards*
London WC2R 3AT

1 November 1996

# Table of Cases

# Table of Statutes

# Table of Statutory Instruments

# Part 1

## Introduction

Chapter 1

# Community Care Assessments: An Overview

## 1.1 Introduction

This book deals, primarily, with community care assessment and service provision decisions under the National Health Service and Community Care Act 1990 after the new system introduced as from 1 April 1993, although other forms of statutory assessment, for example, under the Carers (Recognition and Services) Act 1995, are also considered. It is directed both towards the way in which such decisions should be made, and the scope for challenge if they are reached unlawfully. The principal means of challenge will be by judicial review but other forms of redress, including the statutory complaints machinery, will also be considered.

## 1.2 Community care

The philosophy of community care as expressed in the Government White Paper, *Caring for People* (Cmnd 849), 'means providing the right level of intervention and support to enable people to achieve maximum independence and control over their own lives.'

From 1 April 1993, when the relevant sections of the National Health Service and Community Care Act 1990 (most notably, s 47) came into force, responsibility lies on local authorities for arranging community care for vulnerable groups, including the mentally ill.

The new system places financial control directly in the hands of the purchasing arms of social services' departments across the country. It is the local authority's social services committee (see the Local Authority Social Services Act 1970, s 2, Sched 1) that will, as the resource holder, assess needs and make a decision on the nature of any community care services (as defined by s 46(3): see 1.5, below) to be provided.

## 1.3 The assessment and service provision regime

The general regime for assessing need for community care services is contained in s 47 of the National Health Service and Community Care Act 1990.

Section 47(1) places an individual duty on a local authority, where it appears to it that any person for whom it may provide or arrange for the provision of community care services may be in need of any such services to:

(1) carry out an assessment of his needs for these services (the assessment decision); and

(2) having regard to the results of such assessment then decide whether his needs call for the provision by it of any such services (the services provision decision).

The duties of assessing need and determining any service provision are, conceptually, separate although the decisions will, in practice, often be made together. It is important to note, however, that the factors affecting assessment of need do not necessarily dictate that an authority must decide to provide services commensurate with such need (see Chapters 2 to 4).

There is a qualification to the above duties which is set out in ss 47(5) and 47(6) of the 1990 Act.

Where, in the opinion of the authority, the condition of a person is such that community care services are required as a matter of urgency then such services may be temporarily provided without carrying out a prior assessment of need (s 47(5)). However, as soon as practicable thereafter an assessment of needs is required to be made in accordance with the general s 47 regime (s 47(6)).

There is no provision in the 1990 Act prescribing how s 47 assessments are to be carried out. However, s 47(4) provides that the Secretary of State may give directions as to the manner in which an assessment is to be carried out. In the absence of such directions (no directions have yet been issued), the assessment 'shall be carried out in such manner and take such form as the local authority consider appropriate' (s 47(4)).

Services under the Chronically Sick and Disabled Persons Act 1970 may fall outside the definition of community care services (see 2.3). There is, none the less, a distinct assessment regime for need for such services which is contained in the Disabled Persons (Services, Consultation and Representation) Act 1986 which will continue after 1 April 1993 (see ss 47(2), 47(7) and 47(8) of the 1990 Act). The statutory assessment procedure for disabled persons may, in any event, prove a helpful model of comparison for determining how some assessments should be conducted under the 1990 Act.

## 1.4  Complaints machinery

Section 50(1) of the National Health Service and Community Care Act 1990 inserts s 7B after s 7 of the Local Authority Social Services Act 1970. This enables the Secretary of State to order local authorities to establish a procedure for considering representations (including complaints) in relation to the discharge of, or any failure to discharge, any of their social services functions in respect of a 'qualifying individual'. Such individual is, by s 50(2), defined as a person whom the authority has a power or duty to provide, or to secure the provision of, a service to him and whose need or possible need for such service has (by whatever means) come to the attention of the authority.

An order has been made, and directions given, requiring the establishment of a specific complaints procedure (see Chapter 8) with a rigid timetable for implementation. Often, though not invariably, an applicant disappointed by an assessment or service provision decision will be required to utilise an authority's complaints procedure prior to seeking judicial review (see Appendix 1, Practitioner Checklist). The legality and fairness of an authority's complaints regime is itself subject to judicial review.

## 1.5  Community care services

By s 46(3) of the National Health Service and Community Care Act 1990 the expression 'community care services' is defined as services which a local authority may provide or arrange to be provided under any of the following provisions:

(1) Part III of the National Assistance Act 1948 (provision of accommodation and welfare services for blind, deaf, dumb, mentally disordered and other disabled persons). (Section 2 of the Chronically Sick and Disabled Persons Act 1970 is part of the exercise of functions under s 29 of the National Assistance Act 1948 (and in Part III thereof).) For that reason it has often been assumed that it constitutes a 'community care service' within the meaning of s 46(3) of the 1990 Act. This may not, in fact, be so. The arguments are considered in Chapter 2.

(2) Section 45 of the Health Services and Public Health Act 1968 (promotion of the welfare of old people).

(3) Section 21 of and Sched 8 to the National Health Service Act 1977 (non-residential care of mothers and young children, prevention, care and after-care, home-help and laundry facilities).

(4) Section 117 of the Mental Health Act 1983 (after-care for those persons who have ceased to be detained in hospital and then leave hospital).

The provision of services under s 2 of the Chronically Sick and Disabled Persons Act 1970 and after-care services under s 117 of the Mental Health Act 1983 appear to be individual statutory duties rather than target duties or powers. Ostensibly, nothing in the National Health Service and Community Care Act 1990 operates to convert such duties to powers but the interrelationship between a duty to provide services and the discretionary service provision regime under the 1990 Act is not wholly clear (see 2.3 and 2.6, where this aspect is analysed).

## 1.6  Directions and guidance

An authority's exercise of its social services functions in respect of assessment, service provision and complaints procedures is subject to guidance and directions issued by the Secretary of State.

Section 7 of the Local Authority Social Services Act 1970 provides that:

> Local authorities shall, in the exercise of their social services functions, includ-
> ing the exercise of any discretion . . . act under the general guidance of the
> Secretary of State.

'Social services functions' include community care assessments and service provision decisions as well as the exercise of functions under the various social welfare enactments including Part III of the Children Act 1989 and those comprising 'community care services', and (if different) s 2 of the Chronically Sick and Disabled Persons Act 1970 (see Local Authority Social Services Act 1970, ss 2, 3, 15(2) and Sched 1).

The phrase 'act under the general guidance' is to be contrasted with ss 7A, 7B, 7D and 7E of the Local Authority Social Services Act 1970, as inserted by s 50 of the National Health Service and Community Care Act 1990 (see Materials 1). These latter sections are concerned with directions given by the Secretary of State which:

(1)  shall be given in writing (s 7A);
(2)  may be given to a particular authority or class of authority or to authorities generally (s 7A);
(3)  must be complied with by the authority (ss 7B(3), 7D(3)).

Although less than clearly expressed, the distinction between statutory guidance (ie guidance issued under s 7 of the 1970 Act) and directions appears to be that the former must be taken into consideration, and followed without substantial deviation, by an authority when making assessment, service provision or complaints decisions. Directions must, however, be strictly complied with.

Very little guidance has been issued under s 7 of the Local Authority Social Services Act 1970. A notable exception is the document entitled *Policy Guidance: Community Care in the Next Decade and Beyond* (HMSO, 1990) which has, unequivocally, been issued under statute (see also *Charging for Residential Accommodation Guide* (CRAG)) at Chapter 14, guidance to the Children Act 1989 and the *Policy Guidance* to the Carers (Recognition and Services) Act 1995 (see Materials 4 (M)). Most guidance, such as *The Managers' Guide* or *The Practitioners' Guide* is non-statutory, albeit containing helpful information as to good practice.

The legal effect of the *Policy Guidance* and other guidance has recently been considered by Sedley J, at first instance, in *R v Islington LBC, ex p Rixon* (1996) *The Times*, 17 April. That case involved alleged failure by Islington to make provision according to law for the social, recreational and educational needs of Jonathan Rixon, a disabled service user. Islington argued that the *Policy Guidance* was no more than one of the many factors to which the local authority should have regard when making assessment and service provision decisions. Sedley J, however, rejected this.

Sedley J held that the words 'shall act under' in s 7(1) of the 1970 Act were material and that:

. . . Parliament by s 7(1) has required local authorities to follow the path charted by the Secretary of State's guidance, with liberty to deviate from it where the local authority judges on admissible grounds that there is good reason to do so, but without freedom to take a substantially different course.

He also held that circulars and other non-statutory guidance not issued under s 7(1) must, none the less, be 'conscientiously taken into account' by a local authority social services department. The 'occasional lacuna' would not furnish evidence of disregard but a 'series of lacunae' would. Inferential in the judgment is the proposition that a local authority should provide some reasoning so as to show that it has considered even non-statutory guidance.

No precise formal content is prescribed by statute in respect of directions. However, in practice, directions made under s 7B or 7D of the Local Authority Social Services Act 1970 specify their status and the section under which they are made on their face. Similarly guidance, whether in the form of circulars, letters or other documentation, is usually specific as to its statutory status.

Guidance or directions issued by the Secretary of State which are unlawful are susceptible to judicial review (see, eg: *Laker Airways Ltd v Department of Trade* [1977] QB 643; *R v Secretary of State for Social Services, ex p Lewisham (etc) LBC* (1980) *The Times*, 26 February).

## 1.7  Core documents

The following general guidance (material parts of some of which are reproduced in Materials 3) is particularly relevant to the processes of assessment, service provision and adjudication of complaints:

- The Government White Paper *Caring for People*, Cmnd. 849 ('the Government White Paper').
- *Community Care in the Next Decade and Beyond: Policy Guidance* ('*Policy Guidance*').
- *Care Management and Assessment: Managers' Guide* ('*Managers' Guide*').
- *Care Management and Assessment: Practitioners' Guide* ('*Practitioners' Guide*').
- *Getting the Message across: A Guide to Developing and Communicating Policies, Principles and Procedures on Assessment* ('*Getting the message across*').
- *The Right to Complain: Practice Guidance on Complaints Procedures in Social Services Departments* ('*Right to Complain*').
- *Hospital Discharge Workbook* issued by the Department of Health in 1994.

Apart from the general guidance itself there are numerous Department of Health guidance letters on implementation. These are set out in Materials 5.

Important orders and directions (material parts of which are repro-
duced at Materials 2), to date are:
- Local Authority Social Services (Complaints Procedure) Order
  1990 (SI No 2244).
- National Assistance Act 1948 (Choice of Accommodation)
  Directions 1992, LAC(92)27.
- Complaints Procedure Directions 1990 (Appendix to *Policy
  Guidance*).

There is, finally, a plethora of guidance specific to particular community
care services, the most important of which is contained in Materials 4.

Sometimes guidance in the form of a circular (see, eg, the Laming letter
which was cancelled on 31 March 1994) bears a cancellation date on its
face. The legal effect of cancellation is not, it is submitted, to nullify the
content of the circular which still remains evidence of good practice and
which is still required to be taken into account by social services in their
assessment and service provision decision-making process. In *R v
Gloucestershire CC, ex p Barry* (1996) *The Times*, 12 July, for example, all
the judgments in the Court of Appeal referred to the Laming letter.

## 1.8 Treatment

This book contains an introductory section (Chapters 1 and 2) and four
further parts designed to provide a systematic and practical approach to the
community care legislation.

Part 2 deals with the following substantive questions relating to the pro-
cesses of assessment and service provision:
- How should a local authority determine entitlement to assessment?
  (Chapter 3.)
- How should the authority assess need? (Chapter 4.)
- How should the authority determine service provision? (Chapter 5.)

Part 3 covers procedural fairness in respect of:
- Assessment and service provision decisions (Chapter 6).
- Communication of assessment and service provision decisions
  (Chapter 7).

Part 4 is concerned with remedies in respect of a local authority's default
in the exercise of its functions in relation to assessment and/or service pro-
vision and covers:
- Complaints procedures (Chapter 8).
- Judicial review (Chapter 9).
- The Secretary of State's default powers (Chapter 10).
- The Local Government Ombudsman (Chapter 11).
- The Local Government Monitoring Officer (Chapter 12).
- Private law actions for damages (Chapter 13).

Part 5 is a miscellaneous section containing a chapter on the financial
aspect of assessment (Chapter 14), and a chapter on the increasingly

important topic of hospital discharge and the general overlap between health service and social service functions (Chapter 15).

Finally the Materials section (1 to 5) contains statutory material and documentation relevant to assessment, service provision and complaints procedures in the form of guidance, orders, circulars and directions. There are also practical Appendices including a detailed Practitioner Checklist, Complaints Procedure Guide and Judicial Review Checklist (Appendix 1), and an Appendix (Appendix 2) containing precedents including an imaginary judicial review case study, and specimen letters and decisions relating to the processes already considered.

Chapter 2

# Community Care Assessments: Powers and Duties

## 2.1 Introduction

It has already been seen that the National Health Service and Community Care Act 1990 defines community care services as being those services that a local authority is empowered or under a duty to provide under four enactments. Due to the wide scope of services that a local authority may provide, only the most common services will be referred to in this chapter. Extracts of the relevant statutes and circulars are reproduced (see Materials).

In addition the obligation on an authority to reach a decision regarding a disabled person's need for services under s 2 of the Chronically Sick and Disabled Persons Act 1970 renders it necessary to examine the scope of such services, whether or not they constitute a 'community care service' (see, 2.3 below) and the relationship between the powers and duties to provide the services themselves.

## 2.2 National Assistance Act 1948, s 21

Section 21 of the National Assistance Act 1948 empowers local authorities to provide accommodation for persons aged 18 or over who by reason of age, illness, disability or any other circumstances are in need of care and attention not otherwise available to them.

However, the power to provide such accommodation is converted to a duty by virtue of LAC(93)10, *Approvals and Directions for Arrangements from 1 April 1993 made under sections 21 and 29 of the National Assistance Act 1948* (see Materials 4(B)). The circular also effectively transfers any power to provide accommodation under the National Health Service Act 1977 to s 21 of the 1948 Act.

The circular contains a direction that local authorities are to make arrangements to provide accommodation under s 21 in relation to persons who are 'ordinarily resident' in their area.

A direction is also given that local authorities are to make arrangements to provide temporary accommodation for persons who are in urgent need and, in particular, authorities are to make arrangements to provide accommodation for persons who are, or have been, suffering from mental disorder, or for the purposes of preventing mental disorder. This would include persons discharged from psychiatric hospital where those persons are ordinarily resident in another area.

The circular particularly emphasises approvals for arranging accommodation for people who are drug or alcohol dependent. Further guidance regarding assessments and provision for such persons has been issued under LAC(93)2 (reproduced at Materials 4(F)). The guidance does not have the status of a direction but should be taken into account by authorities.

The circular on the meaning of 'ordinarily resident' within a variety of contexts is reproduced (see Materials 4(J)).

The term 'make arrangements to provide' is intended within the circular to refer to the ability of the authority to contract with, for example, a voluntary/independent organisation or local housing authority in order to provide the service. If the contracted provider cannot provide or arrange for the provision of the service, however, the authority will not have discharged its obligation.

Accommodation under this section has been recognised historically as being limited to residential care homes for the elderly. However, it is clear from s 21(2) that authorities are expected to provide different types of accommodation for all categories of persons to whom the section may apply. Thus the range of accommodation to be provided is very wide, from basic housing or limited warden/alarm supported accommodation, to residential care homes with 24-hour support. An authority which does not make arrangements for wide provision, therefore, may be open to challenge.

The phrase 'accommodation' in s 21 is not defined, but the authors' view is that, taking into account the fact that under s 21(5) an authority is not obliged to provide ancillary services (eg support services connected with the accommodation where this is unnecessary), the definition of 'accommodation' is necessarily wide, since otherwise the authority's discretion as to restriction of ancillary services would be otiose.

The extent of a local authority social services department's duty to provide accommodation under s 21 was the subject of judicial review proceedings brought by asylum seekers who had been excluded from entitlement to housing under the Housing Act 1985 and who were, as a result of recent legislation, unable to claim welfare benefits (*R v London Borough of Hammersmith et al, ex p M, P, A and X* (1996) *The Times*, 10 October). Collins J held that the applicants, although not necessarily disabled, were 'persons in need of care and attention', and as such, having no alternative access to accommodation, were owed a duty under s 21 by the authority. The fact that the applicants did not necessarily require support services ancillary to the accommodation did not entitle the authority to conclude that the duty under s 21 did not apply.

## 2.3  National Assistance Act 1948, s 29 and Chronically Sick and Disabled Persons Act 1970, s 2

**(1)  National Assistance Act, s 29**

This section empowers local authorities to make arrangements for promoting the welfare of disabled persons over the age of 18. For some services, the power is converted to a duty by virtue of directions given under LAC(93)10.

'Disabled persons' are defined as those who are 'blind, deaf or dumb or suffer from a mental disorder of any description and other persons who are substantially and permanently handicapped by illness, injury, congenital deformities or other disabilities as may be prescribed.'

Local authorities are under a general obligation to provide a social work service (whether at home or elsewhere), facilities for social rehabilitation (including overcoming difficulties with mobility or communication), and facilities for social, occupational, recreational and cultural activities. A register must also be kept of persons to whom s 29 relates.

The Secretary of State has approved the making of arrangements for holiday homes, subsidised or free travel and payments towards warden schemes (whether in authority-run or private accommodation). Authorities may make any arrangements for the provision of welfare services for people to whom s 29 applies.

The section, by virtue of the content of the Approvals, extends not only to those 'ordinarily resident' but to any other person (*R v Royal County of Berkshire, ex p Parker* (1996) *The Times*, 15 August).

**(2)  Chronically Sick and Disabled Persons Act 1970, s 2**

The assessment regime under s 47 of the 1990 Act provides that if, during the course of an assessment of need under s 47(1)(*a*), it appears to the local authority that the person is disabled, the authority must reach a decision as to the services he requires under s 4 of the Disabled Persons (Services, Consultation and Representation) Act 1986 without request (s 47(2)).

Section 4 of the 1986 Act places an obligation on the authority to decide whether the needs of the disabled person call for the provision of any services in accordance with s 2(1) of the Chronically Sick and Disabled Persons Act 1970.

The level of service provision under s 2 will normally be crucial as to whether a person is able to remain in their own home with a reasonable quality of life, or has to move to residential accommodation. For this reason, and due to the high level of expenditure incurred by local authorities, the interrelation between the duty under s 2 and resources has been the subject of considerable debate.

Section 2(1) of the 1970 Act states materially:

Where a local authority having functions under section 29 of the National Assistance Act 1948 are satisfied in the case of any person to whom that section applies who is ordinarily resident in their area that it is necessary in order to meet the needs of that person for that authority to make arrangements for all or any of the following matters . . . [list of services] . . . then, subject to the provisions of section 7(1) of the Local Authority Social Services Act 1970 (which requires local authorities in the exercise of certain functions, including functions under the said section 29, to act under the general guidance of the Secretary of State) it shall be the duty of that authority to make those arrangements in exercise of their functions under the said section 29.

The services under s 2 are comprehensive, relating to adaptations to the home, practical assistance in the home, holidays, transport in order to use s 29 services and other similar services, meals and telephones. The full text is set out at Materials 1(G).

The nature of the duty under s 2 was considered in detail by the courts in *R v Gloucestershire County Council, ex p Barry* (1996) *The Times*, 12 July. The case is discussed in more detail in Chapter 5. The Court of Appeal held that once a person has been assessed as being 'in need' of s 2 services, such services must be provided, without regard to the availability of resources. The duty is owed to an individual, rather than a target population, and 'need' is to be given its usual everyday meaning.

In considering the case at first instance, the Divisional Court held that although the s 2 duty applies to functions under s 29 of the National Assistance Act 1948, the authority for the provision of s 2 services is s 2 itself. Therefore, the duty under s 2, whilst related to s 29 functions, stands in its own right and may be actionable if breached. This may give rise to issues regarding authorities' ability to charge for such services, which is discussed further in Chapter 14.

It is clear that once an assessment for need for s 2 services is carried out, and a need is established, an authority cannot seek to exercise its discretion to provide the services under s 47(1)(*b*) of the 1990 Act where another enactment merely empowers the authority to provide the same service. In such circumstances, the duty under s 2 'trumps' any power to provide the same service.

Local authorities must therefore first reach a decision regarding need for s 2 services before proceeding to a service provision decision regarding those other services which they are empowered or under a duty to provide. Although authorities are entitled to meet the assessed need in the most economical way (*Barry*), it is submitted that this will have major implications for authorities, especially when deciding on whether a package of care at home or in residential care (e.g. under s 21 of the 1948 Act) will be provided.

The fact that s 2 services are not specifically referred to in s 46(3) of the 1990 Act as being 'community care services', coupled with the comments by the Divisional Court in the *Barry* case lends support to the proposition that s 2 services are not community care services. Given that need for services under s 29 of the 1948 Act must be assessed under s 47(1)(*a*), and that assessment of need for s 2 services is separately included under s 47(2), this indicates that the argument is correct. However, the position is not entirely clear and the arguments are likely to be aired before the courts in future, specifically with regard to charging issues, given that s 17 of the Health and Social Services and Social Security Adjudication Act 1983 permits charges to be made in respect of 'community care services' only.

## 2.4   Health Services and Public Health Act 1968, s 45

Section 45 of the Health Services and Public Health Act 1968 empowers local authorities to provide services for the elderly in order to promote their welfare.

Paragraph 2 of Circular 19/71 states that its purpose is to:

> . . . enable authorities to make other approved arrangements for services to the elderly who are not substantially and permanently handicapped, and thus to promote the welfare of the elderly generally and so far as possible to prevent or postpone personal or social deterioration or breakdown . . .

It is clear that the circular empowers the authority to provide a wide range of services to a target population, rather than to any particular individual. However, the circular identifies particular groups for whom services, such as day centres, meals, transport, adaptations, home helps, social work support and warden services in accommodation should be provided.

Many of these services may also be provided under s 2 of the Chronically Sick and Disabled Persons Act 1970. However, if a person comes within the definition of 'disabled' under that Act, then the power to provide the service under the 1968 Act is 'trumped' by the duty under the 1970 Act. Even if a person does not come within the definition of 'disabled' their needs for the above services must none the less be assessed under s 47 of the 1990 Act, although there will be a discretion as to whether such services will be provided.

## 2.5   National Health Service Act 1977, s 21 and Sched 8

This section empowers local authorities to provide services for the care of mothers; prevention, care and aftercare; and home help and laundry facilities. However, under LAC(93)10 there is a target duty to provide certain services.

Schedule 8, para 2 approves the making of arrangements by authorities for the care of persons suffering from illness, and for their aftercare, and in particular for centres for training and occupation.

LAC(93)10 converts this power into a duty, specifically for persons who are suffering from, or who have suffered from, a mental disorder. The circular directs that authorities should make arrangements for:

(1) the provision of day centres, training centres for the training or occupation of such persons;

(2) the appointment of sufficient approved social workers (ASWs) for the purposes of the Mental Health Act 1983; and

(3) the provision of social work and related services to help in the identification, diagnosis, assessment and social treatment of mental disorder and to provide social work and social treatment of mental disorder; to provide social work and domiciliary support to people at home and elsewhere.

Therefore, if the authority does not provide such services as is adequate to respond to the need of the area, a challenge may be mounted.

Furthermore, the authority may provide other services, such as:

(1) meals at centres or elsewhere;

(2) remuneration for people at centres;

(3) social work support to prevent impairment in health of families, or to prevent breakdown;

(4) night-sitting services, recuperative holidays and facilities for social and recreational facilities.

In accordance with the 1990 Act, authorities should ensure that when an assessment is carried out under s 47, needs for the above services are assessed and a decision is reached.

Of course, if the authority only assesses for those services which it *does* provide in practice, rather than those services which it is empowered to provide, then it is open to challenge.

Schedule 8, para 3 places a duty on the local authority to provide home help services 'on such a scale as is adequate for the needs of their area or to arrange for the provision on such a scale' for:

> ... households where such help is required owing to the presence of—a person who is suffering from illness, lying in, an expectant mother, aged, handicapped as a result of having suffered from an illness or congenital deformity.

The above duty to provide a home help service (or to contract for its provision) for the needs of the area is a target duty. It could, however, be enforced by an individual if, as a result of inadequate provision, that individual was adversely affected. Note that the duty also applies to those who are in need due to illness, in addition to those persons considered to be 'disabled'.

## 2.6   Mental Health Act 1983, s 117

Under s 117 of the Mental Health Act 1983, a joint duty is placed on both the local social services department and the District Health Authority to provide, in co-operation with relevant voluntary agencies, aftercare services to an individual until such time as a joint agreement is reached between the authorities that the person is no longer in need of such services.

The duty applies to persons subject to detention under ss 3 and 37 of the Mental Health Act 1983, and to persons transferred from prison into the psychiatric hospital system under ss 47 and 48 of that Act.

The 'local social services authority' is the authority for the area in which the person is resident or to which he is sent on discharge by the hospital in which he was detained (s 117(3)).

The duty to an individual under s 117 is unique in the context of the community care framework, being jointly placed upon the local authority and the health authority. The overlap between the assessment structure under s 47 of the 1990 Act and the joint duty under s 117 is complex.

Except in rare cases, a person previously detained under s 3, 37, 47 or 48 of the 1983 Act may be in need of community care services on leaving hospital, and therefore the local authority's duty to assess and reach a service provision decision will be triggered under s 47 of the 1990 Act. However, the way that s 117(2) is phrased indicates that services must be provided based on the needs assessment itself, without recourse to the discretion to provide services under s 47(1)(b). Section 117 may therefore place an absolute duty upon both authorities to meet jointly assessed need, regardless of resources.

The duty is also unusual in that it places an individual duty on the health authority to jointly assess and provide services. Although under s 47(3) of the 1990 Act, where it appears to a local authority that a person may be in need of health services, the authority shall invite the health authority to participate in the assessment, s 117 places a higher obligation on the health authority to assess, and where needed, provide services.

The fact that services must continue to be provided by both authorities until a joint decision is taken that the person is no longer in need of such services, means that the duty does not expire through effluxion of time. The duty arguably continues indefinitely (ie until such joint decision is made). Presumably, monitoring of a person's need must take place before any joint decision is made that need has changed, or ceased to exist. A unilateral decision by either authority that services are no longer required will not discharge the duty.

Although there is a duty under Sched 8 to the National Health Service Act 1977 and LAC(93)10 (see above, 2.4) to provide services for persons suffering from mental disorder, s 117 is a duty to an individual, and may be enforced as such.

The case of *R v Ealing District Health Authority, ex p Fox* [1993] 3 All ER 170 established the principle that joint assessment by health and social services departments of a person's need for aftercare services must take place before the person leaves hospital, and therefore that the duty under s 47 applies to future need. This is strongly supported by the copious guidance on arrangements for people referred to the specialist psychiatric services (see Materials 4(E)).

Section 117(1) states that the duty to provide services arises when the person ceases to be detained and leaves hospital. It would be absurd if the duty only arose on the cessation of liability to detention, as this would exclude persons on trial leave, or those who are conditionally discharged. It is clear that the duty to provide services is triggered on the person leaving hospital, even if still liable to be detained or recalled.

The guidance and circulars published relating to arrangements on discharge apply to all people referred to the specialist psychiatric services, and not just those to whom the duty under s 117 applies. These would include voluntary patients, those in the community who may be in need of support, and patients detained under the shorter sections of the Mental Health Act 1983. Local authorities are under a duty to assess need and reach a decision regarding services for these persons within the usual s 47 structure, taking account of the guidance.

It is evident from the guidance that no person should leave hospital without adequate provision of services. However, lack of provision should not delay discharge, rather the services must be put in place to enable the person to return to the community. Decisions by clinical teams to discharge prior to adequate assessments and care packages being put in place may be actionable by way of judicial review, and local authorities may be forced to comply with their duties in such cases. The impact of the *Policy Guidance* to the 1990 Act on hospital discharge is discussed below in Chapter 15.

The *Advice Note on Discretionary Charges for Adult Social Services* makes it clear that services provided under s 117 may not be charged for. The fact that local authorities are not empowered under the Health and Social Services and Social Security Adjudications Act 1983 to charge for s 117 services means that the cost of such services, even accommodation, arguably must be borne by the local and health authority. (See further Chapter 15 on charging for services, and Materials 4(M)).

## 2.7   Conclusion

This chapter has illustrated the wide range of community care services that local authorities are empowered, or under a duty, to provide. The assessment regime under s 47 of the 1990 Act, coupled with the copious guidance to the various enactments, clearly shows that authorities must assess need for all services, regardless of whether they are actually provided by the authority in practice or not. Failure to assess on this basis will be unlawful.

## Part 2

# Assessments and Service Provision Determination

# Chapter 3

# Entitlement to Assessment

## 3.1 Criteria for entitlement

Entitlement to assessment, under s 47(1)(*a*) of the National Health Service and Community Care Act 1990 is conditioned by a person's apparent need for the provision of community care services that a local authority is empowered to provide or arrange for that individual. However, several questions arise from this ostensibly straightforward statement. They are these:

(1) What degree of need must be established so as to found a duty on the local authority to carry out an assessment?

(2) Must there be an application prior to any duty to assess?

(3) What degree of investigation is an authority required to undertake in order to determine entitlement to assessment?

(4) Will an authority be justified in refusing assessment where apparent need is only for those services which the authority does not or cannot provide?

(5) What circumstances justify judicial review of a failure or refusal to undertake a s 47(1)(*a*) assessment?

## 3.2 Apparent need

A careful reading of ss 47 and 50 of the National Health Service and Community Care Act 1990 suggests that a person's apparent need for community care services is only required to be a 'possible' need. It does not have to appear to be an urgent or pressing need or an actual need (cf the similar considerations under the Housing Act 1985, s 62 and the Education Act 1993, ss 167 and 168).

This appears from the following:

(1) the provision in s 47(1) of the 1990 Act making assessment contingent merely upon the appearance to a local authority that a person 'may' be in need of particular community care services;

(2) the omission, in that section, of any requirement that such apparent need must be urgent;

(3) the definition of a 'qualifying person' in s 50 of the 1990 Act entitling

a person, where the Secretary of State has established a complaints procedure (see Chapter 8), to make representations where:

(a) the authority has a power or duty to provide such services for him, and

(b) his need or 'possible' need for such services has come to the authority's attention: it would, clearly, be otiose to allow a person having merely a 'possible' need to embark on a complaints procedure if some higher threshold test were required for entitlement to assessment.

Contrary to this view, in *R v Mid Glamorgan CC, ex p Miles* (1994) *Legal Action*, January, p 21, the respondent local authority initially refused to assess a serving prisoner who sought a placement in a drug rehabilitation centre after release on parole. Mid Glamorgan social services contended that it was required to assess current rather than future needs and that the applicant could not establish a current need because he had not yet been released on parole. In the event the case was compromised in the applicant's favour without the substantive point being determined.

## 3.3  Must there be an application?

It is apparent that no application is required to be made by or on behalf of a person needing community care services. The *Policy Guidance* states, at para 3.29, that a carer may make an application for assessment but this is merely by way of clarification and does not introduce any restriction on the nature of the duty imposed upon the local authority under s 47(1)(*a*). In the case of disabled persons, s 47(2) of the 1990 Act clarifies that there is no need for any request for an assessment for services under s 2 of the Chronically Sick and Disabled Persons Act 1970 during the course of a s 47(1)(*a*) assessment as would, ordinarily, be required by s 4 of the Disabled Persons (Services, Consultation and Representation) Act 1986.

Not only is there no express requirement for an application for assessment contained in the National Health Service and Community Care Act 1990 itself (cf, eg, the Housing Act 1985 homelessness regime), but it would run counter to:

(1) the fact that assessment must take place once the authority finds an appearance of need (s 47(1)(*a*) of the 1990 Act);

(2) the fact that a person is entitled to invoke any designated complaints procedure if, *inter alia*, his need/possible need has 'by whatever means' come to the attention of the authority (see s 50 of the 1990 Act inserting s 7B into the Local Authority Social Services Act 1970): this expression is, undoubtedly, wide enough to extend beyond a specific application.

This was the *ratio* of *R v GloucestershireCC, ex p RADAR* (unreported, 21 December 1995). In that case Carnwath J held that a local authority did not discharge its duty to assess by sending out a letter to potentially affected persons, offering assessment and then assessing only those who replied. The judge specifically observed that the obligation to make an assessment for community care services does not depend upon a request but, rather, on the 'appearance' of need.

Although a duty to assess arises independent of any application, it is submitted that a local authority cannot compel a service user to accept assessment. Indeed, the *Practice Guidance* on the Carers (Recognition and Services) Act 1995 (para 11.2) contemplates that a user may refuse assessment under s 47 of the 1990 Act. If he does so a carer has, according to the *Practice Guidance*, no right to request a statutory assessment under the 1995 Act. It is, however, submitted that refusal by the service user to submit to an assessment does not relieve social services of the obligation to conduct the assessment, albeit without the user's direct participation (see 5.5).

### 3.4 Investigating entitlement to assessment

It is unclear whether a local authority may simply respond to situations where individual need is brought to its attention or whether there is some further obligation upon it to conduct investigations into potentially vulnerable groups so as to determine entitlement to assessment. The Laming letter (at para 5 see Materials 5) appears to assume the former without directly engaging the issue.

The fact that a complaints regime only affords standing to an individual whose need/possible need has 'come to the attention of the authority' (see s 50 of the National Health Service and Community Care Act 1990, and s 7B of the Local Authority Social Services Act 1970) does not immediately suggest that the authority is required to do more than act upon individual information received by it. If the position were otherwise the right to invoke the complaints machinery would, presumably, be phrased more widely.

In the case of disabled persons, however, local authority social services departments are required, by s 1 of the Chronically Sick and Disabled Persons Act 1970, to survey the need for services for people to whom s 29 of the National Assistance Act 1948 applies, and under LAC(93)10 to maintain a register of persons to whom s 29 applies. It is submitted, therefore, that all persons included in the register are entitled to an assessment under s 47(1)(*a*) of the 1990 Act without request.

### 3.5 Refusal of assessment

Many community care services are provided under a statutory power. May an authority, therefore, decline to assess on the basis that, even were an assessment to be undertaken, there could be no resulting obligation to provide such services?

The answer to this is to be found in the condition requiring assessment contained in the opening sentence of s 47(1) of the National Health Service and Community Care Act 1990. Assessment is required where it appears to the authority 'that any person for whom they may provide or arrange for the provision of community care services may be in need of any such services.'

Accordingly, the relevant criteria are not merely related to apparent need but also to the fact that a particular person is one for whom the authority is permitted to provide designated community care services in respect of those apparent needs.

The fact, therefore, that community care services are not physically available to the service user is not a factor entitling the local authority to refuse to undertake an assessment. In *R v Royal County of Berkshire, ex p Parker* (1996) *The Times*, 15 August, Laws J held that if Parliament had intended the s 47(1)(*a*) duty to be subject to a factual capacity in the authority itself to make provision within its existing arrangements, it could readily have so provided.

A related issue is whether, once assessment is undertaken, an authority must assess for services which it has decided not to provide or which it has no resources to provide. This is considered at 4.3.

In determining whether an assessment may validly be refused, it will accordingly always be important to identify the particular community care service in respect of which an apparent need is contended and the local authority's statutory powers in respect of such service.

## 3.6   Eligibility criteria

Many local authorities purport to lay down eligibility criteria as a threshold to need for assessment. It is, however submitted that this may be unlawful if it precludes any consideration of the individual case. Criteria which prevent actual assessment of need by virtue of a global definition of need can only, sensibly, operate as a fetter on discretion.

## 3.7   Judicial review of a refusal to assess

Judicial review will be potentially available (see, though, Chapter 9 at 9.2), where a local authority acts unlawfully, irrationally or unfairly in refusing to carry out an assessment.

In principle, and having regard to the above discussion, it is suggested that judicial review is likely to arise where an authority:

(1)   adopts an incorrect legal test as to the requisite degree of 'need' justifying assessment or an incorrect test as to the onus or standard of proof: given the wording of s 47(1) of the National Health Service and Community Care Act 1990 it is submitted that there cannot be any onus on an application to establish need or apparent need once the applicant's possible need is brought to the authority's attention; or

(2)   declines (or fails) to make an assessment irrationally in the face of possible need; or

(3) declines to make an assessment without investigation as to whether there is apparent need where such need is contended; or

(4) adopts an incorrect legal test as to its own power to provide or to arrange for the provision of particular community care services; or

(5) declines to make an assessment without affording any reasons for its decision (see *R v Civil Service Appeal Board, ex p Cunningham* [1991] 4 All ER 310, and the discussion at 7.6); or,

(6) fetters its discretion by applying eligibility criteria.

On the other hand it is suggested that judicial review will not be available:

(1) merely because an authority does not pursue an investigation into the need of potentially vulnerable groups (other than those groups which evince apparent need) such as those on the s 29 registers—see 3.4, above;

(2) where an authority declines to assess because it has no statutory power or duty in respect of particular services for which apparent need exists.

# Chapter 4

# Assessing Need

## 4.1 The duty to assess

Section 47(1)(*a*) of the National Health Service and Community Care Act 1990 imposes a duty on a local authority to carry out an assessment of a person's needs for the provision of community care services in circumstances where:

(1) that authority is empowered to provide or arrange for the provision of community care services for that person; and

(2) it appears to that authority that such person may be in need of any such services.

The decision-making process in respect of an assessment must be undertaken lawfully, rationally and fairly. Failure to do so will render the assessment liable to being quashed in judicial review proceedings.

In analysing the scope of the assessment duty, once entitlement to assessment has been established (see Chapter 3), the following substantive issues on legality and rationality arise:

(1) Is the authority required to assess need for community care services which it does not provide, even though statutorily empowered to do so?

(2) Is the authority required to assess need in circumstances where it cannot provide community care services which it is empowered to provide due to lack of resources?

(3) Are resources relevant to the assessment duty?

(4) What is the 'need' that must be assessed?

(5) What enquiries must an authority make to determine need?

(6) Are an authority's assessment duties affected in respect of disabled persons under s 47(2) of the 1990 Act or carers under the Carers (Recognition and Services) Act 1995 or children under Part III of the Children Act 1989?

(7) Are the authority's duties qualified in any way by the possible involvement of other authorities (under s 47(3) of the 1990 Act) or agencies?

(8) Is the duty to assess a continuing one or does it cease upon an assessment decision?

Questions of procedural fairness involving the manner in which assessments should be conducted, the speed within which decisions should be communicated and whether reasons must be provided are separately considered (see Chapters 6 and 7).

## 4.2 Assessing need for services not provided by the authority

It is clear that the assessment regime under the 1990 Act distinguishes between assessment and community care service provision since the duty to assess is separately set out in s 47(1)(*a*) of the Act whereas service provision is contained in s 47(1)(*b*) (see Materials).

There is, in this respect, a direct comparison with ss 167 and 168 of the Education Act 1993, which envisages a separation between the duty on a local education authority to assess special educational needs and the duty to make a statement of such needs in circumstances where the authority is of the opinion that it should determine the special educational provision to be made.

Just as the 1993 Act does not impose a duty on an authority to make or to maintain a statement in respect of every child whose special educational needs are covered by the Act (see *R v Secretary of State for Education and Science, ex p Lashford* [1988] 1 FLR 72 dealing with similar provisions in the Education Act 1981) so, too, the fact that a local authority has assessed a need for community care services that the authority is empowered to provide cannot entail the conclusion that the authority is required to provide them (see Chapter 5 where the implications of this on service provision are considered).

But if this is right it follows that the National Health Service and Community Care Act 1990 contemplates assessment as a service in its own right which can be distinguished from any services that are arranged in consequence (see *Policy Guidance* at para 3.15; para 5 of the Laming letter).

The assessment service that is afforded by s 47(1)(*a*) is one of assessing need for community care services that an authority is empowered to provide for a particular person. Thus, the authority must (whatever decision it arrives at in respect of service provision) investigate need for all services that an authority may provide for a particular individual rather than being limited to those community care services that are actually provided. A limiting of the assessment to need for which there were services that the authority had decided to make available would render such assessment amenable to judicial review. (See, eg para 22 of Summary of Practice Guidance in the *Practitioners' Guide*, Materials 3(D).)

This was confirmed in *R v Royal County of Berkshire, ex p Parker* (1996) *The Times*, 15 August. There, Laws J observed that the s 47(1)(*a*) duty to assess is not conditional upon its being shown that the local authority in question has in place existing arrangements to provide services of a kind which, in the light of the assessment, the service user is in need. The judge held that the duty arises where the local authority possesses the legal power to provide or arrange for the provision of particular community care services.

Paragraph 3.15 of the *Policy Guidance* suggests that an authority should, in assessing need, take into account the types of service that it has decided to make available. Paragraph 2.20 of the *Manager's Guide* is to similar effect. It is submitted, however, that this approach would be unlawful if adopted at the assessment, as opposed to the service provision, stage.

## 4.3    The effect of lack of service resources on assessment of need

As indicated above, the authority's duty to assess need is free-standing from its duty to provide services. It is, therefore, immaterial to assessment that the authority does not have the resources to provide services in respect of which it assesses a need. The impact of lack of resources on service provision is considered at 5.4.

As the Laming letter makes clear, at para 13, there may be circumstances where an authority is entitled to take into account its available resources 'when deciding how to respond to an individual's assessment'. That is, however, analytically different from taking resources into account when assessing need. The latter would be an error of law and potentially susceptible to judicial review.

## 4.4    Resources and assessment

The duty to assess triggered as it is by the appearance of need for community care services cannot, sensibly, be qualified by lack of resources in the assessing authority. However, para 2.17 of the (non-statutory) *Practitioners' Guide* states that:

> Agencies will want to determine their own levels of assessment according to their policies, priorities and available personnel.

In context this must mean that social services are entitled to deploy their resources towards the most cost-effective assessment process consistent with their statutory obligations. This interpretation is supported by para 3.3 of the *Practitioners' Guide* which provides, materially, that:

> . . . the assessment process should be as simple, speedy and informal as possible . . . based on the principle of what is the least that is necessary . . . to understand the needs being presented . . . to justify the investment of public resources.

This does not, however, relieve the local authority of its duty to assess for all services which it is empowered to provide.

## 4.5    What is 'need'?

As has been seen (see 3.1 and 3.2), the touchstone of entitlement to assessment is the 'appearance' of need for community care services. The assessment process itself is directed towards actual need for such services.

'Need' is not defined in the legislation. The *Practitioners' Guide*, however, considers 'need' to be:

> the requirements of individuals to enable them to achieve, maintain or restore an acceptable level of social independence or quality of life, as defined by the particular care agency or authority. (*Practitioners' Guide*: Summary of Practice Guidance, para 11 in Materials 3(D).)

Although the *Practitioners' Guide* goes on, at para 13 of the Summary, to describe 'need' as 'a relative concept' it would appear that the assessment of 'need' engages a judgment rather than a discretion and that social services are required to evaluate a service user's need objectively (see *R v Gloucestershire CC, ex p Barry* (1996) *The Times*, 12 July, per Swinton Thomas LJ and Sir John Balcombe).

In *R v Avon CC, ex p M* [1994] 2 FLR 1006, the court held, materially, that:

(1)  a service user's needs include his psychological needs;
(2)  the assessment under s 47(1)(*a*) of the 1990 Act should be appropriate to the particular needs of the service user.

Consistent with the Care Programme Approach need is not confined to urgent or immediate need (see Chapter 3 at 3.2). Further, the summary of practice guidance contained in the *Practitioners' Guide* states, at para 3, that:

> . . . care management and assessment emphasise . . . dealing with the needs of individuals as a whole rather than assessing needs separately for different services.

## 4.6   Scope and content of enquiries

The legal scope and content of an authority's duty to enquire into a service user's need is to be distinguished (although there is some overlap) from natural justice issues. These are considered in Chapter 6. Failure to carry out adequate enquiry or take relevant factors into account will render an authority's assessment amenable to judicial review subject to whether a particular applicant should, first, exhaust the complaints machinery (see Chapters 8 and 9).

Section 47(4) of the National Health Service and Community Act 1990 empowers the Secretary of State to issue directions as to how assessments shall be carried out. No directions have been issued. In their absence the assessment is to be undertaken 'as the local authority considers appropriate'. As with other areas of public-law decision-making, however, the assessment process must be performed lawfully. In this context Government guidance, both statutory and non-statutory, is material.

According to the Laming letter, at para 12, the assessment should focus on the difficulties for which individuals are seeking assistance. It should take account of all the circumstances relevant to those individuals and, in particular, of:

•    their capacities and incapacities;
•    their preferences and aspirations;

- their living situation;
- the support available from relatives and friends;
- any other sources of help.

The Laming letter also provides a helpful reminder (see para 3), that:

> the assessment process should be structured so that the needs of the individual ie their capacities and incapacities and their circumstances are identified before consideration is given to any requirements for service provision.

When assessing need a local authority must comply substantially with statutory guidance (pre-eminently the *Policy Guidance*), issued under s 7 of the Local Authority Social Services Act 1970. Failure to do so may be corrected by means of judicial review (*R v Islington LBC, ex p Rixon* (1996) *The Times*, 17 April). In *R v North Yorkshire CC, ex p Hargreaves* (1994) *The Times*, 9 November, for example, a local authority's assessment was held to be unlawful as being in breach of paras 3.16 and 3.25 of the *Policy Guidance* (involvement of service user and carer in the assessment process and taking account of their preferences).

Beyond this there are other factors which must, on basic public law principles, also be taken into account during the assessment process. Prominent among these (albeit more likely to be relevant to the service provision decision) are any recommendations as to need made in the particular case by a complaints review panel (see *R v Avon CC, ex p M* (1994) 2 FLR 1006). In *R v Islington LBC, ex p Rixon* (1996) *The Times*, 17 April, Sedley J held that non-statutory guidance, such as the *Practitioners' Guide*, must also be taken into account.

The general principles relating to assessment enquiries are likely to be similar to those developed under the Housing Act 1985 in respect of a local authority's duties to investigate issues of priority need and intentional homelessness. The following are likely to constitute the minimum requirements that a court would place upon the scope of the duty to make a proper enquiry:

(1) enquiries must cover all relevant factors (see *R v Ryedale DC, ex p Smith* (1983) 16 HLR 66);

(2) users should be given the opportunity to explain their circumstances fully and inconsistencies should be less readily relied upon where an applicant's native language is not English (see *R v Surrey Heath BC, ex p Li* (1984) 16 HLR 79);

(3) enquiries need not constitute 'CID-type' enquiries (see *Lally v Royal Borough of Kensington and Chelsea* (1980) *The Times*, 27 March), but the burden of making proper enquiry lies upon the authority rather than the applicant (see *R v Reigate and Banstead DC, ex p Paris* (1984) 17 HLR 103, *R v Gravesham BC, ex p Winchester* (1986) 18 HLR 207);

(4) where medical evidence is provided, the authority should either accept such evidence or make further enquiry: it should not reject

such evidence without making such further enquiry (see *R v Bath City Council, ex p Sangermano* (1984) 17 HLR 94);

(5) basic issues must be put to the user and an authority may not take into account that which the applicant failed to say but was not asked about (see *R v Wandsworth LBC, ex p Rose* (1983) 11 HLR 105);

(6) an authority may rely on hearsay (see *R v Nottingham City Council, ex p Costello* (1989) *The Times*, 14 February).

According to the *Policy Guidance*, at para 3.20:

> assessment arrangements should normally include an initial screening process to determine the appropriate form of assessment. Some people may need advice and assistance which does not call for a formal assessment, others may require only a limited or specialist assessment of specific needs, others may have urgent needs which require an immediate response. Procedures should be sufficiently comprehensive and flexible to cope with all levels and types of need.

These themes are developed further in Chapter 6.

## 4.7   Special cases: disabled persons

Section 47(2) of the National Health Service and Community Care Act 1990 provides that if at any time during a s 47 needs assessment it appears to the local authority that the applicant is a disabled person then the authority shall proceed to make a decision as to the services that he requires under s 4 of the Disabled Persons (Services, Consultation and Representation) Act 1986 without his requesting it to do so under that section and shall inform him that it will be doing so and of his rights under the 1986 Act.

The term 'disabled person' is, by s 47(8) of the 1990 Act, expressed to have the same meaning as in the 1986 Act, namely a person to whom s 29 of the National Assistance Act 1948 applies. This, in turn, takes one back to the s 29 formulation, namely persons

> . . . aged 18 or over, who are blind, deaf or dumb or who suffer from mental disorder of any description and other persons aged 18 or over who are substantially and permanently handicapped by illness, injury or congenital deformity or such other disabilities as may be prescribed by the Minister.

Further, s 2 of the Chronically Sick and Disabled Persons Act 1970 now also applies to children by virtue of the Children Act 1989, which inserts a new s 28A into the 1970 Act.

The 1986 Act is concerned with the assessment of need for, and provision by an authority of, welfare services under s 2(1) of the Chronically Sick and Disabled Persons Act 1970 (see 2.3).

An assessment of whether it is necessary to make arrangements to meet a need for services under s 2 involves the exercise of a judgment similar to that of whether the person is disabled (per Swinton Thomas LJ in *R v Gloucestershire CC, ex p Barry* (1996) *The Times*, 12 July). The local authority is required to decide what is needed as opposed to what is desirable. Where a need is identified there is, then, an absolute duty to make the necessary arrangements (see Chapters 2 and 5).

In making an assessment of a disabled person (whether in respect of the need for services under s 2 of the 1970 Act or other welfare enactments) the local authority is, by s 8(1) of the Disabled Persons (Services, Consultation and Representation) Act 1986, required to have regard to the ability of the user's carer, as defined, to continue to provide care on a regular basis. The term 'carer' means a person, not employed to provide such care by anybody in the exercise of statutory functions, who provides 'a substantial amount of care on a regular basis.'

An assessment of a disabled person ought, in principle, to be similar to those relating to other service users. Paragraph 2.19 of the *Practitioners' Guide* states that:

> . . . where a person appears to be 'disabled' under the terms of the Disabled Persons (Services, Consultation and Representation) Act 1986, the local authority is required to offer a comprehensive assessment, irrespective of the scale of need that is initially present.

However, in *R v Gloucestershire CC, ex p RADAR* (unreported 21 December 1995), Carnwath J observed that the word 'comprehensive' is misleading unless taken to refer merely to the decision required to be taken in respect of disabled persons under s 2 of the Chronically Sick and Disabled Persons Act 1970. The judge expressed doubt as to whether 'comprehensive' in para 2.19 of the *Practitioners' Guide* was intended to bear the same meaning as that used in the table referred to in para 2.17. It is submitted, however, that these views which were *obiter* are incorrect in so far as they apply to the initial assessment of disabled persons. It is the greater vulnerability of disabled persons that merits a comprehensive assessment in the first place.

## 4.8   Special cases: carers

There is no express provision for assessing carers under the 1990 Act (contrast s 8(1) of the Disabled Persons (Services, Consultation and Representation) Act 1986 above). Paragraph 3.29 of the *Policy Guidance* stresses, however, that carers are entitled to request a separate s 47(1)(*a*) assessment if they feel that they require community care services 'in their own right' and that this 'could arise if the care plan of the person for whom they care does not, in their view, adequately address the carer's own needs.' In fact, on general principles it is submitted that carers needing community care services 'in their own right' would not need to make a request for an assessment provided that their apparent need for services had come to the authority's attention. Many (if not most) carers, will, indeed need services in their 'own right' even if this amounts to general social work support.

Other parts of the *Policy Guidance* emphasise the pivotal role of carers in the assessment process (see, eg, para 3.16: participation of carers in the assessment; para 3.18: need for accessible information 'to enable . . . carers to exercise genuine choice and participate in the assessment of their care needs and in the making of arrangements for meeting these needs'; paras 3.25 and 3.28: need to take into account carers' preferences).

The Carers (Recognition and Services) Act 1995 is designed to provide an underpinning statutory framework for the assessment of carers' needs in a statutory community care assessment although nothing in the 1995 Act diminishes the binding nature of the pre-existing statutory *Policy Guidance*. The Act came into force on 1 April 1996.

The effect of s 1(1) and (2) of the 1995 Act is that where (but only where) a local authority is undertaking a s 47(1)(*a*) assessment or an assessment of the needs of a disabled child under Part III of the Children Act 1989 or s 2 of the Chronically Sick and Disabled Persons Act 1970 and an individual (the carer) provides or intends to provide 'a substantial amount of care on a regular basis' for the service user, then the carer may request the local authority to carry out an assessment of the carer's ability to provide and to continue to provide care. If such a request is made the authority must then carry out such an assessment and shall take into account the results of that assessment in making its service provision decision in respect of the service user. The same criteria apply to reassessment (see s 12 of the Interpretation Act 1978).

Excluded from the 1995 Act, by s 1(3), are 'professional' carers, namely those who work under a contract or who provide care as a volunteer for a voluntary organisation. Included, however, are child carers. Where the 1995 Act applies s 8 of the Disabled Persons (Services, Consultation and Representation) Act 1986, is, by s 1(5) of the 1995 Act, disapplied.

Although, by s 1(4) of the 1995 Act, the Secretary of State is empowered to issue directions as to the manner in which a carer's assessment is to be carried out no directions have yet been made. There is, none the less, non-statutory guidance, *Policy Guidance* issued under s 7 of the Local Authority Social Services Act 1970, and a letter (CI(95)12) from Herbert Laming to Directors of Social Services relating to young carers (all reproduced in Materials).

The 1995 Act statutory *Policy Guidance* clarifies, in particular, that:

(1) The term 'carer' includes persons who are not relatives of the service user and who may not be living with the person for whom they are caring (para 6).

(2) The terms 'regular' and 'substantial' in the expression 'a substantial amount of care on a regular basis' are to be interpreted in their everyday sense (para 10).

(3) It will be for local authorities to form their own judgment as to what constitutes 'regular' and 'substantial' and to make their views known (para 11).

(4) Where the carer is either under 18 or the parent of a disabled child, local authorities should consider whether the Children Act 1989 applies (para 13).

(5) Local authorities should continue to follow current policy and practice guidance where a carer does not want their own assessment or where a carer is providing care on less than a substantial and regular basis (para 18).

(6) Carers should be informed about their rights under the 1995 Act (para 19) and local authorities should ensure that it becomes part of routine assessment practice to inform any carer who it appears to be eligible under the 1995 Act of their right to request an assessment (para 20).

(7) A 1995 Act assessment should take account of the carer's circumstances, age, views and preferences, as well as the amount of support available, but it should not automatically assume a willingness to continue caring or to continue providing the same level of support (para 21).

(8) Where the carer is a child the impact of caring may be different as it may affect the child's health and development by the restrictions that providing regular and substantial care might place on the child's educational and leisure opportunities (para 22).

(9) Social service departments should work closely with local education authorities when carrying out assessments of young carers and parents of disabled children (para 31).

## 4.9   Special cases: children

Assessment of children for the provision of care in the community is heavily affected by Part III of the Children Act 1989. There is no discrete statutory duty to assess under this Act but there is a power of assessment contingent on: (a) the facilitating of the duty under s 17 of the Act, and (b) the undertaking of a separate statutory assessment on the child.

Section 17 of the 1989 Act provides, materially, that:

(1) It shall be the general duty of every local authority (in addition to the other duties imposed on them by this Part)—
   (a)  to safeguard and promote the welfare of children within their area who are in need; and
   (b)  so far as is consistent with that duty, to promote the upbringing of such children by their families,
by providing a range and level of services appropriate to those children's needs.
(2) For the purpose principally of facilitating the discharge of their general duty under this section, every local authority shall have the specific duties and powers set out in Part I of Schedule 2.
(3) Any service provided by an authority in the exercise of functions conferred on them by this section may be provided for the family of a particular child in need or for any member of his family, if it is provided with a view to safeguarding or promoting the child's welfare . . .
(5) Every local authority—
   (a)  shall facilitate the provision by others . . . of services which the authority have power to provide by virtue of this section . . .

* * * * *

(10) For the purposes of this Part a child shall be taken to be in need if—

    (a)   he is unlikely to achieve or maintain, or to have the opportunity of achieving or maintaining, a reasonable standard of health or development without the provision for him of services by a local authority under this Part;

    (b)   his health or development is likely to be significantly impaired, or further impaired, without the provision for him of such services; or

    (c)   he is disabled . . .

(11) For the purposes of this Part, a child is disabled if he is blind, deaf or dumb or suffers from mental disorder of any kind or is substantially and permanently handicapped by illness, injury or congenital deformity or such other disability as may be prescribed; and in this Part—

    'development' means physical, intellectual, emotional, social or behavioural development; and

    'health' means physical or mental health.

Part I of Sched 2 of the 1989 Act provides, materially, that:

**3**   Where it appears to a local authority that a child within their area is in need, the authority may assess his needs for the purposes of this Act at the same time as any assessment of his needs is made under—

    (a)   the Chronically Sick and Disabled Persons Act 1970;

    (b)   Part III of the Education Act 1993;

    (c)   the Disabled Persons (Services, Consultation and Representation) Act 1986; or

    (d)   any other enactment . . .

In relation to the Children Act 1989, the Secretary of State has published statutory guidance in respect of Part III (reproduced in Materials 4(I)). Key points in this Guidance are that:

2.4   The definition of 'need' in the Act is deliberately wide to reinforce the emphasis on preventive support and services to families. It has three categories: a reasonable standard of health or development; significant impairment of health or development; and disablement. It would not be acceptable for an authority to exclude any of these three—for example, by confining services to children at risk of significant harm . . .

2.5   In assessing individual need, authorities must assess the existing strengths and skills of the families concerned and help them overcome identified difficulties and enhance strengths. Sometimes the needs will be found to be intrinsic to the child; at other times however it may be that parenting skills and resources are depleted or under-developed and thus threaten the child's well-being. For example, a chronically sick parent may need continuing practical and emotional support of varying degrees of intensity according to the incidence of acute phases of his illness and the developing needs of the child . . .

2.6   The Act envisages family support services being offered to members of a family of a child in need where the service is provided with a view to safeguarding and promoting the child's welfare . . . a local authority may put together a package of services for a family which could include home help . . . The outcome of any service provision under this power should be evaluated to see whether it has met the primary objective, namely to safeguard or promote the child's welfare.

2.7   Good practice requires that the assessment of need should be undertaken

in an open way and should involve those caring for the child, the child and other significant persons. Families with a child in need, whether the need results from family difficulties or the child's circumstances, have the right to receive sympathetic support and sensitive intervention in their family's life . . .
2.10   Once a need has been identified a plan for the best service provision will be required . . .
2.13   The effect of the provision of services to support families may often be to avoid the need to take the child into long-term compulsory care . . .
2.14   . . . Some families . . . reach a stage where they are not able to cope with their own difficulties and are therefore providing inadequate care for their child or are afraid of doing so. They may look to social services for support and assistance. If they do this they should receive a positive response which reduces any fears they may have of stigma or loss of parental responsibility.

## 4.10   Other agencies

Section 47(3) of the National Health Service and Community Care Act 1990 provides that if at any time during a needs assessment under s 47 it appears to the authority that there may be a need for the provision to the applicant of services under the National Health Service Act 1977 (by a District Health Authority) or of any services under the Housing Act 1985 (by a local housing authority), the local authority shall notify the relevant authority and invite them to assist, to such extent as is reasonable in the circumstances, in the making of the assessment.

There is an obvious importance to these other authorities participating in the assessment process given the further requirement of s 47(3) that the local authority undertaking the s 47 assessment must take into account, in arriving at a service provision decision, any services which are likely to be made available for the applicant by that authority.

The meaning of the phrase 'services which are likely to be made available' is unclear but it represents, presumably, a subjective evaluation on the part of the s 47 assessing authority of what services the District Health Authority or local housing authority are, following collaborative assessment under s 47, likely to provide to the applicant.

It is, thus, a *sine qua non* of the service-provision decision that, in the event of an ostensible need for the above-mentioned services that emerges during the assessment, the District Health/local housing authority participate in the s 47 assessment provided that it is reasonable of the assessing authority to invite them to do so.

If either authority refuses unreasonably to participate it is open to the s 47 assessing authority or the individual to seek judicial review of such refusal. Indeed, unless the assessing authority does so it would face difficulty in reaching an informed service-provision decision.

According to para 3.32 of the *Policy Guidance* social services are:

responsible for the involvement of all other agencies in deciding what should be done, by whom and by when, but other agencies will need to make available the staff required for assessment . . . Where a service user has complex needs, it may be necessary to call . . . a case conference; the individual and his carer should then be invited to attend.

The District Health Authority is, necessarily, involved in the assessment of community care services under s 117 of the Mental Health Act 1983 (see Chapter 2) and the reaching of a service provision decision in respect of such services. It would appear, therefore, that s 47(3) of the 1990 Act and para 3.32 of the *Policy Guidance* have only a limited and somewhat formal application to s 117 after-care services.

## 4.11 Reviewing assessment decisions

There is, clearly, power in a local authority to review an assessment once made. Indeed, 'for frail people in the community, frequent reviews and adjustments of their care plans are likely to be needed.' (Laming letter at para 31; see, also, *Policy Guidance* at paras 3.51–3.53).

Such power is not expressly contained in the National Health Service and Community Care Act 1990 but it emerges from general principles of statutory interpretation that permit exercise of a statutory power from time to time unless contrary to the statutory intent (see s 12 of the Interpretation Act 1978).

Further, the requirement in s 47(1)(*a*) of the 1990 Act that an authority must assess an applicant's needs for community care services where there is an apparent need for such services imposes a continuing duty to assess where the authority, notwithstanding an adverse first assessment, considers that there is such apparent need on reconsideration of the matter.

In many circumstances the need for review will arise from an alleged change of circumstances. Conceptually, however, this need not be the case and the care management philosophy attending the community care approach renders it unnecessary. If the authority is, for example, presented with new material or considers that it made a mistake of fact or law it would, undoubtedly, be entitled to review its previous assessment. This is a distinct power and does not require invocation of the complaints machinery in respect of the original assessment.

If a local authority unreasonably refuses to review its decision it would be susceptible to judicial review subject to a user's right (and possibly duty) to invoke the complaints machinery prior to seeking review (see Chapter 9 for a full discussion). A reassessment ought not, provided that there is continuing need, to result in reduction or withdrawal of services even if service provision might be decided in a different way on reassessment (see the Laming letter at para 31, and Chapter 5).

Unreasonable reassessment may itself give rise to liability to judicial review or, more probably, to an applicant invoking the complaints procedure.

Withdrawal of community care services without prior reassessment is unlawful (*R v Gloucestershire CC, ex p Mahfood* (1995) TLR 351).

# Chapter 5

# Service Provision

## 5.1 Scope of the duty

The separation of assessment of need from service provision has already been noted (see Chapter 4).

Section 47(1)(*b*) of the National Health Service and Community Care Act 1990 provides that, following assessment of an individual, the local authority, 'having regard to the results of that assessment, shall then decide whether his needs call for the provision by them' of 'any' community care services.

It seems clear that, after carrying out a needs assessment, an authority (subject to its obligation to comply with absolute statutory duties), retains a discretion to determine the scope of its provision of community care services. This discretion must, however, be exercised in conformity with guidance issued under s 7 of the Local Authority Social Services Act 1970 and may, in some cases (eg hospital discharge, see Chapter 15) be limited by such guidance (see *R v London Borough of Sutton, ex p Tucher*, unreported, 29 October 1996). A decision as to whether particular needs 'call for provision' of 'any' community care services by the authority generally (but see above), entitles social services to make a decision not to provide services even if a need has been established for such services. The discretion must, of course, be exercised lawfully and in accordance with recognised public law principles (see 5.2, below).

This feature of discretion preceding duty is a familar one and is replicated in, for example, ss 167 and 168 of the Education Act 1993 (special educational needs and local authority statements), and in ss 62 to 64 of the Housing Act 1985 (determination of matters giving rise to housing duties).

In the case of disabled persons, as defined (see 4.7), a service provision decision is separately required in respect of services under s 2 of the Chronically Sick and Disabled Persons Act 1970 (see s 47(2) of the 1990 Act). The constituent elements of this decision are examined below (see 5.3, below) and also in Chapter 4 (see 4.7).

The following issues require particular analysis:

(1) the extent of the statutory discretion under s 47(1)(*b*) of the 1990 Act;

(2) the position in relation to community care services that are required (as opposed to permitted) to be provided;

(3)  the relevance (if any) of lack of resources;
(4)  the legality of a service provision policy;
(5)  the extent to which service provision may be reviewed by the pro-
     viding authority;
(6)  the nature of the 'rights' created by a failure to determine service
     provision lawfully or provide services or to review service provision.

## 5.2   The statutory discretion to determine service provision

The principal aim of assessment is to arrive at a decision on whether services should be provided, and in what form (see White Paper (see 1.7) para
3.2.12). Indeed, good practice dictates that communication of the assessment decision will normally involve not merely the results of assessment but
also confirmation of an agreed care plan (see *Policy Guidance* at para 3.24).

It does not follow from this, however, that assessment of a particular
need is, as a matter of law, determinative of a duty to provide services for
which such need is established.

As has been seen (see 4.2), there is a duty to assess need in respect of all
community care services that a local authority is empowered or required to
provide for a particular individual, in circumstances where an apparent
need for such services comes to the attention of the authority (see s 47(1)(a)
of the 1990 Act). But the fact that an authority is empowered to provide
specific services cannot entail the consequence that it must provide them as
soon as need is established for, were this so, a statutory power would automatically become assimilated to a duty.

The wording of s 47(1)(b) reinforces this view. It requires the authority to
make a service provision decision 'having regard to the results' of the assessment. This means that the authority must take the assessment into account
when deciding on its duty to provide community care services but it does not
have to pay 'slavish adherence' to such assessment (see *De Falco v Crawley
BC* [1980] 1 QB 460). It is entitled to exercise its discretion and take factors
other than the assessment into account provided that it does so lawfully.

Any discretion must, to be lawfully exercised, be within the policy and
objects of the relevant statute (*Padfield v Minister of Agriculture, Fisheries
and Food* [1968] AC 997).

In the context of community care this inevitably means that the authority in determining service provision is (unless it is under an absolute duty
to provide services, see below), entitled to have regard to what is available
and affordable, (see White Paper at para 3.2.12). However, a decision based
solely on lack of resources might be susceptible to challenge by way of judicial review on grounds of irrationality. See, for example, *R v Gloucestershire
CC, ex p Mahfood* (1995) TLR 351.

In assessing availability the authority has a duty under s 47(3) of the
National Health Service and Community Care Act 1990 to inform the relevant District Health Authority and/or housing authority if it considers

that there is a need for provision by that authority in the light of the assessment, and to take into account any services likely to be made available by those authorities in reaching decisions on their own service provision.

Clearly, if a District Health or Housing Authority unreasonably refuses to participate in the assessment it will not be possible to evaluate the nature of the services likely to be made available by that authority. In that event it may be that the local authority responsible for assessment/service provision or the individual should seek to judicially review the other authority since, otherwise, an informed service provision decision will be incapable of being made.

Priority may legitimately be given to those whose needs are greatest (see the White Paper at para 3.2.12; Laming letter at para 14). The extent of need is, clearly, at least in part dependent upon the support that is available from carers (see *Policy Guidance* at para 3.27 *et seq*, and the Carers (Recognition and Services) Act 1995) and from other authorities (see s 47(3) of the 1990 Act). Equally clearly, a local authority would err in law if it took into account the fact that a user or his family was unable to meet the cost of service provision since such criterion is wholly unrelated to need. For this reason 'assessment of financial means should . . . follow the assessment of need and decisions about service provision' (see *Policy Guidance* at para 3.31).

In essence the authority has a responsibility (subject to absolute statutory duties) to meet needs within the resources available. The *Policy Guidance* suggests that:

> The aim should be to secure the most cost-effective package of services that meets the user's care needs, taking account of the user's and carers' own preferences . . . [see para 3.25].

Consistent with the philosophy of community care, the *Policy Guidance* sets out a suggested order of preference of service provision (see para 3.24) towards the stated objective of preserving normal living as far as possible:

(1) support for the user in his own home including day and domiciliary care, respite care, the provision of disability equipment and adaptations to accommodation as necessary;

(2) a move to more suitable accommodation, which might be sheltered or very sheltered housing, together with the provision of social services support;

(3) a move to another private household, ie to live with relatives or friends or as part of an adult fostering scheme;

(4) residential care;

(5) nursing home care;

(6) long-stay care in hospital.

As in the case of assessments, the way in which a local authority exercises its discretionary power to determine the level of community care service provision must, being a social services function, be 'under the general guidance' of the Secretary of State (see s 7 of the Local Authority Social Services Act 1970), and 'in accordance with such directions as may be given' by the Secretary of State under s 7A of the 1970 Act as inserted by s 50 of the National Health Service and Community Care Act 1990 (see *R v London Borough of Sutton, ex p Tucher*, unreported, 29 October 1996).

The legal issues associated with these provisions have already been considered (see 1.6). Essentially, the authority is required to follow statutory guidance without substantial deviation, to take non-statutory guidance into account, but must act precisely in accordance with any relevant directions issued. No directions have been issued in relation to service provision. The principal guidance material is set out in Materials 3–4.

A local authority must also have regard to its own published eligibility criteria for service provision and ought not to elevate such criteria into restrictive rules (see below at 5.5).

The *Practice Guidance* states, at para 4.32, that following completion of the care plan any 'unmet needs' should be recorded with reasons. The concept of 'unmet need' is, however, foreign to an absolute statutory duty such as that subsisting under s 2 of the Chronically Sick and Disabled Persons Act 1970 (see 5.4, below), or, it is submitted, s 117 of Mental Health Act 1983.

## 5.3 Mandatory community care services

The provision of home-helps under s 21 of the National Health Service Act 1977, social workers under s 29 of the 1948 Act, accommodation under s 21 of that Act and after-care services under s 117 of the Mental Health Act 1983, appear to constitute mandatory duties as opposed to powers (but note the distinction between 'target' and individual duties in 5.4, below). The same is true (whether or not they constitute 'community care services' as defined by s 46(3) of the 1990 Act) of provision of services under s 2 of the Chronically Sick and Disabled Persons Act 1970.

The fact that at least some of these duties fall within the definition of 'community care services' under s 46(3) of the 1990 Act and, therefore, within the scope of the assessment regime under s 47 suggests, at first sight, that the provision of these services is included within the local authority's general discretion as to service provision under s 47(1)(*b*).

This cannot in fact be so since, otherwise, clear statutory duties would, merely by the creation of a framework for assessment of need, be converted to powers.

The correct construction of s 47(1)(*b*), in this context, is that where assessment of need discloses a need for services that are required to be provided, then the authority must, subject to the question of resources (see 5.4, below), determine that such need calls for the provision of those services.

## 5.4 Lack of resources

Traditionally, courts will not interfere in cases of discretionary allocation of resources (see, eg *R v Hertfordshire CC, ex p Three Rivers District Council*

(1992) *The Times*, 18 March). In practical terms this means that a local authority is unlikely to be subject to a successful judicial review if it declines service provision in respect of community care services that it is empowered, but cannot afford, to provide (see the Laming letter at para 13; *Practitioners' Guide*: Summary of Practice Guidance at para 24). Exceptionally, however, particular parts of statutory guidance issued under s 7 of the Local Authority Social Services Act 1970 may require service provision decisions to be made independent of available financial resources (see eg *R v London Borough of Sutton, ex p Tucher*, unreported, 29 October 1996).

The statutory *Policy Guidance* states, at para 3.25, that:

> . . . local authorities also have a responsibility to meet needs within the resources available and this will sometimes involve difficult decisions where it will be necessary to strike a balance between meeting the needs identified within available resources and meeting the care preferences of the individual.

However, the same considerations do not logically apply in circumstances where there is a statutory obligation to provide particular services (see 5.3, above). There, social services ought not, as a matter of principle, to be allowed to take resources into account since the requirement of the statute would, thereby, be subverted.

It is, however, important to distinguish between two different types of statutory duty, namely:

- target duties, and
- individual duties.

'Target duties' are owed to the population at large rather than to specific individuals. Instances abound in social welfare legislation. Part III of the National Assistance Act 1948 contains examples of target duties (albeit contingent on directions of the Secretary of State) in respect of welfare arrangements (s 29). These (and other target duties) are discussed in more detail in Chapter 2.

Such duties do not cease to be obligations as opposed to powers but the courts have allowed decision-makers to take account of resources in complying with such duties. Put shortly, the 'target' element defines the scope of the duty itself so as to render it less than absolute.

Thus, in *R v Secretary of State for Social Services, ex p Hincks* (1980) 1 BMLR 93, for example, a statutory obligation to provide health services 'necessary to meet all reasonable requirements' was held to be subject to an implied proviso, namely, 'within the resources available' (see, also *R v Barnet, ex p B* [1994] 1 FLR 592; *R v Central Birmingham Health Authority, ex p Walker* (1987) 3 BMLR 32).

Further, breaches of target duties are normally to be dealt with by recourse to the default powers of the Secretary of State (*R v Inner London Education Authority, ex p Ali* (1990) 2 Admin LR 822 at p 829 per Woolf LJ citing his earlier decision in *R v Secretary of State for the Environment, ex p Ward* [1984] 1 WLR 834), and are only properly justiciable in judicial review where there has been not a simple failure but a decision positively to 'stop production' (*R v Secretary of State for the Environment, ex p Ward* [1984] 1 WLR 834; *Meade v Haringey LBC* [1979] 1 WLR 637).

Materially, in *R v Islington LBC, ex p Rixon* (1996) *The Times*, 17 April, Sedley J rejected the applicant's submission that s 29 of the National Asssistance Act 1948 became converted from a target duty to an individual duty by virtue of the inter-relationship between that section (as a 'community care service' under s 46(3) of the National Health Service and Community Care Act 1990) and s 47(1)(*b*) of the 1990 Act. The judge's dismissal of that argument (if right) means that nothing in the assessment and service provision decision regime created in the 1990 Act operates to prevent resources from being taken into account by a local authority when making a service provision decision in respect of a service provided under a target duty.

Individual duties in the 'community care service' statutory provisions are very much the exception rather than the rule. Probably, the duty under s 117 of the Mental Health Act 1983 (after-care services for formerly compulsorily detained mentally disordered patients) falls into this category. Whether or not a 'community care service' (see 2.3), services provided under s 2 of the Chronically Sick and Disabled Persons Act 1970 also involve duties owed to an individual person.

In respect of such individual duties (assuming that they are interpreted as such), it seems likely that the resources or lack of resources available to social services may not be taken into account in reaching a service provision decision.

The issue was central to *R v Gloucestershire CC, ex p Barry* (1996) *The Times*, 12 July, in the context of the duty under s 2 of the Chronically Sick and Disabled Persons Act 1970. There, the Court of Appeal (by a majority), held that a local authority is not entitled to take into account the availability of resources when carrying out its duties under s 2 of the 1970 Act, save only to the extent that it may make the necessary arrangements in the most economical way open to it.

Gloucestershire CC had assessed the applicant, a 79-year-old gravely disabled man, under s 2 as needing home care services at a certain level. The council withdrew his cleaning services and reduced his laundry provision on the ground that it had been necessary to do so due to the shortage of financial resources by virtue of lack of funding from Central Government. No lawful reassessment of need was carried out prior to withdrawal/reduction of services and this, the Divisional Court (at first instance: see *sub nom R v Gloucestershire CC, ex p Mahfood* (1995) TLR 351) held to be unlawful.

However, the Divisional Court (per McCowan LJ and Waller J) held that the local authority would not have erred in law had it, on a reassessment, taken the restricted availability of its financial resources into account when assessing 'need' and the arrangements necessary to meet that need under s 2. The Divisional Court held, however, that once the authority had identified 'need' and the arrangements necessary to meet the need, it was under an absolute duty to provide the services and could not use budgetary difficulties as a reason for non-provision, albeit that it could reassess need, etc, and reduce provision in the light of its reassessment.

The Court of Appeal (Swinton Thomas LJ and Sir John Balcombe, with Hirst LJ dissenting, see (1996) *The Times*, 12 July), held essentially that:

(1) The s 2 duty was, plainly, individually orientated.

(2) 'Need' is an ordinary English word and means a 'basic or essential requirement'.

(3) The existence of a 'need' is a question of assessment and judgment rather than the exercise of a discretion.

(4) A third party's resources or the needs of others were irrelevant to the making of a judgment as to the need of a particular disabled person.

(5) Once the assessment of need and the necessary arrangements to meet that need has been made resources might well be relevant to the manner in which provision is made to meet the need (eg, an assessed need for cleaning and laundry services might be met by laundry being done at home or by being taken away).

Applying the above principles to the facts, the appeal in Mr Barry's case was allowed. A conjoined appeal (*R v Lancashire CC, ex p RADAR and Gilpin*) was dismissed, but see 15.5). There is an appeal pending before the House of Lords in the *Barry* case.

## 5.5   Legality of a service provision policy

Decisions are often taken against a background of general policy. If the policy is lawful and is applied fairly, judicial review will be inappropriate.

It follows from the reasoning in 5.3 above, that any policy not to make service provision available for community care services that are mandatory would be unlawful and, therefore, challengeable in the courts.

However, a policy may, legitimately, be formulated in respect of discretionary service provision. Such policy must, however, not prevent consideration of 'all the issues which are relevant to each individual case as it comes up for decision' (see *Stringer v Minister of Housing and Local Government* [1970] 1 WLR 1281 at p 1298, per Cooke J).

Sometimes, departure from a lawful policy may itself be unlawful. In *R v Home Secretary, ex p Ruddock* [1987] 2 All ER 518, for example, Taylor J held that the Secretary of State was bound by a duty of fairness not to depart from published guidelines on the issuing of warrants for telephone tapping, albeit that the applicant was unaware of the terms of such guidelines. This is, in a sense, the converse of policy operating as a fetter on discretion and connotes that policy may occasionally act to circumscribe discretion, or at least to set limits to the extent to which discretion may be exercised without affording an opportunity to an applicant of making representations as to why existing policy ought not to be altered (see, also, *R v Secretary of State for the Home Department, ex p Asif Khan* [1984] 1 WLR 1337).

Given the statutory requirement for publication of community care plans under s 46(1) of the 1990 Act, and the fact that good practice dictates that authorities should produce accessible information as to departmental aims and priorities (see *Getting the Message Across* at pp 10–11), there is a clear need for careful drafting of any relevant policy so as not to frustrate a user's legitimate expectation if a particular policy is departed from in an individual case.

## 5.6   Reviewing service provision

It is axiomatic that care needs for which services are being provided should be reviewed regularly by further assessment (see Materials, *Policy Guidance* at para 3.51, and Laming letter at para 31).

As a result of the Divisional Court decision in *R v Gloucestershire CC, ex p Mahfood* (see 5.4, above) it is now clear that an authority has no power to make a new determination reducing its service provision without a prior re-assessment of need. The reason for this is that a determination as to service provision is contingent upon a decision as to need (see s 47(1) of the 1990 Act).

It is submitted that the situation is different where an authority's level of resources has risen so that it may now provide community care services for which a need was established on assessment but for which, previously, there were no resources available.

In such circumstances, an authority may increase the level of its services without going through the reassessment process since, *ex hypothesi*, there is no point in the assessment process but circumstances do require the exercise of the power to determine increased provision (see s 12 of the Interpretation Act 1978). Further, the language of s 47(1)(*b*) of the 1990 Act would appear to allow redetermination of service provision based upon the original assessment in circumstances where no new need was being contended.

Whether, following reassessment, an authority could act to reduce the determined level of service provision, in the absence of a diminished need, is open to doubt. The Divisional Court judgment in *R v Gloucestershire CC, ex p Mahfood* (above) does not grapple with this issue because, there, the definition of 'need' was held to be in part a function of resources. The cases on legitimate expectation referred to at 5.5, above (*ex p Ruddock*; *ex p Khan*) suggest that the withdrawal of a benefit or advantage conferred as the result of an assurance or past practice will not be permitted by the courts unless the overwhelming public interest requires it and then only following representations. It follows that this is another area where a plea of lack of available resources may not assist the authority (see the Laming letter at para 31; see also 5.4, above).

## 5.7   Service provision and the courts

The issue here is the nature of the legal remedies theoretically available to a user in respect of:

(1)   the authority's failure to determine service provision lawfully or at all;

(2)   the authority's failure to review service provision lawfully or at all;

(3)   the authority's failure to provide the requisite level of service having reached a determination that such level is required to be provided.

In *Cocks v Thanet District Council* [1983] 2 AC 286, the House of Lords considered whether ss 4, 5 and 6 of the Housing (Homeless Persons) Act 1977 created any private law, as opposed to public law, rights. The leading speech was delivered by Lord Bridge who said:

> It is for the housing authority, once the duty to inquire has arisen, to make the appropriate inquiries and to decide whether they are satisfied, or not satisfied as the case may be, of the matters which will give rise to the limited housing or the full housing duty. These are essentially public law functions.

Lord Bridge contrasted this with the legal position once a decision had been reached. He observed:

> On the other hand, the housing authority are charged with executive functions. Once a decision has been reached by the housing authority which gives rise to the temporary, the limited or the full housing duty, rights and obligations are immediately created in the field of private law.

It has already been noted at 5.1 that the homelessness decision-making model is directly parallel to that of service provision. Applying the principles of the House of Lords in *Cocks v Thanet* (see also *Mohram Ali v Tower Hamlets* [1992] 3 WLR 208; *Tower Hamlets LBC v Abdi*, unreported, 16 September 1992; *London Borough of Hackney v Lambourne*, unreported, 27 November 1992), the following seems clear:

(1)   The sole mode of legal challenge to a failure to determine service provision lawfully or at all is by way of judicial review since this is a decision-making function of the authority reached prior to any private law duty arising.

(2)   For the same reason as in (1), judicial review is the only means of challenging a failure to review service provision lawfully or at all.

(3)   Where a decision has been reached as to service provision, either initially or on review by the authority, such authority is then charged with the 'executive function' of implementation which is an obligation probably enforceable in private law, including a claim for damages (see Chapter 13).

Issues may arise as, for example, to whether judicial review may properly be sought before exhausting any available complaints machinery, or as to the scope of any potential damages claim in private law where service provision is withdrawn by virtue of an unlawful decision. These matters are separately considered in the chapters on remedies (see Chapters 9 to 13 and the Practitioners' Checklist in Appendix 1).

## Part 3

Natural Justice in the Conduct and
Communication of Assessment

# Chapter 6

# Conducting the Assessment

## 6.1  Fairness of assessment

This chapter is concerned with the fairness of the assessment process (including any re-assessment by way of review, see 6.7). Aspects of fairness relevant to the decision reached (the giving of reasons, for example) are discussed in Chapter 7.

If an assessment is not conducted in accordance with the requirements of natural justice or procedural propriety it will, in principle, be susceptible to judicial review (see *Council of Civil Service Unions v Minister for the Civil Service* [1985] AC 374).

The National Health Service and Community Care Act 1990 is, largely, silent as to how an assessment should be carried out. This does not mean, however, that natural justice is irrelevant. As Byles J observed in *Cooper v Wandsworth Board of Works* (1863) 14 CBNS 180 at p 194:

> a long course of decisions . . . establish, that although there are no positive words in a statute requiring that the party shall be heard, yet the justice of the common law will supply the omission of the legislature.

Where it is clear that additional steps are needed to achieve justice and will not frustrate the apparent purpose of the legislation the court will readily imply them into the Act (see, eg, per Lord Reid in *Wiseman v Borneman* [1971] AC 297 at p 308).

There are, in any event, two statutory provisions that provide additional underpinning for the implication of natural justice into the assessment process.

As has been seen, ss 7 and 7A of the Local Authority Social Services Act 1970 require a local authority, exercising social services functions, to act (respectively) 'under' guidance of the Secretary of State or 'in accordance with' directions issued by the Secretary of State. A large amount of guidance has already been given (see, eg, Materials 3 to 5), which is clearly (in part) designed to ensure fairness in the undertaking of authorities' assessment procedures. This guidance must, in so far as it is statutory (eg, the *Policy Guidance*), be complied with without substantial deviation, and in so far as it is non-statutory (eg, the *Practitioners' Guide*) be taken account of when conducting assessments and followed in spirit if not to the letter (see 1.6, where the legal effect of guidance is considered).

Secondly, s 47(4) of the 1990 Act provides for the giving of directions by the Secretary of State as to the manner in which an assessment is to be carried out. In the absence of such directions (none have yet been given) the assessment 'shall be carried out in such manner and take such form as the local authority consider appropriate.' This discretion must, clearly, be exercised in such a way as to achieve fairness in the assessment process in order to fall within the policy and objects of the Act (*Padfield v Minister of Agriculture, Fisheries and Food* [1968] AC 997).

## 6.2    Scope of natural justice in the assessment procedure

It is sometimes said that natural justice has two limbs, namely: (i) the rule against bias, and (ii) the right to be heard (see *Kanda v Government of Malaya* [1962] AC 322 at 337).

In the context of community care service assessments, however, the particular aspects of fairness likely to be relevant are:

(1)  legitimate expectation; and,

(2)  the right to be heard.

Legitimate expectation will be relevant where a local authority has (as it should: see Laming letter at paras 10 and 11) published criteria as to its assessment procedures/criteria for eligibility, or has developed a practice of conducting assessments, and then seeks to depart from such criteria or practice (see 6.3, below).

Procedural fairness in allowing a user to put his case as to need embraces a number of aspects. In *Ridge v Baldwin* [1964] AC 40 (at p 65) Lord Reid emphasised that the appropriate test for ensuring that a person has had the opportunity of putting his case was what a reasonable man would consider to be fair in the particular circumstances. This general statement of principle requires scrutiny of several different stages of the assessment process (see below).

## 6.3    Legitimate expectation

The notion of 'legitimate expectation' has greatly extended the boundaries of natural justice to the point where it can be said to approximate to a requirement of administrative fairness in a wide range of situations.

As formulated by Lord Diplock in *Council of Civil Service Unions v Minister for the Civil Service* [1985] AC 374, legitimate expectation affords a form of protection against adverse decisions inconsistent with some benefit or advantage where the decision-maker has conferred such benefit or advantage as a result of past practice or assurance. As stated by Lord Diplock, and in most of the case law since, the concept has, primarily, been applied in a procedural manner so as to ensure that no such adverse decision will be taken without first giving the affected party an opportunity of making representations as to why the particular benefit/advantage should not be withdrawn.

It would, none the less, be unwise to view legitimate expectation as a solely procedural concept. Two modern decisions (*R v Home Secretary, ex p Khan* [1984] 1 WLR 1337; *R v Same, ex p Ruddock* [1987] 1 WLR 1482), show that the doctrine comes close to permitting the conferment of a substantive benefit as opposed merely to a right to make representations. In *Khan*, Parker LJ went so far as to suggest that a new policy could only be adopted against the recipient of a circular after considering whether the overriding public interest demanded it. In a recent case in the community care field the Court of Appeal appeared to accept that legitimate expectation was capable of conferring a substantive benefit (see *R v Devon CC, ex p Baker* [1995] 1 All ER 73).

Local authorities are advised to publish, in accessible form, information about their care services, including authorities' criteria for determining when services should be provided and the assessment procedures showing how and where to apply for an assessment, and giving information about how to make representations and complaints (see *Policy Guidance* at para 3.18 and 'Care Programming Approach', see Materials 3(B) and 4(E)).

It seems likely that if a local authority were to depart from published criteria (or from past practice) as to either its manner of conducting assessments, or its criteria for assessing need, without at least affording a user the opportunity of making representations and, perhaps also, without considering whether the wider public interest required such departure, it would render itself susceptible to judicial review.

In *Khan*, the Secretary of State was held by a majority of the Court of Appeal to be bound by a circular limiting the ambit of his discretion to turn down an application for entry clearance for a child. Exactly the same principle appears to be relevant to an authority's published information upon which a user or his representatives rely.

## 6.4 Pre-assessment considerations

All the guidance issued emphasises the importance of local authorities presenting clear and accessible published information about their assessment practices in a form which reaches users (see, also, 5.3, above). This is consistent with the importance that natural justice accords to a person being given notice of a hearing so as to be able to put his case properly (see *R v Thames Magistrates' Court, ex p Polemis* [1974] 1 WLR 1371).

According to the *Managers' Guide*, at para 2.5, such information should, as a matter of good practice, include:
- the range of needs for which the agency accepts responsibility;
- the aims, priorities and objectives of the agency;
- the types of services available from all sectors and the needs for which they cater;
- the criteria determining access to resources;

- the referral, assessment and review procedures within and between agencies;
- the entitlements of users and carers to information, participation and representation, including provision for equal opportunities;
- the charging policies;
- the standards by which the agency will monitor its performance, including response times to referrals;
- complaints and feedback procedures.

Failure to provide information in sufficiently clear form could, itself, form a ground of challenge in judicial review proceedings.

## 6.5    Participants in assessment process

The individual service user and normally, with his agreement, any carers should, so far as possible, be involved throughout an assessment (see *Policy Guidance* at para 3.15). Failure to do so may render an assessment unlawful (*R v North Yorkshire CC, ex p Hargreaves* (1994) *The Times*, 9 November). Such involvement follows, inevitably, from the statutory scheme of assessment which is to determine individual need for community care services. Additionally, natural justice may require that a service user be permitted the use of a representative to put his case for him if desired (cf *R v Leicestershire City JJ, ex p Barrow* [1991] 2 QB 260). Failure to permit a user, carer or representative access to the assessment procedure would render an authority, *prima facie*, amenable to judicial review.

There may be circumstances where the assessment is so straightforward as to involve minimum participation by the user or someone acting on his behalf (see 6.6, below). More likely to arise, however, is the situation where a user either does not want to or is unable to participate actively.

Clearly, a user cannot be forced to participate in an assessment against his will. A local authority is, none the less, under a duty to make an assessment in any case where apparent need for community care services capable of being provided by the authority is brought to its attention (see s 47(1) of the 1990 Act).

Thus, in circumstances where the user is unwilling to participate in an assessment such assessment must take place on the basis of the information brought before the authority by the carer or other third party or on the basis of information that it would otherwise seek an assessment. If the carer does not wish to participate it is unlikely that he may, thereafter, complain as to a breach of natural justice by the authority by reason of his not having made representations (see, eg *R v Nailsworth Licensing JJ, ex p Bird* [1953] 1 WLR 1046).

The position is slightly different where a user is unable to participate actively. The *Policy Guidance*, at para 3.16, indicates in general terms that in such circumstances 'it is even more important that he or she should be helped to understand what is involved and the intended outcome.' (See also *Children Act Guidance* at Materials 4.)

This does not, however, deal with the overall problem of procedural fairness. Section 3(6) of the Disabled Persons (Services, Consultation and Representation) Act 1986 will, when in force, require an authority, during an assessment under that Act, to provide such services as in its view are necessary to ensure that any mental or physical incapacity does not prevent the making of representations by or on behalf of a disabled person.

As a matter of principle it would seem that similar assistance should be given, where appropriate, for the purpose of an assessment under the 1990 Act. Indeed, ss 47(5) and (6) of the 1990 Act provide some support for this view empowering, as they do, the provision of community care services without assessment where the condition of a service user is such that, in the authority's view, he requires such services as a matter of urgency.

Given the statutory context it is submitted that an authority should, in all but the simplest case, permit oral representations to be made by a user or his representative. Where a carer's interests may be in conflict with the user's wishes, there should be separate representation (see *Guidance to the Carers Act* at Materials 4).

Participants in assessment from the authority's perspective are considered below.

## 6.6 The assessment

It is clear that every assessment must be handled on its merits. Arrangements should normally include an initial screening process to determine the appropriate form of assessment (see *Policy Guidance* at para 3.20; Laming letter at para 10). However, the screening process should not be so perfunctory as to prevent a service user being assessed for all services, within a reasonable time.

Some people may only require advice and assistance without formal assessment. In other cases assessment may, in practice, already have taken place as where, for example, a patient has already been assessed for discharge from hospital. In the latter case, subject to the user wishing to make further representations, the prior assessment will probably form the basis of the assessment decision (see White Paper at para 3.2.11; see also *Policy Guidance* at paras 3.41–3.45).

Other cases will, inevitably, be more complex and require more elaborate procedures. Such procedures 'should be sufficiently comprehensive and flexible to cope with all levels and types of need presented by different client groups.' (See *Policy Guidance* at para 3.20.)

The *Managers' Guide* contains a table (reproduced in Materials 3), containing a model for six possible types of assessment according to the type of need and the services to be considered and giving an indication of the type of staff, number of agencies involved and an example of a service outcome.

Where an apparent need is simple and defined the simplest type of assessment carried out by reception or administrative staff is likely to be sufficient. At the top end of the scale a comprehensive assessment will be required for ill-defined, high risk and severe need and this should be carried out by professionally qualified and/or specialist professional staff on a multiple agency basis. In all assessments GPs ought generally, as a matter of good practice to be consulted (see *Policy Guidance* at paras 3.47 and 3.48; Laming letter at para 9).

In all cases where a local authority, in assessing need, proposes to act on the basis of information not available to the user so that the user is not alerted to what is in the local authority's mind, such information must be disclosed to the user or his representative and failure to do so is a breach of natural justice (see *Mahon v Air New Zealand Ltd* [1984] AC 808; *R v Mental Health Review Tribunal, ex p Clatworthy* [1985] 3 All ER 699). A related consideration, underpinned by statute, is that confidential health and personal social services information on a service user should not be disclosed to other agencies for the purpose of assessment without obtaining the user's written consent to such disclosure (*Policy Guidance* at para 3.50). If a user is unable to consent to disclosure, the Official Solicitor may be approached.

## 6.7   Consultation and the reassessment process

It is now established that community care services may not be withdrawn without a prior reassessment of need (*R v Gloucestershire CC, ex p Mahfood* (1995) TLR 351). Similarly, there must be a prior reassessment before service provision is reduced or met in a different way. The same considerations of fairness necessarily apply to a reassessment as they do to an assessment.

Additionally, however, it may be important that before any withdrawal of services there is full consultation with those likely to be affected. This stems from the legitimate expectation which the service user or users may have from any past practice, or promise of consultation.

In *R v Devon CC, ex p Baker* [1995] 1 All ER 73, for example, residents of a home for the elderly were held to have a legitimate expectation of consultation about closure. Similarly, but even more extensively, in *R v Wandsworth LBC, ex p Beckwith* (1995) *The Times*, 5 June (a case decided at first instance by Potts J and not overruled on this point by the House of Lords), the court held that the duty to consult (where it arises) extends to residents of other homes only indirectly affected by the closure of a particular residential care home.

More difficult is the question of whether legitimate expectation of consultation before withdrawal could be based on the past practice of provision of the service. Plainly, the service user has a legal entitlement to reassessment before withdrawal of services. It seems unlikely, however, that the courts would (in the absence of a promise or past practice of consultation) require more than a reassessment of need before permitting withdrawal of services. A decision to withdraw services where there was no evidence, on reassessment, or reduced need for the service might, however, be challengeable either on legitimate expectation or other recognised public law principles.

Consultation, when required, requires (per Webster J in *R v Secretary of State for Social Services, ex p Association of Metropolitan Authorities* [1986] WLR 1 at p 4):

> . . . the communication of a genuine invitation to give advice and a genuine consideration of that advice . . . [I]t must go without saying that to achieve consultation sufficient information must be supplied by the consulting to the consulted party to enable it to tender helpful advice. Sufficient time must be given by the consulting to the consulted party. Sufficient, in that context, does not mean ample, but at least enough to enable the relevant purpose to be fulfilled. By helpful advice . . . I mean sufficiently informed and considered information or advice about aspects of the form or substance of the proposals, or their implications for the consulted party, being aspects material to the implementation of the proposal, as to which the party consulted might have relevant information or advice to offer.

# Chapter 7

# Communication of Decisions

## 7.1 Introduction

The National Health Service and Community Care Act 1990 is silent as to the form or timing of assessment and service provision decisions. In this chapter the following particular problems are addressed:

- Given that assessment and service provision determination are separate processes (see Chapter 4) must decisions in respect of each be delivered separately?
- Must such decision(s) be in writing?
- What is the minimum content of each decision?
- Do reasons have to be provided?
- Within what timescale must such decision(s) be given?
- To whom should such decisions be communicated?

## 7.2 Separate decisions?

Although assessment is, conceptually, separate from service provision determination the only 'decision' that a local authority is statutorily required to come to is one on whether it should provide community care services (see s 47(1)(b) of the 1990 Act). The assessment process is a necessary constituent of such a decision because the authority must make its decision 'having regard to the results of the assessment'.

Thus, whilst it is clear that assessment means that the authority will have to 'decide' on a particular applicant's needs for community care services under s 47(1)(a) of the 1990 Act, it is apparent that the authority's 'decision' is necessarily contained in the service provision determination itself. The authority makes a single decision but it contains separate constitutive elements.

## 7.3 Decision in writing?

Nothing in the National Health Service and Community Care Act 1990 expressly requires that the authority's assessment or service provision determinations must be recorded in writing.

It is submitted that there is no such universal requirement for, if it were otherwise, an unnecessary burden would be placed upon local authorities habitually conducting informal assessments and making service provision decisions of a straightforward nature.

This view is supported by the *Managers' Guide* which (at para 2.24) observes that decisions 'in respect of simple needs' may be communicated 'on a verbal basis'. However, given the probable requirement that most assessment/service provision decisions provide reasons (see below), it is likely that the courts would require written decisions in relation to anything other than an objectively straightforward case. The *Managers' Guide* and *Policy Guidance* (see, respectively, para 2.24 and para 3.27) indicate that a written decision should be given where an assessment results in the offer of a continuing service but, whilst correct, this is almost certainly not the only situation in which an authority's decision should be given in writing. Certainly, a decision in writing should always be supplied on request (*Policy Guidance* at para 3.27). According to para 4.37 of the *Practitioners' Guide* care plans 'should be set out in concise written form, linked with the assessment of need' (see also *R v Islington LBC, ex p Rixon* (1996) *The Times*, 17 April).

## 7.4 Content of assessment decision

The objective of assessment is to determine individual need for community care services that a local authority is empowered to provide or arrange for the provision of (see s 47(1)(*a*) of the 1990 Act).

Thus, an authority's assessment should define an individual's specific needs in relation to identified community care services irrespective of whether the authority had decided to provide such services. A useful definition of 'need' in this context is 'the requirement of individuals to enable them to achieve, maintain or restore an acceptable level of social independence or quality of life' (see *Practitioners' Guide*: Summary of Practice Guidance at para 11).

The assessment should, it is submitted, be reasoned (see below). On that basis it should explain, intelligibly, the material upon which it has determined need. If there is material before it, or representations made, which the authority has rejected, the basis for such rejection should be clearly set out. From a practical perspective the assessment should be clearly demarcated in the decision and separated from the service provision element of the reasoning.

## 7.5 Content of service provision decision

Section 47(1)(*b*) of the National Health Service and Community Care Act 1990 requires a service provision decision to be made (having regard to the authority's assessment) of whether the applicant's needs call for provision by the authority of any service for which need is established. The criteria affecting such a decision have already been considered (see Chapter 5).

The content of a decision as to service provision connotes the following:
(1) determination of the issue of whether the applicant's needs (as

recorded in the assessment) call for the provision by the authority of particular services and, if so, what services;

(2)  the reasons for that decision including identification of the material relied up by the authority in arriving at such decision (see below) and indicating why, if it be the case, that material before it, or representations made, were rejected;

(3)  reference to the existence of a complaints procedure (see *Policy Guidance* at para 6.29).

In practice, once needs have been assessed, any decision to provide particular community care services or arrange for the provision of such services should (if possible) be set out in the form of a care plan (see *Policy Guidance* at para 3.24). The plan should make clear the extent to which an individual's needs qualify for assistance under the authority's eligibility criteria for services (see Laming letter at para 15).

The *Policy Guidance* (ibid) suggests that a care plan should be agreed and 'care planning' is defined in Appendix B of the *Guidance* as:

> the process of negotiation between assessor, applicant, carers and other relevant agencies on the most appropriate ways of meeting assessed needs within available resources and incorporating them into an individual care plan.

This is, necessarily, subject to the authority's obligations under s 7 of the Local Authority Social Services Act 1970. If agreement is not possible the points of difference should be recorded (*Policy Guidance* at para 3.25).

The decision should (see *Policy Guidance* at para 3.26, and Laming letter at para 15) include agreement as to what is to be done, by whom and by when, with clearly identified points of access to each of the relevant agencies for the service user, carers and for the service manager.

A model outline of a care plan is proposed in the *Practitioners' Guide* as consisting of the following:

- the overall objectives
- the specific objectives of:
  — users
  — carers
  — service providers
- the criteria for measuring the achievement of these objectives
- the services to be provided by which personnel/agency
- the cost to the user and the contributing agencies
- the other options considered
- any point of difference between the user, carer, care-planning practitioner or other agency
- any unmet need with reasons—to be separately notified to the service planning system
- the named person(s) responsible for implementing, monitoring and reviewing the care plan
- the date of the first planned review.

In *R v Islington LBC, ex p Rixon* (1996) *The Times*, 17 April, Sedley J held that the respondent authority's care plan was unlawful in failing to comply in material respects with the above-mentioned *Practitioners' Guide* as to content, specification of objectives, achievement of agreement on implementation by all those involved, leeway for contingencies and the identification and feeding back of assessed but still unmet need. The judge rejected the respondent's submission that the content of a care plan was not justiciable by way of judicial review. Crucially, he held that the authority should have had regard to the relevant parts of the *Practitioners' Guide* in formulating its care plan and that, 'whilst the occasional *lacuna* would not furnish evidence of such a disregard, the [above] series of *lacunae* . . . does . . . suggest that the . . . guidance has been overlooked.' *Rixon* was applied in *R v London Borough of Sutton, ex p Tucher*, unreported, 29 October 1996, where mandamus was awarded to compel the respondent council to issue a care plan within 21 days in conformity with para 3.25 of the Policy Guidance and with the above-cited parts of the *Practitioners' Guide*.

## 7.6 Reasons

A failure to provide reasons may afford a basis for challenging an assessment or service provision decision on the ground that it constitutes procedural impropriety or unfairness. This is so even though nothing in the National Health Service and Community Care Act 1990 expressly requires the giving of reasons.

In a landmark decision, the Court of Appeal in *R v Civil Service Appeal Board, ex p Cunningham* [1991] 4 All ER 310 held that: (i) there is, except as laid down by statute, no general duty in English law to give reasons for a decision, but that (ii) natural justice may, in appropriate circumstances, require the giving of reasons.

The regulating principle is that:

> Unless the citizen can discover the reasoning behind the decision, he may be unable to tell whether it is reviewable or not and so he may be deprived of the protection of the law. A right to reasons is therefore an indispensable part of a sound system of judicial review. (See Wade and Forsyth, *Administrative Law*, 7th edn (OUP) at p 542.)

This was the reasoning of the majority of the Court of Appeal in *Cunningham*. Lord Donaldson of Lymington MR who gave the leading judgment in that case, ended his decision with the words:

> I would therefore dismiss the appeal not only upon the ground of legitimate expectation . . ., but also upon the broader ground that fairness requires a tribunal such as the board to give sufficient reasons for its decision to enable the parties to know the issues to which it addressed its mind and that it acted lawfully.

McCowan LJ, in reaching the same conclusion, stated:

> I am influenced by the following factors:
> 1   There is no appeal from the board's determination of the amount of compensation.
> 2   In making that determination the board is carrying out a judicial function.

3    The board is susceptible to judicial review.
4    The procedure provided for by the code, that is to say the provision of a recommendation without reasons, is insufficient to achieve justice.
5    There is no statute which requires the courts to tolerate that unfairness.
6    The giving of short reasons would not frustrate the apparent purpose of the code.
7    It is not a case where the giving of reasons would be harmful to the public interest.

These considerations drive me to the view that this is a case where the board should have given reasons . . .

In essence, therefore, where a 'fully judicial body' (per Lord Donaldson MR at p 318j), susceptible to judicial review and from which there is no right of appeal, gives a decision in a case where to give reasons would prejudice neither the purpose of the material statute nor the public interest, that body ought to give reasons for its decision, so that the individual affected thereby may know whether the decision was made lawfully.

The reasoning in *Cunningham* has been strengthened in later cases. In *R v Secretary of State for the Home Department, ex p Doody* [1994] 1 AC 531 the House of Lords, after approving *Cunningham*, observed (per Lord Mustill) that it may be that the very importance of the decision to the individual—as where personal liberty is involved—is such that a decision must contain reasons. In *R v Universities Funding Council, ex p Institute of Dental Surgery* [1994] 1 WLR 242 Sedley J held that a duty to give reasons exists not only where a decision deals with matters which the courts guard zealously (such as personal liberty) but also where a decision is 'aberrant' or calls for an explanation.

These decisions strongly suggest that a local authority making assessment and service provision decisions in the field of community care is performing functions which render it liable in law to provide reasons for such decisions. Assuming that to be right, such authority must (independent of policy guidance) provide reasons for its decisions which are both 'adequate and intelligible' (see *Re Poyser and Mills Arbitration* [1964] 2 QB 247).

Failure to provide such reasons may lead to judicial review although if lack of reasons is the sole substantive ground for review the court may simply order the authority to provide reasons rather than quash the decision itself.

## 7.7   Time within which decisions must be reached

No express time limits are laid down in the National Health Service and Community Care Act 1990 for the communication of assessment or service provision decisions. None the less such decisions should be made timeously (see White Paper at para 3.2.11; *Practitioners' Guide* at para 3.3).

Unreasonable delay in determination of assessment or service provision may lead to judicial review. In *R v Secretary of State for the Home Department, ex p Phansopkar* [1976] QB 606, for example, *mandamus* was granted requiring the Home Secretary to determine applications for certificates proving a right of abode in a reasonable time.

What constitutes unreasonable delay in the context of community care assessments is a matter of fact and degree. Possibly, such delay must be *Wednesbury* unreasonable in the sense that no reasonable local authority could have delayed for such a period (see *R v IRC, ex p Opman International UK* [1986] 1 WLR 568; *R v Secretary of State for the Home Department, ex p Rofathullah* [1989] QB 219). However, as seen above, lack of resources cannot be used as an excuse for failure to assess and absence of resources cannot of themselves justify unreasonable delay in assessment. Further, if an authority were to give no indication of when it might assess that in itself might afford a challenge by way of judicial review. The courts are, however, traditionally reluctant to interfere in the context of the time within which a public body should perform its functions and deploy its resources (see *Rofathullah*, per Purchas LJ).

In urgent cases a local authority may provide community care services prior to any assessment (s 47(4) of the 1990 Act). Delay in arranging an assessment should not preclude the provision of such services or be used as a reason to delay service provision. However, where community care services are provided without prior assessment, an assessment must be carried out 'as soon as practicable thereafter' (s 47(5) of the 1990 Act). Statutory guidance issued under s 7 of the Local Authority Social Services Act 1970 may require a service provision decision to be taken within a particular time where failure to do so will contravene the guidance itself (see *R v London Borough of Sutton, ex p Tucher*, unreported, 29 October 1996).

## 7.8  Recipient of decisions

The service user and carer must, clearly, be provided with the assessment/service provision decision. With the user's permission assessment information should be passed on to those responsible for care delivery (see *Policy Guidance* at para 3.26).

Additionally, service users have a general right under the Access to Personal Files Act 1987 and the Access to Personal Files (Social Services) Regulations 1989 to know what information is held about them by social services and housing departments and to copies of that information on payment of a small fee. The relevant information must be provided within 40 days. Certain information is, however, exempt from the statutory requirements, being information:

(1)  about other persons (without their consent);
(2)  about the physical or mental health of the service user where the health authority states that disclosure would harm that person's or another person's physical or mental health;
(3)  for the prevention or detection of crime;
(4)  protected by legal privilege.

Also of relevance is the Access to Health Records Act 1990, (which allows access to records by legal advisors), and consideration should be given to use of the Official Solicitor and/or the Court of Protection in cases of legal incapacity.

# Part 4

## Legal Remedies

# Chapter 8

# Complaints Procedures

## 8.1  Legal source of complaints procedures

Section 7B of the Local Authority Social Services Act 1970 (as inserted by s 50 of the National Health Service and Community Care Act 1990) creates machinery for a complaints procedure to be set up where a local authority has improperly discharged, or failed to discharge, any of its social services functions. The term 'social services functions' is, clearly, wide enough to embrace, and does embrace, assessments or service provision decisions under the 1990 Act (see ss 2, 3 and 15(2) of and Sched 1 to the Local Authority Social Services Act 1970). Additionally, the *Policy Guidance*, at para 6.5, clarifies that '. . . it will be open to authorities at their discretion to deal with a complaint not covered by section 7B under the standard procedure.'

By s 7B(1) of the 1970 Act the Secretary of State is empowered to require, by order, local authorities to establish a procedure for considering any representations (including any complaints) made to them by a 'qualifying individual' or anyone acting on his behalf in relation to the discharge of, or failure to discharge, any of an authority's social services functions in respect of that individual. The Local Authority Social Services (Complaints Procedure) Order 1990 provides, somewhat repetitively, that:

> Every local authority shall establish a procedure for considering any representations (including any complaints) which are made to them by a qualifying individual, or anyone acting on his behalf, in relation to the discharge of, or any failure to discharge, any of their social services functions in respect of that individual.'
> A person is a 'qualifying individual', under s 7B(2), if:
> 
> (a) the authority have a power or a duty to provide, or to secure the provision of, a service for him; and,
> (b) his need or possible need for such a service has (by whatever means) come to the authority's attention.

Local authorities are, by s 7B(3), bound to comply with any directions of the Secretary of State as to the procedure to be adopted in considering representations, and as to the taking of any necessary action in consequence thereof. They must also give such publicity to their procedures as they consider appropriate (see s 7B(4)).

The Secretary of State has issued directions as to the creation of complaints procedures by virtue of the Complaints Procedure Directions 1990 (reproduced in Materials 2). In addition, helpful practice guidance is contained in the *Policy Guidance* and in the *Right to Complain* (see 1.7). This guidance must be taken into account by an authority in so far as the guidance is not reproduced in the directions (see s 7 of the 1970 Act).

The *Policy Guidance* also states (at para 6.9) that such guidance is not exhaustive and that in formulating or revising its complaints procedures an authority may find it helpful to refer, for example, to the code of practice on complaints procedures issued by the Local Authority Associations and the Commission for Local Administration in 1978, and to the booklet *Open to Complaints: Guidelines for Social Services Complaints Procedures* published by the National Consumer Council (with the National Institute for Social Work) in 1988.

Given that complaints in respect of an authority's failure to perform its social services functions are required to be considered under a specific complaints regime, a user will need to consider carefully whether such procedure (or specific stage of the procedure) constitutes an alternative remedy so as to preclude judicial review of an assessment or service provision decision before the procedure is exhausted (see also Practitioner Checklist in Appendix 1).

Materially, in *R v Gloucestershire CC ex p RADAR* (unreported, 21 December 1995) Carnwath J held that judicial review was more suitable for litigating 'a general issue of principle'. In *R v Devon CC, ex p Baker* [1995] 1 All ER 73 the court was prepared to entertain judicial review in what was regarded as a 'developing' area of the law. It is also significant that in recent cases the courts have accepted a discrete monitoring role in considering such cases.

This issue is considered in more detail in Chapter 9, and the observations made in respect of susceptibility to judicial review in this chapter must be read as being subject to that issue.

## 8.2 Publicising the complaints regime

Although publicity for an authority's complaints procedures is left to the authority's discretion (see s 7B(4) of the Local Authority Social Services Act 1970), the *Policy Guidance* (at para 6.26) suggests three potential methods, being:

(1) Leaflets explaining the procedure in simple terms and referring to the role of the Local Government Ombudsman and to the separate leaflet, *Complaint about the Council?* The leaflet should also give the name, address and telephone number of the person responsible for administering the procedure and be widely accessible to all, including ethnic minorities and blind people.

(2) Notices displayed in the authority's offices.

(3) Visual and oral presentations.

In addition, an assessment or service provision decision should itself contain reference to the authority's complaints procedure (see Chapter 8, and *Policy Guidance* at para 6.29).

Failure to publicise an authority's complaints procedure so as to deny a user any effective opportunity of having his complaint heard would be susceptible to judicial review either as a breach of the authority's discretion under s 7B(4) of the 1970 Act (see *Padfield v Minister of Agriculture Fisheries and Food* [1968] AC 997) or, more simply, as a violation of natural justice.

By contrast, if an authority has given full publicity to its complaints procedure then if such published procedures were to be departed from a user or those acting on his behalf should be given 'full and serious consideration whether there is some overriding public interest' justifying such departure (see *R v Secretary of State for the Home Department, ex p Asif Khan* [1984] 1 WLR 1337). Failure to do so could give rise to a challenge to any substitute procedure as a breach of the user's legitimate expectation. However, if the procedure adopted is fair and does not lead to injustice then, even if there is variation from the authority's published procedures, an application for judicial review would be unlikely to succeed given that 'the so-called rules of natural justice are not engraved on tablets of stone' (see *Lloyd v McMahon* [1987] AC 625 at p 702), and that the procedure ought not to be operated inflexibly (see 8.3, below). Ideally, however, an authority's published procedures should state clearly that departure from stages of the procedure may be necessary according to the circumstances of the individual case.

## 8.3   Stages of the procedure

There are three stages to an authority's complaints procedure. These are:
  (1)   the informal or problem-solving stage;
  (2)   the formal or registration stage;
  (3)   the review stage.

By Direction 4(1) of the 1990 Directions the local authority must appoint one of its officers to assist the authority in the co-ordination of all these stages of its consideration of a complaint. The authority must also ensure that all members or officers involved in the handling of complaints are familiar with the procedures contained in the Directions (see Direction 4(2)).

Nothing in an authority's complaints regime is intended to affect other potential avenues of complaint, such as the right of a user to approach a local councillor, or to complain (if appropriate) to the Mental Health Act Commission (see *Policy Guidance* at paras 6.34 and 6.35). An authority may lawfully refuse access to its complaints procedure in respect of anonymous complaints or complaints of a general nature unconnected with the performance of the authority's social services functions (see *Policy Guidance* at para 6.5).

However, it is not open to an authority to refuse access to its complaints machinery on the basis that an alternative complementary method of recourse is available to a user since this would constitute unlawful delegation of power (see *Barnard v National Dock Labour Board* [1953] 2 QB 18), as well as falling foul of the authority's express statutory obligation to maintain a complaints procedure.

## 8.4 The informal stage

Direction 5(1) of the Complaints Procedure Directions 1990 provides that where a local authority receives representations from a qualifying individual (see 8.1, above) it should, first, attempt to resolve the matter informally.

There are a number of points to be made as to the implementation of this preliminary stage of the complaints procedure:

(1) The fact that this stage is categorised as 'informal' does not mean that it is 'casual' (see the *Right to Complain* at para 4.3). Its purpose is to solve problems at the earliest possible stage and pursuing every case to the final stage would undermine this concept (*Right to Complain* at para 4.8). Representations may, at this stage, be oral (see *Policy Guidance* at para 6.17). Although the 1990 Directions are not entirely clear on this point it seems that informal representations need not be recorded under Direction 9 since the recording of representations appears to constitute the registration stage and the commencement of formal time limits (see below).

(2) The informal stage should not, however, be used as a device to prevent or dissuade users from making a formal complaint (*Right to Complain* at para 4.5). Procedures operated in this way would be liable to challenge on judicial review as being void for improper motives (see *Wheeler v Leicester City Council* [1985] AC 1054).

(3) But disregard of this stage by an authority may be justified in appropriate circumstances (see *Policy Guidance* at para 6.30). This reflects the principle that inflexible application of a procedure in the name of fairness may itself produce unfairness (here delay) and, therefore, be unlawful (see *R v Police Complaints Board, ex p Madden* [1983] 1 WLR 447). For example, serious allegations may require the involvement of senior staff at an early stage and a more formal process (*Policy Guidance*, ibid). Certainly, if a complainant wishes to go straight to the formal stage of the procedure he should be helped to do so (*Right to Complain* at para 4.9).

(4) For similar reasons, different procedures from the conventional complaints regime may need to be utilised. The *Policy Guidance* (para 6.30) suggests that where allegations indicate the commission of a criminal offence, and such allegations are serious and substantial, the police should be informed immediately and local procedures contained in an authority's standing orders should be followed.

(5) Procedures for reviewing assessment and service provision decisions (see 9.7) may overlap, to some extent, with the informal (or even registration) stage of the complaints procedure. It may be that a complaint is really a request for reconsideration of the assessment. As already seen, any review of an assessment decision should make reference to how a complaint may be pursued further (see *Policy Guidance* at para 6.29). Further, at the registration stage a complaint about a particular decision will be referred to the original decision-maker to see and take action on it (*Right to Complain* at para 4.13).

(6) Although the 1990 Directions do not appear to require an authority to provide support for complainants at the informal stage, the *Policy Guidance*, at para 6.28, makes it clear that such support and encouragement should be available at the earliest stage since by providing it 'the chances of resolving the matter there and then increase.'

## 8.5   The registration stage

Direction 5(2) of the 1990 Directions stipulates that if the matter cannot be resolved to the complainant's satisfaction, the local authority must give or send to him an explanation of the registration and review stages of the complaints procedure (as set out in the Directions) and ask him to submit a written representation if he desires to proceed.

The requirement that a complainant be sent or given an explanation of the procedure set out in the Directions is strict and is likely to be regarded as mandatory so that it will be fatal to disregard it (see, eg, *Grunwick Processing Laboratories Ltd v ACAS* [1978] AC 277). This requirement differs from the general exhortation to authorities to publish their complaints procedures (see above), since it is not the authority's particular procedure but, rather, the procedure contained in the 1990 Directions that must be provided. Further, the information must be provided directly to the complainant as opposed to being published generally.

It is at this stage that the authority is, by Direction 5(3), required to offer assistance and guidance to the complainant on the use of the complaints procedure or, at least, to provide advice as to where the complainant may obtain such advice and guidance.

Those providing such support must ensure that a complainant's representations reflect what the complainant wishes to say and should ask the complainant to sign it (*Right to Complain* at para 4.10).

Whilst there may be technical arguments open to a local authority that it cannot be held to have acted unlawfully in respect of inadequate representations upon which a third party, rather than the authority, has advised, the general duty to act fairly probably requires the authority to ensure that there is no ambiguity in the representations presented to it. In particular, the term 'representations' has a specific meaning under Direction 2(1) of the 1990 Directions and means representations (including complaints) referred to in s 7B(1) of the Local Authority Social Services Act 1970. Section 7B(1) necessitates that representations must be 'in relation to the discharge of, or any failure to discharge' any social services functions of the authority in respect of the complainant.

The next stages of the registration stage may be summarised thus:

(1)  Every representation received must be registered (Direction 9). This does not preclude an oral hearing but it seems clear that the registration stage is envisaged, primarily, as a formal written record of complaint and response thereto.

(2)  Such registered complaint must be considered and responded to within 28 days of the authority receiving the complaint. If this is not possible an explanation of the position must be provided to the complainant within the first 28 days including the reason why it is not possible and an indication of when a response may be expected. A full response must, in any event, be given within three months (Direction 6(1)).

(3)  These time limits would, almost certainly, be regarded by a court as mandatory and would, accordingly, justify judicial review if breached (see, though, the tactical considerations in relation to judicial review at Chapter 9). The authority is, by Direction 9, required to record whether the time limit has been complied with.

(4)  The authority must notify in writing the result of its consideration to:
   (a)  the complainant,
   (b)  (where different) the person on whose behalf the complaint was made 'unless the local authority consider that that person is not able to understand it or it would cause him unnecessary distress', and
   (c)  any other person who the authority considers has 'sufficient interest' in the case (Direction 7(1)).

It is unclear who could fall within category (b) above given that the complainant is, by Direction 2(1), expressed to mean a 'qualifying individual' under s 7B(2) of the 1970 Act (see above), and only such persons have standing to invoke the complaints procedures at all. Further, it is unclear as to why only that category of persons is exempt from notification in the event of incapacity to understand or distress. However, persons having a 'sufficient interest' is a potentially wide class and probably extends to anyone affected by or involved in the response. Although the Directions do not expressly so stipulate, the authority's response should advise the complainant what further options are open should he remain dissatisfied (see *Policy Guidance* at para 6.14).

(5)  There is no express requirement in the Directions for the authority's notification to be reasoned, but this may be thought to be implicit in the obligation to notify 'the result of their consideration' in writing.

(6) Arrangements must be made so that where a complainant asks (within 28 days of notification) for the authority's response to be reviewed, a panel constituted by the authority meets within 28 days of the authority's receipt of the complainant's request (see Direction 7(2) and (3)). So far as the authority is concerned the time limits would probably be regarded by a court as mandatory and give rise, potentially, to judicial review if breached. It seems likely that an authority has a discretion to extend time for the complainant to seek review by the authority's panel in the interests of fairness.

(7) The authority must record its own notification and whether it (and, presumably, the complainant) has complied with the time limits in respect of the meeting of the panel (Direction 9).

Investigation of a complaint, at the registration stage, may need to be conducted by an investigator. The legal principles relevant to the type of enquiry to be conducted are similar to those in respect of assessment enquiries (see Chapter 4). A useful practice guide is contained as an Appendix to the *Right to Complain* and is reproduced in Materials 2. Although the *Practice Guide* does not itself require the investigator's report or recommendations to the authority to be disclosed to the complainant, it is submitted that the complainant is entitled to disclosure of such material in order that he may comment upon it to the authority. In the absence of disclosure judicial review may lie since the complainant has not, in that event, been entitled to put his case properly or to make informed representations on matters which might be of concern to the investigator (see *R v Mental Health Review Tribunal, ex p Clatworthy* [1985] 3 All ER 699). This is particularly so given that the complainant is entitled to an oral hearing (see below) before the review panel and the investigator's report may be highly relevant to the representations that a complainant wishes to make before the panel.

## 8.6 The review stage

The review stage is the final stage of the stipulated complaints procedure and arises where a complaint has not been satisfactorily resolved at either the informal or registration stages. It involves formal consideration of the complaint by a panel of the authority.

Direction 2(1) of the 1990 Directions defines 'panel' as meaning a panel of three persons, at least one of whom must be an independent person. Direction 2(3) defines an 'independent person' as:

> a person who is neither a member nor an officer of that authority, nor where the local authority have delegated any of its social services functions to any organisation, a person who is a member of or employed by that organisation, nor the spouse of any such person.

It is the 'independent person' who should chair the panel (see *Policy Guidance*, Annex A at para 4). Helpful guidance as to how local authorities have selected an independent person is contained at paras 4.22 *et seq* of the *Right to Complain*.

As indicated above, the review panel should meet within 28 days of the user's request for review. The panel has the task of reconsidering *de novo* the authority's notification. It seems clear that the panel is engaged in such reconsideration, ie *de novo* of the notification decision rather than in a process akin to judicial review since Direction 7(3) of the 1990 Directions requires the panel to consider the matter together with any oral or written submissions as the complainant or the local authority wish it to consider.

It is also plain from the wording of Direction 7(3) that the complainant is, in contrast to the usual procedure at the registration stage, entitled to an oral hearing. This is reinforced by Annex A of the *Policy Guidance* at para 5 which advises that complainants should be notified in writing at least ten days beforehand of the time and venue of the meeting and that they should be invited to attend.

The conduct of the hearing is informal. Complainants should be told of their right to be accompanied by a representative. Although the *Policy Guidance* (Annex A, para 5) indicates that a representative should not be a professional barrister or solicitor, it is submitted that professional representation may be justified if, for example, a local authority was permitted to be professionally represented, or difficult points of law are involved. A panel would err in law if it held that, notwithstanding the *Policy Guidance*, it had no discretion to allow professional representatives to attend (see, eg, *R v Home Secretary, ex p Tarrant* [1985] QB 251). Care should be taken to ensure that particular disabilities or language difficulties are catered for so as ensure fairness. In an appropriate case, therefore, Annex A, para 5 of the *Policy Guidance* might be held to be unlawful.

The regulation of procedure before the panel is, in principle, at the tribunal's discretion. Thus, a tribunal may (and in an appropriate case must) permit the calling of witnesses and their cross-examination as part of the review procedure and as part of the principles of natural justice. In any event, a complainant or his representative should be permitted to make oral representations prior to the local authority. Other persons may, subject to the consent of the panel, attend part of the proceedings to make further submissions but will normally only be allowed to attend the hearing whilst making such submissions (*Policy Guidance*, Annex A at para 5). Clearly, the making of oral submissions does not affect a complainant's right to make representations in writing additionally or alternatively (see Direction 7(3)).

The panel is required to decide on its recommendations and record them in writing within 24 hours of the end of the meeting (Direction 8(1)). However, if it decides to take into consideration a matter on which it has not heard submissions it should alert the complainant and accord to him an opportunity of being heard (see *R v Mental Health Review Tribunal, ex p Clatworthy* [1985] 3 All ER 699). It must send written copies of its recommendations (Direction 8(2)) to:

(1) the local authority,
(2) the complainant,
(3) (if appropriate) the person on whose behalf the representations were made, and
(4) any other person who the local authority considers has sufficient interest in the case.

The reasons for the panel's recommendations must be recorded in writing (Direction 8(3)) and, presumably (though the Directions are unclear) communicated to the same persons to whom the recommendations are sent (as indicated in para 7 of Annex A to the *Policy Guidance*). If a panel member disagrees with the majority recommendation, the letter should record that member's view and the reason for it (Annex A, *ibid*).

An authority is not bound to accept the recommendations of the panel (but see below). It has 28 days in which to decide whether to accept such recommendations and what action to take in the light of those recommendations (Direction 8(4)). As with the panel it should alert a complainant to any matter which it proposes to consider upon which it has not, through the panel, received submissions (see *R v Mental Health Review Tribunal, ex p Clatworthy* [1985] 3 All ER 699). The authority must, within that period, notify in writing the persons to whom the recommendations were sent of its decision/action and of their reasons (*ibid*).

Clearly, any errors of law or unfairness of procedure during the review stage will render the decision/action of the authority susceptible to judicial review. However, subject to the issue of whether judicial review may be sought as an alternative to invoking the complaints procedure at all, or as an alternative to following such procedure through to the review stage (see Chapter 9), if the complaints regime is utilised and taken to the final stage it is unlikely that an error of law or breach of natural justice at earlier stages of the procedure may be sought to be reviewed if the final review stage has been conducted lawfully and fairly (see *Calvin v Carr* [1980] AC 574; *Lloyd v McMahon* [1987] AC 625).

By virtue of Direction 9 of the 1990 Directions the local authority must record each representation received before the panel, together with the outcome both before the panel and before the authority. It must also record whether the time limits within which the panel and the local authority is, respectively, required to act at the review stage have been complied with. As with other time periods it is likely that failure to comply would be regarded as mandatory provisions although the practicalities of seeking judicial review in respect of non-compliance are dubious (see Chapter 9).

## 8.7 Review panel recommendations

In *R v Avon CC, ex p M* [1994] 2 FLR 1006 Henry J held that a social services department which refused to adopt a review panel's recommendations acted unlawfully by failing to give the recommendations of the panel sufficient weight.

The decision demonstrates the importance that the courts attach to recommendations of a review panel which are, as has been seen, required to be reasoned. None the less, a local authority is not bound by such recommendations. In *R v North Yorkshire CC, ex p Hargeaves* (1994) *The Times*, 9 November, Dyson J did not accept that the *Avon* case was authority for the proposition that review panel recommendations were of binding effect. It is submitted that, in order to justify a departure from the recommendations of a review panel, a local authority would have to provide adequate and intelligible reasons for such a departure (see *R v Islington LBC, ex p Rixon* [1995] *The Times* 17 April) in the context of the need for reasons to justify the departure from guidance (both statutory and non-statutory).

Chapter 9

# Judicial Review

## 9.1 Nature and scope of the remedy

Judicial review is a supervisory remedy whereby the High Court exercises control over the means by which public bodies perform their statutory duties and powers. The relevant procedure is contained in Ord 53 of the Rules of the Supreme Court, and in s 31 of the Supreme Court Act 1981 (for an outline of the procedure see below at 9.8).

It is available to a person with a 'sufficient interest' in the matter to which the application relates and will, accordingly, include any service user affected by an assessment or service provision decision or a decision relating to charging for services. Pressure groups will also have standing in a case engaging a general principle although such groups will rarely obtain more than declaratory relief (see *R v Gloucestershire CC, ex p RADAR* (1995) unreported, 21 December).

In the context of community care the scope of judicial review will extend, principally, to a local authority's policies, procedures and decisions (or unreasonable delay in reaching such decisions) in respect of:

- entitlement to assessment (see Chapter 3);
- assessment (see Chapters 4, 6 and 7);
- service provision (see Chapters 5, 6 and 7);
- complaints by a qualifying individual (see Chapter 8);
- charging (see Chapter 14).

Additionally, judicial review may lie if the Secretary of State has unlawfully exercised (or failed to exercise) his default powers (see Chapter 10) or, exceptionally, against unlawful directions or policy guidance issued by the Secretary of State (see Chapter 1).

Judicial review is a particular kind of remedy. It is concerned with legality rather than merits. As Lord Hailsham LC stated in *Chief Constable of North Wales Police v Evans* [1982] 1 WLR 1155 at p 1160:

> It is important to remember in every case that the purpose . . . is to ensure that the individual is given fair treatment by the authority to which he has been subjected and that it is no part of that purpose to substitute the opinion of the judiciary or of individual judges for that of the authority constituted by law to decide the matters in question.

It is also important to bear in mind that judicial review is discretionary. This means that, even if a service user or other applicant establishes a *prima facie* case, the High Court may still refuse relief. In community care cases the court may well refuse relief if it considers that an alternative remedy should have been utilised. Given the possibility, for example, of invoking the complaints regime or the Secretary of State's default powers where a local authority has reached an unfair assessment or service provision decision, an applicant and his legal advisers should consider carefully whether judicial review is a sensible immediate option to challenge the decision. This issue is considered at 9.7, below.

The outline that follows is directed towards clarifying the grounds for judicial review and the remedies available, together with a summary of the main procedural provisions. Appendix 2 contains an exemplary case study.

## 9.2   Grounds for obtaining judicial review

In *Council of Civil Service Unions v Minister for the Civil Service* [1985] AC 374 ('the CCSU case') Lord Diplock (at p 410) observed that:

> one can conveniently classify under three heads the grounds on which administrative action is subject to control by judicial review. The first ground I would call 'illegality', the second 'irrationality' and the third 'procedural impropriety.' That is not to say that further development on a case by case basis may not in course of time add further grounds.

The distinction between illegality and irrationality is nowhere better developed than in the judgment of Lord Greene MR in *Associated Provincial Picture Houses Ltd v Wednesbury Corpn* [1948] 1 KB 223.

As to illegality he stated that:

> the Court is entitled to investigate the action of the local authority with a view to seeing whether it has taken into account matters which it ought not to take into account, or conversely, has refused to take into account matters which it ought to take into account.

He went on to observe, in respect of irrationality:

> . . . once that question is answered in favour of the local authority, it may still be possible to say that, although the local authority have kept within the four corners of the matters which they ought to consider, they have nevertheless come to a conclusion so unreasonable that no reasonable authority could ever have come to it. In such a case, again, I think the Court can interfere.

Procedural impropriety is, essentially, non-observance of the rules of natural justice. This demands, in the context of the community care legislation, that a user is given a fair hearing. What constitutes a fair hearing will shift according to various factors that have already been considered (see Chapters 5 and 7) including, most notably, the subject matter of the assessment or complaint (see *Russell v Duke of Norfolk* [1949] 1 All ER 109 at p 118, per Tucker LJ). The fairness of a hearing may also embrace the doctrine of legitimate expectation (see 6.3). Additionally, the time within which a decision is communicated and whether such decision is adequately reasoned are facets of natural justice albeit that they follow the hearing itself (see Chapter 7).

## 9.3 Available remedies

The following final forms of relief are, under RSC, Ord 53, r 1, obtainable on judicial review:
- the prerogative orders of certiorari, prohibition or mandamus;
- a declaration or injunction.

It is also possible for damages to be awarded, but only as a private as opposed to a public law remedy. This is demonstrated by the requirement under Ord 53, r 7(1) that the court determining the application for judicial review must be satisfied that damages could have been awarded at the time of making the application if, instead of seeking judicial review, the proceedings had been commenced by action.

In its modern form certiorari lies to quash a decision for invalidity. Prohibition prevents a local authority (or other respondent) from acting unlawfully. Mandamus requires performance of a specific duty in public law. These remedies can only be obtained by way of final order (see s 29 of the Supreme Court Act 1981). The interim equivalent of prohibition and mandamus is the injunction (see 9.4, below) which can also be obtained, though in practice it is rarely sought, as a final order. A declaration, as in private law, lies to declare the law though it, too, lies solely as a final form of relief (see *IRC v Rossminster* [1980] AC 952, per Lord Wilberforce at p 1079).

The normal remedies in respect of allegedly unlawful assessment/service provision or complaints decisions will be certiorari to quash the decision and mandamus to require re-determination of the user's application according to law.

If the authority's decision ought, on its own reasoning, to compel service provision or the acceptance of the user's complaint then it may be possible to argue that the court should, on judicial review, order the authority (in addition to quashing the decision) to remit the matter to the authority with a direction to reconsider it and reach a decision in accordance with the findings of the court (see Ord 53, r 9(4)). However, a direction of this kind is rare and would appear to be less apposite to assessment decisions which, by their nature, are less specific in point of determination.

It would, generally, be premature for a user to seek prohibition to prevent an authority from arriving at a particular decision but such circumstances might arise as where, for example, a manifestly unlawful procedure was being followed to the user's detriment.

Failure on the part of a local authority to give a decision, or reasons therefor, or to review a decision would be reviewable by means of an order of mandamus (see *R v Home Secretary, ex p Phansopkar* [1976] QB 606).

Declaratory relief, rather than a prerogative order, is likely to be relevant if application is made against the Secretary of State in respect of directions or policy guidance because certiorari applies to 'judicial' rather than legislative action (see Wade and Forsyth, *Administrative Law* 7th edn (OUP) at p 887). Where the Secretary of State has unlawfully refused to exercise his default powers, the correct remedy would be certiorari to quash such decision and mandamus to compel exercise of the power. An unlawful exercise of default powers might involve a local authority in seeking, on judicial review, certiorari and prohibition to prevent the continued exercise of the power. In both these cases, however, declaratory relief would also be appropriate.

## 9.4   Interim relief on judicial review

In order to obtain interlocutory injunctive relief in judicial review an applicant must show that he has a real prospect of success at the hearing and that the balance of convenience favours the making of such order. In the case of a mandatory injunction it is necessary to show a strong *prima facie* case of breach of duty (see *R v Kensington and Chelsea Royal LBC, ex p Hammell* [1989] QB 518). Undertakings as to damages (save, generally, in legal aid cases) will usually be required although the court has jurisdiction not to require such undertaking (see *R v London Borough of Lambeth and Caballito Properties Ltd, ex p Sibyll Walter*, unreported, 2 February 1989).

In a community care (as in a homelessness) case the need for interim relief will usually lie in respect of maintenance (or continued maintenance) of service provision. It is submitted that, in an appropriately strong case, the court may be prepared to grant interim injunctive relief to compel service provision, eg, where a service provision decision has been made, but no services provided. This is especially likely (so as to preserve the *status quo*) where community care services have been provided and are then withdrawn. It is, indeed, the prospect of obtaining such interim relief that often justifies the use of judicial review rather than exhausting other alternative remedies (see 9.7, below).

In *R v Gloucestershire CC, ex p Mahfood* (1995) TLR 351, for example, the applicant service users were notified of a proposed withdrawal of services. They sought interim injunctions on their applications for leave to apply for judicial review so as to preserve the *status quo*. In the event, the respondent local authority undertook to continue to provide services until the hearing of the substantive application.

There have been cases where the court has indicated a willingness to grant interim relief to compel an assessment under s 47(1)(*a*) of the National Health Service and Community Care Act 1990 preparatory to a service provision decision. In cases where social services do not deny a statutory obligation to assess the use of judicial review in this fashion may be a useful tactic in enforcing timeous assessments. However, it is questionable whether interim relief should lie if the very issue engaged is whether the authority is legally required to assess at the time when the judicial review proceedings are brought. Further, very careful consideration should be given in this type of case to whether the complaints procedure is not a viable alternative remedy.

Interim injunctive relief is now also obtainable against the Crown (contrast *Factortame v Secretary of State* [1989] 2 WLR 997 overruled in *M v The Home Office* [1994] 1 AC 377).

Apart from interim injunctive relief the court also has jurisdiction to order a stay of proceedings (equivalent to a prohibitory injunction) under Ord 53, r 3(10)(*a*) against both the Crown (see *R v Secretary of State for Education, ex p Avon CC* [1991] QB 558), and respondent local authorities, where the relief sought is an order of prohibition or certiorari. A stay of proceedings has no real advantages over interim injunctive relief because an undertaking as to damages is still, in practice, required as much for a stay of proceedings as for an injunction.

## 9.5 Discretion to refuse relief

Because of the discretionary nature of judicial review it cannot be assumed that victory is assured to an otherwise meritorious applicant. In community care cases the most likely reasons for relief being refused in the court's discretion are:

(1) delay, and
(2) the existence of an alternative remedy.

These are considered below.

However, relief may also be refused for a variety of other discretionary reasons. The most usual bases are: because of an applicant's conduct (*Fulbrook v Berkshire Magistrates' Courts Committee* (1970) 69 LGR 75), or waiver (*R v Williams, ex p Phillips* [1914] 1 QB 608); or because the court does not discern the need for any order, as where a remedy is considered to be futile (*R v Secretary of State for Social Services, ex p Association of Metropolitan Authorities* [1986] 1 WLR 1), or unnecessary (*R v Monopolies and Mergers Commission, ex p Argyll Group plc* [1986] 1 WLR 763). These factors are by no means exhaustive (see, eg, *R v Secretary of State for Social Services, ex p Cotton* (1985) *The Times*, 14 December: relief refused because it would be 'administratively inconvenient').

## 9.6 Delay

Order 53, r 4(1) provides that an application for leave to move for judicial review:

> shall be made promptly and in any event within three months from the date when grounds for the application first arose unless the Court considers that there is good reason for extending the period within which the application shall be made.

This provision must be read with s 31(6) of the Supreme Court Act 1981 which stipulates that where the court considers that there has been undue delay in applying for judicial review it may refuse to grant leave to make the application or any relief sought:

> if it considers that the granting of the relief sought would be likely to cause substantial hardship to, or substantially prejudice the rights of, any person or would be detrimental to good administration.

At the leave stage an applicant must show an arguable case. Generally the application is made *ex parte* (see 9.9 below). In *R v Stratford on Avon DC, ex p Jackson* [1985] 1 WLR 1319 the court held as follows:

(1) an application for leave may be made within three months, yet still not be made 'promptly' so as to be out of time;

(2) in deciding whether to extend time the court should not be influenced by criteria applicable to private law cases; the fact that an applicant has had difficulty in obtaining legal aid will provide a good reason to extend time;

(3) any application for leave made outside the three-month outer time limit will constitute 'undue delay' within the meaning of s 31(6) of the Supreme Court Act 1981 so that the court's discretion to extend time will need to be invoked.

In *R v Dairy Produce Quotas Tribunal, ex p Caswell* [1990] 2 WLR 1320, the House of Lords approved the above reasoning and upheld the following general test:

(1) at the leave stage the judge must refuse leave if the application is not made promptly or within three months, unless the applicant establishes good reason to extend time;

(2) even if the judge would otherwise have extended time he may refuse leave if he considers that there is substantial hardship/prejudice or detriment to good administration under s 31(6) of the Supreme Court Act 1981;

(3) in practice he will usually grant leave, if good reason is shown, leaving the issue of prejudice, etc to be decided at the full hearing.

In community care cases, the most usual reason for delay will be the length of time taken in processing an applicant's legal aid application. As the decision in *Jackson* shows (see above), this will usually provide a sufficient reason for extending time although delay on the part of an applicant's solicitor in obtaining legal aid cannot be prayed in aid (see, eg, *R v Tavistock General Commissioners, ex p Worth* [1985] STC 564).

Care should be taken in pursuing other remedies such as an authority's complaints machinery or default powers of the Secretary of State.

Whilst the court is likely to consider that prior resort to other (not necessarily alternative) remedies affords a good reason for extending time for applying for leave to move, it would be sensible for those advising applicants either to extract a concession from the local authority that it will not take a time point if subsequent application for judicial review proves to be necessary or, alternatively, to lodge an application for leave to move but invite the court to adjourn it while the other remedies are pursued (see Ord 53, r 3(8) by way of analogy).

In considering the issue of delay the court does not penalise applicants especially where there is no hardship or prejudice to third parties (see, eg *R v Local Commissioner, ex p Croydon LBC* [1989] 1 All ER 1033, at p 1041 per Woolf J). On the other hand it cannot and should not be assumed that, even in a social welfare context, the court will not infer delay by an applicant and refuse to grant leave to move or substantive relief even within the three-month period (see, especially, *R v Secretary of State for Health, ex p Alcohol Recovery Project* (1993) COD 344).

## 9.7 Alternative remedies

The existence of an alternative remedy is not, of itself, a basis for refusing judicial review. Such remedy may not be designed to achieve the same objective as review. For example, a right of appeal often relates to merits rather than to legality.

Where, however, a free-standing alternative remedy does exist the court's views will be determined by whether such remedy is legally more convenient. Convenience is dictated not only for the parties but also in the public interest (see *R v Huntingdon DC, ex p Cowan* [1984] 1 WLR 501).

A useful case for these advising service user applicants is *ex p Waldron* [1986] QB 824. There (at p 852) Glidewell LJ held that choice of remedy ought to depend upon whether an alternative statutory remedy:

- would resolve the question fully;
- would be quicker;
- demanded special knowledge.

The major problem facing applicants in community care cases will be whether to invoke a local authority's statutory complaints procedure or to seek judicial review.

It seems clear that the courts could regard the complaints regime, where available, as constituting an alternative remedy to judicial review since the statutory machinery is expressly designed to assist complaints 'in relation to the discharge of, or any failure to discharge' any of an authority's social services functions in respect of particular applicants (see s 7A of the Local Authority Social Services Act 1970). Even where the complaints procedure is not statutorily available it may still be an alternative remedy in view of the authority's discretion to use it outside its statutory scope (see para 6.5 of the *Policy Guidance*). The same cannot be said of failure to exercise Secretary of State's default powers (see Chapter 10).

Whilst the complaints regime might well resolve a complaint fully and require a degree of specialised knowledge, it is submitted that a principal determining factor in whether an applicant should proceed through the complaints machinery or seek judicial review is the availability of interim service provision in judicial review cases as opposed to the complaints machinery.

Certainly, an authority has power to provide services in emergency cases (see s 47(5) of the National Health Service and Community Care Act 1990 and 7.7). There is, however, no ostensible power to provide services where a decision has been taken not to do so under the s 47 of the 1990 Act. Such cases are, *ex hypothesi*, not emergency cases and to provide interim services would contradict the authority's own decision.

In those circumstances, assuming the applicant to have a strong *prima facie* case, judicial review (together with an expedited hearing) may be quicker in providing community care services given the availability of interim injunctive relief under Ord 53 (see 9.4, above).

A second reason for proceeding by way of judicial review rather than complaint is if the case involves a 'general issue of principle' (per Carnwath J in *R v Gloucestershire CC, ex p RADAR* (1995) unreported, 21 December). The complaints process may be more suitable for relief in an individual case where no discrete point of law is engaged, but judicial review is generally more appropriate where, otherwise, an applicant would have to argue points of law without the benefit of legal representation (*R v London Borough of Sutton, ex p Tucher*, unreported, 29 October 1996). Thus, although the respondent local authority initially raised the issue of alternative remedy in *R v Gloucestershire CC, ex p Mahfood and Others* (1995) TLR 351, the court made it plain that it was willing to entertain a challenge based on the issue of whether resources were relevant to a decision under s 2 of the Chronically Sick and Disabled Persons Act 1970. So, too, in *R v Gloucestershire CC, ex p RADAR* (above) Carnwath J regarded the issue of whether a local authority's duty to assess or reassess under s 47(1)(*a*) of the 1990 Act was complied with by sending out an 'offer' letter as raising a question of general principle suitable for judicial review rather than the complaints procedure. See, also, *R v Devon CC, ex p Baker* [1995] 1 All ER 73. The courts have also indicated that they are willing to perform a monitoring role in community care cases (see, eg, *R v Surrey CC and Kingston and District Community NHS Trust, ex p Richardson*, unreported, 17 June 1996).

In children's cases it is important to bear in mind s 1(2) of the Children Act 1989 which provides that:

> In any proceedings in which any question with respect to the upbringing of a child arises, the court shall have regard to the general principle that any delay in determining the question is likely to prejudice the welfare of the child.

This may be a powerful argument for invoking judicial review as opposed to the complaints process.

Finally, it is important to bear in mind that the complaints procedure may be extremely lengthy and that judicial review, if an expedited hearing is obtained, may result in the provision of urgent services at a far earlier stage.

Considerations of alternative remedy apart, there is an important overlap between judicial review and the complaints procedure. It is submitted that a letter before action threatening judicial review should be treated by a local authority as a complaint in parallel to the judicial review proceedings and responded to accordingly.

## 9.8 Outline of the judicial review procedure

Before seeking judicial review, practitioners should ensure that a letter before action is sent to the local authority setting out the applicant's case and allowing the authority a reasonable opportunity to respond.

There are three stages to a judicial review application. These are:
- the application for leave to move;
- the interlocutory stage;
- final hearing.

(See, also, *Practitioner Checklist* in Appendix 1.) For a detailed exposition of the judicial review procedure, see Gordon *Judicial Review: Law and Procedure* (Sweet & Maxwell 1996).

## 9.9 Application for leave to move for judicial review

The application for leave is usually made *ex parte*. It is designed to satisfy the court that the applicant has an arguable case. As Lord Diplock succinctly expressed it in *IRC v National Federation of Self-Employed and Small Businesses Ltd* [1982] AC 617 at p 644:

> ... If on a quick perusal of the material then available, the court thinks that it discloses what might on further consideration turn out to be an arguable case in favour of granting to the applicant the relief claimed, it ought, in the exercise of a judicial discretion, to give him leave to apply for that relief. The discretion that the court is exercising at this stage is not the same as that which it is called upon to exercise when all the evidence is in and the matter has been fully argued at the hearing of the application.

Notwithstanding that the application for leave does not necessarily involve an in-depth examination, an applicant has a duty to make full disclosure at the leave stage of all material matters and failure to do so may result in the grant of leave being set aside.

An applicant is required to seek leave to move for judicial review, under Ord 53, r 3(2), by filing in the Crown Office of the High Court:
- a notice in Form 86A (see Appendix 2);
- a supporting affidavit verifying the facts relied on (see Appendix 2).

The above documents should be contained in an indexed and paginated bundle together with a list of essential reading (see *Practice Direction* [1994] 1 WLR 1551).

Such application may be made *ex parte* 'on the papers'. This merely entails waiting for the decision of a High Court judge on the papers filed in the Crown Office. If the judge refuses leave the applicant may:

(1) renew the application by lodging Form 86B in the Crown Office within ten days of notice of refusal of leave under Ord 53, r 3(5): an oral *ex parte* hearing before a High Court judge will then be fixed by the Crown Office;

(2) further renew (if unsuccessful) to the Court of Appeal within seven days of refusal of leave at the oral hearing, under Ord 59, r 14(3):

different documents are required to bring the matter before the Court of Appeal for oral hearing.

It is possible to seek an oral rather than a paper hearing initially. If so, this must be requested expressly in Form 86A (see Ord 53, r 3(3)). Such oral hearing may be *ex parte* although there is a growing practice of serving the respondent so that he may assist the court. In the latter event an 'opposed *ex parte*' hearing takes place with the respondent making brief submissions before the single judge as to why leave should not be granted or, as appropriate, interim relief should not be granted. If an applicant is unsuccessful at the oral hearing stage his only further recourse is to renew to the Court of Appeal within seven days (see above).

The decision whether to seek an oral or paper hearing often involves tactical considerations. However, where interim relief is being sought an oral hearing should always be requested and the papers served on the respondent prior to seeking leave. This was emphasised in *R v Kensington and Chelsea Royal LBC ex p Hammell* [1989] QB 518 where, at p 539, Parker LJ observed as follows:

> ... where an application for interim relief is intended to be made, the applicant would be well advised to give notice to the other party that such an application is being made in order that the other party may, if he so wishes, attend and assist the court by filling in any gaps in the information which may be available and thereby enable the matter to be dealt with properly at the first hearing and dispense with the necessity of having a second hearing. I can therefore say no more than that notice that an ex parte application for interim relief is going to be made would be an advisable step in all cases.

Applicants in community care cases will frequently require an expedited hearing since, otherwise, there is often a year or more to wait between the grant of leave to move and the full hearing. If expedition is obtained the court should be asked to abridge time for service of the respondent's evidence from the usual 56 days to a lesser period so as to enable expedition to take place as soon as possible (see *Practice Note (Judicial Review: Affidavit in Reply)* [1989] 1 WLR 358). It is often sensible to seek an oral hearing of the leave application in such cases because of judges' reluctance to grant expedition on the papers.

Sometimes a respondent local authority will concede the application prior to the grant of leave but following issue of proceedings. In (but only in) a 'very clear case' costs may be sought (*R v Royal Borough of Kensington and Chelsea, ex p Ghebregiogis* (1994) COD 502).

## 9.10   The interlocutory stage

The papers (Form 86A/affidavit/notice of motion) must be served on the respondent and other persons 'directly affected' by the decision complained of within 14 days following the grant of leave. They must also be lodged in the Crown Office within that period together with an affidavit of service (see, generally, Ord 53, r 5).

Most forms of interlocutory relief are available in judicial review, including amendment of the Form 86A (see Ord 20, rr 7 and 8, and Ord 53, r 6(2)), and extension of time under Ord 3, r 5. Application should be made on notice of motion to the court having jurisdiction to determine the substantive application. The motion should be supported by affidavit. Those interlocutory applications relating only to the movement of a case within the Crown Office list should be made to the Master of the Crown Office on summons supported by affidavit.

The most important applications from an applicant's point of view are:

- discovery and inspection under Ord 24;
- leave to cross-examine the deponent of any affidavit under Ord 38, r 2(3)).

There is no automatic discovery in judicial review, and the case law indicates that discovery is more difficult to obtain under Ord 53 than in a private law action (see *R v Secretary of State for the Home Office, ex p Harrison* [1988] 3 All ER 86). However, in an appropriate case discovery will be ordered. In the community care context it will frequently be important to know the basis upon which an assessment/service provision or complaint decision was made.

From a respondent's point of view the most important interlocutory applications are:

(1) applications to set aside the grant of leave under Ord 32, r 6 (such applications should be made only rarely where there has been material non-disclosure or where the applicant has no arguable case);

(2) extension of time for filing affidavit evidence under Ord 3, r 5 (such application should be made before the expiry of time for compliance).

Prior to the full hearing the applicant should prepare a paginated bundle of documents for the use of the court. It will also be important for the applicant's counsel to prepare a skeleton argument for the court (which will need to be filed and served) five working days before the hearing and for the respondent's counsel to prepare an opposing skeleton argument two working days beforehand.

If the case is compromised an agreed order may be handed in to the Crown Office signed by the parties. Because of the public law nature of the proceedings reasons must be given for any compromise (see *Practice Direction (Crown Office List: Uncontested Proceedings)* [1982] 1 WLR 979; see Appendix 2 for a precedent).

Where the respondent compromises proceedings in an attempt to defuse matters and stave off probable defeat the court may award costs (*R v Liverpool CC, ex p Newman* (1993) COD 65). The court may be prepared to assess the relative strength of the parties' arguments on the substantive issues in order to determine a disputed costs issue (see *R v Holderness BC, ex p James Robert Developments Ltd* (1992) 66 P & CR 46).

## 9.11   Final hearing

The full hearing consists of oral argument by both sides. Except where cross examination is allowed (which is highly exceptional), the hearing will take the form of legal argument upon the Form 86A and affidavits.

Costs normally follow the event subject to the usual limitations imposed by the grant of a legal aid certificate. There is a right of appeal, with leave, to the Court of Appeal within 28 days of the sealing of the order.

# Chapter 10

# Default Powers of the Secretary of State

## 10.1 Nature of the power

Section 50 of the National Health Service and Community Care Act 1990 inserts a new s 7D into the Local Authority Social Services Act 1970.

By s 7D(1) of the 1970 Act if the Secretary of State is satisfied that any local authority has failed, without reasonable excuse, to comply with any of its duties which are social services functions (other than a duty under the Children Act 1989), he may make an order declaring that authority to be in default with respect to the duty in question.

Any declaration made under s 7D(1) may be supplemented by directions requiring the local authority to comply with its duty within such specified period as the Secretary of State considers is necessary (see s 7D(2)). Any direction not complied with is enforceable, at the suit of the Secretary of State, by mandamus (s 7D(3)).

The default power under s 7D is characteristic of many similar powers in social services legislation generally. In the context of challenging assessment or service provision decisions or, indeed, the manner in which an authority has responded to a complaint it is clear that a local authority is exercising a social services function. Thus, invoking the default powers of the Secretary of State may be a potential alternative remedy to judicial review (but see below).

In this chapter the following questions are considered:

(1) Which of the local authority's social services functions are susceptible to exercise of the default powers?

(2) What constitutes a 'reasonable excuse' so as to prevent the Secretary of State from exercising his default powers?

(3) Are default powers an alternative remedy to judicial review?

(4) Does the existence of a default power preclude the bringing of a private law action?

(5) What remedy does an applicant have if the Secretary of State refuses to exercise his default powers?

## 10.2 Functions subject to default powers

Section 7D(1) of the Local Authority Social Services Act 1970 applies to 'duties' which are social services functions. Axiomatically, there is a fundamental distinction in administrative law between a duty and a power. Thus, in circumstances in which a local authority has a discretion as opposed to a duty to exercise a particular social services function the default powers of the Secretary of State cannot be exercised under the 1970 Act.

In relation to assessment, service provision and complaint adjudication many of the social services functions required to be performed by local authorities are mandatory and are, therefore, subject to exercise of the Secretary of State's default powers.

The duties of a local authority under s 47 of the National Health Service and Community Care Act 1990 are:

(1)  to carry out an assessment (s 47(1)(a));
(2)  to decide, in the light of the assessment, whether an individual's needs call for the provision by the authority of particular community care services (s 47(1)(b)).

Clearly, also, an authority has a duty, at least in public law, to provide services which it decides that an individual's needs call for it to provide.

In respect of complaints, a local authority has a duty to establish a complaints procedure and to administer it (see s 7B of the Local Authority Social Services Act 1970).

However, a local authority has a measure of discretion as to its conclusions on assessment (see Chapter 4), as to service provision decisions (see Chapter 5), and as to complaints decisions (see Chapter 8). Whilst it is true that discretionary powers must not be abused so as to thwart the policy of an Act of Parliament (see *Padfield v Minister of Agriculture, Fisheries and Food* [1968] AC 997), it is submitted that the default power machinery is not intended to regulate the manner in which a local authority exercises its discretion even where it is contended that discretionary powers have been abused. Default powers are intended to be exercised in respect of statutory duties which have not been complied with as opposed to the duty that the common law imposes not to abuse statutory discretion.

This view is supported by the expression 'without reasonable excuse' (see below) set out in s 7D(1). The notion of the Secretary of State examining the legality of the manner in which a local authority has exercised its discretion, and the authority seeking to provide a reasonable excuse for such exercise, is contrary to the purpose of the default power regime which is 'an administrative device of last resort which is rarely used and which has as its object the internal efficiency of the executive machinery of the State' (see Wade and Forsyth *Administrative Law*, 7th edn (OUP) at p 758).

## 10.3  Reasonable excuse

A local authority may seek to excuse non-performance of a social services statutory duty. If, in the Secretary of State's view, the authority's explanation of non-compliance is reasonable then he may not exercise the default power.

It is apparent that what constitutes a reasonable excuse is, generally, for the Secretary of State to determine in his discretion (see s 7D(1) which begins: 'if the Secretary of State is satisfied . . .').

It is, largely, a question of fact. Certainly, ignorance of or mistake concerning the statutory requirement cannot provide a reasonable excuse for non-compliance (see, eg, *R v Philip Reid* [1973] 1 WLR 1283).

However, lack of resources may well constitute a reasonable excuse for non-provision of services that the authority has determined it must provide even if it is no defence to judicial review proceedings seeking declaratory relief that such duty is owed (see Chapter 5).

For general guidance for applicants alleging unlawful failure to exercise default powers, see *R v Kent CC, ex p Bruce* (1986) *The Times*, 2 August.

## 10.4   Alternative remedy?

It is apparent from the above discussion that the default power cannot constitute an alternative remedy to judicial review (see, also, *R v Devon CC, ex p Baker* [1995] 1 All ER 73).

The only likely circumstances, in the present context, in which default powers might be apposite would be where a local authority has simply refused to assess or to create a complaints regime or to provide services in respect of which it had the resources and a duty to provide or where it had plainly disregarded a direction of the Secretary of State.

It does not follow from this, however, that the default power machinery, even where applicable, truly constitutes an alternative remedy to judicial review. As has been observed, default powers are not really a species of legal remedy at all, and certainly not equally convenient so as to preclude judicial review (see *R v Leicester Guardians* [1899] 2 QB 632 at p 639, per Darling J). They are '. . . suitable for dealing with a general breakdown of some public service caused by a local authority's default, but . . . quite unsuitable as a remedy for defaults in individual cases . . .' (Wade and Forsyth, *Administrative Law*, 7th edn (OUP) at p 758).

## 10.5   Default powers and actions for damages

It is sometimes said that the courts will not intervene if Parliament has provided another remedy even if this prevents individuals from bringing actions for breach of statutory duty.

Two cases—*Wyatt v Hillingdon LBC* (1978) 76 LGR 727 and *Southwark LBC v Williams* [1971] Ch 734—are often cited. In both instances private law rights contended for by individuals were held by the courts to be enforceable solely by means of specific default procedures vested in the Secretary of State.

However, a better explanation of the *Wyatt* and *Southwark* cases is that the nature of the duty sought to be enforced in place of a particular default power made it unsuitable for enforcement in private law at all. If an authority's failure to provide services is actionable in private law (for which see

Chapter 13) then the existence of an independent default procedure ought, in principle, to be irrelevant (see, eg, *Meade v Haringey LBC* [1979] 1 WLR 637). The more difficult question, examined in Chapter 13, is whether an authority's failure to provide services can afford an individual right to damages.

## 10.6   Failure to exercise default powers

If the Secretary of State irrationally fails to exercise his default powers he is himself potentially amenable to judicial review (see, eg, *R v Secretary of State for the Environment, ex p Ward* [1984] 1 WLR 834). Probably, standing for judicial review would not be restricted to those persons directly owed duties under the National Health Service and Community Care Act 1990 (*Ward's* case, above).

# Chapter 11

# The Local Government Ombudsman

## 11.1  Source of powers

Since the foundation of the Commission for Local Administration in England under the Local Government Act 1974, Ombudsmen have been appointed to investigate complaints by individuals with regard to local authority maladministration and/or injustice.

## 11.2  Scope of power

In investigating allegations of maladministration, the Ombudsman has exercised wide powers which are not necessarily limited to those issues which might be justiciable by way of an action for judicial review. The approach taken is based on equitable principles. For example, issues concerning delay in taking appropriate action, failure to investigate an issue thoroughly, failure to comply with legal requirements or provide adequate information, and general policy issues (such as prioritising cases for assessment/provision) illustrated by individual cases might be investigated. Therefore, a case based on unfairness, whilst not necessarily *Wednesbury* unreasonable, may come within the remit of the Ombudsman.

Complaints need not necessarily be made by individuals as in appropriate cases the Ombudsman may investigate issues raised by unincorporated or incorporated associations on behalf of a group of affected individuals.

## 11.3  Requirements before investigation

According to the Local Government Ombudsman's Office, a strict policy is operated whereby the Ombudsman will not investigate a complaint unless the local authority's complaints procedure has first been exhausted. Given that the powers of the Ombudsman are generally accepted to be wider than that of the Complaints Review Panels, this policy may itself be open to challenge in appropriate cases. Although s 26(5) of the Local Government Act 1974 precludes investigation by the Ombudsman until the local authority has been afforded a reasonable opportunity of investigating the same complaint, it is submitted that this does not necessarily entail prior exhaustion of the statutory complaints procedure.

The Ombudsman will also refuse to investigate complaints where the matter at issue occurred more than 12 months before the complaint is made. However, exceptions may be made with 'good cause'. This might apply to a situation where the local authority's own complaints procedure has resulted in delay.

Issues which have already been referred to a tribunal or minister, or which are likely to be brought before the courts, are unlikely to be investigated, unless the Ombudsman considers that it would be inequitable to expect the individual to commence proceedings in the particular circumstances of the case.

## 11.4   Available remedies

If the Ombudsman makes a finding of maladministration or injustice, he may recommend unlimited financial compensation. In the past, the level of compensation has been relatively low, but an analysis of cases over recent months shows a marked increase in recommended awards. The local authority is empowered to pay the compensation.

The Ombudsman may also recommend the implementation of any other lawful remedy. In practice, however, most individuals seeking services will have been provided with them by the time the lengthy investigation is completed. In several cases, recommendations have been made that the authority should amend priority systems, or ensure that structures are put in place to avoid injustice in future.

If the authority refuses to implement the recommendations after the second report stage, then the Local Government Ombudsman may force the authority to publish the Ombudsman's findings in the press. In addition, an action for judicial review might be appropriate, although this may present a problem in terms of time limits.

## 11.5   Choice of remedy

The appropriateness of making a complaint to the Local Government Ombudsman is discussed in the Practitioner Checklist (Appendix 1).

In general, the remedy is most appropriate where the complaints procedure has not secured adequate relief, and only in non-urgent cases. The process is lengthy, although some complaints are resolved at an early stage. However, adding the time for the authority's own complaints procedure to be exhausted, many individuals will be deterred from utilising this remedy.

Where policy issues are at stake, which might not warrant an action for judicial review (for whatever reason), or where compensation is appropriate, a complaint to the Ombudsman should be considered carefully.

Chapter 12

# The Local Government Monitoring Officer

## 12.1 Function of the monitoring officer

Under s 5 of the Local Government and Housing Act 1989, each local authority must appoint a monitoring officer who has a duty to report on potential or actual illegalities on the part of the authority concerned, as well as maladministration or injustice.

The section empowering the officer to report is reproduced (see Materials 1) and relates to any decision, omission or proposal by the authority or its committees, subcommittees, or an individual officer.

## 12.2 Remedy

In the event that the monitoring officer prepares a report in the circumstances described above, the authority/committee concerned must convene a meeting to consider the report within 21 days of receipt. Until the investigation of the report is finalised, the decision (or proposed decision) is suspended.

## 12.3 Effect of remedy

Practitioners have reported (in relation to homelessness cases) that in some authorities, this is an effective remedy. However, it is unclear as to how efficacious it is in community care cases, as it appears to be rarely used.

Failure to prepare a report may, of course, in appropriate cases, lay the authority open to challenge by way of judicial review. Indeed, several authorities have not appointed a monitoring officer at all. The Secretary of State's default powers may be used in such cases to ensure an officer is designated.

Chapter 13

# Action for Damages

## 13.1 The problems

None of the remedies discussed in Chapters 8 to 12 are designed to result in an award of damages for a service user unlawfully deprived of community care services although, presumably, a local authority could, in its discretion, make a payment of compensation following adjudication of a complaint made to it (*a fortiori* if a review panel recommended an award of compensation: see *R v Avon CC, ex p M* (1994) 2 FLR 1006). Also, a local authority may comply with recommendations of the Ombudsman to pay compensation (see Chapter 11).

In order to obtain compensation through the courts a service user would have to establish a cause of action in private law against the authority. The nature of private law claims against public authorities for damages was analysed comprehensively by the House of Lords in the landmark decision in *X and Others (Minors) v Bedfordshire CC (and conjoined appeals)* [1995] 3 All ER 353 ('the *Bedfordshire* case') as, essentially comprising:

(1) an enforceable claim by reason of a direct breach of statutory duty without the need to prove breach of a duty of care or by reason of a breach of a common law duty of care arising from the imposition of the statutory duty or from the performance of it ('breach of statutory duty'); and/or

(2) misfeasance in public office, ie the failure to exercise, or the exercise of, statutory powers either with the intention to injure the plaintiff or in the knowledge that the conduct was unlawful.

Misfeasance in public office is, in practice, very difficult to prove. That apart, the general difficulty of bringing a private law claim for damages in the community care field is that in this area of the law few actionable private law rights would appear to be created. This is so whether the claim lies for breach of statutory duty alone or whether the claim arises in negligence, being (in the context of a public authority's actions), the breach of a common law duty of care in the performance of a statutory obligation. Nothing in the National Health Service and Community Care Act 1990 expressly removes this difficulty or expressly opens the way for additional damages actions merely by creating an individual assessment regime.

## 13.2 Breach of statutory duty for non-provision of services

The National Health Service and Community Care Act 1990 in no way alters the pre-existing duty imposed, or power conferred, on a local authority to provide 'community care services' under the provisions of the relevant social welfare enactments.

However, as has been seen, many of these statutes—even where they impose duties—are phrased in terms of general ('target') rather than individual obligations. Further, for the most part, the exercise of social service functions under such enactments engages a discretion on the part of the authorities concerned. Both these elements militate against conferment of private law rights.

In the *Bedfordshire* case, Lord Browne-Wilkinson clarified the following:

(1) a breach of statutory duty *simpliciter* (ie without the need for any common law duty of care) does not, of itself, give rise to any private law cause of action;

(2) there is no general rule by reference to which it can be decided whether a statute does create such a right of action;

(3) if the statute provides no other remedy for its breach and the Parliamentary intention to protect a limited class is shown there may be a private right of action 'since otherwise there is no method of securing the protection the statute was intended to confer';

(4) the mere existence of some other statutory remedy is not necessarily decisive;

(5) statutory provisions establishing a regulatory system or a scheme of social welfare for the benefit of the public at large are unlikely to confer a private right of action: the cases where a private right of action for breach of statutory duty have been held to arise are all cases in which the statutory duty has been very limited and specific as opposed to general administrative functions imposed on public bodies and involving the exercise of administrative discretions; in determining whether a duty of care subsists in respect of the imposition of a statutory duty and/or the manner of its performance there is a distinction between the manner in which a statutory discretion is or is not exercised and the manner in which the statutory duty is implemented in practice: only if a statutory discretion is exercised outside the ambit of the discretion conferred can there exist a *prima facie* common law duty of care; before imposing a common law duty of care, consider whether:

   (a) the function is non-justiciable (such as, eg, discretion involving policy considerations),

   (b) the damage is reasonably foreseeable,

   (c) there is a proximity of relationship between the parties, and

   (d) it is fair, just and reasonable to impose a duty of care;

(6) courts should be extremely reluctant to impose a common law duty

of care in the exercise of discretionary powers or duties conferred by Parliament for social welfare purposes.

Although the *Bedfordshire* case was concerned, specifically, with legislation relating to education and to the protection of children (in that case, child abuse), and although Lord Browne-Wilkinson emphasised in his speech that 'each case turns on the provisions in the relevant statute', it is clear that the decision is of direct application to community care legislation and that the principles laid down would be applied to all the 'social services functions' laid down in Sched 1 to the Local Authority Social Services Act 1970.

On that basis, of the various statutes which set out the range of 'community care services' (see s 46(3) of the 1990 Act), it has been said that s 117 of the Mental Health Act 1983 alone may be an exception to statutory provisions that read more like general duties to provide certain services for people in the area than duties owed to particular individuals.

In *R v Ealing District Health Authority, ex p Fox* [1993] 1 WLR 373 Otton J held that the duty under s 117 was a duty in favour of an individual. He held, materially, as follows:

> the duty is not only a general duty but a specific duty owed to the applicant to provide him with aftercare services until such time as the district health authority and local social services authority are satisfied that he is no longer in need of such services . . .

So, too, and whether or not it constitutes a 'community care service', s 2(1) of the Chronically Sick and Disabled Persons Act 1970 also constitutes an individual rather than a 'target' duty (see 2.4).

However, in respect both of s 117 of the 1983 Act and of s 2 of the 1970 Act, there exist 'alternative' statutory remedies, namely the default powers of the Secretary of State. For reasons already suggested, the statutory remedy is unlikely to preclude judicial review. In the case of s 2(1) services, however, it has been held to exclude a private law claim for damages (see *Wyatt v Hillingdon LBC* (1979) 76 LGR 727).

It is, none the less, arguable, following the *Bedfordshire* case, that the mere existence of a default power is not determinative of the question of whether a private law right exists and that the decision in *R v Gloucestershire CC, ex p Barry* (1996) *The Times*, 12 July, demonstrates that s 2(1) imposes an absolute statutory duty independent of financial resources and one that does not involve any statutory discretion (see 5.4). On those premises it may be that a court would hold, exceptionally, that s 2(1) of the 1970 Act and, possibly, s 117 of the Mental Health Act 1983 do confer private law rights.

It is unlikely (subject to 13.3, below) that failure to provide any of the other 'community care services' as defined by s 46(3) of the 1990 Act affords a basis for a private law claim for damages.

## 13.3   Relevance of a service provision decision

Different considerations may apply, however, once a service provision decision is made in the applicant's favour.

Section 47(1)(*b*) of the National Health Service and Community Care Act 1990 creates a duty to make a decision as to whether an individual's needs call for service provision by the authority. The ostensible duty is simply one of arriving at a decision. However, following an authority's decision that it is called upon to provide particular community care services it is arguable that there is a further implied duty in private law (there is almost certainly a public law duty) to provide such services and that failure to do so gives rise to an actionable claim against the authority for damages for breach of statutory duty.

Certainly, the Laming letter (at para 13) assumes such liability for it indicates that:

> . . . once the authority has indicated that a service should be provided to meet an individual's needs and the authority is under a legal obligation to provide it or arrange for its provision then the service must be provided . . .

Provided that s 47(1) of the 1990 Act does create such implied obligation (and the point is not free from doubt), Lord Bridge's analysis in *Cocks v Thanet DC* [1983] 2 AC 286 (see 5.7), applies. The starting point for a damages claim will be the stage at which the authority reaches its service provision decision.

If a service provision decision is taken that results in the withdrawal of services it is difficult to spell out any corresponding statutory duty that would give rise to a corresponding action for damages. The rationale of executive action depends upon the authority making a decision and failing to give effect to it. If, however, the decision is subsequently replaced by a later decision the first decision lapses and any 'rights' that a service user has in respect of an unlawful later decision lie in public law.

## 13.4   Interrelationship with other remedies

An application for damages may be joined to judicial review proceedings where there is a private law as well as a public law claim. This will, undoubtedly, be the case where an authority has failed to implement a favourable service provision decision since such failure renders the authority liable to mandamus as well as to a possible damages claim for breach of statutory duty.

Although the Secretary of State's default powers may properly be exercised in respect of an authority's failure to provide services where it has made a favourable service provision decision there is no reason in principle why, if a damages claim lies, it should not be proceeded with instead of or in addition to seeking the exercise of such powers (see Chapter 13).

## 13.5 Other actions for breach of statutory duty

It is possible that an authority's failure to carry out an assessment or to make a service provision decision within a reasonable period (both being individual duties) may give rise to a statutory duty, breach of which affords an individual the right to seek damages for breach of statutory duty prior to the making of a service provision decision in the service user's favour. Certainly, a failure by a local authority to implement its own complaint adjudication may give rise to private law rights in the same way as failure to provide services following a favourable service provision may do (see above).

# Part 5

## Miscellaneous

Chapter 14

# Charging for Services

## 14.1 Policy behind the 1990 Act

One of the policies behind the National Health Service and Community Care Act 1990 is that services are to be provided in the most cost-effective manner. Paragraph 5 of the DoE Circular 10/92 states:

> The Government's policy remains that care should be provided to people as far as possible in their existing housing where this is their preference and it is practicable and cost effective to do so.

Furthermore, the local authorities providing such services may be able to recover all or part of the cost of those services from the service user. An assessment of a user's means (ie capital and income) will follow the needs assessment and service provision decision.

In this chapter the following questions are examined:

(1) Can a local authority charge for its services, whether residential or non-residential?

(2) How much can the authority charge?

(3) How does an authority assess the means of a service user and will the value of the home be taken into account?

(4) What happens if the service user does not or cannot pay?

Relevant enactments are s 22 of the National Assistance Act 1948, National Assistance (Assessment of Resources) Regulations 1992, Local Authority Circular (95) 7 *Charging for Residential Accommodation Guide* (CRAG) amendment no 5, CRAG amendment no 6 (LAC(95)21), CRAG no 7 (LAC(96)9). National Assistance (Assessment of Resources) (Amendment) Regulations 1995 and 1996 and Health and Social Services and Social Security Adjudications Act 1983.

## *Charging for residential accommodation*

## 14.2 General principles on accommodation charges

Under s 22(2) of the National Assistance Act 1948 (Part III), as modified by s 44 of the 1990 Act, a local authority is obliged to charge for providing long-term residential accommodation. This also applies to accommodation provided under s 29 of the 1948 Act (although may not apply to such services provided under s 117 Mental Health Act 1983, see 2.5).

Generally, the charges for accommodation are to be set at the 'standard rate'. Under s 22 of the 1948 Act local authorities are required to set the standard rate for local authority homes at an amount equivalent to the full cost to the authority of providing any accommodation. Thus, it is submitted that it is unlawful to set a standard rate that represents anything other than the exact cost of the placement. The standard rate for accommodation in homes not managed by the local authority will be the gross cost to the local authority of providing or purchasing the accommodation under a contract with the independent sector homes (s 26(2)).

In all cases where accommodation is provided in premises maintained by the independent sector, the person becomes liable to reimburse the local authority for the full amount that the authority has paid the independent sector organisation for the accommodation. As with those cases where the authority itself has provided the accommodation, the authority must assess the means of the applicant to determine how much of the total cost he can afford after the needs assessment has taken place and a service provision decision been made.

The general policy is that a resident is to be charged according to his means and the local authority must assess his ability to pay using the National Assistance (Assessment of Resources) Regulations 1992, as amended by the National Assistance (Assessment of Resources) (Amendment) Regulations 1995 and 1996.

In no case, however, are a resident's resources after payment of the accommodation charges to be reduced below the 'Personal Expenses Allowance' (PEA) (and any disregarded income available), which at the time of writing is £13.75 per week. Under para 1.024A of CRAG, residents should not be charged for extra activities which are part of the residential care package negotiated in the contract as these should be included in the standard charge, but where a separate package of services has been arranged, the authority may charge the resident extra for those services under the guidelines for discretionary charging powers for non-residential services (see below) subject to the means assessment and such charges are likely to be minimal in most cases. It is arguable, however, that it would not be reasonable to expect a user to pay for such services which reduces his income below the PEA. In some circumstances, the local authority has discretion to raise the level of the PEA above the prescribed minimum (see 14.18, below).

## 14.3  Respite care

See also 'temporary residents' at 14.19(2), below.

Local authorities have a discretion to charge for up to eight weeks' respite care in a residential home. If a period of respite care exceeds eight weeks, then they must charge for the accommodation.

Under para 3.005 of CRAG an assessment of ability to pay is not required for the first eight weeks of a temporary stay. It will be for the local authority to decide in each case whether to make a means assessment during this period and where no assessment is made, the charges may be the amount it appears reasonable to the local authority for the resident to pay. Exercise of this discretion should be carefully monitored.

## 14.4 Means assessment

The processes and procedures that the local authority must embark upon in order to assess the means of a service user are now set out in the National Assistance (Assessment of Resources) Regulations 1992 as amended by the National Assistance (Assessment of Resources) (Amendment) Regulations 1995 and 1996. Detailed guidance is also to be found in Local Authority Circular (95) 7, issued in March 1995 entitled *Charging for Residential Accommodation Guide* which incorporates four previous issues of the guidance and amendments no 6 and 7. The guidance is issued under s 7(1) of the Local Authority Social Services Act 1970 and as such is binding.

The regulations and guidance provide complex and detailed provisions as to the carrying out of a means assessment and is essential reading for all practitioners involved in this area, as the points below represent only a summary of the main guidance.

## 14.5 Income

A resident's resources are either capital or income. In general, income payments are ones which are made in respect of a period and form part of a series of payments (whether or not payments are received regularly). In general, income is taken into account for the period equivalent to that which it represents. It is treated in one of three ways:
- taken into account in full,
- partly disregarded, or
- fully disregarded.

## 14.6 Income taken fully into account

Income taken fully into account includes:
(1) Most Social Security benefits.
(2) Retirement, occupational and widows pensions.
(3) Trust income.
(4) Income from certain disregarded capital—where the capital asset is the normal dwelling of a temporary resident (less costs to cover housing commitments), where capital is the dwelling which the resident intends to occupy as his home, where it is the former dwelling of the resident which is occupied by a partner or relative of the resident who is over 60, under 16 or whom the resident is liable to maintain,

or who is incapacitated (this list not exhaustive). In some situations, income from these sources, which covers mortgage payments, payments for water rates and council tax, may be disregarded.

(5) Income from subletting a part of the property which is not part of the living accommodation.
(6) Income from renting part or the whole of the property, where the value of the property exceeds £16,000.
(7) Third-party payments made to meet higher fees.
(8) Trust income (see para 10 of CRAG).

## 14.7 Income partly disregarded

A few rare types of income attract a £10 disregard. Of most note are charitable and voluntary payments (including payments made from charitable motives) which may either be subject to the £10 disregard or fully disregarded (see para 10 of Sched 3 to the 1992 Regulations and para 8.051 to 8.057 of CRAG). A 'one off' payment is treated as capital under reg 22.

Annuity income from home income plans and income from subletting, from boarders and mortgage protection insurance policies may be disregarded either in part or in total.

## 14.8 Income fully disregarded

Types of income which are fully disregarded include:
(1) Some benefits, eg attendance allowance and the care component of DLA (for temporary residents) and the part of income support which is paid in respect of home commitments for temporary residents.
(2) Certain charitable and voluntary payments.
(3) Child support maintenance payments and child benefit/one parent benefit (unless the child is accommodated with the resident).
(4) Council tax benefit.
(5) Income in kind.
(6) Social fund payments.
(7) Work expenses paid by employer, and expenses paid to voluntary workers.

## 14.9 Notional income

A resident may be treated as having an income which he does not actually receive in a variety of situations. This may include income which is paid to the local authority by the third party to contribute towards the fees of a home, income which would be available on application or which is due but has not been paid, or income which the resident has disposed of. (See also 'notional capital' at 14.12, below.)

Third-party payments for arrears of charges for residential accommodation made directly to the local authority will not be treated as notional income.

Certain income cannot be counted as notional income such as income payable under a discretionary trust, family credit or disability working allowance, refund of income tax, housing benefit or the mobility component of DLA, or any potential entitlement to severe disablement allowance. However, unclaimed social security benefits (with some exceptions) and occupational pensions which have not been claimed will be taken into account.

Some income which is due but not paid will be treated as notional income with exceptions such as an occupational pension which has not been paid due to an insufficiency of resources.

As with the rules on capital (see 14.13, below), if the local authority are satisfied that the resident has deprived himself of income in order to reduce the charge payable for his accommodation, he may be treated as possessing that income (reg 17).

Evidence of deprivation will need to be produced to the local authority and in order for it to be taken into account as notional income, the purpose of the disposable income to avoid or reduce a charge must be the significant motive in making the disposal.

## 14.10 Earnings

The employed applicant's earnings will be treated as income and will consist of any remuneration or profit derived from the employment, including any bonus or commission, payments in lieu of notice, some holiday pay, any retainer, expenses not wholly, exclusively and necessarily incurred in the performance of the duties of employment, and statutory sick pay.

Earnings do not, however, include any payment in kind, occupational pension, or work expenses which arise wholly, exclusively and necessarily in connection with employment. Where employment has ended, any earnings paid, or due to be paid, shall be fully disregarded.

After a figure for gross earnings have been arrived at, deductions are made for income tax, national insurance contribution and an allowance of one-half of the weekly contributions towards an occupational or personal pension scheme.

For those residents who have been self-employed, income tax, national insurance contributions, stock purchases, half of any sum paid to a personal pension scheme, transport costs wholly related to the business, stationery and advertising costs, are deducted from gross earnings. Where self-employment has ended, any earnings paid or due to be paid are fully disregarded.

## 14.11 Capital

A resident with capital of more than £16,000 is liable to pay the standard charge for accommodation if in a local authority home, or the full amount of the contracted fee if in an independent-sector home. If a resident has more than £16,000 there is no need to make a wider assessment of his ability to pay. Where a resident is one of a couple, the resident is liable to pay the standard rate or full contracted fee if they have more than £16,000 in their own right, or if their share of jointly held capital is more than £16,000. Capital of £10,000 or less is fully disregarded (reg 20). The aim is that a person with such capital (ie, over £10,000 should use those resources first, before relying upon public funds to pay for his accommodation.

If a person's capital exceeds £16,000 and the full charge is made, the position should be monitored by the authority on a regular basis to avoid overcharging when capital levels reduce to £16,000. This is often not carried out and arguably, is the responsibility of the authority rather than the paying individual.

Examples of capital include buildings, land, building society and bank accounts, cash, stocks and shares, National Savings Certificates, and capital held by the Court of Protection (the list is not exhaustive).

Where a resident has £16,000 or less but more than £10,000, the resident's ability to pay is assessed in the normal way with regard to income and a notional tariff weekly income of £1 for every complete £250 or part of £250 over £10,000 is added to the weekly income as part of the assessment. Schedule 4 to the 1992 Regulations lists items of capital that are to be disregarded, for example:

- property in specified circumstances (see below),
- surrender value of any life insurance policy,
- payments in kind from a charity,
- payments from particular trusts or funds,
- funds held in trust for another person,
- social fund payments,
- reversionary interests, etc.

Some capital assets listed in Sched 4 are disregarded for 26 weeks or longer where the local authority consider this to be appropriate. These include:

- capital received from the sale of a former home where the capital is to be used by the resident to buy another home (within a specified period),
- premises which the resident intends to occupy as his home where essential repairs or alterations are required,
- money acquired specifically for repairs to or a placement of the resident's home or personal possessions,
- assets of any business owned (or part owned) by the resident in which he was self-employed, where the person intends to take up work again when he is fit to do so.

(The list is not exhaustive).

Arrears of most benefits will not be treated as capital for up to 52 weeks; rather they will be treated as income over the period for which they are payable.

In some cases, income is to be treated as capital. These include:

- tax refunds,
- holiday pay,
- income from a capital asset, eg building society interest or dividends from shares,
- bounty payments,
- advance of earnings or loan from employer,
- irregular charitable and voluntary payments.

A payment by a third party directly to the local authority to clear arrears of charges for residential accommodation will not be treated as belonging to the resident.

Specific rules as to how capital assets are to be valued can be found in reg 23 of the 1992 Regulations and para 6.011, etc of CRAG.

## 14.12   Notional capital

In some circumstances, a resident may be treated as possessing a capital asset even where he does not *actually* possess it. If the actual capital exceeds the capital limits, it is not necessary to consider the question of notional capital. Notional capital may, however, be capital if it would be available to him if he applied for it, or which is paid to a third party in respect of the resident, or capital which the resident has deprived himself in order to reduce the amount of charge he has to pay.

This does not include:

(1) Capital held in a discretionary trust.
(2) Capital held in a trust derived from a payment in consequence of a personal injury.
(3) Any loan which could be raised against the capital asset which is disregarded, for example, the home (reg 25(2)).

## 14.13   Deprivation of capital

The local authority may treat a resident as still in possession of an asset if it feels that a resident has deprived himself of a capital asset in order to reduce his accommodation charge (reg 25). The onus is on the resident to prove that he no longer has the resource, eg production of a trust deed, deed of gift, receipts for expenditure or proof that debts have been repaid. Examples of where a person has deprived themselves of capital might include the transfer of the property to someone else, where capital has been reduced by living extravagantly, where substantial expenditure has been incurred, where a lump sum payment has been made to someone else, or where money has been put into a trust which cannot be revoked.

The local authority may only take into account capital assets which have been disposed of if the significant motive for deprivation of the asset has been to avoid a charge for accommodation. Where the capital asset has been used to repay a debt, the asset should not be treated as notional capital where this was reasonable. Obviously, the timing of the disposal will be taken into account where considering the purpose of a disposal. Examples are given in CRAG at para 6.063.

If the local authority is of the opinion that the resident has disposed of capital in order to avoid the charge or to reduce the charge payable, the authority has discretion whether to treat the resident as having the capital and assess the charge payable accordingly. If the asset was transferred within six months of the date when the resident moved into the residential accommodation, the authority may use the provisions of s 21 of the Health and Social Services and Social Security Adjudications Act 1983 to transfer the relevant part of the charges to the recipient of the asset.

## 14.14  Treatment of property

For most service users their main concern when entering residential care will be whether the main dwelling home must be sold in order to pay charges for residential accommodation. Schedule 4 of the Regulations and para 7 of CRAG provide detailed guidance as to whether the value of the home is to be taken into account or disregarded indefinitely. Local authorities also have an element of discretion over whether to take the value of the property into account when assessing the level of charges.

Normally, the value of a main dwelling occupied by a resident as his home should be ignored if he is a temporary resident in a care or nursing home. This is the case if the person intends to return to the dwelling and it is still available to him, or he is taking reasonable steps to dispose of the property in order to acquire another more suitable property for him to return to. This applies to only one dwelling.

If the resident no longer occupies the dwelling as his home, its value should still be disregarded where it is occupied in whole or in part by:

(1)  The resident's partner or former partner (except where divorced or estranged).

(2)  A relative of the resident or member of his family who is aged 60 or over, or is aged under 16 and is a child whom the resident is liable to maintain, or is incapacitated.

Under the provisions above, 'relatives' includes parents, children and spouses of children, step-relatives, siblings, grandparents, uncles, aunts, nephews and nieces, and partners or any 'close' relatives.

Whether a person is 'incapacitated' is not defined in the Regulations, but the guidance assumes that it would be reasonable to conclude that a relative is incapacitated if in receipt of disability benefits or where the degree of incapacity is equivalent to that required to qualify for one of those benefits.

The local authority also has an important discretion to disregard property in which the third party continues to live where it considers it reasonable to do so. This is particularly important for carers who may not be relatives. Often the exercise of this discretion may be challenged, especially if the authority operates a fixed policy, disregarding individual circumstances.

Aside from the exceptions listed above, the value of the property will be taken into account when computing capital if the service user is the legal or beneficial owner. Where there is no beneficial interest in the property, no account should be taken of the value of the property, but where the resident is the sole beneficial owner of the property the capital value should be taken into account in full.

## 14.15 Valuation of the home

Paragraph 6 of CRAG details the valuation of a beneficial interest and items such as the expenses of sale, and in some situations debts secured on assets, may be taken into account.

Where there is joint beneficial ownership of property, the interest in the property is to be valued as capital and the value of the interest is calculated as the actual share in the proceeds of the sale to a willing buyer (at the time of assessment) less the cost of transferring the interest to the buyer (usually 10 per cent) and any incumbrance.

## 14.16 Jointly owned assets other than the home

Joint capital (non-land) assets are considered to be equally shared by the owners regardless of the true position, eg a joint bank account balance will be divided in half to obtain the capital valuation.

## 14.17 Couples and liable relatives

Under the National Assistance Act 1948, the local authority has no power to assess a couple according to their joint resources. Each person entering residential care should be assessed according to their individual means, although the liability of a married person to maintain their spouse should be considered in each case. Likewise, there are no powers for the local authority to use the assessment regulations as a basis for assessing how much a liable spouse should be able to contribute towards the cost of residential accommodation. Nevertheless, under s 42 of the 1948 Act, a man is liable to maintain his wife, and a woman is liable to maintain her husband. It should be noted that this does not apply to unmarried couples even though they live together as husband and wife. As married couples are also to maintain one another under social security legislation, if income support is in payment to a resident, it is not usually worth the local authority pursuing maintenance from the remaining spouse.

It is strange that although the liable relative rules are to be taken into account in considering whether a spouse should contribute towards the cost of residential care, para 11.005 of CRAG states that an authority cannot demand that a spouse provides details of his resources, and local authorities should not use assessment forms for the residents which require information about the means of the spouse. It is difficult to see how a local authority can come to a conclusion as to the amount that a liable relative should pay if the information cannot be requested. However, CRAG operates as mandatory guidance on authorities and therefore joint assessment forms should not be used.

Guidance is given in para 11.006 of CRAG as to the steps to be taken in considering whether to pursue a liable relative for payments. In general, the Department of Health does not consider it appropriate to expect spouses to reduce their resources to income support levels in order to pay maintenance to a resident and ultimately, the question of the 'appropriate' amount of maintenance can only be decided by the courts.

As for payments which are being made by liable relatives to persons in residential accommodation, these will be taken into account when considering the weekly income of a resident and the assessment of means, and so will include maintenance for a divorced spouse.

The payments which are excluded from being taken into account for assessment of means include payments which arise from a property settlement following separation or divorce (these are treated as capital), the first £250 of payments made as a gift, payments made to a third party in respect of the resident if it is unreasonable to take it into account, and any child support maintenance payments.

A liable relative payment is either a periodical payment or a non-periodical payment.

(1) *Periodical payments:* These are payments that are made or due to be made (and whether in advance or in arrears) to the resident at regular intervals pursuant to a court order or maintenance agreement, or otherwise in an established pattern. They do not include payments before the resident was provided with accommodation. The payments are calculated on a weekly basis, whether the payments are made on a weekly or monthly basis, or by irregular lump sums, as long as the payments are due to be made on a weekly basis.

(2) *Non-periodical payments:* For persons in receipt of income support, if a non-periodical liable relative payment (LRP) is received, the local authority will divide the payment by the amount of income support normally in payment plus any disregards which would be applicable if the payment was a regular payment of earnings.

Where income support is not in payment, the non-periodical payment should be taken into account over the number of weeks calculated by dividing a payment by the difference between the standard charge and the charge a resident was previously paying.

Special rules apply to cases where periodical and non-periodical payments are made, and these are set out in para 11 of CRAG.

## 14.18  Personal expenses allowance

Under para 5.001 of CRAG, the personal expenses allowance (PEA) is intended to enable residents to have money to spend as they wish, for example, on stationery, personal toiletries, treats and small presents for friends and relatives. In emergencies, the local authority may supply replacement clothing. In assessing a resident's ability to pay for his accommodation, the local authority is required to ensure that he retains an amount for personal expenses (s 22(4) of the National Assistance Act 1948) which is currently £13.75 per week.

Under s 22(4) of the 1948 Act, local authorities have the power to vary the amount of the PEA. Examples include someone who does not qualify as a 'less dependent' resident, and therefore cannot be assessed under the rules described below at 14.19 but who none the less needs to retain more of his income in order to help him lead a more independent life. It would also include a situation where a person in residential accommodation has a dependent child, where the needs of the child should be taken into account when setting the PEA. It might also include a situation where a person temporarily in residential accommodation receives income support including an amount for a partner who remains at home, where the local authority should consider the needs of the person at home in setting the PEA. This might also apply to a situation where the person in residential accommodation is the main recipient of the couples' overall income, eg occupational pension, where the local authority might increase the resident's PEA to allow some of that income to pass to the partner remaining in the home. Local authorities should address this issue as part of the means assessment, without waiting for the spouse to make representations.

## 14.19 Special groups

### (1) Less-dependent residents

Before April 1993, local authorities had powers to arrange for the provision of residential accommodation under both the National Assistance Act 1948 and the National Health Service Act 1977. The powers in the latter legislation to provide accommodation were repealed from 1 April 1993 by the National Health Service and Community Care Act 1990. Therefore, from that date, all adult residential accommodation placements made by the local authorities will be made under the National Assistance Act 1948. Therefore, a charge must be made for the accommodation (subject to the discretion to charge for placements up to eight weeks in duration).

For residents placed in accommodation under the 1977 Act, accommodation was provided mainly for people who were able to live more independently than those accommodated under the 1948 Act but who nevertheless required some degree of caring support. Local authorities were not required to make charges for such accommodation, but were empowered to make a reasonable charge where appropriate. Therefore, residents were often left with more money for their personal use than the PEA because they were seen as needing extra money for, eg the cost of food or household expenses or travel to work.

Examples of less-dependent residents might include a person who lives in local authority accommodation that does not provide board, or a person living in private or voluntary sector accommodation which is not required to be registered under the Registered Homes Act 1984 as a residential care or nursing home. Under reg 2 of the 1992 Regulations and para 2.09 of CRAG, 'board' means at least one cooked or prepared meal provided by someone other than the resident or his family that is eaten in the accommodation, where the cost of the meal is included in the standard rates.

Charges for such residents are therefore left entirely to the discretion of the local authority in deciding how much of a person's income to disregard, but full reasons for the decision not to exercise discretion to increase the PEA should be given by the authority in each case. Failure to exercise such discretion lawfully, or failure to provide reasons for a decision, may be open to challenge by way of judicial review.

### (2)   Temporary residents (including respite care)

A local authority has discretion whether to charge for the first eight weeks of a temporary stay. It may decide to make an assessment of the person's ability to pay and where no assessment is made, the charge of the amount it appears reasonable to the local authority for the resident to pay (s 22(5A) of the 1948 Act) (see 14.3, above).

After eight weeks, the local authority must charge the resident at the standard rate and carry out an assessment of his ability to pay under the provisions below. The definition of temporary residence allows the local authority to regard a person's stay as temporary if it is likely to last for any period not exceeding 52 weeks, or in exceptional circumstances, is unlikely to substantially exceed 52 weeks (reg 2(1)). In para 3 of CRAG it is recognised that a stay which was initially expected to be permanent may turn out to be temporary and *vice versa*. From the time when it is decided a placement is temporary or permanent, according to the circumstances of the situation, the appropriate charging rules must be applied.

In assessing a person's ability to pay, the dwelling normally occupied as the resident's home is to be disregarded if the resident intends to return to occupy that dwelling and it is still available or he is taking reasonable steps to dispose of the property in order to acquire another more suitable home to which he will return. For other capital assets, the rules as to charging are as set out in the paragraphs above (relating to 'permanent' placements and capital).

As for income, if income support and housing benefit are in payment, they are in general disregarded in computation of income for charging purposes. In addition, extra costs, such as water rates and mortgage payments/service charges not met by income support or housing benefit, insurance premiums, etc, may also be disregarded. Income support may be paid for home commitments for up to 52 weeks on admission to residential accommodation (para 26 of Sched 3 to the 1992 Regulations).

Where neither income support nor housing benefit are in payment, income is calculated according to the rules on 'permanent' placements, and then amounts are disregarded as it appears reasonable to allow in respect of home commitments such as mortgage payments/service charges, insurance premiums, standard charges for fuel, water rates, etc. In any case where attendance allowance or the DLA care component is in payment, this should be completely ignored.

### (3) Students

Special rules apply to students. See regs 4 and 39 of the 1992 Regulations, and para 12 of CRAG.

## 14.20 Transitional provisions: effect on benefits

Transitional provisions under the Social Security Benefits (Amendments Consequential Upon the Introduction of Community Care) Regulations 1992 gave protection to residents who were already in residential accommodation before the introduction of the new rules in April 1993 and who would financially be worse off were the new rules to apply to them immediately. The provisions applied to persons in accommodation provided under Part III of the National Assistance Act 1948 immediately before 12 April 1993, subject to income and capital limits (Sched 1 to the 1992 Consequential Amendments Regulations).

The provisions did not apply to new residents placed in residential accommodation between 1 April and 12 April 1993, less-dependent residents, people accommodated under para 2 of Sched 8 to the National Health Service Act 1977, people accommodated under s 29(4)(c) of the 1948 Act, people in accommodation under Part III of the 1948 Act who are already paying the standard charge, and people who also have income of which less than £1 is being disregarded (the list is not exhaustive). The transitional provisions terminated in April 1996.

For some residents in independent residential care or nursing homes on 31 March 1993, there may be a 'preserved right' to income support, protecting residents from the new changes introduced by the 1990 Act. The regulations prescribing those residents who will be entitled to preserved rights are complex and are beyond the scope of this edition.

For those persons covered by the transitional provisions, there is a 'preserved right' to the higher levels of income support. From April 1996, all residents will be liable to pay the charge assessed under the new rules from the first four weeks following the annual benefits review. For detailed guidance as to the effect of the transitional provisions, see para 13 of CRAG.

## 14.21 Residential charges: enforcement

Once the means assessment has been carried out, and a person has been assessed as being required to make payment for residential services, the local authority finance department will generally send bills direct to the service user. Many local authorities send bills to the resident's spouse or other relative but this should not be done as a matter of course given that the resident is the person liable to pay the charges.

Depletion in capital and/or changes in the level of income should be monitored constantly by the local authority, and new means assessments carried out at the appropriate time to ensure that the resident is not being overcharged.

In the majority of cases, a person's main capital asset will be the former home and obviously, unless the property is sold, there will be insufficient capital to pay the charges on a weekly or monthly basis. In such circumstances, it is open to the local authority to apply to place a legal charge upon the property, which would be realisable when the property is sold, or the resident dies.

Disputes regarding means assessments will not entitle the local authority to delay provision of the placement. Further, inability to pay charges (where there has been deprivation of income/capital) does not enable the authority to fail to provide, or withdraw a service.

The amount of the legal charge will depend on the level of the accruing bill for residential charges, together with the legal costs of the local authority (if appropriate). Under Health and Social Services and Social Security Adjudications Act 1983, local authorities are empowered to enforce a legal charge in this way, but cannot claim interest on the accruing sum. Many local authorities are seeking to place charges on property under the Local Government Act 1972, which allows for the charging of interest, but guidance from the Department of Health indicates that the power under the 1983 Act to place a charge on a property should be used (being specifically directed to such a situation) and therefore interest should not be charged.

In many cases, the capital value of the home will be insufficient to fund several years in residential care. As referred to above, when capital deterioration reaches £16,000 the resident's means should be re-assessed in the normal way in order to ascertain whether the full charge should still be demanded, or whether the local authority needs to contribute towards the cost of residential care.

## *Charges for non-residential services*

### 14.22    Charges for non-residential services

Relevant provisions are the *Advice Note on Discretionary Charges for Adult Social Services* (January 1994) (LAC(94)1).

#### (1)    The legislation

Section 17(1) of the Health and Social Services and Social Security Adjudications Act 1983, which came into force in January 1984, gives authorities a discretionary power to recover charges for such services as the authority considers reasonable.

Under s 17(2), this applies to services provided under s 29 of the National Assistance Act 1948 (welfare arrangements for disabled persons), s 45(1) of the Health Services and Public Health Act 1968 (welfare of old people), Sched 8 to the National Health Service Act 1977 (care of mothers and young children, prevention of illness and care and after-care and home-help and laundry facilities), para 1 of Part II of Sched 9 to the Health and Social Services and Social Security Adjudications Act 1983 (meals and recreation for old people), other than the provision of services for which payment may be required under s 22 or s 26 of the National Assistance Act 1948.

However, it is open to a service user under s 17(3) to satisfy the authority that his means are insufficient for it to be 'reasonably practicable' for him to pay that (otherwise) reasonable amount.

Local Authority Circular (94) 1 reminds local authorities of these powers to charge for some non-residential services for adults. It states:

> the Government's view, confirmed in the Community Care White Paper 'Caring for People' of 1989 and in the subsequent policy guidance, has consistently been that users who can pay for such services should be expected to do so taking into account their ability to pay.

According to the *Advice Note on Discretionary Charges for Adult Social Services*, published January 1994 for use by the Social Services Inspectorate, charges may be recovered under s 17 for the services listed in s 2(1) of the Chronically Sick and Disabled Persons' Act 1970 'as these services are arranged by local authorities in exercise of their functions under s 29 of the 1948 Act'. However, according to the Divisional Court judgment given in the '*Gloucestershire* cases' at first instance on 16 June 1995, it is clear that the court considered that s 2 services under the 1970 Act stood distinct and separate from s 29 of the 1948 Act. It therefore remains unclear as to whether local authorities may charge for services provided under s 2 of the 1970 Act and this is a point which is likely to come before the courts in the near future. Whether a service purportedly provided under s 2 could be charged for in this situation where the service could be provided under one of the other enactments covered by s 17 of the Health and Social Services and Social Security Adjudications Act 1983 is also a moot point.

The *Advice Note* also makes it clear that charges may not be made for services provided under s 117 of the Mental Health Act 1983 (which may include home-care services and accommodation. See further 2.5, above). In addition, charges may not be made for providing advice about the availability of services or for community care assessment.

Where local and health authorities arrange jointly for social care services (other than under s 117 of the Mental Health Act), local authorities may only recover the cost of the social care element of the services so provided.

**(2)   Discretion to reduce or waive a charge**

In general, a local authority may have a charging policy for individual services. This should not be applied so rigidly as to fail to take account of individual circumstances. Under the *Advice Note*, when setting charges, local authorities 'should take account both of the full cost of providing the service and within that of what recipients can reasonably be expected to pay'. Under s 17(3) of the 1983 Act, the user has the right to ask the authority for a review of the charge if he considers that the charges are not affordable. It is for the user to satisfy the local authority that their means are insufficient to pay the amount they would otherwise be charged.

Although the *Advice Note* states that the Government does not consider there should be automatic exemption from charges for people on benefits, it states, 'representations from people receiving Welfare Benefits and those on very low incomes should, however, be given sympathetic consideration. Authorities will want to bear in mind that these benefits cannot be increased to enable the recipient to meet charges for care'. It is difficult to see how people in receipt of benefits may reasonably be expected to pay charges for services arising from their disability.

**(3)   The assessment of means—who is to pay?**

Authorities may only charge the person receiving the service and should have regard only to that individual's means in assessing his ability to pay. Normally, this means that parents and other members of a user's family cannot be required to pay the charges, except to the extent that they may be managing the resources of the user, and that their own resources should not be taken into account (*Advice Note*).

In assessing ability to pay authorities may take into account all types of income including benefits (except the mobility component of DLA) and income from capital. The *Advice Note* emphasises that it is the overall financial position of the user which should be taken into account, including whether they have access to income from any other source, and whether the charges will result in the service user being left without the means to pay for any other necessary personal care, including extra expenditure that may be incurred because of the user's disability.

**(4)   Refusal or inability to pay**

It is clear from LAC (94) 1 that ability to pay should not influence decisions on the services that are provided, and the assessment of financial means should therefore follow the care assessment. Paragraph 3.31 of the *Policy Guidance* states:

> The provision of services, whether or not the local authority is under a statutory duty to make provision, should not be related to the ability of the user or their families to meet the costs . . . the assessment of financial means should, therefore, follow the assessment of need and decisions about service provision.

It would therefore be unlawful for a local authority to take a potential user's means into account during the assessment or service provision decision process or to use the means assessment as a reason for delaying practical provision of services.

Once someone has been assessed as needing a service, that service cannot be withdrawn even if he or she refuses to pay the charge required. Any decision to withdraw or reduce service provision on this basis will be open to challenge. Non-payment will not entitle the local authority to withdraw the service that it has agreed to provide, although there is a right to summary enforcement in the magistrates' court as a civil debt (see s 17(4)). This is 'without prejudice to any other method of recovery' of the debt, but withdrawal of the service cannot be categorised as a method of 'recovery'. In some cases, local authorities may seek to place a charge on a property for unpaid charges for services.

## 14.23  Conclusion

The debate surrounding charging for services is likely to continue. Authorities will need to ensure that any charging policy is exercised lawfully and fairly, with due regard to individual circumstances. Proposals for the introduction of private insurance schemes for payment of residential care charges will, it is submitted, only affect minimal numbers of users, and unless (and until) new comprehensive social policy legislation is introduced, charging issues are likely to be further aired before the courts.

Chapter 15

# Hospital Discharge and the Role of NHS Bodies in Community Care Decision Making

## 15.1 Introduction

The overlap of responsibility between the National Health Service and local authorities has for some time been in issue, but has come to the fore with the advent of the National Health Service and Community Care Act 1990.

The shift in social policy planning towards community based services, the closure of the old asylums, phasing out of continuing care hospital beds and the introduction of NHS Trusts have all led to a greater tightening of budgetary boundaries.

Paragraph 1.11 of the *Policy Guidance* states:

> The objective must be to provide a service in which the boundaries between primary health care, secondary health care and social care do not form barriers seen from the perspective of the service user. Care must be focused on meeting the needs of individuals and their carers appropriately and sensitively. This objective must be a priority in collaborative planning involving health and local authorities.

This chapter aims to place the responsibility of the NHS and local authorities within a legal context. The relevant guidance can be found at Materials 4.

## 15.2 Assessment

Many people admitted to hospital for treatment, whether on a short- or long-term basis, may be in need of community care services, and continuing health and/or social care services on or before discharge. The duty on social services departments to assess under s 47 of the 1990 Act is often triggered on admission, especially where treatment that may seriously affect the person's ability to resume normal daily living is contemplated.

Although the duty to assess need for community care services under s 47 of the 1990 Act lies with social services departments of local authorities, the stated aim of assessment according to the *Policy Guidance* is that all needs for care services are considered (para 3.32). See also *R v Royal County of Berkshire, ex p Parker* (1996) *The Times*, 15 August.

We have already seen that s 47(3) places an obligation on local authority social services departments to invite housing departments and the health service to participate in the assessment process, where there may be a need for such services. The *Policy Guidance* stresses the need for strong links to be established between all agencies to ensure that proper assessments are carried out.

Guidance on hospital discharge and the arrangements for ensuring assessments are completed prior to final discharge planning have recently been published in place of existing guidance. LAC(95)5/HSG(95)8, *NHS Responsibilities for meeting continuing healthcare needs* and LAC(95)17/HSG(95)39, *Discharge from NHS inpatient care of people with continuing health or social care needs: arrangements for reviewing decisions on eligibility for NHS continuing inpatient care* are reproduced at Materials 4(H).

The *Hospital Discharge Workbook* (Materials 3(F)) published in 1994 is not issued under s 7 of the Local Authority Social Security Services Act 1970, and as such, does not have status of a direction. However, it does reflect many principles contained within the *Policy Guidance* and must be seen by authorities and health agencies as providing a framework for good practice.

The *Workbook* refers to the Patients' Charter as stating:

> The Charter Standard is that before you are discharged from hospital a decision should be made about any continuing health or social care needs you may have. Your hospital will agree arrangements for meeting these needs with agencies such as community nursing services and local authority social services departments before you are discharged. You, and with your agreement, your carers will be consulted and informed at all stages.

The *Workbook* states that assessment of social care and health needs should take place at an early stage, on a multidisciplinary basis and that decisions should be made with full consultation. There should be a written care plan provided and agreed, and that wherever practicable individuals be allowed to return to their own homes.

There is no doubt that an assessment must be carried out and a service provision decision reached prior to discharge given that para 3.44 of the *Policy Guidance* states that:

> Subject always to consumer choice, patients should not leave hospital until the supply of essential community care services has been agreed with them, their carers and all the authorities concerned.

The guidance on *NHS responsibilities for continuing healthcare needs* also requires that an assessment on a multidisciplinary basis must be undertaken in cases where residential/nursing home care or a package of support at home may be needed (para 17).

Therefore, if discharge is implemented prior to the assessment and service provision procedure having been completed, at least as far as essential services are concerned, a hospital Trust may lay itself open to challenge by way of judicial review. In the alternative, the Trust may consider bringing proceedings against a local authority to compel it to comply with its duty to assess and reach a decision under s 47 of the 1990 Act.

In a recent landmark decision, a local authority's failure to reach a final service provision decision (thereby preventing the applicant from leaving hospital) was deemed to be unlawful. The court ordered the authority to reach a decision under s 47(1)(b) of the 1990 Act in the form of a care plan, in accordance with para 3.24 of the *Policy Guidance*. Furthermore, the court did not consider the use of the local authority's complaints procedure to be a true alternative remedy, given that discrete points of law were involved (*R v London Borough of Sutton, ex p Tucher*, unreported, 29 October 1996).

As far as a potential applicant is concerned, any attempt to discharge prior to the assessment having completed and a service provision decision reached may give rise to an action for judicial review against both the Trust/health authority to restrain discharge and to ensure that the local authority complies with its obligations.

'Essential services' are not defined in the *Policy Guidance* but the authors' view is that these would include accommodation and services in a person's own home which support an acceptable quality of life, both in terms of physical and mental health. A patient does not have a complete veto over discharge by refusing a reasonable package of essential services, but this will depend on the assessed needs and the individual concerned (see further below).

## 15.3  The decision to discharge

Although the responsibility for making decisions under s 47 of the 1990 Act rests with local authorities, the decision to discharge from hospital will invariably come from the medical team itself.

The guidance referred to above relating to NHS responsibilities for meeting continuing health care needs sets down time limits within which health authorities, NHS Trusts and other hospitals and local authorities should agree:

• local policies and eligibility criteria for continuing health care;
• information to be given to patients and their carers as to how discharge procedures will work and the local arrangements for continuing health or social care support.

Trusts should ensure that these policies are adhered to, or face a potential challenge by way of judicial review from local authorities or patients themselves. Likewise, local authorities should be aware of the need to follow their own policies.

A decision to discharge a patient taken by a medical team applying only the eligibility criteria for continuing inpatient care may therefore be open to challenge, as such decisions are not merely matters of clinical opinion. Any decision to discharge where there may be continuing health or social care needs which have not been assessed and provided for may be subject to judicial review.

Paragraph 20 of the hospital discharge guidance states that the decision to discharge will be the responsibility of the consultant (in consultation with the multidisciplinary team) taking into account the results of the assessment and the local eligibility criteria. Paragraph 21 of the guidance gives examples of the types of decisions that may be made, from continuing inpatient care, a period of rehabilitation, placement in a nursing/residential home, to a package of social and health care at home.

Communication of the decision should be in the form of an agreed written care plan, which adequately reflects the assessment and decision making process (*Policy Guidance*, para 3.24). If no such plan is produced, both the health and social services departments risk challenge.

## 15.4   Hospital or discharge?

If a patient wishes to challenge a decision to discharge, on the basis that he requires continuing inpatient care in a hospital or nursing home, guidance on arranging for reviewing decisions on eligibility for continuing inpatient care has been published, providing for the right to appeal to a review panel (Materials 4(H)). The review panels must be operative as from 1 April 1996.

It is important to note that the review panel procedure cannot be used where decisions regarding a package of care at home are in dispute, or where there is a dispute between health or social services regarding funding. It is only concerned with the proper application of the eligibility criteria, including whether the proper procedures have been followed in reaching the decision regarding discharge. For other disputes regarding the care package at home, for example, the local authority's complaints procedure or an action for judicial review should be utilised (see Chapters 8 and 9).

Eligibility criteria should not be applied so rigidly that the circumstances of each case are not considered on their own merits. To do so might fetter discretion and as such, lay the criteria and/or its application, open to challenge.

As with the local authority's complaints procedure, attempts to resolve a complaint should be made informally. If the patient is still dissatisfied, he or any carer may ask the health authority to review the decision to discharge. Normally the health authority will seek the view of a panel consisting of three members, one of whom should be independent. The panel should convene within two weeks of the request, and the normal rules relating to natural justice will apply.

The health authority does have the right not to convene a review panel, but it should be borne in mind that although such a decision may be made only in very clear cases, full reasons should be given in order to avoid a challenge.

The outcome of the review must be communicated in writing to the patient and hospital/consultant. Although the role of the panel is advisory, its recommendations should not be departed from save in exceptional circumstances, with full reasons.

## 15.5  Challenging the package of care

In most cases, the decision as to whether a person requires continuing inpatient care in hospital will not be as much in dispute as the decision as to where a patient will go on discharge.

The decisions most often complained of are those which offer only residential or nursing home care as opposed to a package of care in the patient's own home. Although the local authority is entitled to meet the assessed needs of a person in the most economical way, potential applicants should consider whether the assessment has been properly carried out, ie has it addressed the psychological needs of the person concerned as well as the need for physical care and attention?

A prime example is that of the assessed need for '24-hour care' raised in the recent *Lancashire* case (see 5.4 above). Although it is true that such a need could be met in a variety of settings, it must be questioned as to whether the assessment was properly conducted, dealing with all relevant matters, including the psychological impact of a move to residential care. The authors take the view that the issues in this case might be differently argued in future.

The guidance on hospital discharge restates the principle that a patient has the right to refuse to be discharged into a nursing or residential care home (para 27). In such cases the local authority should work with hospital and community staff, the patient and carers to explore other options. It is important to note that para 29 of the guidance states:

> If these other options have been rejected it may be necessary for the hospital, in consultation with the health authority, social services department and, where necessary the housing authority, to implement discharge to the patient's home or alternative accommodation, with a package of health and social care within the options and resources available.

As the patient may refuse discharge into a nursing or residential care home, it would appear that the patient has a veto over discharge in such cases until a package of essential care services is established at home. If the patient is 'disabled' within the meaning of the Chronically Sick and Disabled Persons Act 1970, the local authority must (under s 47(2) of the 1990 Act) make a decision regarding the need for services under s 2 of the 1970 Act, and furthermore, must meet that assessed need without regard to the available resources, whether such services are deemed to be 'essential' or not.

For other disputes regarding the proposed package of care, attention should be given to the scope and adequacy of the assessment, as well as the service provision decision and its legality. In some cases, where discharge is unlikely to take place within several weeks, consideration should be given to the use of the local authority or NHS complaints procedures. In more urgent cases, an application for judicial review may be warranted.

## 15.6   Joint NHS/local authority funding

Health authorities have statutory powers under s 28A of the National Health Service Act 1977 to make payments to local authorities and other agencies for the purchase of personal social services, education for disabled people and housing. This includes arrangements under 'joint finance' schemes for capital and service projects.

Guidance on such arrangements has been published in LAC(92)17 and HSG(92)43.

The guidance requires health and local authorities to work closely together in preparing community care plans to develop jointly commissioned and funded social services provision. It is envisaged that during this process, arrangements will be agreed between health authorities and local authorities for health finance to be used for personal social services (eg meals on wheels) and housing for individual and/or client groups.

In particular, emphasis is placed on the ability of health authorities to make 'dowry payments' (jointly or alone) to social services departments in respect of patients who were, or are, in long-stay hospital environments but are moving, or have been moved, into the community with a package of services. In appropriate cases, health finance may be spent on social services rather than on health services. The guidance states:

> Health authorities have been funded to care for these people, and it is therefore for them to fund their transfer into the community . . . When an individual patient is discharged from a long stay hospital, the DHA responsible for his hospital care must agree with the receiving local authority the care to be provided and any financial arrangements so that current and future responsibility for providing or contributing to the cost of that care is clear. (para 8 and 9)

In respect of patients already in the community where changes to the level of provision are required in order to prevent breakdown of a placement, the guidance states:

> Where no agreement had been made between the DHA responsible for hospital care before discharge and the LA about respective responsibilities, the HA should assist the LA eg in arranging a joint assessment of need and, if the resecuring or reprovisioning of care leads the LA to incur additional expenditure, the HA will be expected to use its powers under s 28A to assist the LA to fund the care. (para 10).

The guidance recognises that expecting health authorities to have some responsibility for long-stay patients who were discharged some years ago may represent an additional burden, but considers that it would be wrong to expect local authorities to take total responsibility, if no fixed arrangements were made on discharge.

A precondition of joint funding agreements is that the specific guidance on s 28A payments annexed to the guidance is followed. Specifically, any expenditure must be recommended by a Joint Consultative Committee, the health authorities remain accountable for the way the funds are spent, and the NHS retains an interest in any capital developments purchased using such funds.

Directions issued by the Secretary of State regarding payments under s 28A set out maximum periods for which payments may be made. The periods vary depending on whether the payment is in respect of capital projects, or to voluntary organisations, or for 'dowry' purposes. For dowry payments, if in respect of an individual, the maximum period is seven years, extendable to 13 years.

Decisions by Joint Consultative Committees may be subject to judicial review proceedings, and decisions made by health authorities may also be subject to scrutiny by the courts.

## 15.7   NHS complaints

As from 1 April 1996 a new framework for the investigation of NHS complaints came into effect. Directions have been issued to health authorities, NHS Trusts and special health authorities to implement the new procedures. The new system is in addition to existing complaints regimes, such as the Health Service Ombudsman, FHSA procedures and the new guidance on hospital discharge (see 15.2, above).

The Government's policy and objectives were set out in EL(95)37, and interim guidance has been superseded by detailed guidance published in March 1996 entitled *Guidance on Implementation of the NHS Complaints Procedure*. It has not been possible to reproduce the guidance in this edition and a brief summary of the procedure is set out below.

Trusts/health authority boards/family health services authorities are required to establish formal complaints procedures and take steps to ensure the arrangements are well publicised. Any existing patient, or former patient, or a person on their behalf may make a complaint. Authorities are required to designate a complaints manager to oversee the process.

Complaints should normally be made within six months of the incident or its discovery (provided that this is within 12 months) but there is discretion to extend this time limit in appropriate cases.

The first stage is for the complaint to be resolved through the local resolution process, which must be established by each relevant authority. The Chief Executive of the Trust/health authority must respond in writing to a complainant. There are recommended time limits for this process.

If no satisfactory outcome is achieved at this stage, the complainant may request that a referral is made to the Independent Review Panel. This should be done within 28 days of the result of the local resolution process.

Panel Convenors must be appointed by each authority. It is for the convenor to decide, on receipt of a signed statement from the complainant, whether a Review Panel should be set up in accordance with the guidance. The Panel is generally seen as being a last resort. Again, there are recommended time limits within which decisions to refer to a Panel must be made and communicated.

The Panel will normally comprise three members who are independent of the authority/Trust complained of. Depending on the nature of the complaint, the members may have clinical experience, or may include a lay member. Complex clinical complaints may be investigated by independent clinical assessors either prior to or as part of the review process. Wide discretion is given to authorities/Trusts as to how the panel process operates, but in general, it is envisaged that no oral hearing will take place and complaints will usually be investigated through a combination of receipt of written information and/or interviews with relevant parties.

The Panel has no power to make formal recommendations, but may make suggestions as to how the complaint should be resolved. There are recommended time limits for communication of Panel reports.

Following any final Panel report, the complainant may wish to take further action, by way of legal proceedings or by a complaint to the Health Services Ombudsman.

At the time of writing this edition, as the new system has just been introduced, no information is available as to the efficacy of the procedure in resolving complaints. For most cases involving community care issues, however, the hospital discharge review process may be more relevant.

## 15.8   NHS decision-making

Any decision made by a health authority, NHS Trust or any individual employed within the NHS structure must, as a matter of course, comply with the general principles of public decision-making, eg fairness, relevancy, etc.

In addition, such bodies must take into account guidance in the form of circulars where not specifically directed to do so. There does not, at first sight, appear to be an NHS equivalent for s 7 of the Local Authority Social Services Act 1970 (directing authorities to act under guidance of the Secretary of State).

However, the National Health Service Act 1977 provides for the Secretary of State to issue directions to Regional Health Authorities, who may in turn direct District Health Authorities to exercise health service functions. District Health Authorities are empowered to issue directions to other bodies, which would include NHS Trusts (ss 13 to 17).

Section 5 of the National Health Service and Community Care Act 1990 empowers the Secretary of State to establish NHS Trusts in order to manage and own hospitals in place of Regional Health Authorities, and each Trust has the functions conferred on it by Sched 2 to the 1990 Act.

Paragraph 6(2) of Sched 2, Part II to the 1990 Act states:

An NHS Trust shall comply with any directions given to it by the Secretary of State with respect to all or any of the following matters—

(e) compliance with guidance or directions given (by circular or otherwise) to health authorities, or particular descriptions of health authorities . . .

Although the Secretary of State has not specifically directed that the *Policy Guidance* to the 1990 Act should be followed by health authorities and NHS Trusts, it is addressed to these bodies as well as local authorities. Under s 2 of the National Health Service Act 1977, the Secretary of State has power to:

do any other thing whatsoever which is calculated to facilitate, or is conducive to, the discharge of such a duty.

The *Policy Guidance* has been afforded mandatory status (see 1.16, above) with regard to local authority functions. It would be surprising if the residual power under s 2 of the National Health Service Act 1977 did not provide for a parallel to s 7 of the Local Authority Social Services Act 1970, binding health authorities and NHS Trusts alike.

Copious guidance has been issued to both health and local authorities in relation to hospital discharge arrangements, particularly for persons who have been, or are, suffering from mental disorder. Extracts of all relevant guidance are reproduced at Materials 4.

## 15.9  Conclusion

Since the introduction of the 1990 Act, attention has been focused on local authority social services functions, decreasing resources, and unmet need. The National Health Service has, over recent years, as a result of policy development, limited its provider role markedly with regard to joint social and health needs.

It is hoped that this chapter has analysed some of the legal issues affecting both local and health authorities, in order to illustrate how the NHS is not immune from challenge or responsibility for joint planning and provision of services, even those traditionally thought to be the remit of social services departments.

The 'seamless thread' between health and social care provision must be the responsibility of careful planning and individual decision-making.

# Materials

# Contents

# Materials 1

# Statutory Material

*Where provisions have been amended by a later enactment, they are printed in their amended form.*

Contents

## A. National Health Service and Community Care Act 1990

**46.**—(3) In this section—

'local authority' means the council of a county, a metropolitan district or a London borough or the Common Council of the City of London;

'community care services' means services which a local authority may provide or arrange to be provided under any of the following provisions—

  (*a*) Part III of the National Assistance Act 1948;

  (*b*) section 45 of the Health Services and Public Health Act 1968;

  (*c*) section 21 of and Schedule 8 to the National Health Service Act 1977; and

  (*d*) section 117 of the Mental Health Act 1983; and

'private carer' means a person who is not employed to provide the care in question by any body in the exercise of its functions under any enactment.

**Assessments of needs for community care services**

**47.**—(1) Subject to subsections (5) and (6) below, where it appears to a local authority that any person for whom they may provide or arrange for the provision of community care services may be in need of any such services, the authority—

    (*a*)  shall carry out an assessment of his needs for those services; and

    (*b*)  having regard to the results of that assessment, shall then decide whether his needs call for the provision by them of any such services.

(2) If at any time during the assessment of the needs of any person under subsection (1)(*a*) above it appears to a local authority that he is a disabled person, the authority—

    (*a*)  shall proceed to make such a decision as to the services he requires as is mentioned in section 4 of the Disabled Persons (Services, Consultation and Representation) Act 1986 without his requesting them to do so under that section; and

    (*b*)  shall inform him that they will be doing so and of his rights under that Act.

(3) If at any time during the assessment of the needs of any person under subsection (1)(*a*) above, it appears to a local authority—

    (*a*)  that there may be a need for the provision to that person by such District Health Authority as may be determined in accordance with regulations of any services under the National Health Service Act 1977, or

    (*b*)  that there may be a need for the provision to him of any services which fall within the functions of a local housing authority (within the meaning of the Housing Act 1985) which is not the local authority carrying out the assessment,

the local authority shall notify that District Health Authority or local housing authority and invite them to assist, to such extent as is reasonable in the circumstances, in the making of the assessment; and, in making their decision as to the provision of the services needed for the person in question, the local authority shall take into account any services which are likely to be made available for him by that District Health Authority or local housing authority.

(4) The Secretary of State may give directions as to the manner in which an assessment under this section is to be carried out or the form it is to take but, subject to any such directions and to subsection (7) below, it shall be carried out in such manner and take such form as the local authority consider appropriate.

(5) Nothing in this section shall prevent a local authority from temporarily providing or arranging for the provision of community care services for any person without carrying out a prior assessment of his needs in accordance with the preceding provisions of this section if, in the opinion of the authority, the condition of that person is such that he requires those services as a matter of urgency.

(6) If, by virtue of subsection (5) above, community care services have been provided temporarily for any person as a matter of urgency, then, as soon as practicable thereafter, an assessment of his needs shall be made in accordance with the preceding provisions of this section.

(7) This section is without prejudice to section 3 of the Disabled Persons (Services, Consultation and Representation) Act 1986.

(8) In this section—

'disabled person' has the same meaning as in that Act; and

'local authority' and 'community care services' have the same meanings as in section 46 above.

*    *    *    *    *

**Powers of the Secretary of State as respects social services functions of local authorities**

**50.** After section 7 of the Local Authority Social Services Act 1970 (local authorities to exercise social services functions under guidance of the Secretary of State) there shall be inserted the following sections—

**'Directions by the Secretary of State as to exercise of social services functions**

7A.—(1) Without prejudice to section 7 of this Act, every local authority shall exercise their social services functions in accordance with such directions as may be given to them under this section by the Secretary of State.

(2) Directions under this section—

(a) shall be given in writing; and

(b) may be given to a particular authority, or to authorities of a particular class,or to authorities generally.

**Complaints procedure**

7B.—(1) The Secretary of State may by order require local authorities to establish a procedure for considering any representations (including any complaints) which are made to them by a qualifying individual, or anyone acting on his behalf, in relation to the discharge of, or any failure to discharge, any of their social services functions in respect of that individual.

(2) In relation to a particular local authority, an individual is a qualifying individual for the purposes of subsection (1) above if—

(a) the authority have a power or a duty to provide, or to secure the provision of, a service for him; and

(b) his need or possible need for such a service has (by whatever means) come to the attention of the authority.

(3) A local authority shall comply with any directions given by the Secretary of State as to the procedure to be adopted in considering representations made as mentioned in subsection (1) above and as to the taking of such action as may be necessary in consequence of such representations.

(4) Local authorities shall give such publicity to any procedure established pursuant to this section as they consider appropriate.

**Inquiries**

7C.—(1) The Secretary of State may cause an inquiry to be held in any case where, whether on representations made to him or otherwise, he considers it advisable to do so in connection with the exercise by any local authority of any of their social services functions (except in so far as those functions relate to persons under the age of eighteen).

(2) Subsections (2) to (5) of section 250 of the Local Government Act 1972 (powers in relation to local inquiries) shall apply in relation to an inquiry under this section as they apply in relation to an inquiry under that section.

**Default powers of Secretary of State as respects social services functions of local authorities**

7D.—(1) If the Secretary of State is satisfied that any local authority have failed, without reasonable excuse, to comply with any of their duties which are social services functions (other than a duty imposed by or under the Children Act 1989), he may make an order declaring that authority to be in default with respect to the duty in question.

(2) An order under subsection (1) may contain such directions for the purpose of ensuring that the duty is complied with within such period as may be specified in the order as appear to the Secretary of State to be necessary.

(3) Any such direction shall, on the application of the Secretary of State, be enforceable by mandamus.

**Grants to local authorities in respect of social services for the mentally ill**

7E. The Secretary of State may, with the approval of the Treasury, make grants out of money provided by Parliament towards any expenses of local authorities incurred

(*a*)  in connection with the exercise of their social services functions in relation to persons suffering from mental illness; or

(*b*)  in making payments, in accordance with directions given by the Secretary of State to voluntary organisations which provide care and services for persons who are, or have been, or are likely to become dependent upon alcohol or drugs.'

## B.  National Assistance Act 1948 Part III (as amended)

**Duties of local authorities to provide accommodation**

21.—(1)  Subject to and in accordance with the provisions of this Part of this Act, a local authority may with the approval of the Secretary of State, and to such extent as he may direct shall, make arrangements for providing—

(*a*)  residential accommodation for persons aged 18 or over who by reason of age, illness, disability or any other circumstances are in need of care and attention which is not otherwise available to them; and

(*aa*)  residential accommodation for expectant and nursing mothers who are in need of care and attention which is not otherwise available to them.

(2)  In making any such arrangements a local authority shall have regard to the welfare of all persons for whom accommodation is provided, and in particular to the need for providing accommodation of different descriptions suited to different description of such persons as are mentioned in the last foregoing subsection.

\*    \*    \*    \*    \*

(4)  Subject to the provisions of section 26 of this Act, accommodation provided by a local authority in the exercise of their functions under this section shall be provided in premises managed by the authority or, to such extent as may be determined in accordance with the arrangements under this section, in such premises managed by another local authority as may be agreed between the two authorities and on such terms, including terms as to reimbursement of expenditure incurred by the said other authority, as may be so agreed.

(5)  References in this Act to accommodation provided under this part thereof shall be construed as references to accommodation provided in accordance with this and the five next following sections, and as including references to board and other services, amenities and requisites provided in connection with the accommodation except where in the opinion of the authority managing the premises their provision is unnecessary.

(6)  References in this Act to a local authority providing accommodation shall be construed, in any case where a local authority agree with another local authority for the provision of accommodation in premises managed by the said other authority, as references to the first-mentioned local authority.

(7) Without prejudice to the generality of the foregoing provisions of this section, a local authority may—

    (*a*)   provide, in such cases as they may consider appropriate, for the conveyance of persons to and from premises in which accommodation is provided for them under this Part of the Act;

    (*b*)   make arrangements for the provision on the premises in which accommodation is being provided of such other services as appear to the local authority to be required.

(8) Nothing in this section shall authorise or require a local authority to make any provision authorised or required to be made (whether by that or by any other authority) by or under any enactment not contained in this Part of this Act or authorised or required to be provided under the National Health Service Act 1977.

**Charges to be made for accommodation**

**22.**—(1) Subject to section 26 of this Act, where a person is provided with accommodation under this Part of this Act the local authority providing the accommodation shall recover from him the amount of the payment which he is liable to make in accordance with the following provisions of this section.

(2) Subject to the following provisions of this section, the payment which a person is liable to make for any such accommodation shall be in accordance with a standard rate fixed for that accommodation by the authority managing the premises in which it is provided, and that standard rate shall represent the full cost to the authority of providing that accommodation.

(3) Where a person for whom accommodation in premises managed by any local authority is provided, or proposed to be provided, under this Part of this Act satisfies the local authority that he is unable to pay therefor at the standard rate, the authority shall assess his ability to pay, and accordingly determine at what lower rate he shall be liable to pay for the accommodation:

(4) In assessing for the purposes of the last foregoing subsection a person's ability to pay, a local authority shall assume that he will need for his personal requirements such sum per week as may be prescribed by the Minister, or such other sum as in special circumstances the authority may consider appropriate.

(4A) Regulations made for the purposes of subsection (4) of this section may prescribe different sums for different circumstances.

(5) In assessing as aforesaid a person's ability to pay, a local authority shall give effect to regulations made by the Secretary of State for the purposes of this subsection except that, until the first such regulations came into force, a local authority shall give effect to Part III of Schedule 1 to the Supplementary Benefits Act 1976, as it had effect immediately before the amendments made by Schedule 2 to the Social Security Act 1980.

(5A) If they think fit, an authority managing premises in which accommodation is provided for a person shall have power on each occasion when they provide accommodation for him, irrespective of his means, to limit to such amount as appears to them reasonable for him to pay the payments required from him for his accommodation during a period commencing when they begin to provide the accommodation for him and ending not more than eight weeks after that.

\*    \*    \*    \*    \*

(8) Where accommodation is provided by a local authority in premises managed by another local authority, the payment therefor under this section shall be made to the authority managing the premises and not to the authority providing accom-

modation, but the authority managing the premises shall account for the payment to the authority providing the accommodation.

### Provision of accommodation in premises maintained by voluntary organisations

**26.**—(1) Subject to subsections (1A) and (1B) below, arrangements under section 21 of this Act may include arrangements made with a voluntary organisation or with any other person who is not a local authority where—

(a) that organisation or person manages premises which provide for reward accommodation falling within subsection (1)(a) or (aa) of that section, and

(b) the arrangements are for the provision of such accommodation in those premises.

(1A) Subject to subsection (1B) below, arrangements made with any voluntary organisation or other person by virtue of this section must, if they are for the provision of residential accommodation with both board and personal care for such persons as are mentioned in section 1(1) of the Registered Homes Act 1984 (requirement of registration), be arrangements for the provision of such accommodation in a residential care home which is managed by the organisation or person in question, being such a home in respect of which that organisation or persons—

(a) is registered under Part 1 of that Act, or

(b) is not required to be so registered by virtue of section 1(4)(a) or (b) of that Act (certain small homes) or by virtue of the home being managed or provided by an exempt body;

and for this purpose 'personal care' and 'residential care home' have the same meaning as in that Part of that Act.

(1B) Arrangements made with any voluntary organisation or other person by virtue of this section must, if they are for the provision of residential accommodation where nursing care is provided, be arrangements for the provision of such accommodation in premises which are managed by the organisation or person in question, being premises—

(a) in respect of which that organisation or person is registered under Part II of the Registered Homes Act 1984, or

(b) which, by reason only of being maintained or controlled by an exempt body, do not fall within the definition of a nursing home in section 21 of that Act.

(1C) Subject to subsection (1D) below, no such arrangements as are mentioned in subsection (1B) above may be made by an authority for the accommodation of any person without the consent of such District Health Authority as may be determined in accordance with regulations.

(1D) Subsection (1C) above does not apply to the making by an authority of temporary arrangements for the accommodation of any person as a matter of urgency; but, as soon as practicable after any such temporary arrangements have been made, the authority shall seek the consent required by subsection (1C) above to the making of appropriate arrangements for the accommodation of the person concerned.

(1E) No arrangements may be made by virtue of this section with a person who has been convicted of an offence under any provision of—

(a) the Registered Homes Act 1984 (or any enactment replaced by that Act); or

(b) regulations made under section 16 or section 26 of that Act (or under any corresponding provisions of any such enactment).

(2) Any arrangements made by virtue of this section provide for the making by

the local authority to the other party thereto of payments in respect of the accommodation provided at such rates as may be determined by or under the arrangements and subject to subsection (3A) below the local authority shall recover from each person for whom accommodation is provided under the arrangements the amount of the refund which he is liable to make in accordance with the following provisions of this section.

(3) Subject to subsection (3A) below a person for whom accommodation is provided under any such arrangements shall, in lieu of being liable to make payment therefor in accordance with section 22 of this Act, refund to the local authority any payments made in respect of him under the last foregoing subsection;

Provided that where a person for whom accommodation is provided, or proposed to be provided, under any such arrangements satisfies the local authority that he is unable to make a refund at the full rate determined under that subsection, subsections (3) to (5) of section 22 of this Act shall, with the necessary modifications, apply as they apply where a person satisfies the local authority of his inability to pay at the standard rate as mentioned in the said subsection (3).

(3A) Where accommodation in any premises is provided for any person under arrangements made by virtue of this section and the local authority, the person concerned and the voluntary organisation or other person managing the premises (in this subsection referred to as 'the provider') agree that this subsection shall apply—

    (*a*)   so long as the person concerned makes the payments for which he is liable under paragraph (*b*) below, he shall not be liable to make any refund under subsection (3) above and the local authority shall not be liable to make any payment under subsection (2) above in respect of the accommodation provided for him;

    (*b*)   the person concerned shall be liable to pay to the provider such sums as he would otherwise (under subsection (3) above) be liable to pay by way of refund to the local authority; and

    (*c*)   the local authority shall be liable to pay to the provider the difference between the sums paid by virtue of paragraph (*b*) above and the payments which, but for paragraph (*a*) above, the authority would be liable to pay under subsection (2) above.

(4) Subsections (5A), (7) and (9) of the said section 22 shall, with the necessary modifications, apply for the purposes of the last foregoing subsection as they apply for the purposes of the said section 22.

(4A) Section 21(5) of this Act shall have effect as respects accommodation provided under arrangements made by virtue of this section with the substitution for the reference to the authority managing the premises of a reference to the authority making the arrangements.

(5) Where in any premises accommodation is being provided under this section in accordance with arrangements made by a local authority, any person authorised in that behalf by the authority may at all reasonable times enter and inspect the premises.

\*    \*    \*    \*    \*

(7) In this section the expression 'voluntary organisation' includes any association which is a housing association for the purposes of the Housing Act 1936, or the Housing (Scotland) Acts, 1925 to 1946 and 'exempt body' means an authority or body constituted by an Act of Parliament or incorporated by Royal Charter.

**Exclusion of powers to provide accommodation under this Part in certain cases**

**26A.**—(1) Subject to subsection (3) of this section, no accommodation may be provided under section 21 or section 26 of this Act for any person who immediately before the date on which this section comes into force was ordinarily resident in relevant premises.

(2) In subsection (1) 'relevant premises' means—

(*a*) premises in respect of which any person is registered under the Registered Homes Act 1984;

(*b*) premises in respect of which such registration is not required by virtue of their being managed or provided by an exempt body;

(*c*) premises which do not fall within the definition of a nursing home in section 21 of that Act by reason only of their being maintained or controlled by an exempt body; and

(*d*) such other premises as the Secretary of State may by regulations prescribe; and in this subsection 'exempt body' has the same meaning as in section 26 of this Act.

(3) The Secretary by State may by regulations provide that, in such cases and subject to such conditions as may be prescribed, subsection (1) of this section shall not apply in relation to such classes of persons as may be prescribed in the regulations.

(4) The Secretary of State shall by regulations prescribe the circumstances in which persons are to be treated as being ordinarily resident in any premises for the purposes of subsection (1) of this section.

(5) This section does not affect the validity of any contract made before the date on which this section comes into force for the provision of accommodation on or after that date or anything done in pursuance of such a contract.

**Welfare arrangements for blind, deaf, dumb and crippled persons, etc**

**29.**—(1) A local authority may, with the approval of the Secretary of State, and to such extent as he may direct in relation to persons ordinarily resident in the area of the local authority shall make arrangements for promoting the welfare of persons to whom this section applies, that is to say persons aged 18 or over who are blind, deaf or dumb, or who suffer from mental disorder of any description and other persons aged 18 or over who are substantially and permanently handicapped by illness, injury, or congenital deformity or such other disabilities as may be prescribed by the Minister.

\* \* \* \* \*

(4) Without prejudice to the generality of provisions of subsection (1) of this section, arrangements may be made thereunder—

(*a*) for informing persons to whom arrangements under that subsection relate of the services available for them thereunder;

(*b*) for giving persons instruction in their own homes or elsewhere in matters of overcoming the effects of their disabilities;

(*c*) for providing workshops where such persons may be engaged (whether under a contract of service or otherwise) in suitable work, and hostels where persons engaged in the workshops, and other persons to whom arrangements under subsection (1) of this section relate and for whom work or training is being provided in pursuance of the Disabled Persons (Employment) Act 1944, or the Employment and Training Act 1973 may live;

(*d*) for providing persons to whom arrangements under subsection (1) of this section relate with suitable work (whether under a contract of service or otherwise) in their own homes or elsewhere;

(e)  for helping such persons in disposing of the produce of their work;

(f)  for providing such persons with recreational facilities in their own homes or elsewhere;

(g)  for compiling and maintaining classified registers of the persons to whom arrangements under subsection (1) of this section relate.

(4A)  Where accommodation in a hostel is provided under paragraph (c) of subsection (4) of this section—

(a)  if the hostel is managed by a local authority, section 22 of this Act shall apply as it applies where accommodation is provided under section 21;

(b)  if the accommodation is provided in a hostel managed by a person other than a local authority under arrangements made with that person, subsections (2) to (4A) of section 26 of this Act shall apply as they apply where accommodation is provided under arrangements made by virtue of that section; and

(c)  section 32 and 43 of this Act shall apply as they apply where accommodation is provided under sections 21 to 26;

and in this subsection references to 'accommodation' include references to board and other services, amenities and requisites provided in connection with the accommodation, except where in the opinion of the authority managing the premises or, in the case mentioned in paragraph (b) above, the authority making the arrangements their provision is unnecessary.

\*   \*   \*   \*   \*

(6)  Nothing in the foregoing provisions of this section shall authorise or require—

(a)  the payment of money to persons to whom this section applies, other than persons for whom work is provided under arrangements made by virtue of paragraph (c) or paragraph (d) of subsection (4) of this section or who are engaged in work which they are enabled to perform in consequence of anything done in pursuance of arrangements made under this section; or

(b)  the provision of any accommodation or services required to be provided under the National Health Service Act 1977 or the National Health Service (Scotland) Act 1947.

**Recovery of cost of assistance from persons liable for maintenance**

**43.**—(1)  Where assistance is given or applied for by reference to the requirements of any person (in this section referred to as a person assisted) the local authority concerned may make a complaint to the court against any other person who for the purposes of this Act is liable to maintain the person assisted.

(2)  On a complaint under this section the court shall have regard to all the circumstances and in particular to the resources of the defendant, and may order the defendant to pay such sum, weekly or otherwise, as the court may consider appropriate.

(3)  For the purposes of the application of the last foregoing subsection to payments in respect of assistance given before the complaint was made, a person shall not be treated as having at the time when the complaint is heard any greater resources than he had at the time when the assistance was given.

**Cross references**
See also LAC(93)10—*Approvals and Directions for arrangements from 1 April 1993 made under sections 21 and 29 of the National Assistance Act 1948* (1993).

See also National Assistance Act 1948 (Choice of Accommodation) Directions 1992, LAC(92)27.

## C. Local Authority Social Services Act 1970

**Local authority to establish social services committee**

**2.**—(1) Every local authority shall establish a social services committee and, subject to subsection (3) below, there shall stand referred to that committee all matters relating to the discharge by the authority of—

    (*a*) their functions under the enactments specified in the first column of Schedule 1 to this Act (being the functions which are described in general terms in the second column of that Schedule); and

    (*b*) such other of their functions as, by virtue of the following subsection, fall within the responsibility of the committee.

(2) The Secretary of State may by order designate functions of local authorities under any other enactment for the time being in force as being appropriate for discharge through a local authority's social services committee other than functions which by virtue of that or any other enactment are required to be discharged through some other committee of a local authority; and any functions designated by an order under this section which is for the time being in force shall accordingly fall within the responsibility of the social services committee.

**Business of Social Services Committee**

**3.**—(1) A local authority may delegate to their social services committee any of their functions matters relating to which stand referred to the committee by virtue of section 2 of this Act (hereafter in this Act referred to as 'social services functions') and, before exercising any of those functions themselves, the authority shall (unless the matter is urgent) consider a report of the committee with respect to the matter in question.

(2) Nothing in section 2 of this Act prevents a local authority from referring to a committee other than their social services committee a matter which by virtue of that section stands referred to the social services committee and which in the authority's opinion ought to be referred to the other committee on the ground that it relates to a general service of the authority; but before referring any such matter the authority shall receive and consider a report of the social services committee with respect to the subject matter of the proposed reference.

\* \* \* \* \*

**Local authorities to exercise social services functions under guidance of Secretary of State**

**7.**—(1) Local authorities shall, in the exercise of their social services functions, including the exercise of any discretion conferred by any relevant enactment, act under the general guidance of the Secretary of State.

**Citation, interpretation, commencement and extent**

\* \* \* \* \*

**15.**—(2) In this Act 'functions' includes powers and duties and 'social services functions' has the meaning given by section 3 of this Act.

\* \* \* \* \*

SCHEDULE 1

Section 2

ENACTMENTS CONFERRING FUNCTIONS ASSIGNED TO SOCIAL
SERVICES COMMITTEE

| Enactment | Nature of functions |
|---|---|
| Children and Young Persons Act 1933 (c 12) | |
| Part III | Protection of the young in relation to criminal and summary proceedings; children appearing before court as in need of care, protection or control; committal of children to approved school or care of fit person, etc. |
| Part IV | Remand homes, approved schools and children in care of fit persons. |
| National Assistance Act 1948 (c 29) | |
| Sections 21 to 27 | Provision of residential accommodation for the aged, infirm, needy, etc. |
| Sections 29 and 30 | Welfare of persons who are blind, deaf, dumb or otherwise handicapped or are suffering from mental disorder; use of voluntary organisations for administration of welfare schemes. |
| Sections 43 to 45 | Recovery of costs of providing certain services. |
| Section 48 | Temporary protection of property belonging to persons in hospital or accommodation provided under Part III of the Act, etc. |
| Section 49 | Defraying expenses of local authority officer applying for appointment as receiver for certain patients. |
| Section 56(3) except so far as it relates to an offence under section 47(11). | Prosecution of offences. |
| Disabled Persons (Employment) Act 1958 (c 33) | |
| Section 3 | Provision of facilities for enabling disabled persons to be employed or work under special conditions. |
| Mental Health Act 1959 (c 72) | |
| Section 8 and the Registered Homes Act 1984 so far as its provisions relate to mental nursing homes | Welfare and accommodation of mentally disordered persons. |
| Mental Health (Scotland) Act 1984 | |
| Section 10 | Welfare of certain persons while in hospital in Scotland. |

| *Enactment* | *Nature of functions* |
|---|---|
| Health Visiting and Social Work (Training) Act 1962 (c 33) | |
| Section 5(1)(*b*), and as extended by section 45(9) of the Health Services and Public Health Act 1968 (c 46) | Research into matters relating to local authority welfare services. |
| Section 5(1)(*c*) | Research into matters relating to functions of local authorities. |
| Children and Young Persons Act 1963 (c 37) | |
| Part I | Powers relating to young persons in need of care, protection or control; further provisions for protection of the young in relation to criminal proceedings. |
| Health Services and Public Health Act 1968 (c 46) | |
| Section 45 | Promotion of welfare of old people. |
| Section 65 | Financial and other assistance to voluntary organisations. |
| Social Work (Scotland) Act 1968 (c 49) | |
| Sections 75(2) and 76(4) | Reference for consideration, etc of case of child in care whose parent moves to Scotland and transfer of child. |
| Family Law Reform Act 1969 (c 46) | |
| Section 7 (4) | Supervision of ward of court. |
| Children and Young Persons Act 1969 (c 54) | |
| The whole Act except section 9 in so far as they assign functions to a local authority in their capacity of a local education authority. | Care and other treatment of children and young persons through court proceedings. |
| Chronically Sick and Disabled Persons Act 1970 (c 44) | |
| Section 1 | Obtaining information as to need for, and publishing information as to existence of, certain welfare services. |
| Section 2 | Provision of certain welfare services. |
| Section 18 | Provision of certain information required by Secretary of State. |
| Sections 6 and 7B of this Act | Appointment of director of social services, etc; provision and conduct of complaints procedure. |
| Children Act 1975 (c 72) | |
| Part II | Application by local authority for revocation of custodianship order; inquiries carried out by local authority in custodianship cases. |

| Enactment | Nature of functions |
|---|---|
| Adoption Act 1976 (c 36) | Maintenance of Adoption Service; functions of local authority as adoption agency; applications for orders freeing children for adoption; inquiries carried out by local authorities in adoption cases; care, possession and supervision of children awaiting adoption. |
| Supplementary Benefits Act 1976 Schedule 5 | Provision and maintance of resettlement units for persons without a settled way of living. |
| National Health Service Act 1977 Schedule 8 | Care of mothers and young children; prevention, care and after-care; home-help and laundry facilities. |
| Residential Homes Act 1980 Sections 1 to 7 | Registration of disabled or old persons' homes and residential homes for mentally disordered persons. |
| Mental Health Act 1983 (c 20) Parts II, III and VI | Welfare of the mentally disordered; guardianship of persons suffering from mental disorders including such persons removed to England and Wales from Scotland or Northern Ireland; exercise of functions of nearest relative of persons so suffering. |
| Sections 66, 67, 69(1) | Exercise of functions or nearest relative in relation to applications and references to Mental Health Review Tribunals. |
| Section 114 | Apppointment of approved social workers. |
| Section 115 | Entry and inspection. |
| Section 116 | Welfare of certain hospital patients. |
| Section 117 | After care of detained patients. |
| Section 130 | Prosecutions. |
| Registered Homes Act 1984 (c 23) Part I | Registration of Residential Care Homes. |
| Public Health (Control of Disease) Act 1984 (c 22) Section 46(2) and (5) | Burial or cremation of person dying in accommodation provided under Part III of the National Assistance Act 1948, and recovery of expenses from his estate. |

| *Enactment* | *Nature of functions* |
| --- | --- |
| Housing Act 1985<br>    Section 72(*b*) | Co-operation in relation to homeless persons and persons threatened with homelessness. |
| Children Act 1989 | Welfare reports. |
| The whole Act, in so far as it confers functions on a local authority within the meaning of that Act. | Consent to application for residence order in respect of child in care. |
| | Family assistance orders. |
| | Functions under Part III of the Act (local authority support for children and families). |
| | Care and supervision. |
| | Protection of children. |
| | Functions in relation to community homes, voluntary homes and voluntary organisations, registered children's homes, private arrangements for fostering children, child minding and day care for young children. |
| | Inspection of children's homes on behalf of Secretary of State. |
| | Research and returns of information. |
| | Functions in relation to children accommodated by health authorities [National Health Service trusts] and local education authorities or in residential care, nursing or mental nursing homes or in independent schools. |
| National Health Service and Community Care Act 1990 (c 19)<br>    Section 46 | Preparation of plans for community care services. |
|    Section 47 | Assessment of needs for community care services. |
| Education Act 1993<br>    Section 166 | Help for local education authority in exercising functions under Part III of the Act. |
| Carers (Recognition and Services) Act 1995 (c 12)<br>    Section 1 | Assessment of ability of carers to provide care. |

## D.  Health Services and Public Health Act 1968

**Promotion by local authorities of the welfare of old people**

45.—(1) A local authority may with the approval of the Secretary of State, and to such extent as he may direct, shall make arrangements for promoting the welfare of old people.

\* \* \* \* \*

(3) A local authority may employ as their agent for the purposes of this section any voluntary organisation or any person carrying on professionally or by way or trade or business, activities which consist of or include the provision of services for old people, being an organisation or person appearing to the authority to be capable of promoting the welfare of old people.

(4) No arrangements under this section shall provide—

(a)  for the payment of money to old people except in so far as the arrangements may provide for the remuneration of old people engaged in suitable work in accordance with the arrangements;

(b)  for making available any accommodation or services required to be provided under the National Health Service Act 1977.

**Cross references**

See also Circular 19/71 (welfare of the elderly—implementation of section 45 of the Health Services and Public Health Act 1968).

## E.  National Health Service Act 1977

**Local social services authorities**

21.—(1) Subject to paragraphs (d) and (e) of section 3 (1) above, the services described in Schedule 8 to this Act in relation to—

(a)  care of mothers,

(b)  prevention, care and after-care,

(c)  home-help and laundry facilities,

are functions exercisable by local social services authorities, and that Schedule has effect accordingly.

**Cross references**

1  (See further for more details).

2  And see also Circular LAC(93)10, *Approvals and Directions for Arrangements from 1 April 1993 made under Schedule 8 to the NHSA 1977 and sections 21 and 29 of the NAA 1948* (1993).

\* \* \* \* \*

**Co-operation between health authorities and local authorities**

22.—(1) In exercising their respective function health authorities, family health services authorities and local authorities shall cooperate with one another in order to secure and advance the health and welfare of the people of England and Wales.

(2) There shall be committees, to be called joint consultative committees, who shall advise bodies represented on them on the performance of their duties under section (1) above, and on the planning and operation of services of common concern to the authorities.

\* \* \* \* \*

**Power to make payments towards expenditure on community services**

28A.—(1) This section applies to the following authorities—

(*a*) a District Health Authority; and

(*b*) a special health authority established for a London Post-Graduate Teaching Hospital.

(2) An authority to whom this section applies may, if they think fit, make payments:

(*a*) to a local social services authority towards expenditure incurred or to be incurred by them in connection with any function which, by virtue of section 2(1) or (2) of the Local Authority Social Services Act 1970, is to be performed through their social services committee, other than functions under section 3 of the Disabled Persons (Employment) Act 1958;

(*b*) to a district council, towards expenditure incurred or to be incurred by them in connection with their functions under section 8 of the Residential Homes Act 1980 or Part II of Schedule 9 to the Health and Social Services and Social Security Adjudications Act 1983 (meals and recreation for old people);

(*c*) to an authority who are a local education authority for the purposes of the Education Acts 1944 to 1981, towards expenditure incurred or to be incurred by them in connection with their functions under those Acts, in so far as they perform those functions for the benefit of disabled persons;

(*d*) to an authority who are a local authority for the purposes of the Housing Act 1957, towards expenditure incurred or to be incurred by them in connection with their functions under Part V of that Act (provision of housing accommodation; and

(*e*) to the following bodies, in respect of expenditure incurred or to be incurred by them in connection with the provision of housing accommodation,—

(i) a housing association, as defined in section 189(1) of the Housing Act 1957, which is registered by the Housing Corporation under section 13 of the Housing Act 1974;

(ii) the Commission for the New Towns;

(iii) a new town development corporation;

(iv) an urban development corporation established under the local Government, Planning and Land Act 1980;

(v) the Housing Corporation; and

(vi) the Development Board for Rural Wales.

(3) A payment under this section may be made in respect of expenditure of a capital or of a revenue nature or in respect of both kinds of expenditure.

(4) No payment shall be made under this section in respect of any expenditure unless the expenditure has been recommended for a payment under this section by a joint consultative committee on which the authority proposing to make the payment are represented.

(5) The Secretary of State may by directions prescribe conditions relating to payments under this section.

(6) The power to give such directions may be exercised so as to make, as respects the cases in relation to which it is exercised, the same provision for all cases, or different provision for different cases or different classes of case, or different provision as respects the same case or class of case for different purposes.

(7) Without prejudice to the generality of subsection (5) above, the power may be exercised—

(*a*)  so as to make different provisions for England and Wales and different provision for different districts in either; and

(*b*)  so as to require, in such circumstances as may be specified—

    (i)  repayment of the whole or any part of a payment under this section;

    (ii)  payment, in respect of property acquired with money paid under this section, of an amount representing the whole or part of an increase in the value of the property which has occurred since its acquisition.

(8)  No payment shall be made under this section in respect of any expenditure unless the conditions relating to it—

(*a*)  accord with the evidence given by the joint consultative committee in making the recommendation for a payment under this section in respect of the expenditure in question; and

(*b*)  conform with the conditions prescribed for payments with that description under subsection (5) above.

(9)  Where expenditure which has been recommended by a joint consultative committee for a payment under this section is expenditure in connection with services to be provided by a voluntary organisation—

(*a*)  the authority who are to make the payment may make payments to the voluntary organisation towards the expenditure incurred or to be incurred by the organisation in connection with the provision of those services, instead of or in addition to making payments under subsection (2) above; and

(*b*)  an authority of one of the descriptions specified in paragraph (*a*), (*b*), (*c*), or (*d*) of subsection (2) above and who have received payments under that subsection may make out of the sums paid to the payments to the voluntary organisation towards expenditure incurred or to be incurred by the organisation in connection with the provision of those services,

but no payment shall be made under this subsection except subject to conditions—

    (i)  which conform with the conditions prescribed for payments of that description under subsection (5) above; and

    (ii)  which accord with the advice given by the joint consultative committee in recommending the expenditure for a payment under this section.

\*  \*  \*  \*  \*

## SCHEDULE 8

Section 21

## LOCAL SOCIAL SERVICES AUTHORITIES

### *Care of mothers and young children*

1.—(1)  A local social services authority may, with the Secretary of State's approval, and to such extent as he may direct, shall make arrangements for the care of expectant and nursing mothers (other than for the provision of residential accommodation for them).

### *Prevention, care and after-care*

2.—(1)  A local social services authority may, with the Secretary of State's approval, and to such extent as he may direct, shall make arrangements for the purpose of the prevention of illness and for the care of persons suffering from illness and for the after-care of persons who have been so suffering and in particular for—

\*    \*    \*    \*    \*

    (*b*)   the provision, for persons whose care is undertaken with a view to preventing them from becoming ill, persons suffering from illness and persons who have been so suffering, of centres or other facilities for training them or keeping them suitably occupied and the equipment and maintenance of such centres;

    (*c*)   the provision, for the benefit of such persons as are mentioned in paragraph (*b*) above, of ancillary or supplemental services; and

    (*d*)   for the exercise of the functions of the authority in respect of persons suffering from mental disorder who are received in guardianship under Part II or Part III of the Mental Health Act 1983 (whether the guardianship of the local social services authority or other persons).

Such an authority shall neither have the power nor be subject to a duty to make under this paragraph arrangements to provide facilities for any of the purposes mentioned in section 15(1) of the Disabled Persons (Employment) Act 1944.

\*    \*    \*    \*    \*

(3) The Secretary of State may make regulations as to the conduct of premises in which, in pursuance of arrangements made under this paragraph, are provided for persons whose care is undertaken with a view to preventing them from becoming sufferers of mental disorder within the meaning of that Act of 1983 or who are, or have been, so suffering, facilities for training them or keeping them suitably occupied.

\*    \*    \*    \*    \*

*Home-help and laundry facilities*

3.—(1) It is the duty of every local social services authority to provide on such a scale as is adequate for the needs of their area, or to arrange for the provision on such a scale as is so adequate, of home-help for households where such help is required owing to the presence of—

    a person who is suffering from illness, lying-in, an expectant mother, aged, handicapped as a result of having suffered from illness or by congenital deformity,

and every such authority has power to provide or arrange for the provision of laundry facilities for households for which home-help is being, or can be, provided under this sub-paragraph.

\*    \*    \*    \*    \*

## F.   Mental Health Act 1983 (as amended)

**After-care**

**117.—(1)** This section applies to persons who are detained under section 3 above, or admitted to a hospital in pursuance of a hospital order made under section 37 above, or transferred to a hospital in pursuance of a transfer direction made under section 47 or 48 above, and then cease to be detained and whether or not immediately after so ceasing leave hospital.

(2) It shall be the duty of the District Health Authority and of the local social

services authority to provide, in co-operation with relevant voluntary agencies, after-care services for any person to whom this section applies until such time as the District Health Authority and the local social services authority are satisfied that the person concerned is no longer in need of such services; but they shall not be so satisfied in the case of a patient who is subject to after-care under supervision at any time while he remains so subject.

(3) In this section 'the District Health Authority' means the District Health Authority for the district, and 'the local social services authority' means the local social services authority for the area in which a person concerned is resident or to which he is sent on discharge by the hospital in which he was detained.

**Cross references**
1 See also Circular HSG(90)23/LASSL(90)11/HSG(94)5, *Care Programme Approach.*
2 See also HSG(94)5, *Introduction of Supervision Registers for Mentally Ill People from 1 April 1994.*
3 And see LASSL(94)4/HSG(94)27, *Guidance on the Discharge of Mentally Disordered People and their Continuing Care in the Community.*
4 And see EL(93)68, *Assessment of need of services for mentally disordered offenders and others with similar needs.*

## G. The Chronically Sick and Disabled Persons Act 1970

**Information as to need for and existence of welfare services**
**1.**—(1) It shall be the duty of every local authority having functions under section 29 of the National Assistance Act 1948 to inform themselves of the number of persons to whom that section applies within their area and for the need for the making by the authority of arrangements under that section for such persons.

(2) Every such local authority—
(*a*) shall cause to be published from time to time at such times and in such manner as they consider appropriate general information as to the services provided under arrangements made by the authority under the said section 29 which are for the time being available in their area; and
(*b*) shall ensure that any such person as aforesaid who uses any other service provided by the authority (whether under any such arrangements or not) is informed of any other of those services which in the opinion of the authority is relevant to his needs and of any service provided by any other authority or organisation which in the opinion of the authority is so relevant and of which particulars are in the authority's possession.

(3) This section shall come into operation on such date as the Secretary of State may by order made by statutory instrument appoint.

**Provision of welfare services**
**2.**—(1) Where a local authority having functions under section 29 of the National Assistance Act 1948 are satisfied in the case of any person to whom that section applies who is ordinarily resident in their area that it is necessary in order to meet the needs of that person for that authority to make arrangements for all or any of the following matters, namely—
(*a*) the provision of practical assistance for that person in his home;
(*b*) the provision for that person of, or assistance to that person in obtaining, wireless, television, library or similar recreational facilities;
(*c*) the provision for that person of lectures, games, outings or other recre-

ational facilities outside his home or assistance to that person in taking advantage of educational facilities available to him;

(d) the provision for that person of facilities for, or assistance in, travelling to and from his home for the purpose of participating in any services provided under arrangements made by the authority under the said section 29 or, with the approval of the authority, in any services provided otherwise than as aforesaid which are similar services which could be provided under such arrangements;

(e) the provision of assistance for that person in arranging for the carrying out of any works of adaptation in his home or the provision of any additional facilities designed to secure his greater safety, comfort or convenience;

(f) facilitating the taking of holidays by that person, whether at holiday homes or otherwise and whether provided under arrangements made by the authority or otherwise;

(g) the provision of meals for that person whether in his home or elsewhere;

(h) the provision for that person of, or assistance to that person in obtaining, a telephone and any special equipment necessary to enable him to use a telephone,

then, subject to the provisions of section 7(1) of the Local Authority Social Services Act 1970 (which requires local authorities in the exercise of certain functions, including functions under the said section 29, to act under the general guidance of the Secretary of State) it shall be the duty of that authority to make those arrangements in exercise of their functions under the said section 29.

### Duties of housing authorities

**3.**—(1) A local housing authority in discharging their duty under section 8 of the Housing Act 1985 to consider housing conditions in their district and the needs of their district with respect to the provision of further housing accommodation shall have regard to the special needs of chronically sick or disabled persons.

### Application of Act to authorities having functions under the Children Act 1989

**28A.** This Act applies with respect to disabled children in relation to whom a local authority have functions under Part III of the Children Act 1989 as it applies in relation to persons to whom section 29 of the National Assistance Act 1948 applies.

#### Cross references
1 See also DHSS Circular 12/70.
2 See also Circular No 45/71 (guidance on the general implications for local authorities of the coming into operation of this section), and Circular No 69/71 (which requests local authorities to inform the Secretary of State about the progress they have made in implementing this section), and LAC(87)6 (which gives guidance on the amendments made to this section by the Disabled Persons (Services, Consultation and Representation) Act 1986).

## H. Disabled Persons (Services, Consultation and Representation) Act 1986

### Services under section 2 of the 1970 Act: duty to consider needs of disabled persons

**4.** When requested to do so by—

(a) a disabled person

(b) his authorised representative, or

(c) any person who provides care for him in the circumstances mentioned in section 8,

a local authority shall decide whether the needs of the disabled person call for the provision by the authority of any services in accordance with section 2(1) of the 1970 Act (provision of welfare services).

\* \* \* \* \*

**Duty of local authority to take into account abilities of carer**

**8.**—(1) Where—

(*a*) a disabled person is living at home and receiving a substantial amount of care on a regular basis from another person (who is not a person employed to provide such care by any body in the exercise of its functions under any enactment), and

(*b*) it falls to a local authority to decide whether the disabled person's needs call for the provision by them of any services for him under any of the welfare enactments,

the local authority shall, in deciding that question, have regard to the ability of that other person to continue to provide such care on a regular basis.

(2) Where that other person is unable to communicate, or (as the case may be) be communicated with, orally or in writing (or in each of those ways) by reason of any mental or physical incapacity, the local authority shall provide such services as, in their opinion, are necessary to ensure that any such incapacity does not prevent the authority from being properly informed as to the ability of that person to continue to provide care as mentioned in subsection (1).

\* \* \* \* \*

## I. Carers (Recognition and Services) Act 1995

*(Came into force on 1 April 1996.)*

**Assessment of ability of carers to provide care**

**1.**—(1) Subject to subsection (3) below, in any case where—

(*a*) a local authority carry out an assessment under section 47 (1) (*a*) of the National Health Service & Community Care Act 1990 of the needs of a person ('the relevant person') for community care services, and

(*b*) an individual ('the carer') provides or intends to provide a substantial amount of care on a regular basis for the relevant person,

the carer may request the local authority, before they make their decision as to whether the needs of the relevant person call for the provision of any services, to carry out an assessment of his ability to provide and to continue to provide care for the relevant person; and if he makes such a request, the local authority shall carry out such an assessment and shall take into account the results of that assessment in making that decision.

(2) Subject to subsection (3) below, in any case where—

(*a*) a local authority assess the needs of a disabled child for the purposes of Part III of the Children Act 1989 or section 2 of the Chronically Sick and Disabled Persons Act 1970, and

(*b*) an individual ('the carer') provides or intends to provide a substantial amount of care on a regular basis for the disabled child,

the carer may request the local authority, before they make their decision as to whether the needs of the disabled child call for the provision of any services, to carry out an assessment of his ability to provide and to continue to provide care for the disabled child; and if he makes such a request, the local authority shall carry out such an assessment and shall take into account the results of that assessment in making that decision.

(3) No request may be made under subsection (1) or (2) above by an individual who provides or will provide the care in question—

(a) by virtue of a contract of employment or other contract with any person; or

(b) as a volunteer for a voluntary organisation.

(4) The Secretary of State may give directions as to the manner in which an assessment under subsection (1) or (2) above is to be carried out or the form it is to take but, subject to any such directions, it shall be carried out in such manner and take such form as the local authority consider appropriate.

(5) Section 8 of the Disabled Persons (Services, Consultation and Representation Act 1986 (duty of local authority to take into account ability of carers) shall not apply in any case where—

(a) an assessment is made under subsection (1) above in respect of an individual who provides the care in question for a disabled person; or

(b) an assessment is made under subsection (2) above.

(6) In this section—

'community care services' has the meaning given by section 46(3) of the National Health Service and Community Care Act 1990;

'child' means a person under the age of eighteen;

'disabled child' means a child who is disabled within the meaning of Part III of the Children Act 1989;

'disabled person' means a person to whom section 29 of the National Assistance Act 1948 applies;

'local authority' has the meaning given by section 46(3) of the National Health Service and Community Care Act 1990; and

'voluntary organisation' has the same meaning as in the National Assistance Act 1948.

\* \* \* \* \*

**4.** There shall be paid out of money provided by Parliament any increase attributable to this Act in the sums payable out of money so provided under any other enactment.

**Cross references**

See Carers (Recognition and Services) Act 1995 Policy Guidance and Practice Guide

## J.  Children Act 1989

### PART I

### INTRODUCTORY

**Welfare of the child**

**1.**—(1) When a court determines any question with respect to—

(a)  the upbringing of a child; or

(b)  the administration of a child's property or the application of any income arising from it,

the child's welfare shall be the court's paramount consideration.

(2) In any proceedings in which any question with respect to the upbringing of a child arises, the court shall have regard to the general principle that any delay in determining the question is likely to prejudice the welfare of the child.

(3) In the circumstances mentioned in subsection (4), a court shall have regard in particular to—

(a) the ascertainable wishes and feelings of the child concerned (considered in the light of his age and understanding);

(b) his physical, emotional and educational needs;

(c) the likely effect on him of any change in his circumstances;

(d) his age, sex, background and any characteristics of his which the court considers relevant;

(e) any harm which he has suffered or is at risk of suffering;

(f) how capable each of his parents, and any other person in relation to whom the court considers the question to be relevant, is at meeting his needs;

(g) the range of powers available to the court under this Act in the proceedings in question.

*     *     *     *     *

**Provision of services for children in need, their families and others**

**17.**—(1) It shall be the general duty of every local authority (in addition to the other duties imposed on them by this Part)—

(a) to safeguard and promote the welfare of children within their area who are in need; and

(b) so far as is consistent with that duty, to promote the upbringing of such children by their families,

by providing a range and level of services appropriate to those children's needs.

(2) For the purpose principally of facilitating the discharge of their general duty under this section, every local authority shall have the specific duties and powers set out in Part I of Schedule 2.

(3) Any service provided by an authority in the exercise of functions conferred on them by this section may be provided for the family of a particular child in need or for any member of his family, it is provided with a view to safeguarding or promoting the child's welfare.

(4) The Secretary of State may by order amend any provision of Part I of Schedule 2 or add any further duty or power to those for the time being mentioned there.

(5) Every local authority—

(a) shall facilitate the provision by others (including in particular voluntary organisations) of services which the authority have power to provide by virtue of this section, or section 18, 20, 23 or 24; and

(b) may make such arrangements as they see fit for any person to act on their behalf in the provision of any such service.

(6) The services provided by a local authority in the exercise of functions conferred on them by this section may include giving assistance in kind or, in exceptional circumstances, in cash.

(7) Assistance may be unconditional or subject to conditions as to the repayment of the assistance or of its value (in whole or in part).

(8) Before giving any assistance or imposing any conditions, a local authority shall have regard to the means of the child concerned and of each of his parents.

(9) No person shall be liable to make any repayment of assistance or of its value

at any time when he is in receipt of income support or family credit under the Social Security Act 1986.

(10) For the purposes of this Part a child shall be taken to be in need if—

    (a)  he is unlikely to achieve or maintain, or to have the opportunity of achieving or maintaining, a reasonable standard of health or development without the provision for him of services by a local authority under this Part;

    (b)  his health or development is likely to be significantly impaired, or further impaired, without the provision for him of such services; or

    (c)  he is disabled,

and 'family', in relation to such a child, includes any person who has parental responsibility for the child and any other person with whom he has been living.

(11) For the purposes of this Part, a child is disabled if he is blind, deaf or dumb or suffers from mental disorder of any kind or is substantially and permanently handicapped by illness, injury or congenital deformity or such other disability as may be prescribed; and in this Part—

'developments' means physical, intellectual, emotional, social or behavioural development; and

'health' means physical or mental health.


*Provision of accommodation for children*

**Provision of accommodation for children: general**

**20.**—(1) Every local authority shall provide accommodation for any child in need within their area who appears to them to require accommodation as a result of—

    (a)  there being no person who has parental responsibility for him;

    (b)  his being lost or having been abandoned; or

    (c)  the person who has been caring for him being prevented (whether or not permanently, and for whatever reason) from providing him with suitable accommodation or care.

(2) Where a local authority provide accommodation under subsection (1) for a child who is ordinarily resident in the area of another local authority, that other local authority may take over the provision of accommodation for the child within—

    (a)  three months of being notified in writing that the child is being provided with accommodation; or

    (b)  such other longer period as may be prescribed.

(3) Every local authority may provide accommodation for any child in need within their area who has reached the age of sixteen and whose welfare the authority consider is likely to be seriously prejudiced if they do not provide him with accommodation.

(4) A local authority may provide accommodation for any child within their area (even though a person who has parental responsibility for him is able to provide him with accommodation) if they consider that to do so would safeguard or promote the child's welfare.

(5) A local authority may provide accommodation for any person who has reached the age of sixteen but is under twenty-one in any community home which takes children who have reached the age of sixteen if they consider that to do so would safeguard or promote his welfare.

(6) Before providing accommodation under this section, a local authority shall, so far as is reasonably practicable and consistent with the child's welfare—

    (a)  ascertain the child's wishes regarding the provision of accommodation; and (*b*) give due consideration (having regard to his age and understanding) to such wishes of the child as they have been able to ascertain.

(7) A local authority may not provide accommodation under this section for any child if any person who—

(*a*) has parental responsibility for him; and

(*b*) is willing and able to—

    (i) provide accommodation for him; or

    (ii) arrange for accommodation to be provided for him,

objects.

(8) Any person who has parental responsibility for a child may at any time remove the child from accommodation provided by or on behalf of the local authority under this section.

(9) Subsections (7) and (8) do not apply while any person—

(*a*) in whose favour a residence order is in force with respect to the child; or

(*b*) who has care of the child by virtue of an order made in the exercise of the High Court's inherent jurisdiction with respect to children,

agrees to the child being looked after in accommodation provided by or on behalf of the local authority.

(10) Where there is more than one such person as is mentioned in subsection (9), all of them must agree.

(11) Subsections (7) and (8) do not apply where a child who has reached the age of sixteen agrees to being provided with accommodation under this section.

\* \* \* \* \*

*Duties of local authorities in relation to children looked after by them*

**General duty of local authority in relation to children looked after by them**

**22.**—(1) In this Act, any reference to a child who is looked after by a local authority is a reference to a child who is—

(*a*) in their care; or

(*b*) provided with accommodation by the authority in the exercise of any functions (in particular those under this Act) which stand referred to their social services committee under the Local Authority Social Services Act 1970.

(2) In subsection (1) 'accommodation' means accommodation which is provided for a continuous period of more than 24 hours.

(3) It shall be the duty of a local authority looking after any child—

(*a*) to safeguard and promote his welfare; and

(*b*) to make such use of services available for children cared for by their own parents as appears to the authority reasonable in his case.

(4) Before making any decision with respect to a child whom they are looking after, or proposing to look after, a local authority shall, so far as is reasonably practicable, ascertain the wishes and feelings of—

(*a*) the child;

(*b*) his parents;

(*c*) any person who is not a parent of his but who has parental responsibility for him; and

(*d*) any other person whose wishes and feelings the authority consider to be relevant,

regarding the matter to be decided.

(5) In making any such decision a local authority shall give due consideration—

(a) having regard to his age and understanding, to such wishes and feelings of the child as they have been able to ascertain;

(b) to such wishes and feelings of any person mentioned in subsection (4)(b) to (d) as they have been able to ascertain; and

(c) to the child's religious persuasion, racial origin and cultural and linguistic background.

\*    \*    \*    \*    \*

### Co-operation between authorities

**27.**—(1) Where it appears to a local authority that any authority mentioned in subsection (3) could, by taking any specified action, help in the exercise of any of their functions under this Part, they may request the help of that other authority specifying the action in question.

(2) An authority whose help is so requested shall comply with the request if it is compatible with their own statutory or other duties and obligations and does not unduly prejudice the discharge of any of their functions.

(3) The authorities are—

(a) any local authority;

(b) any local education authority;

(c) any local housing authority;

(d) any health authority or National Health Service trust; and

(e) any person authorised by the Secretary of State for the purposes of this section.

### Consultation with local education authorities

**28.**—(1) Where—

(a) a child is being looked after by a local authority; and

(b) the authority propose to provide accommodation for him in an establishment at which education is provided for children who are accommodated there;

they shall, so far as is reasonably practicable, consult the appropriate local education authority before doing so.

(2) Where any such proposal is carried out, the local authority shall, as soon as is reasonably practicable, inform the appropriate local education authority of the arrangements that have been made for the child's accommodation.

(3) Where the child ceases to be accommodated as mentioned in subsection (1)(b), the local authority shall inform the appropriate local education authority.

(4) In this section 'the appropriate local authority' means—

(a) the local education authority within whose area the local authority's area falls; or

(b) where the child has special educational needs and a statement of his needs is maintained under Part III of the Education Act 1993, the local education authority who maintain the statement.

### Recoupment of cost of providing services etc

**29.**—(1) Where a local authority provide any service under section 17 or 18, other than advice, guidance or counselling, they may recover from a person specified in subsection (4) such charge for the service as they consider reasonable.

(2) Where the authority are satisfied that that person's means are insufficient for it to be reasonably practicable for him to pay the charge, they shall not require him to pay more than he can reasonably be expected to pay.

(3) No person shall be liable to pay any charge under subsection (1) at any time when he is in receipt of income support, family credit or disability working allowance under Part VII of the Social Security Contributions and Benefits Act 1992.

(4) The persons are—

(a) where the service is provided for a child under sixteen, each of his parents;

(b) where it is provided for a child who has reached the age of sixteen, the child himself; and

(c) where it is provided for a member of the child's family, that member.

(5) Any charge under subsection (1) may, without prejudice to any other method of recovery, be recovered summarily as a civil debt.

(6) Part III of Schedule 2 makes provision in connection with contributions towards the maintenance of children who are being looked after by local authorities and consists of the re-enactment with modifications of provisions in Part V of the Child Care Act 1980.

(7) Where a local authority provide any accommodation under section 20(1) for a child who was (immediately before they began to look after him) ordinarily resident within the area of another local authority, they may recover from that other authority any reasonable expenses incurred by them in providing the accommodation and maintaining him.

(8) Where a local authority provide accommodation under section 21(1) or (2)(a) or (b) for a child who is ordinarily resident within the area of another local authority and they are not maintaining him in—

(a) a community home provided by them;

(b) a controlled community home; or

(c) a hospital vested in the Secretary of State, or any other hospital made available pursuant to arrangements made by a District Health Authority,

they may recover from that other authority any reasonable expenses incurred by them in providing the accommodation and maintaining him.

(9) Where a local authority comply with any request under section 27(2) in relation to a child or other person who is not ordinarily resident within their area, they may recover from the local authority in whose area the child or person is ordinarily resident any reasonable expenses incurred by them in respect of that person.

\* \* \* \* \*

## SCHEDULE 2

Sections 17, 23 and 29

## LOCAL AUTHORITY SUPPORT FOR CHILDREN AND FAMILIES

### PART I
### PROVISION OF SERVICES FOR FAMILIES

*Identification of children in need and provision of information*

1.—(1) Every local authority shall take reasonable steps to identify the extent to which there are children in need within their area.

(2) Every local authority shall—

(a) publish information—

(i)    about services provided by them under sections 17, 18, 20 and 24; and

(ii)    where they consider it appropriate, about the provision by others (including, in particular, voluntary organisations) of services which the authority have power to provide under those sections; and

(b)    take such steps as are reasonably practicable to ensure that those who might benefit from the services receive the information relevant to them.

### Maintenance of a register of disabled children

2.—(1) Every local authority shall open and maintain a register of disabled children, within their area.

(2) The register may be kept by means of a computer.

### Assessment of children's needs

3. Where it appears to a local authority that a child within their area is in need, the authority may assess his needs for the purposes of this Act at the same time as any assessment of his needs is made under—

(a)    the Chronically Sick and Disabled Persons Act 1970;

(b)    Part III of the Education Act 1993;

(c)    the Disabled Persons (Services, Consultation and Representation) Act 1986; or

(d)    any other enactment.

\*    \*    \*    \*    \*

### Provision for disabled children

6. Every local authority shall provide services designed—

(a)    to minimise the effect on disabled children within their area of their disabilities; and

(b)    to give such children the opportunity to lead lives which are as normal as possible.

### Provision to reduce need for care proceedings etc

7. Every local authority shall take reasonable steps designed—

(a)    to reduce the need to bring—

(i)    proceedings for care or supervision orders with respect to children within their area;

(ii)    criminal proceedings against such children;

(iii)    any family or other proceedings with respect to such children which might lead to them being placed in the authority's care; or

(iv)    proceedings under the inherent jurisdiction of the High Court with respect to children;

(b)    to encourage children within their area not to commit criminal offences; and

(c)    to avoid the need for children within their area to be placed in secure accommodation.

### Provision for children living with their families

8. Every local authority shall make such provision as they consider appropriate for the following services to be available with respect to children in need within their area while they are living with their families—

(*a*)  advice, guidance and counselling;

(*b*)  occupational, social, cultural or recreational activities;

(*c*)  home help (which may include laundry facilities);

(*d*)  facilities for, or assistance with, travelling to and from home for the purpose of taking advantage of any other service provided under this Act or of any similar service;

(*e*)  assistance to enable the children concerned and his family to have a holiday.

*Family centres*

9.—(1) Every local authority shall provide such family centres as they consider appropriate in relation to children within their area.

(2) 'Family centre' means a centre at which any of the persons mentioned in sub-paragraph (3) may—

(*a*)  attend for occupational, social, cultural or recreational activities;

(*b*)  attend for advice, guidance or counselling; or

(*c*)  be provided with accommodation while he is receiving advice, guidance or counselling.

(3) The persons are—

(*a*)  a child;

(*b*)  his parents;

(*c*)  any person who is not a parent of his but who has parental responsibility for him;

(*d*)  any other person who is looking after him.

*Maintenance of the family home*

10. Every local authority shall take such steps as are reasonably practicable, where any child within the area who is in need and whom they are not looking after is living apart from his family—

(*a*)  to enable him to live with his family; or

(*b*)  to promote contact between him and his family,

if, in their opinion, it is necessary to do so in order to safeguard or promote his welfare.

*Duty to consider racial groups to which children in need belong*

11. Every local authority shall, in making any arrangements—

(*a*)  for the provision of day care within their area; or

(*b*)  designed to encourage persons to act as local authority foster parents,

have regard to the different racial groups to which children within their area who are in need belong.

\*   \*   \*   \*   \*

## K.  Health and Social Services and Social Security Adjudications Act 1983

**Charges for local authority services in England and Wales**

**17.**—(1) Subject to subsection (3) below an authority providing a service to which this section applies may recover such charge (if any) for it as they consider reasonable.

(2) This section applies to services provided under the following enactments—

(a) section 29 of the National Assistance Act 1948 (welfare arrangements for blind, deaf, dumb and crippled persons);

(b) section 45 (1) of the Health Services and Public Health Act 1968 (welfare of old people);

(c) Schedule 8 to the National Health Service Act 1977 (care of mothers and young children, prevention of illness and care and after-care and home help and laundry facilities);

(d) section 8 of the Residential Homes Act 1980 (meals and recreation for old people); and

(e) paragraph 1 of Part II of Schedule 9 to this Act other than the provision of services for which payment may be required under section 22 or 26 of the National Assistance Act 1948.

(3) If a person—

(a) avails himself of a service to which this section applies, and

(b) satisfies the authority providing the service that his means are insufficient for it to be reasonably practicable for him to pay for the service the amount which he would otherwise be obliged to pay for it,

the authority shall not require him to pay more for it than it appears to them that it is reasonably practicable for him to pay.

(4) Any charge under this section may, without prejudice to any other method of recovery, be recovered summarily as a civil debt.

\* \* \* \* \*

### Recovery of sums due to the local authority where persons in residential accommodation have disposed of assets

**21.**—(1) Subject to the following provisions of this section, where—

(a) a person avails himself of Part III accommodation; and

(b) that person knowingly and with the intention of avoiding charges for the accommodation—

　　(i) has transferred any asset to which this section applies to some other person or persons not more than six months before the date on which he begins to reside in such accommodation; or

　　(ii) transfers any such asset to some other person or persons while residing in the accommodation; and

(c) either—

　　(i) the consideration for the transfer is less than the value of the asset; or

　　(ii) there is no consideration for the transfer,

the person or persons to whom the asset is transferred by the person availing himself of the accommodation shall be liable to pay to the local authority providing the accommodation or arranging for its provision the difference between the amount assessed as due to be paid for the accommodation by the person availing himself of it and the amount which the local authority receive from him for it.

### Arrears of contributions charged on interest in land in England and Wales

**22.**—(1) Subject to subsection (2) below, where a person who avails himself of Part III accommodation provided by a local authority in England, Wales or Scotland—

(a) fails to pay any sum assessed as due to be paid by him for the accommodation; and

(b) has a beneficial interest in land in England and Wales,

the local authority may create a charge in their favour on his interest in the land.

(2) In the case of a person who has interests in more than one parcel of land the charge under this section shall be upon his interest in such one of the parcels as the local authority may determine.

(2A) In determining whether to exercise their power under subsection (1) above and in making any determination under subsection (2) above, the local authority shall comply with any directions given to them by the Secretary of State as to the exercise of those functions.

(3) Any interest in the proceeds of sale of land held upon trust for sale is to be treated, subject to subsection (8) below, as an interest in land for the purposes of this section.

(4) Subject to subsection (5) below, a charge under this section shall be in respect of any amount assessed as due to be paid which is outstanding from time to time.

(5) The charge on the interest of a joint tenant in the proceeds of sale of land held upon trust for sale shall be in respect of an amount not exceeding the value of the interest that he would enjoy in those proceeds if the joint tenancy was severed but the creation of such a charge shall not sever the joint tenancy.

(6) On the death of a joint tenant in the proceeds of sale of land held upon trust for sale whose interest in the proceeds is subject to a charge under this section—

    (*a*)  if there are surviving joint tenants, their interests in the proceeds; and

    (*b*)  if the land vests in one person, or one person is entitled to have it vested in him, his interest in it,

shall become subject to a charge for an amount not exceeding the amount of the subsection (5) above.

(7) A charge under this section shall be created by a declaration in writing made by the local authority.

(8) Any such charge, other than a charge on an interest in the proceeds of sale of land, shall in the case of unregistered land be a land charge of Class B within the meaning of section 2 of the Land Charges Act 1972 and in the case of registered land be a registrable charge taking effect as a charge by way of legal mortgage.

\*    \*    \*    \*    \*

**Interest on sums charged on or secured over interest in land**

**24.**—(1) Any sum charged on or secured over an interest in land under this Part of this Act shall bear interest from the day after that on which the person for whom the local authority provided the accommodation dies.

(2) The rate of interest be such reasonable rate as the Secretary of State may direct or, if no such direction is given, as the local authority may determine.

**Cross references**

1 See circular LAC(94)1 (incorporated into Circular LAC(95)7—CRAG No. 5 (charges for residential accommodation guide)).

2 See also LAC(95)21—CRAG amendment No. 6 and LAC(96)9—CRAG amendment No. 7.

3 See also Advice Note for use by Social Services Inspectorate on Discretionary Charges for Adult Social Services (January 1994).

# L.   Community Care (Residential Accommodation) Act 1992

**Arrangements for provision of residential accommodation in premises managed by voluntary organisations etc**

**1.**—(1) The following subsections shall be substituted for subsections (1) and (1A) of section 26 of the National Assistance Act 1948 (arrangements for provision of accommodation in premises maintained by voluntary organisations etc) in place of those set out in section 42(2) of the National Health Service and Community Care Act 1990—

'(1) Subject to subsections (1A) and (1B) below, arrangements under section 21 of this Act may include arrangements made with a voluntary organisation or with any other person who is not a local authority where:

    (a) that organisation or person manages premises which provide for reward accommodation falling within subsection (1)(a) and (aa) of that section, and

    (b) the arrangements are for the provision of such accommodation in those premises.

(1A) Subject to subsection (1B) below, arrangements made with any voluntary organisation or other person by virtue of this section must, if they are for the provision of residential accommodation with both board and personal care for such persons as are mentioned in section 1(1) of the Registered Homes Act 1984 (requirement of registration), be arrangements for the provision of such accommodation in a residential care home which is managed by the organisation or person in question, being such a home in respect of which that organisation or person—

    (a) is registered under Part I of that Act, or

    (b) is not required to be so registered by virtue of section 1(4)(a) or (b) of that Act (certain small homes) or by virtue of the home being managed or provided by an exempt body;

and for this purpose "personal care" and "residential care home" have the same meaning as in that Part of that Act.

(1B) Arrangements made with any voluntary organisation or other person by virtue of this section must, if they are for the provision of residential accommodation where nursing care is provided, be arrangements for the provision of such accommodation in premises which are managed by the organisation or person in question, being premises—

    (a) in respect of which that organisation or person is registered under Part II of the Registered Homes Act 1984, or

    (b) which, by reason only of being maintained or controlled by an exempt body, do not fall within the definition of a nursing home in section 21 of that Act.

(1C) Subject to subsection (1D) below, no such arrangements as are mentioned in subsection (1B) above may be made by an authority for the accommodation of any person without the consent of such District Health Authority as may be determined in accordance with regulations.

(1D) Subsection (1C) above does not apply to the making by an authority of temporary arrangements for the accommodation of any person as a matter of urgency; but, as soon as practicable after any such temporary arrangements have been made, the authority shall seek the consent required by subsection (1C) above to the making of appropriate arrangements for the accommodation of the person concerned.

(1E) No arrangements may be made by virtue of this section with a person who has been convicted of an offence under any provision of—

    (a) the Registered Homes Act 1984 (or any enactment replaced by that Act); or

    (b) regulations made under section 16 or section 26 of that Act (or under any corresponding provisions of any such enactment)'.

(2) In consequence of subsection (1) above the following enactments are hereby repealed, namely—

(a) section 42(2) of the National Health Service and Community Care Act 1990; and

(b) section 2(5)(a) of the Registered Homes (Amendment) Act 1991; and, in section 42(3) of that Act of 1990, for 'At the end of subsection (2) of that section' there shall be substituted. 'In section 26 of that Act (arrangements for provision of accommodation in premises maintained by voluntary organisations etc.), at the end of subsection (2)'.

\*     \*     \*     \*     \*

## M.  Local Government and Housing Act 1989

### Designation and reports of monitoring officer

**5.**—(1) It shall become duty of every relevant authority—

(a) to designate one of their officers (to be known as 'the monitoring officer') as the officer responsible for performing the duties imposed by this section; and

(b) to provide that officer with such staff, accommodation and other resources as are, in his opinion, sufficient to allow those duties to be performed;

and the officer so designated may be the head of the authority's paid service but shall not be their chief finance officer.

(2) It shall be the duty of a relevant authority's monitoring officer, if it at any time appears to him that any proposal, decision or omission by the authority, by any committee, sub-committee of the authority or by any joint committee on which the authority are represented constitutes, has given rise to or is likely to or would give rise to—

(a) a contravention by the authority, by any committee, sub-committee or officer of the authority or by any such joint committee of any enactment or rule of law or of any code of practice made or approved by or under any enactment; or

(b) any such maladministration or injustice as is mentioned in Part III of the Local Government Act 1974 (Local Commissioners) or Part II of the Local Government (Scotland) Act 1975 (which makes corresponding provision for Scotland),

to prepare a report to the authority with respect to that proposal, decision or omission.

(3) It shall be the duty of a relevant authority's monitoring officer—

(a) in preparing a report under this section to consult so far as practicable with the head of the authority's paid service and with their chief finance officer; and

(b) as soon as practicable after such a report has been prepared by him or his deputy, to arrange for a copy of it to be sent to each member of the authority.

\*     \*     \*     \*     \*

(5) It shall be the duty of a relevant authority and of any such committee as is mentioned in subsection (4) above—

(a) to consider any report under this section by a monitoring officer or his deputy at a meeting held not more than twenty-one days after copies of the report are first sent to members of the authority or committee; and

(b) without prejudice to any duty imposed by virtue of section 115 of the Local Government Finance Act 1988 (duties in respect of conduct involving contravention of financial obligations) or otherwise, to ensure that no step is taken for giving effect to any proposal or decision to which such a report relates at any time while the implementation of the proposal or decision is suspended in consequence of the report; and nothing in section 101 of the Local Government Act 1972 or in section 56 of, or Schedule 10 or 20, to the Local Government (Scotland) Act 1973 (delegation) shall apply to the duty imposed by virtue of paragraph (a) above.

(6) For the purposes of paragraph (b) of subsection (5) above the implementation of a proposal or decision to which a report under this section relates shall be suspended in consequence of the report until the end of the first business day after the day on which consideration of that report under paragraph (a) of that subsection is concluded.

(7) The duties of a relevant authority's monitoring officer under this section shall be performed by him personally or, where he is unable to act owing to absence or illness, personally by such member of his staff as he has for the time being nominated as his deputy for the purposes of this section.

*    *    *    *    *

## N.  Community Care (Direct Payments) Act 1996

*England and Wales*

**Direct payments**

1.—(1) Where—

(a) an authority have decided under section 47 of the National Health Service and Community Care Act 1990 (assessment by local authorities of needs for community care services ) that the needs of a person call for the provision of any community care services, and

(b) the person is of a description which is specified for the purposes of this subsection by regulations made by the Secretary of State,

the authority, may if the person consents, make to him, in respect of his securing the provision of any of the services for which they have decided his needs call, a payment of such amount as, subject to subsections (2) and (3) below, they think fit.

(2) If—

(a) an authority pay under subsection (1) above at a rate below their estimate of the reasonable cost of securing the provision of the service concerned, and

(b) the payee satisfies the authority that his means are insufficient for it to be reasonably practicable for him to make up the difference,

the authority shall so adjust the payment to him under that subsection as to avoid there being a greater difference than that which appears to them to be reasonably practicable for him to make up.

(3) In the case of a service which, apart from this Act, would be provided under section 117 of the Mental Health Act 1983 (after-care), an authority shall not pay

under subsection (1) above at a rate below their estimate of the reasonable cost of securing the provision of the service.

(4) A payment under subsection (1) above shall be subject to the condition that the person to whom it is made shall not secure the provision of the service to which it relates by a person who is of a description specified for the purposes of this subsection by regulations made by the Secretary of State.

(5) The Secretary of State may by regulations provide that the power conferred by subsection (1) above shall not be exercisable in relation to the provision of residential accommodation for any person for a period in excess of such period as may be specified in the regulations.

(6) If the authority by whom a payment under subsection (1) above is made are not satisfied, in relation to the whole or any part of the payment—

(a) that it has been used to secure the provision of the service to which it relates, or

(b) that the condition imposed by subsection (4) above, or any condition properly imposed by them, has been met in relation to its use,

they may require the payment or, as the case may be, the part of the payment to be repaid.

(7) Regulations under this section may—

(a) make different provision for different cases, and

(b) include such supplementary, incidental, consequential and transitional provisions and savings as the Secretary of State thinks fit.

(8) The power to make regulations under this section shall be exercisable by statutory instrument which shall be subject to annulment in pursuance of a resolution of either House of Parliament.

(9) In this section, 'community care services' has the same meaning as in section 46 of the National Health Service and Community Care Act 1990.

### Relationship with other functions

**2.**—(1) Except as provided by subsection (2) below, the fact that an authority make a payment under section 1(1) above shall not affect their functions with respect to the provision under the relevant community care enactment of the service to which the payment relates.

(2) Where an authority make a payment under section 1(1) above, they shall not be under any obligation to the payee with respect to the provision under the relevant community care enactment of the service to which the payment relates as long as they are satisfied that the need which calls for the provision of the service will be met by virtue of the payee's own arrangements.

(3) In subsections (1) and (2) above, references to the relevant community care enactment, in relation to the provision of a service, are to the enactment under which the service would fall to be provided apart from this Act.

### Consequential amendments

**3.**—(1) The Local Authority Social Services Act 1970 shall be amended as follows:

(2) In section 7B(2) (persons entitled to use the procedure for complaining about the discharge of a local authority's social services functions) there shall be inserted at the end 'or if he is in receipt of payment from the authority under the Community Care (Direct Payments) Act 1996'.

(3) In Schedule 1 (enactments conferring functions assigned to social services committee) at the end there shall be added—

| 'Community Care (Direct Payments) Act 1996. | Functions in connection with the making of payments to persons in respect of their securing the provision of community care services.' |

\*　\*　\*　\*　\*

# Materials 2

# Relevant Orders, Directions and Regulations

*Contents*

## A.  Local Authority Social Services (Complaints Procedure) Order 1990 (SI No 2244)

The Secretary of State for Health, in exercise of the powers conferred by section 7B(1) of the Local Authority Social Services Act 1970, and of all other powers enable him in that behalf, hereby makes the following Order:—

**Citation and commencement**

**1.** This Order may be cited as the Local Authority Social Services (Complaints Procedure) Order 1990 and shall come into force on 1st April 1991.

**Complaints procedure**

**2.** Every local authority shall establish a procedure for considering any representations (including any complaints) which are made to them by a qualifying individual, or anyone acting on his behalf, in relation to the discharge of, or any failure to discharge, any of their social services functions in respect of that individual.

\*　\*　\*　\*　\*

## B. Policy Guidance: Complaints Procedure Directions 1990

### Arrangement of Directions

#### PART 1—INTRODUCTORY
1. Interpretation
2. Citation and commencement

#### PART II—REPRESENTATIONS AND THEIR CONSIDERATION
3. Exclusions
4. Preliminaries
5. Local Authority action
6. Consideration by local authority
7. Notification to complainant and reference to panel
8. Recommendations

#### PART III—MONITORING OF OPERATION OF PROCEDURE
9. Monitoring of operation of procedure

#### PART IV—GENERAL
10. Exclusion from scope of procedures

The Secretary of State for Health, in the exercise of the powers conferred by section 7B(3) of the Local Authority Social Services Act 1970 (1970 c 42. Section 7B was inserted by section 50 of the National Health Service and Community Care Act 1990 (c 19)) and all other powers enabling him in that behalf, hereby gives the following directions to local authorities:

### PART I—Introductory

#### CITATION AND COMMENCEMENT

1    These Directions may be cited as the Complaints Procedure Directions 1990 and shall come into force on 1st April 1991.

#### INTERPRETATION

2(1)    In these Directions, unless the content otherwise requires
'the Act' means the Local Authority Social Services Act 1970;
'complainant' means a person specified in section 7B(2) or anyone acting on his behalf, making any representation including a complaint to the local authority in relation to the discharge of, or any failure to discharge, any of their social services functions in respect of that individual;
'independent person' has the meaning assigned by paragraph (3) and
'panel' means a panel of 3 persons at least one of whom must be an independent person as defined in paragraph (3);
'representations' means representations (including complaints) referred to in section 7B(1).
2(2)    In these Directions, unless the context requires otherwise—
    (a)    any reference to a numbered section is to the section in the Act bearing that number,
    (b)    any reference to a numbered direction is to the direction in these Directions

bearing that number, and any reference to a numbered paragraph, is to the paragraph of that direction bearing that number.

2(3)   The expression 'independent person' in these Directions means a person who is neither a member nor an officer of that authority, nor, where the local authority have delegated any of its social services functions to any organisation, a person who is a member of or employed by that organisation, nor the spouse of such person.

### PART II—Representations and their Consideration

### EXCLUSIONS

3.   These Directions shall not apply to any representations, (including complaints) to which section 26(3) of the Children Act 1989 applies, made on or after the day upon which that section of the Act comes into force (a day has not yet been appointed for this section to come into force).

### LOCAL AUTHORITY ACTION

4.   The local authority shall appoint one of their officers to assist the authority in the co-ordination of all aspects of their consideration of the representations.

4(1)   The local authority shall appoint one of their officers to assist the authority in the co-ordination of all aspects of their consideration of the representations.

4(2)   The local authority shall ensure that all members or officers involved in the handling of representations under section 7B(1) are familiar with the procedures set out in these Directions.

### PRELIMINARIES

5(1)   Where a local authority received representations from any complainant they shall attempt to resolve the matter informally.

5(2)   If the matter cannot be resolved to the satisfaction of the complainant, the local authority shall give or send to him an explanation of the procedure set out in these Directions and ask him to submit a written representation if he wishes to proceed.

5(3)   The local authority shall offer assistance and guidance to the complainant on the use of this procedure, or give advice on where he may obtain it.

### CONSIDERATION BY LOCAL AUTHORITY

6(1)   The local authority shall consider the representations and formulate a response within 28 days of their receipt, or if this is not possible, explain to the complainant within that period why it is not possible and tell him when he can expect a response, which shall in any event be within 3 calendar months of receipt of the representations.

6(2)   The representations may be withdrawn at any stage by the complainant, in which case the procedure set out in these Directions (other than direction 9 and 11) shall no longer apply to that case.

### NOTIFICATION OF COMPLAINANT AND REFERENCE TO PANEL

7(1)   The local authority shall notify in writing the result of their consideration to—

(*a*) the complainant;

(*b*) the person on whose behalf the representations were made, unless the local authority consider that that person is not able to understand it or it would cause him unnecessary distress;

(*c*) any other person who the local authority considers has sufficient interest in the case.

7(2)  If the complainant informs the authority in writing within 28 days of the date on which the notification mentioned in paragraph (1) is sent to him that he is dissatisfied with that result and wishes the matter to be referred to a panel for review, the local authority shall appoint a panel (including any independent person) to consider the matter which the local authority shall refer to it.

7(3)  The panel shall meet within 28 days of the receipt of the complainant's request for review by the local authority to consider the matter together with any oral or written submissions as the complainant or the local authority wish the panel to consider.

## RECOMMENDATIONS

8(1)  Where a panel meets under direction 7, it shall decide on its recommendations and record them in writing within 24 hours of the end of the meeting.

8(2)  The panel shall send written copies of their recommendations to—

(*a*) the local authority,

(*b*) the complainant,

(*c*) if appropriate, the person on whose behalf the representations were made, and

(*d*) any other person who the local authority considers has sufficient interest in the case.

8(3)  The panel shall record the reasons for their recommendations in writing.

8(4)  The local authority shall consider what action they ought to take, and notify in writing the persons specified in paragraph (1)(*b*), (*c*) and (*d*) of the local authority's decision and of their reasons for taking that decision and of any action which they have taken or propose to take within 28 days of the date of the panel's recommendations.

## PART III—Monitoring

## MONITORING OF OPERATION OF PROCEDURE

9.  The local authority shall keep a record of each representation received, the outcome of each representation, and whether there was compliance with the time limits specified in directions 6(1), 7(3) and 8(1) and 8(4).

## PART IV—General

## EXCLUSION FROM SCOPE OF PROCEDURES

10.—These Directions shall apply only to representations in respect of matters arising on or after the date when an order made under section 50 of the National Health Service and Community Care Act 1990 comes into force (1990 c 19).

Signed by authority of the Secretary of State for Health.

Minister of State for Health

## C.    National Assistance Act 1948 (Choice of Accommodation) Directions 1992 and LAC(92)27

The Secretary of State in exercise of the powers conferred by section 7A of the Local Authority Social Services Act 1970 and of all other powers enabling her in that behalf hereby makes the following Directions:—

### Citation, commencement and extent

1(1)    These Directions may be cited as the National Assistance Act 1948 (Choice of Accommodation) Directions 1992 and shall come into force on 1st April 1993.
(2)    These Directions extend only to England.

### Local authorities to provide preferred accommodation

2.    Where a local authority have assessed a person under section 47 of the National Health Service and Community Care Act 1990 (assessment) and have decided that accommodation should be provided pursuant to section 21 of the National Assistance Act 1948 (provision of residential accommodation), the local authority shall, subject to paragraph 3 of these Directions, make arrangements for accommodation pursuant to section 21 for that person at the place of his choice within the United Kingdom (in these Directions called 'preferred accommodation') if he has indicated that he wishes to be accommodated in preferred accommodation.

### Conditions for provision of preferred accommodation

3.    Subject to paragraph 4 of these Directions the local authority shall only be required to make or continue to make arrangements for a person to be accommodated in his preferred accommodation if—
   (a)    the preferred accommodation appears to the authority to be suitable in relation to his needs as assessed by them;
   (b)    the cost of making arrangements for him at his preferred accommodation would not require the authority to pay more than they would usually expect to pay having regard to his assessed needs;
   (c)    the preferred accommodation is available;
   (d)    the persons in charge of the preferred accommodation provide it subject to the authority's usual terms and conditions, having regard to the nature of the accommodation, for providing accommodation for such a person under Part III of the National Assistance Act 1948.

### Preferred accommodation outside local authority's usual limit

4(1)    Subject to sub-paragraphs (2) and (3), paragraph 3(b) of these Directions shall not apply to a local authority which make arrangements which cost more than the local authority would usually expect to pay in order to provide a person with their preferred accommodation if a third party's contribution to that person (which is treated as that person's resources as assessed under the National Assistance (Assessment of Resources) Regulations 1992 is such that he can reasonably be expected to pay for the duration of the arrangements an amount which is at least equal to the difference between—
   (a)    the cost which the local authority would usually expect to pay for accommodation having regard to the person's assessed need, and
   (b)    the full standard rate for that accommodation as specified in section 22(2)

of the National Assistance Act 1948 (liability to pay full cost of local authority accommodation, the 'standard rate') or pursuant to section 26(2) to (4) of that Act (liability to pay full cost of other accommodation arranged by local authority).

(2)   Sub-paragraph (1) shall not apply in respect of cases in which the third party's contributions are made by a person who is liable under section 42 of the National Assistance Act 1948 to maintain the person who wishes to be provided with preferred accommodation.

(3)   Nothing in these Directions shall prevent a local authority from making or continuing to make arrangements for a person to be accommodated in his preferred accommodation where the cost of making such arrangements is more than the local authority would usually expect to pay having regard to the person's assessed needs.

23 December 1992

Signed by authority of the Secretary of State

---

## Guidance
## National Assistance Act 1948 (Choice of Accommodation) Directions 1992

### Purpose

1.   Under new community care arrangements social services authorities will increasingly be making placements in residential and nursing home care. This direction is intended to ensure where that happens that people are able to exercise a genuine choice over where they live.

2.   It also gives people the right to enter more expensive accommodation than they would otherwise have been offered if there is a third party willing and able to pay the difference in cost.

3.   This direction is intended to formalise the best practice which most authorities would in any case have adopted. It sets out the minimum that individuals should be able to expect. It is not, however, intended to mark the limits of the choice that authorities may be able to offer people. Even where not required to act in a certain way by this direction, authorities should exercise their discretion in a way that maximises choice as far as possible within available resources.

### Summary

4.   If after an assessment of need an authority decides to provide residential care for someone either permanently or temporarily, it will make a placement on their behalf in suitable accommodation.

5.   If the individual concerned expresses a preference for particular accommodation ('preferred accommodation') within the UK the authority must arrange for care in that accommodation, provided

- the accommodation is suitable in relation to the individual's assessed needs
- to do so would not cost the authority more than it would usually expect to pay for accommodation for someone with the individual's assessed needs
- the accommodation is available
- the person in charge of the accommodation is willing to provide accom-

modation subject to the authority's usual terms and conditions for such accommodation.

6.   If a resident requests it, the authority must also arrange for care in accommodation more expensive than it would normally fund provided there is a third party willing and able to pay the difference between the cost the authority would usually expect to pay and the actual cost of the accommodation.

### Preferred Accommodation

7.   As with all aspects of service provision, there should be a general presumption in favour of people being able to exercise choice over the service they receive. The limitations on authorities' legal obligation to provide preferred accommodation set out in the direction are not intended to deny people reasonable freedom of choice, but simply to ensure that authorities are able to fulfil their obligations for the quality of service provided and for value for money. The terms of the direction are explained more fully below. Where for any reason an authority decides not to arrange a place for someone in their preferred accommodation it must have a clear and reasonable justification for that decision which relates to the criteria of the direction.

## SUITABILITY OF ACCOMMODATION

7.1   Suitability will depend on the authority's assessment of individual need. Each case must be considered on its merits.

7.2   Consequently accommodation will not necessarily be suitable simply because it satisfies registration standards. On the other hand accommodation will not necessarily be unsuitable simply because it fails to conform with the authority's preferred model of provision, or meet the letter of a standard service specification.

7.3   This direction does not affect Section 26(1D) of the National Assistance Act 1948 as inserted by the NHS and Community Care Act 1990 which prevents an authority making arrangements for residential care with anyone convicted of an offence under the Registered Homes Act 1984. Similarly, the direction does not require an authority to contract with any accommodation where for any other reason it is prevented by law from doing so.

## COST

7.4   The test should be whether the cost of preferred accommodation is more than the authority would usually expect to pay for someone with the same assessed needs as the individual concerned. This is not necessarily the same as the cost that the authority would in fact have incurred had the particular individual not decided to exercise their right to choose, since that might be either higher or lower than the authority would usually pay. For example, the cost of a one particular placement at a given time might be determined by the fortuitous availability for whatever reason of a place below the cost that an authority would usually expect to meet, or else by the temporary unavailability of accommodation at the authority's usual price.

7.5   The cost being compared should be gross costs before income from charging. Given the different amounts that authorities will recover from individuals by way of charges it would not be possible to determine a usual net cost an authority would expect to pay.

7.6   Costs will vary around the country. There may be circumstances where an authority might judge the need to move to another part of the country to be an integral part of an individual's assessed needs (eg in certain cases to be near a relative), and therefore one of the factors to be considered in determining what the authority would usually expect to pay.

7.7 Costs may also vary according to the type of care. For example, the cost an authority might usually expect to pay for respite care might be different from its usual cost for permanent care.

## AVAILABILITY

7.8 A place in an individual's preferred accommodation may not always be available immediately. If the client wishes, authorities should where appropriate be willing to consider making temporary or intermediate arrangements until a place becomes available.

## CONDITIONS

7.9 In order to ensure that they are able to exercise proper control over the use of their funds, authorities need to be able to impose certain technical conditions, for example in relation to payment regimes, review, access, monitoring, audit, record keeping, information sharing, insurance, sub-contracting etc.

7.10 The contract conditions required of preferred accommodation should be broadly the same as those it would impose on any other similar operation. Stricter conditions should never be used as a way of avoiding a placement. As with suitability, account should be taken of the nature and location of the accommodation. There may be reasons why it would be reasonable to adapt standard conditions and unreasonable not to. For example, authorities should take into account the fact that homes in other areas, or those which take residents from many areas, may have geared themselves to the normal requirements of other authorities.

7.11 In setting their usual terms and conditions authorities are reminded that Part II of the Local Government Act 1988 stipulates that they may not specify non-commercial considerations in contracts.

### More expensive accommodation

8. The direction also places a duty on authorities to make placements in more expensive accommodation than they would usually expect to provided there is a third party able and willing to pay the difference. A third party in this case might be a relative (but not a liable relative, see 11.13), a friend, or any other source.

9. This direction applies only where a resident explicitly chooses to enter accommodation other than that which the authority offers them, and where that preferred accommodation is more expensive than the authority would usually expect to pay.

10. This direction does not mean that authorities may set an arbitrary ceiling on the amount they are willing to contribute towards residential care and require third parties routinely to make up the difference. If challenged an authority would need to be able to demonstrate that its usual cost was sufficient to allow it to provide people with the level of service they could reasonably expect did the possibility of third party contributions not exist.

11. Similarly, the direction is not intended to allow authorities to require third party contributions in cases where the authority itself decides to offer someone a place in unusually expensive accommodation—for example, where there is at the time in question no suitable accommodation available at the authority's 'usual cost'.

## RESPONSIBILITY FOR COSTS OF ACCOMMODATION

11.1    When making arrangements for residential care for an individual under the National Assistance Act 1948, an authority is responsible for the full cost of that accommodation. Therefore where an authority places someone in a more expensive accommodation it must contract to pay the accommodation's fees in full. The third party's contribution will be treated as part of the resident's income for charging purposes and the authority will be able to recover it in that way.

11.2    The prospective resident in these cases will therefore need to demonstrate that there is a third party able and willing to pay the difference between the authority's normal cost and the accommodation's actual fees.

11.3    In order to safeguard both residents and authorities from entering arrangements which are likely to fail, the third party must reasonably be expected to be able to continue to contribute for the duration of the arrangements. Authorities should assure themselves that there is every chance that the third party will continue to have the resources to make the required payments.

11.4    Authorities will be aware that under Section 26(3A) of the National Assistance Act 1948 (as inserted by the NHS and Community Care Act 1990), it is open to them to agree with both the resident and the person in charge of their accommodation that instead of paying a contribution to the authority, the resident may pay the same amount direct to the accommodation with the authority paying the difference. In such a case the third party would also pay the accommodation direct on behalf of the resident. However, it should be noted that even where there is such an agreement for the resident to make direct payments, the authority continues to be liable to pay the full cost of the accommodation should either the resident or relative fail to pay the required amount.

11.5    Authorities should also note that because arrangements under section 26(3A) of the 1948 Act require the agreement of all parties, it would not be reasonable for them to refuse people their preferred accommodation on the grounds that they (or their preferred accommodation) would not enter such an arrangement.

## THE AMOUNT OF THE THIRD PARTY CONTRIBUTION

11.6    The amount of the third party contribution should be the difference between the actual fee for the accommodation and the amount that otherwise the authority would usually have expected to pay for someone with the individual's assessed needs. In determining this amount the authority should apply the same consideration as above (7.4–7.8), except that in these cases it will need to state a precise figure in each case.

11.7    The amount of the third party contribution should be calculated on gross costs, ie the difference between the preferred accommodation's fees and the fees that an authority would usually expect to pay. The fact that residents might not have been able to meet the full cost of the accommodation that the authority would otherwise have arranged does not affect their ability to benefit from this part of the direction. When the third party's contribution has been taken into account, the cost net of charges to an authority of the more expensive accommodation should be the same as it would have been in accommodation at the authority's usual price.

## PRICE INCREASE

11.8    Arrangements between the authority, resident and third party will need to be reviewed from time to time to take account of changes to the accommodation's fees and also changes to the amount the authority would usually expect to pay. These may not change at the same rate, and residents and third parties should be told that there cannot be a guarantee that any increases in the accommodation's fees will automatically be shared evenly between the authority and third party should the particular accommodation's fees rise more quickly than the costs the authority would usually expect to pay for similar people. An authority may find it useful to agree with the resident and third party that the third party's contribution will be reviewed on a regular basis.

## RESPONSIBILITIES OF RESIDENTS AND THIRD PARTIES

11.9    Authorities should make clear to residents and third parties the basis on which arrangements are to be made when they seek to exercise their right to more expensive preferred accommodation. It should be clear from the outset to the resident, third party and person providing the accommodation.

- that failure to keep up payments will normally result in the resident having to move to other accommodation
- that an increase in the resident's income will not necessarily lessen the need for a contribution, since the resident's own income will be subject to charging by the authority in the normal way
- that a rise in the accommodation's fees will not automatically be shared equally between authority and third party
- that if the accommodation fails to honour its contractual conditions, the authority must reserve the right to terminate the contract

11.10    Authorities may wish to consider making a binding legal agreement with the third party to this effect, though they should note there are restrictions on the ability of charitable contributors to enter into such contracts.

## SUITABILITY AND CONDITIONS

11.11    The criteria of suitability, and willingness to provide on the basis of normal conditions should be applied in the same way as for other preferred accommodation (para 7.1 ff).

11.12    An exception to this is that it would be reasonable to expect providers entering this kind of arrangement to agree to do so on the basis that the authority has the right, subject to notice, to terminate the contract should the third party's payments cease or cease to be adequate.

## LIABLE RELATIVES

11.13    Because they may already be obliged to contribute to the cost of accommodation, these arrangements do not apply to relatives liable to contribute to the cost of accommodation under section 42 of the National Assistance Act 1948. In other words, for the purposes of this direction such people cannot act as third parties for the care of the relative to whose care they are already obliged to contribute.

11.14    However, although the direction imposes no legal duty to do so, there is no reason why authorities should not enter in similar arrangements with liable relatives who have the resources both to meet their liability and make an additional third party payment. Indeed, there is no reason why authorities should not, at the request of the resident, arrange more expensive accommodation for someone who can from their own resources afford to pay the additional cost.

### People already resident in residential care

12    People already placed by an authority in residential accommodation have the same rights under this direction as those who have yet to be placed. An individual who wishes to move to different or more expensive accommodation may seek to do so on the same basis as anyone about to enter residential care for the first time.

### People who are unable to make their own choices

13    There will be cases in which prospective residents are unable to express a preference for themselves. It would be reasonable to expect authorities to act on the preferences expressed by their carers in the same way that they would on the resident's own wishes, unless exceptionally that would be against the best interests of the resident.

### Effect on tendering, effect on block contracting

14    Many authorities will already be consulting on, or involved in formal tendering and contracting procedures. As this direction is intended simply to formalise best practice, there should be no conflict between it and arrangements authorities have already made.

15    However, authorities will need to review their arrangements to see if any further action is needed. In particular, where authorities have already published details of their contracting policies, they will need to inform prospective providers of any amendments to that policy required in the light of this direction.

16    For example, where authorities are conducting, or have completed, exercises designed to draw up closed lists of approved suppliers they will need to make it clear that as a result of this direction such a list cannot now be regarded as an exhaustive statement of those providers with whom the authority will contract. It would not be reasonable for an authority to use as a test of the suitability of accommodation its presence on or absence from a previously compiled list of approved suppliers. The direction does not, however, prevent an authority having a list of preferred providers with which it will contract where a potential resident expresses no preference for particular accommodation, nor from recommending such providers to prospective residents.

## Information

17    For individuals to be able to exercise genuine choice they need information about the options open to them. They should be given fair and balanced information with which to make the best choice of accommodation. Authorities should explain to individuals their rights under this direction. Individuals should be told explicitly that they may allow the authority to make a placement decision on their behalf, that they may choose from a preferred list (if the authority operates such a system) or if they wish that they are free to choose any accommodation which is likely to meet their needs subject to the constraints set out in this direction. Authorities might consider including this in a leaflet for prospective residents and their carers.

## Complaints

18    Complaints about the application of this direction and decisions taken in individual cases will fall within the scope of authorities' statutory complaints

procedures. As in all aspects of their activity, authorities should ensure that prospective residents are aware of the existence of the complaints procedure and of their rights under it.

## D. National Assistance (Assessment of Resources) Regulations 1992

(Not reproduced in this publication)

**Cross references**

1 See also National Assistance Act 1948 (Choice of Accommodation) (Amendment) Directions (1993)—LAC (93) 18.

2 See also National Assistance (Assessment of Resources) Regulations Amendment No 2 1994.

3 See also National Assistance (Assessment of Resources) (Amendment) Regulations 1995 (SI No 858).

4 See also National Assistance (Assessment of Resources) (Amendment No.2) Regulations 1995.

5 See also LAC (95) 7—*Charges for Residential Accommodation Guide*—Amendment No 5 (CRAG).

6 See also LAC(95)21 CRAG Amendment No 6.

7 See also LAC(96)9—CRAG Amendment No 7.

8 See also Discretionary Charges for Adult Social Services—Advice Note for use by the Department of Health Social Services Inspectorate (1994).

# Materials 3

# General Guidance

*Contents*

## A.  White Paper, 'Caring for People—Community Care in the Next Decade and Beyond'

2.2  Community care means providing the right level of intervention and support to enable people to achieve maximum independence and control over their own lives. For this aim to become a reality, the development of a wide range of services provided in a variety of settings is essential. These services form part of a spectrum of care, ranging from domiciliary support provided to people in their own homes, strengthened by the availability of respite care and day care for those with more intensive care needs, through sheltered housing, group homes and hostels where increasing levels of care are available, to residential care and nursing homes and long-stay hospital care for those for whom other forms of care are no longer enough.

2.3  While this White Paper focuses largely on the role of statutory and independent bodies in the provision of community care services, the reality is that most care is provided by family, friends and neighbours. The majority of carers take on these responsibilities willingly, but the Government recognises that many need help to be able to manage what can become a heavy burden. Their lives can be made much easier if the right support is there at the right time, and a key responsibility of statutory service providers should be to do all they can to assist and support carers. Helping carers to maintain their valuable contribution to the spectrum of care is both right and a sound investment. Help may take the form of providing advice and support as well as practical services such as day, domiciliary and respite care.

2.4   Social care and practical assistance with daily living are key components of good quality community care. The services and facilities, at presently largely the responsibility of social services authorities, which will be essential to enable people to live in the community include help with personal and domestic tasks such as cleaning, washing and preparing meals, with disablement equipment and home adaptations, transport, budgeting and other aspects of daily living. Suitable good quality housing is essential and the availability of day care, respite care, leisure facilities and employment and educational opportunities will all improve the quality of life enjoyed by persons with care needs.

2.5   The government recognises that some people will continue to need residential or nursing home care. For such people, this form of care should be a positive choice. And there will be others, in particularly elderly and seriously mentally ill people and some people with serious mental handicaps together with other illnesses or disabilities, whose combination of health and social care needs is best met by care in a hospital setting. There will be a continuing need for this form of care.

2.12   The policy of successive governments has been to promote community based services which encourage and prolong independent living. The Government sees the development of community care as set out in this White Paper as a reinforcement of this objective. It places particular emphasis on the following priorities:

**First,** promoting positive and healthy lifestyles among all age groups through health education and the development of effective health surveillance and screening programmes and so reducing as far as possible the need for in-patient and residential care;

**Second,** promoting through planning agreements between health authorities, primary care services, local authorities and the independent sector, coherent networks of local services designed to encourage and assist people to live dignified and independent lives in their own homes;

**Third,** providing for those who require it a full range of facilities which would include acute hospital in-patient services, continuing health provision including specialist departments of geriatric medicine, and therapy services as well as the full range of social services;

**Fourth,** avoiding unnecessary institutional care by ensuring that decisions on the provisions of services are made on the basis of a careful assessment of need;

**Fifth,** ensuring improved access to information about local and national facilities including respite care, and a greater involvement of patients, clients and carers in the development of services.

## Principles of assessment

3.2.3   The objective of assessment is to determine the best available way to help the individual. Assessments should focus positively on what the individual can and cannot do, and could be expected to achieve, taking account of his or her personal and social relationships. Assessments should not focus only on the user's suitability for a particular existing service. The aim should be first to review the possibility of enabling the individual to continue to live at home even if this means arranging a move to a different accommodation within the local community, and if that possibility does not exist, to consider whether residential or nursing home care would be appropriate.

3.2.5   All agencies and professions involved with the individual and his or her problems should be brought in to the assessment procedure when necessary. These may include social workers, GPs, community nurses, hospital staff such as consultants in geriatric medicine, psychiatry, rehabilitation and other hospital specialties, nurses, physiotherapists, occupational therapists, speech therapists, continence advisers, community psychiatric nurses, staff involved with vision and hearing impairment, housing officers, the Employment Department's Resettlement Officers and its Employment Rehabiliation Service, home helps, home care assistants and voluntary workers.

3.2.6   Assessment should take account of the wishes of the individual and his or her carer, and of the carers' ability to continue to provide care, and where possible should include their active participation. Effort should be made to offer flexible services which enable individuals and carers to make choices.

3.2.7   The Government proposes that the responsibility for ensuring that an assessment is made should be a specific duty of the local authority. This does not mean that other agencies should be excluded, nor that local authorities can or should take decisions on services managed by other agencies. A single individual should be responsible for ensuring that each case is dealt with effectively. Indeed, an essential skill which case co-ordinators will need to deploy will be to manage the involvement, contribution, co-operation and partnership between the local authority and the other authorities and professions involved in providing services. The Government expects all those concerned to contribute positively to such arrangements.

3.2.8   There are a number of ways in which an individual may seek help and may therefore need an individual assessment. For example, he or she may apply for local authority home care services or a place in a local authority residential care home, or may request services under the Disabled Persons (Services, Consultation and Representation) Act 1986. In addition, it will now be possible for an individual to ask for local authority funding towards the cost of a place in a private residential or nursing home, or for the provision of domiciliary care. Local authorities should aim to develop a common process for all these situations, and to ensure that an individual is offered the help needed irrespective of the basis on which their first contact with the authority is made.

3.2.9   There will be a wide range of referral routes, or entry points, into the assessment procedure and local authorities should ensure that means of referral are widely publicised. They should also establish, and make public, criteria of eligibility for assessment, and the way in which their assessment processes will work.

3.2.11   Each assessment should, of course, be handled on its merits, but simplicity should be the key. Contributions can be sought quickly and informally and it is not always necessary for all contributors to attend meetings. Assessments should be carried out timeously. The government does not wish to see an elaborate and bureaucratic pattern of costly and time consuming case conferences established, nor does it want to see a duplication of effort. For instance, where a patient has already been assessed for discharge from hospital, this should form the basis of the assessment decision.

3.2.12   The aim of assessment should be to arrive at a decision on whether services should be provided, and in what form. Assessments will therefore have to be made against a background of stated objectives and priorities determined by the local authority. Decisions on service provision will have to take account of what is available and affordable. Priority must be given to those whose needs are greatest. As part of its planning machinery, every local authority should monitor the outcomes of its assessment process, and the implications of these outcomes for future development of services.

3.3.2    People's care needs may change over time and therefore need to be monitored. Where an individual's needs are complex or significant levels of resources are involved, the Government sees considerable merit in nominating a 'case manager' to take responsibility for ensuring that individuals' needs are regularly reviewed, resources are managed effectively and that each service user has a single point of contact. The 'case manager' will often be employed by the social services authority, but this need not always be so. He or she may or may not be the designated person responsible for the original assessment and design stages.

3.4.1    Once a package of care has been designed, it will be the responsibility of the social services authority to ensure that the agreed services are in place. Health authorities and other agencies will be expected to arrange the delivery of any components of care which they have agreed to provide as part of the package. The Government will expect local authorities to make use wherever possible of services from voluntary, 'not for profit' and private providers insofar as this represents a cost effective care choice. Social services authorities will continue to play a valuable role in the provision of services, but in those cases where they are still the main or sole providers of services, they will be expected to take all reasonable steps to secure diversity of provision.

## Housing and community care

3.5.1    If dependent people are to be helped to continue living in the community, then their homes must be places where it is possible to provide the care they need. The Government believes that housing is a vital component of community care and it is often the key to independent living . . .

3.5.2    With increasing disability, people may only be able to stay in their own homes if these are suitably adapted. Adaptations may include the provision of handrails, chair lifts and alarm systems connected to sheltered housing and the availability of wardens. They may also include more substantial adaptions to the dwelling . . .

3.5.3    People who are more severely disabled might be helped by a move to some form of specialised accommodation, such as purpose designed housing for people in wheelchairs, or core and cluster developments for people with mental handicaps. There are also various forms of sheltered and very sheltered housing for elderly disabled people. This option should be primarily for those who want and need it, after an assessment of their care needs.

3.5.4    Social services authorities will need to work closely with housing authorities, housing associations and other providers of housing of all types in developing plans for a full and flexible range of housing. Where necessary, housing needs should form part of the assessment of care needs and the occupational therapist may have a key role here.

## Domiciliary and day care services

3.6.1    A range of domiciliary and day care services and facilities, at present largely the responsibility of social services authorities, are available to enable people to continue to live in the community. These include help with personal care and domestic tasks, such as dressing, cleaning, washing and preparing meals; with transport, budgeting, disability equipment and adaptations to homes; and with basic daily living. In addition, day care, respite care and leisure facilities are available to provide support for individuals and carers.

3.6.2   However, the provision of such services is uneven and poorly co-ordinated and there is a tendency to match clients to services, rather than services to client needs.

## Residential and nursing home care

3.7.2   From April 1991 local authorities will be responsible, in collaboration with health care professionals, for assessing the needs of new applicants for public support for residential or nursing home care. If, after assessment, it is decided that a residential care or nursing home place represents the right choice for the person involved, it will be the responsibility of the social services authority to arrange a place in a suitable home. The type of home to be chosen should be dependent on the outcome of the assessment; a nursing home place should be secured only if the assessment establishes a need for nursing care as the whole or main component of the care required.

## Consumer choice

3.7.8   For many people, entering residential care or a nursing home will mean moving permanently from their own homes and neighbourhoods where they may have lived for a long time. This can be a difficult step but one which may be made easier if approached positively. The Government believes that, subject to the availability of resources, people should be able to exercise the maximum possible choice about the home they enter. The preference of relatives and other carers should also be taken carefully into account. If relatives or friends wish, and are able, to make a contribution towards the cost of care, an individual may decide to look for a place in a more expensive home. The arrangements made by the social services authority should be sufficiently flexible to permit this.

## Charges for services

3.8.1   Under present arrangements local authorities are required to charge what residents in homes can afford, up to the full economic cost of their care. Authorities are able, but not required, to charge for day and domiciliary care. These arrangements will be preserved. In practice many consumers of personal social services cannot afford the full cost of the service, and ability to pay does not and should not in any way influence decisions on the services to be provided. This accords with the Government's general policy on charges for local services; those able to meet all or part of the economic costs should be expected to do so. Moreover, effective costing and charging procedures can be valuable in achieving the best use of resources across the range of personal social services and local social services authorities will be expected to develop them.

## Other personal social services

3.8.5   Local authorities have statutory powers to charge for other personal social services for adults (Health and Social Services and Social Security Adjudications Act 1983 section 17). If a user represents that they cannot afford to pay the charge the local authority are statutorily required to reduce the charge to such amount (if any) as appears reasonable to them. The Government proposes to preserve these arrangements, which will apply equally to services provided through other agencies. This provision permits charging for home help, home care, meals provision and day care services. Local authorities also provide other services for which it would not be appropriate to charge including social work support, occupational therapy, advice and assessment of client needs. These services, including assessments under the new arrangements described in 3.2.1–3.2.13, will continue to be provided free of charge.

\*    \*    \*    \*    \*

## B. Policy Guidance

### Chapter 1: Introduction

1.1 The White Paper 'Caring for People' and the National Health Service and Community Care Act 1990 (the Act) set out the Government's policy framework for community care in the next decade and beyond. The policy builds on the best of good practice which already exists. It aims to enable people to live an independent and dignified life at home, or elsewhere within the community, for as long as they are able and wish to do so. The key objectives are:

- to promote the development of domiciliary, day and respite services to enable people to live in their own homes wherever feasible and sensible;
- to ensure that service providers make practical support for carers a high priority;
- to make proper assessment of need and good care management the cornerstone of high quality care;
- to promote the development of a flourishing independent sector alongside good quality public services;
- to clarify the responsibilities of agencies and so make it easier to hold them to account for their performance;
- to secure better value for taxpayers' money by introducing a new funding structure for social care.

1.2 This booklet sets out the formal policy guidance from the Department. It is primarily addressed to local authority services departments (SSDs) and health authorities. The definition of health authorities for the purposes of this guidance is set out in the glossary but it includes FHSAs who together with DHAs have a particularly important role in community care. It will also be of value to other agencies, such as housing authorities, housing associations, the voluntary and private sectors and to organisations of and for users and carers. In developing the policy framework the booklet treats the Act as though it were now in force.

\* \* \* \* \*

1.4 Policy guidance sets out WHAT is expected of health authorities and local authorities to meet the Government's proposals on community care. It provides the framework within which the delivery of community care should be planned, developed, commissioned and implemented locally. It leaves maximum scope for innovation and flexibility at local level, whilst being sufficient to enable Ministers to monitor and review progress towards national policy objectives.

\* \* \* \* \*

### Good practice information and material

1.6 The Department will offer further material to assist authorities. This will be designed to help them decide HOW to give effect to this policy guidance. It will offer examples and models of effective practice and offer options of how to tackle management and professional issues locally. Much of the material is being prepared by the SSI development groups which have already provided professional advice in preparation of the policy guidance. Good practice material is also being prepared by a CIPFA/ADSS Financial Management Project and other projects which the Department is sponsoring. Appendix D of this booklet lists some examples of information and other material which authorities might also find helpful in bringing the policy into practice.

**Collaboration**

1.7   Effective local collaboration is the key to making a reality of community care. All the authorities and agencies which contribute to the care of vulnerable people in their own community need to be involved in preparing and developing plans and services to meet these local needs. They need to be aware of and respect each other's roles, responsibilities and objectives and to build relationships based on this mutual understanding and respect.

**Links between health care and social care**

1.8   The interface between health care and social care is a key area in planning, assessment, care management, commissioning and service delivery. Neither the White Paper nor the Act change the existing responsibilities of the NHS which will continue to be responsible for continuous health care as outlined in the White Paper. Social care is the responsibility of certain local authorities (County, Metropolitan District and London Borough Councils and the Common Council of the City of London). The Government's policy enables and encourages these authorities to develop a mixed economy of care by entering into contracts with both private and voluntary organisations for the provision of social care services. This will in future include nursing home care currently purchased by individuals funded by DSS income support. SSDs will continue to be able to provide services directly.

1.9   The objective must be to provide a service in which the boundaries between primary health care, secondary health care and social care do not form barriers seen from the perspective of the service user. How this is done will reflect the way local and health authorities work together and organise their resources. Care must be focused on meeting the needs of individuals and their carers appropriately and sensitively. This objective must be a priority in collaborative planning involving health and local authorities. (See Chapter 2—Planning). The key to effective collaboration is reaching agreements based on a clear understanding of those areas which are now the responsibility of the DHA, FHSA or SSD and those for which they will in future be the commissioner. Changes to existing practices must not result from unilateral disengagement by any party from services for which they currently take responsibility and provide resources.

**Primary health care**

1.10   Primary health care is an integral part of care in the community. Community health service staff (district nurses and health visitors, community psychiatric and mental handicap nurses, and therapy services managed by DHAs, GPs and practice nursing and primary health teams) play key roles in community care. It is therefore essential that these DHAs and FHSAs are involved in joint planning with SSDs. Collaboration in planning is discussed further in Chapter 2. As planning unfolds into activity, collaboration is expected to extend into joint service arrangements. All the professions mentioned have parts to play. Joint planning and commissioning should lead to ongoing joint operational activity in assessment, individual care planning, service delivery and review.

1.11   Joint assessment and review require more emphasis than is common now because they underpin the provision of services. The GP can contribute uniquely to this. GPs know the social and health care needs of their patients and are trusted sources of advice. They are frequently the first port of call for those with needs for community services. It is essential that SSDs and FHSAs work closely to ensure that the contribution GPs can make to community care is fully realised. This will require careful and creative local discussions. These should recognise and build upon the major role that GPs now play as providers of community care through their monitoring of patients' health and well-being, the information and advice they can provide, and the effect that their provision of general medical services has on the ability of dependent and vulnerable people to remain at home.

## Links between housing and community care

1.12   Section 46 of the Act imposes a duty on LAs to consult housing authorities and housing associations when drawing up their community care plans. Appropriate housing can play an important part in allowing those with community care needs to remain within the community. The Department of the Environment expects to produce a circular for Housing Authorities in the New Year which will provide guidance on the links between housing, social services authorities and other providers of community care. SSDs should take account of this guidance when drawing up their community care plans. As with health authorities, it will be important that effective relationships are developed and built upon to provide a seamless service for service users. This will require SSDs to put an emphasis on discussion, understanding and agreement in the planning of services rather than unilateral decision making.

1.13   The general aim of supporting people at home longer will have a number of broad consequences, for instance in relation to housing supply and demand. However, changes are likely to happen slowly at first and there should be time to make the necessary adjustments.

*    *    *    *    *

## Links with the Children Act

1.18   The community care policies set out in 'Caring for People' and the Act apply to adult services. There is much common ground between these policies and those which underlie the Children Act. Within SSDs and health authorities there will be a need to relate adult care policies to those for children. In both areas there is an objective of maintaining the individual within his or her family environment whenever possible. Assessment of individual needs followed by planned delivery of services subject to review or a complaints procedure with an independent element is common to both. This should provide the basis for a consistent approach to planning services for the two groups. There is a particular need to give attention to what happens when, at the age of 18, children's services are replaced by those designed for adults. This is particularly important for those who are disabled. The changing needs of both the young adult and his or her carer need to be sensitively handled during this transitional stage. Separate guidance is being prepared on the Children Act which will address this interface in more detail.

*    *    *    *    *

## Chapter 2: Community Care Planning

## SSDs' community care plans

2.25   In their plans SSDs should identify:

## Assessment

- the care needs of the local population taking into account factors such as age distribution, problems associated with living in inner city areas or rural areas, special needs of ethnic minority communities, the number of homeless or transient people likely to require care;

*and in plans from 1 April 1993*

- how the care needs of individuals approaching them for assistance will be assessed;
- how service needs identified following the introduction of systematic assessment will be incorporated into the planning process.

## Services

- the client groups for whom they intend to arrange services. The Department does not wish to be prescriptive about how these are categorised but groupings should show evidence of a balanced consideration of the needs of such groups as dependent elderly people, those with disabilities whether of a learning, physical or sensory nature and those whose need for social care may be intermittent such as those affected by HIV/AIDS or women suffering domestic violence. Plans should include services for people with multiple and low incidence disabilities and will be required to include services for mentally ill people (including those with dementia), and those who misuse drugs and/or alcohol;
- how priorities for arranging services are determined;
- how they intend to offer practical help, such as respite care, to carers;
- how they intend to develop domiciliary services.

*     *     *     *     *

### Chapter 3: Care Management and Assessment

## Introduction

3.1   This chapter contains guidance for local and health authorities on care management including assessing and meeting the individual needs of adults for community care services. While local authorities will be under a statutory duty only to carry out the assessment of care needs, such arrangements should, as a matter of good practice, be set in the context of a care management system. Assessment of children's care needs, including disabled children, will be covered in the guidance of implementing the Children Act 1989. The assessment of disabled children (Part III of the Children Act 1989, and Sections 5 and 6 of the Disabled Persons' Services, Consultation and Representation Act 1986, and the Education Act 1981) will need to key into the assessment arrangements for adults, to ensure a smooth transition for those requiring care, both as children and adults.

*     *     *     *     *

## Objectives of care management systems

3.3   Care management will play a key part in achieving the Government's objectives for community care by:

- ensuring that the resources available (including resources transferred in due course from social security) are used in the most effective way to meet individual care needs;

- restoring and maintaining independence by enabling people to live in the community wherever possible;
- working to prevent or to minimise the effects of disability and illness in people of all ages;
- treating those who need services with respect and providing equal opportunities for all;
- promoting individual choice and self-determination, and building on existing strengths and care resources; and
- promoting partnership between users, carers and service providers in all sectors, together with organisations of and for each group.

3.4   SSDs will be in the lead in setting up care management arrangements which will involve other providers of care, especially health and housing authorities, but also agencies in the independent sector. SSDs should set out their arrangements for assessment in their community care plans (CCPs).

3.5   To achieve the objectives set out in para 2.3; care management systems should aim to:

- respond flexibly and sensitively to the needs of users and their carers;
- allow a range of options;
- intervene no more than is necessary to foster independence;
- prevent deterioration;
- concentrate on those with the greatest needs.

\* \* \* \* \*

3.7   Care management is based on a needs-led approach which has two key aspects:

- a progressive separation of the tasks of assessment from those of service provision in order to focus on needs, where possible having the tasks carried out by different staff;
- a shift of influence from those providing to those purchasing services.

It will have its greatest impact where most of the processes involved are carried out by a single care manager who has some measure of responsibility for a devolved budget.

3.8   It is recognised that care management will usually be introduced in stages. Organisational structures, procedures, practices and attitudes will need to be adapted over time to achieve a needs-led approach to assessment and the delivery of services.

3.9   For the purpose of this guidance, care management in its most comprehensive form covers three distinct processes;

- assessment of the user's circumstances in the round, including support required by carers;
- design of a 'care package' in agreement with users, carers and relevant agencies, to meet the identified needs within the care resources available, including help from willing and able carers. Any preferred solutions which prove unavailable either because of resource constraints or because the services have not been developed will be fed back into the planning process;
- implementation and monitoring of the agreed package; review of the outcomes for users and carers; and any necessary revision of service provision.

\* \* \* \* \*

**Assessment**

3.15   Although assessment is a service in its own right it can be distinguished from the services that are arranged as a consequence. The needs-led approach pre-supposes a progressive separation of assessment from service provision. Assessment does not take place in a vacuum: account needs to be taken of the local authority's criteria for determining when services should be provided, the types of service they have decided to make available and the overall range of services provided by other agencies, including health authorities.

3.16   The individual service user and normally, with his or her agreement, any carers should be involved throughout the assessment and care management process. They should feel that the process is aimed at meeting their wishes. Where a user is unable to participate actively it is even more important that he or she should be helped to understand what is involved and the intended outcome.

*   *   *   *   *

3.18   To enable users and carers to exercise genuine choice and participate in the assessment of their care needs and in the making of arrangements for meeting these needs, local authorities should publish readily accessible information about their care services. This should be compiled in consultation with health and housing authorities and other service providers. The information should cover residential care homes, nursing homes and other community care facilities available in all sectors. It should include the authority's criteria for determining when services should be provided and the assessment procedures, showing how and where to apply for an assessment and giving information about how to make representations and complaints.

3.19   The assessment and care management process should take into account particular risk factors for service users, carers and the community generally; abilities and attitudes; health (especially remediable conditions or chronic conditions requiring continuing health care) and accommodation and social support needs.

3.20   Assessment arrangements should normally include an initial screening process to determine the appropriate form of assessment. Some people may need advice and assistance which do not call for a formal assessment, others may require only a limited or specialist assessment of specific needs, others may have urgent needs which require an immediate response. Procedures should be sufficiently comprehensive and flexible to cope with all levels and types of need presented by different client groups.

*   *   *   *   *

**Care plans**

3.24   Once needs have been assessed, the services to be provided or arranged and the objectives of any intervention should be agreed in the form of a care plan. The objective of ensuring that service provision should, as far as possible, preserve or restore normal living implies the following order of preference in constructing care packages which may include health provision, both primary and specialist, housing provision and social services provision:

- support for the user in his or her own home including day and domiciliary care, respite care, the provision of disability equipment and adaptations to accommodation as necessary;
- a move to more suitable accommodation, which might be sheltered or very sheltered housing, together with the provision of social services support;

- a move to another private household, ie, to live with relatives or friends or as part of an adult fostering scheme;
- residential care;
- nursing home care;
- long-stay care in hospital.

3.25    The aim should be to secure the most cost-effective package of services that meets the user's care needs, taking account of the user's and carers' own preferences. Where supporting the user in a home of their own would provide a better quality of life, this is to be preferred to admission to residential or nursing home care. However, local authorities also have a responsibility to meet needs within the resources available and this will sometimes involve difficult decisions where it will be necessary to strike a balance between meeting the needs identified within available resources and meeting the care preferences of the individual. Where agreement between all the parties is not possible, the points of difference should be recorded. Failure to satisfy particular needs can result in even greater burdens on particular services, for example where a person becomes homeless as a result of leaving inappropriate accommodation which has been provided following discharge from hospital.

3.26    Decisions on service provision should include clear agreement about what is going to be done, by whom and by when, with clearly identified points of access to each of the relevant agencies for the service user, carers and for the care manager. No agency's resources should be committed without its prior agreement. However, where the agencies have agreed as a result of the assessment and care planning process to provide a service, they will be expected to deliver it. With the service user's permission, the assessment information should be passed on to those responsible for care delivery. This applies particularly to any risks that may be associated with the care of the user.

## Carers

### Role of carers in assessment

3.27    Service users and carers should be informed of the result of the assessment and of any services to be provided. In the case of carers, due regard should be had to confidentiality, particularly where the carer is not a close relative. Where care needs are relatively straightforward the most appropriate way of conveying decisions can best be determined taking individual circumstances into account. A written statement will normally be needed if a continuing service is to be provided. Written statements should always be supplied on request.

3.28    Most support for vulnerable people is provided by families, friends and neighbours. The assessment will need to take account of the support that is available from such carers. They should feel that the overall provision of care is a shared responsibility between them and the statutory authorities and that the relationship between them is one of mutual support. The preferences of carers should be taken into account and their willingness to continue caring should not be assumed. Both service users and carers should therefore be consulted—separately, if either of them wishes—since their views may not coincide. The care plan should be the result of a constructive dialogue between service user, carer, social services staff and those of any other agency involved.

### Carers own needs

3.29    Carers who feel they need community care services in their own right can ask for a separate assessment. This could arise if the care plan of the person for whom they care does not, in their view, adequately address the carer's own needs.

### Rights of disabled people

3.30   In accordance with Section 47(2) of the Act, if, at any time during their assessment, an individual is found to be a person to whom Section 29 of the National Assistance Act 1948 applies, the authority must so inform them, advise them of their rights and make a decision as to their need for services, as required by Section 4 of the Disabled Persons' (Services, Consultation and Representation) Act 1986. Once an individual's need for welfare services, specified in Section 2 of the Chronically Sick and Disabled Persons Act 1970, has been established, the authority must make necessary arrangements to meet it.

### Charges for Services

3.31   Separate guidance will be issued in due course on the powers and duties of local authorities to charge for personal social services (including community care services). This will include the statutory charging arrangements under Section 22 of the 1948 Act for residential and nursing home care and discretionary schemes under Section 17 of the Health and Social Services and Social Security Adjudications Act 1983 for charges for welfare services. It is expected that local authorities will institute arrangements so that users of services of all types pay what they can reasonably afford towards their costs. But the provision of services, whether or not the local authority is under a statutory duty to make provision, should not be related to the ability of the user or their families to meet the costs, and delegated budgeting systems should take this into account. The assessment of financial means should, therefore, follow the assessment of need and decisions about service provision.

### Collaboration with other agencies

3.32   Under the Act SSDs will have a legal duty to assess users' needs for community care services, that is welfare services provided under the enactments listed in Section 46(3) of the Act. However, the aim of assessment should be to ensure that all needs for care services are considered. Collaboration with health authorities and local housing authorities will therefore be of particular importance. Section 47(3) of the Act will require SSDs to bring apparent housing and health care needs to the attention of the appropriate authority and invite them to assist in the assessment. Arrangements for assessment and care management need to be addressed jointly by local agencies and roles and responsibilities agreed within those arrangements. As well as considering health and housing needs, staff from the local housing and health authorities may be able to offer expert advice on, and contribute to, the assessment of community care needs. Accommodation related needs, including the possible need for sheltered or very sheltered housing, will sometimes be an element in the assessment of community care need. The local authority is responsible for the involvement of all other agencies in deciding what should be done, by whom and by when, but other agencies will need to make available the staff needed for assessment. Information about the costs of community care services available from all agencies should, as far as possible, be made available to appropriate staff carrying out assessments, to assist them in arriving at cost-effective proposals.

3.33   All relevant agencies should be involved in the assessment process before commitments are made. It will be necessary to ensure that there are well-established links between SSDs, health authorities and local housing departments, particularly where urgent decisions may be needed. SSDs should recognise that the assessment process they originate may be used by other agencies to assist them in fulfilling their statutory responsibilities, for example by local housing authorities in assessing homelessness applications. Any requirements flowing from this should be taken into account in the assessment arrangements.

3.34   Where an individual's care needs appear to fall entirely outside the responsibility of the local authority it will usually be sufficient to refer the person to the appropriate agency and to notify that agency accordingly. A record should be made of such referrals. Care should be taken that individuals are not repeatedly referred from one agency to another.

3.35   Where a service user has complex needs, it may occasionally be necessary to call together staff from all the agencies concerned for a case conference; the individual and his or her carers should then be invited to attend. However, except in difficult cases, it should be possible to conduct consultations either informally in writing or by telephone (with a written record) to avoid delay and limit the demands on scarce professional skills. The number of people attending a conference should be kept small enough to permit a full exchange and appreciation of views.

## Assessment of nursing care needs

3.36   The statutory responsibilities of health authorities to meet health care needs are unchanged. This means that health authorities can continue to make contractual arrangements for nursing home placements, subject to local agreements. Detailed arrangements for care management and assessment will need to be developed locally to take account of the changes in the NHS which have resulted from 'Working for Patients', in particular the separation of the purchasing and providing functions.

3.37   The new arrangements create opportunities to assess the possibilities for supporting users with nursing care needs through community nursing services whether in their own homes, or in residential care homes, or in sheltered or very sheltered housing. Agreement will be needed between health and local authorities about the services each are to provide for such users and the criteria for admission to hospital, nursing home or other residential accommodations as part of the planning process (see Chapter 2).

3.38   The Act requires SSDs to obtain health authority consent before placing users in nursing homes except in the case of arrangements made as a matter of urgency. This provision is aimed at assisting collaborative planning and at ensuring that nursing home care is chosen only when it is a better way of meeting the user's overall care needs than the use of the community nursing service or admission to hospital. It is expected that health authority approval will normally be obtained through participation in the assessment process.

3.39   Appropriate medical and nursing advice should always be sought when admission to residential or nursing home care is being considered. No changes are being made to procedures for admission to hospital. Short-term admission will have a positive role in providing for both acute care and rehabilitation.

## Urgent admissions to residential or nursing home care or to hostels

3.40   Under the Act, services may be provided without assessment in cases where they are required urgently. Urgent admissions to nursing homes do not require the consent of the health authority. Authorities will need to negotiate arrangements for emergency care. Voluntary and private agencies providing such services on behalf of statutory authorities should be informed what resources they can commit and for how long without reference to the authority. Assessment must be carried out as soon as possible afterwards.

## Hospital admissions and discharges

3.41   The decision to admit to, or to discharge from, hospital is taken primarily on medical grounds but it also has to take account of social and other factors. Wherever these factors come into play, there should be close consultation between health authorities and SSDs. It is most undesirable that anyone should be admitted to, or remain in, hospital when their care could be more appropriately provided elsewhere.

3.42   Local assessment arrangements for services required by a patient following discharge from hospital will need to be reviewed in the light of the new responsibilities local authorities will have. As explained in existing circulars on hospital discharge (HC(89)5 and LAC(89)7) health authorities, in conjunction with local authorities, are responsible for designating staff to develop, implement and monitor individual discharge plans. To ensure the continuity of health and social care the local authority and NHS staff working in the community and GPs should be given adequate notice of discharge to enable them to assess and provide for any community care needs, especially where residential or nursing home care may be a possible choice. Local housing authorities may also need to be involved.

3.43   Health Authorities should bear in mind that responsibility for assessing and meeting needs for community social services (including nursing home care where the user is expected to contribute to the cost) rests with the SSDs. Subject to any arrangements agreed between authorities, local authorities should not be expected to endorse decisions about an individual's care needs, or ways of meeting them, taken by health authorities in advance of a recognised community care assessment.

3.44   Subject always to consumer choice, patients should not leave hospital until the supply of at least essential community care services has been agreed with them, their carers and all the authorities concerned. Patients who have lost their homes should not be expected to leave hospital until suitable accommodation has been arranged. In such cases early liaison with the local housing authority is essential.

3.45   Further guidance on discharge from psychiatric hospitals is contained in Chapter 7 and in the forthcoming interdisciplinary guidelines for good practice in discharge and after-care procedures.

## Family health services authorities

3.46   Local Authorities will need to agree with FHSAs arrangements which ensure that the GP's contribution to the assessment of need can be brought to bear effectively. Both authorities should ensure that GPs are given sufficient information on assessment procedures to enable them to be involved effectively in the assessment process and to advise patients. In the preparation of the information FHSAs, on behalf of local authorities, should consult local professional committees. There should be no need for complex arrangements.

## General practitioners

3.47   It is expected that, as a matter of good practice, GPs will wish to make a full contribution to assessment. It is part of the GP's terms of service to give advice to enable patients to avail themselves of services provided by a local authority.

3.48   Where advice is needed by the local authority in the course of assessment, this should be obtained from the GP orally (eg by telephone) as far as possible. A record should be kept of the advice given. In addition to the information that only the patient's own GP can provide, local authorities may, on occasion, also require a clinical examination or an interpretation of the medical report provided by the GP. Local authorities should, therefore, be aware that GPs have a personal duty to and a relationship with their patients, and may not be best placed to act in addition as an assessor on the authority's behalf. In such circumstances local authorities may wish other practitioners to act in this capacity.

## Role for independent agencies in assessment

3.49   Where a specialist service—for example as at drug and alcohol centres—is provided by a voluntary body under arrangements with a SSD, it will be possible to include assessment of needs in relation to such services in contract arrangements. Voluntary organisations may, in addition, have a role in providing expert advice in assessments. Contracts may also provide for agencies to make decisions about service provision but, in such cases, contracts should include arrangements for the SSD to specify both the overall resources the agency may commit in this way and the maximum amount which may be spent on any one user. Formal overall responsibility for decisions on service provision will remain with the SSD, which will be responsible for assessing need for any additional services lying outside the specialist concern of the voluntary body.

## Confidentiality of health and personal social services information

3.50   The Data Protection Act 1984 and orders made under it, the Access to Personal Files Act 1987 and related regulations, and the Access to Health Records Act 1990 and the obligations to safeguard health and personal social services information, will affect the use authorities make of information they receive or hold, and the circumstances in which this can be disclosed. Proper assessment, the design of appropriate packages of care and the arrangement of services, will sometimes depend on agencies being able to share information. The need for this should be explained to the service user and his or her written consent first obtained. Detailed guidance is given in circulars LAC(87)10, LAC(88)16, LAC(88)17, HC(FP)(88)22 and LAC(89)2.

## Review of care needs

3.51   Care needs for which services are being provided, should be reviewed at regular intervals. This review, especially where it relates to complex needs, should wherever possible, be undertaken by someone, such as a care manager, not involved in direct service provision, to preserve the needs-led approach. The projected timing of the first review should be stated in the original care plan. However, reviews may take place earlier if it is clear that community care needs have changed. Reviews may also be needed to services already being provided before the introduction of the new arrangements.

3.52   The purpose of the review is to establish whether the objectives, set in the original care plan, are being, or have been met and to increase, revise or withdraw services accordingly. Reviews should also take account of any changes in needs or service delivery policies. The other purpose of reviews are to monitor the quality of services provided and, in particular, to note the views of service users and carers and any changes in their wishes or preferences. These views should be fed back into service planning, together with any identified shortfalls in provision.

3.53   The type of review will vary according to need but all those involved in the original care planning should be consulted. Large-scale review meetings should rarely be necessary. All relevant agencies, service users and carers should be notified of the results of the review, subject to the same constraints of confidentiality as the care plan.

\*   \*   \*   \*   \*

## Chapter 6: Complaints Procedures

### Introduction

6.1   This chapter gives guidance to local authorities on the implementation of the provisions of Section 7B of the Local Authority Social Services Act 1970 inserted by Section 50 of the National Health Service and Community Care Act 1990 (the 1990 Act) and on the directions made by the Secretary of State under Section 7B of the 1970 Act concerning arrangements for dealing with complaints.

6.2   The Act requires local authorities to establish a procedure for considering any representations (including any complaints) which are made to them with respect to the discharge of their social services functions or about any failure to discharge those functions.

\*   \*   \*   \*   \*

### Qualifying individual

6.4   Complaints must be made by and must be in respect of a 'qualifying individual'; or be made by someone acting on behalf of that individual. A person is a 'qualifying individual' if:

- a local authority has a power or duty to provide, or to secure the provision of, a social service for him; and
- his need or possible need for such a service has (by whatever means) come to the attention of the authority.

### Scope

6.5   The intention of the Act is to allow access to a statutory procedure to anyone who is likely to want to make representations, including complaints about the actions, decisions or apparent failings of a SSD; and to allow any other person to act on behalf of the individual concerned. The procedure excludes only those for whom the authority has no power or duty to provide a service. Complaints of a general nature which are not concerned with an individual case are also likely to fall outside the statutory definition, as are anonymous complaints. It will be open to authorities at their discretion to deal with a complaint not covered by section 7B under the standard procedure.

\* \* \* \* \*

6.7 Complaints can result from an unresolved problem or from a measure of dissatisfaction or disquiet about the organisation, about the implementation of decisions, about the quality and appropriateness of services, or about their delivery or non-delivery.

\* \* \* \* \*

## Other guidance

6.9 Authorities will be required within the statutory framework and in the light of the Department's guidance to devise or modify their own arrangements. This guidance is not exhaustive. In reviewing or setting up their procedure authorities may find it helpful to refer, for example, to the code of practice on complaints procedures issued by the Local Authority Associations and the Commission for Local Administration in 1978; and to the booklet 'Open to Complaints: guidelines for social services complaints procedures' published by the National Consumer Council (with the National Institute for Social Work) in 1988. Social Services Inspectorate practice guidance on the organisation and operation of procedures and on training will be published separately.

## Objectives

6.10 SSDs' complaints procedures should:
   (i) provide an effective means of allowing service users or their representatives to complain about the quality or nature of social services;
   (ii) ensure complaints are acted on;
   (iii) aim to resolve complaints quickly and as close to the point of service delivery as is acceptable and appropriate;
   (iv) give those denied a service an accepted means of challenging the decision made;
   (v) provide in defined circumstances for the independent review of a complaint;
   (vi) give managers and councillors an additional means of monitoring performance and the extent to which service objectives are being achieved.

\* \* \* \* \*

## Complaints procedure

*Essential requirements*
6.14 The complaints procedures established by authorities should be uncomplicated, accessible to those who might wish to use them and understood by all members of staff. They should reflect the need for confidentiality at all stages. The essential requirements are contained in the directions at Appendix C. They require authorities to:
   • designate an officer to assist in the co-ordination of all aspects of the consideration of complaints;
   • ensure that the arrangements made clearly identify the key stages in the complaints procedure and the responsibility of staff at each of those stages;
   • ensure that members and staff of the authority are familiar with the

arrangements made, and that those arrangements clearly identify the key stages in the complaints procedure and the responsibility of staff at each of those stages;

- consider and respond to every registered complaint within 28 days of receipt of the complaint and, where this is not possible, give an explanation of the position to the complainant within the first 28 days and make a full response within 3 months;
- address their response to the person from whom the complaint was received, and also, where different, to the person on whose behalf the complaint was made and to any other persons who appear to have a sufficient interest or are otherwise involved or affected. The response should advise the complainant what further options are open should he or she remain dissatisfied;
- make arrangements so that where a complainant asks (within 28 days) for the authority's response to a registered complaint to be reviewed, a panel constituted by the authority meets within 28 days of the authority's receipt of the complainant's request;
- ensure that the panel's recommendation is recorded in writing within 24 hours of the completion of their deliberations; and is sent (formally) to the authority, to the complainant and to anyone acting on his behalf;
- decide on their response to the recommendation of a panel and make their decision known in writing to the person who requested the review, and where different, the person on whose behalf the request was made and any other persons as appear to have a sufficient interest or are otherwise involved or affected within 28 days of the date of recommendation. The letter should explain the authority's decision and the reasons for it;
- keep a record of all complaints received and the outcome in each case; and identify separately those cases where the time limits imposed by the directions have been breached.

*     *     *     *     *

*Form of complaint*

6.17    There should be no requirement in the first instance for complaints to be written down. Where a complainant wishes to pursue a matter that cannot be resolved informally the complaint should, however, be made in writing, whether by the complainant or by someone (who might be a member of staff) on the complainant's behalf. It is at this point that a complaint is 'registered'.

*Response to complaints*

6.18.    The aim at all stages in the procedure should be to avoid delay and to keep the complainant properly informed. A prompt response at the outset will increase the possibility of that response being accepted. (An interim reply in response to a registered complaint should be unusual.) Similarly, a member of staff might profitably ask what outcome the complainant would find satisfactory, and might discuss with the complainant, especially where a complaint has been registered, when and how the authority will respond. In considering a response account should be taken of the possible need to offer redress, bearing in mind the complainant's hopes and aspirations.

6.19.    The directions include a requirement to tell the complainant and others with an interest in a registered complaint about the outcome of the authority's investigation. The need for others to know about the authority's response will depend on the circumstances of the individual case. For example, where members of staff are implicated in a complaint they are likely to have an interest in the outcome. In general, the aim should be to keep the number of those informed to an essential minimum, not least in the interests of maintaining confidentiality.

\* \* \* \* \*

## Publicity

6.26 Service users, carers and their representatives will need to be properly informed about the authority's social services policy, the assessment process and criteria for service provision (see Chapter 3). The complaints procedure itself must be publicised in accordance with Section 7B(4) of the 1970 Act. This requirement might be met by using:

- *Leaflets*
  These should explain the procedure in straightforward terms and should include a reference to the role of the Commissioner for Local Administration (the Ombudsman) and to the separate leaflet 'Complaint about the Council?'. The leaflet should give the name, address and telephone number of the designated officer or of the person responsible for oversight of the procedure, and of organisations to whom those individuals might turn for advice. It should be made widely available. Where necessary, authorities will need to make available versions of their leaflet in ethnic minority languages and in braille.
- *Notices*
  These should be displayed in the authority's offices. They should also be supplied—with leaflets—to agencies offering independent advice.
- *Visual and oral presentations*
  Authorities may wish to discuss with voluntary organisations and other local groups how information about the complaints procedure should be made available to those with sensory handicaps, the housebound and those whose first language is not English or who do not speak English.

\* \* \* \* \*

## Support for complainants

6.28 In setting up their complaints procedures, authorities will wish to consider how best to ensure provision of the support and encouragement service users and others will need if the procedure is to be effective. Direction 5(3) places a particular responsibility on authorities in this respect. Support may on occasions be provided from outside the authority. But making an immediate offer of help, and giving the complainant the opportunity to explain and discuss a concern when it first arises, the chances of resolving the matter there and then increase. A positive response of this kind will also allay any fears complainants might have about the consequences of voicing a complaint.

## Assessment decisions

6.29 The notification of the outcome of an assessment should include a reference to the complaints procedure. Where a complaint is subsequently received, the grounds for the decision made might first need to be reconsidered by the officer responsible for the assessment in the light of the matters raised in the complaint.

The subsequent reply should say how the complaint may be pursued further. If the complainant remains dissatisfied, the complaint should then be registered and dealt with accordingly.

## Special cases

6.30   An inflexible application of the complaints procedure in all cases would clearly be inappropriate. There will be circumstances in which the earlier stages of the procedure should be bypassed; or an entirely different route taken. Where serious allegations are made senior staff will need to be involved at the outset. Where such allegations suggest that a criminal offence may have been committed the relevant local procedure, which may be contained in the authority's standing orders, should be followed. Where the allegation is serious and substantial the police must be notified immediately.

*     *     *     *     *

## Elected members

6.34   The complaints procedure should not affect in any way the right of an individual or organisation to approach a local councillor for advice or assistance. The procedure should, however, indicate clearly how complaints made to councillors which cannot be resolved on the spot should be handled.

## Mental Health Act 1983

6.35   The Mental Health Act Commission has responsibility, under the Mental Health Act, for overseeing the detention and treatment of compulsorily detained patients; and a general responsibility for the care, treatment and after-care of all mentally disordered people. Mentally disordered people and their carers may complain directly to the Commission.

## Children Act 1989 and Disabled Persons (Services, Consultation and Representation) Act 1986

6.36   Complaints about the discharge by the authority of any of their functions under Part III of the Children Act 1989 will be dealt with under the procedure established under Section 26(3) of that Act once it comes into force and not under the complaints procedure introduced under the 1970 Act. Complaints from people with disabilities which do not fall to be considered under the Children Act procedure, whether about services provided or about decisions on what services are or are not to be provided following an assessment of needs, should be dealt with under the 1970 Act procedure.

*     *     *     *     *

## Annex A
## Review Panels

1   The directions specify that the review panel appointed by the authority at the request of a person dissatisfied with a local authority's written response to his or her registered complaint should be made up of 3 people, at least one of whom should be an independent person.

2   Authorities may individually or jointly wish to draw up a list of independent persons suitable and willing to act as an independent member of a panel so that they can act quickly when the need arises. The people appointed should, where possible, have experience relevant to the subject matter of the complaint. The list should reflect the ethnic make up of the local population and should be prepared in consultation with voluntary groups, other agencies and perhaps independent professionals to ensure that independence is demonstrably built into the procedure. In some areas a standing panel appointed for a period (perhaps not exceeding 3 years) might be an effective arrangement. Otherwise a panel could be convened for each occasion.

3   Independent persons should be given a letter of appointment explaining the duties they will be required to carry out, describing the expenses and other payments to which they may be entitled and drawing attention to important issues such as confidentiality. Authorities will need to consider what training or other support they might wish to provide for independent persons and perhaps other panel members. (This might be dealt with by joint initiatives between authorities).

4   The directions require the panel to meet within 28 days of the receipt of a request for a review. The designated officer might oversee arrangements for appointing the Chairman and other panel members and convening the meeting. The Chairman should be an independent person. Other members of the panel may be independent persons or councillors or other persons whom the authority consider suitable.

5   Complainants should be notified in writing at least 10 days beforehand of the time and venue of the meeting and be invited to attend. Complainants should also be informed of the name and status of the panel members, specifying which members are independent persons, which officers of the authority will be present, and of their right to make written submissions to the panel before the meeting, and to make oral submissions at the meeting. Complainants should be told of their entitlement to be accompanied by another person who would be entitled to be present at the whole meeting and to speak on their behalf if they so wish. This person should not be a barrister or solicitor acting in a professional capacity. In arranging a meeting, the authority may need to consider what provision should be made for complainants whose first language may not be English, or those who may have mobility problems or special communication needs.

6   The meeting should be conducted as informally as possible. The chairman of the panel should open the meeting by explaining its purpose, proposed procedures and with a reminder about confidentiality. The complainant (or a person accompanying him or her) should be given the opportunity to make an oral submission before the authority's representative does. Other people may attend the meeting to make oral submissions if requested to do so by the complainant, subject to the consent of the panel, but will normally only be allowed to be present for that part of the meeting.

7   The panel is required by direction to record its recommendation within 24 hours of the meeting and to notify in writing the complainant, the authority and where appropriate others with an interest. The letter of notification should explain simply and clearly the recommendations **and the reasons for them**. If a panel member disagrees with the majority recommendation the letter should also record that member's view, and the reason for it.

8   Under the terms of the system for payment of members' allowance which comes into force next year it will be possible for authorities to meet travelling and

subsistence costs incurred by councillors in the course of their duties as members of review panels. Payment of attendance allowance will be governed by the definition of 'approved duties' which at present does not cover service on review panels. The Department is discussing with the Department of Environment a possible widening of the definition. Authorities will be notified of the result in due course.

9   Legislation will not specify the basis of payments to independent panel members who for this purpose could be regarded as consultants. Authorities are free to make arrangements in line with their usual practice.

10   Authorities are also free to decide whether to reimburse the travelling and other expenses of complainants, their representatives or anyone else attending review panels.

## C. Managers' Guide

### Section 2

### Assessment Arrangements

**Publishing information**

2.4   Authorities should be in a position to publish information about their **assessment practices** prior to April 1993.

2.5   This information should, as a matter of good practice, include:
- the range of needs for which the agency accepts responsibility
- the aims, priorities and objectives of the agency, partly derived from the national objectives set out in the policy guidance
- the types of services available from all sectors, setting out the range of needs for which they cater
- the criteria determining access to resources
- the referral, assessment and review procedures within and between agencies
- the entitlements of users and carers to information, participation and representation, including provision for equal opportunities
- the charging policies
- the standards by which the agency will monitor its performance, including response times to referrals
- complaints and feedback procedures.

\*     \*     \*     \*     \*

**Determining the level of assessment**

2.12   Local Authorities and other care agencies already have systems for receiving referrals and allocating a response. It will be necessary for them to **re-examine these systems** in order to establish that they are consistent with a **needs-led**, rather than a service-led, approach. For example, in the past, a request for a home help has usually been passed automatically to the home care organiser. What is required now is an assessment system that:
- gives access to a range of services, once the needs have been identified
- does not presuppose the service outcome in the initial assessment response

2.13   This means moving away from separate assessment procedures for different services to an integrated assessment system that offers a graded response according to the type and level of need. This requires a specifically defined process for allocating the appropriate form of assessment.

2.15   The following model sets out six possible levels of assessment according to the type of need and the services to be considered. These give an indication of the type of staff, number of agencies involved and an example of a service outcome.

**Assessing need**

2.20   Assessment staff will, wherever possible, cease to be linked to specific services. Instead, a **range of vocationally and professionally qualified staff** will be available to assess needs of differing levels of severity and complexity. Beyond them, there will be defined access to a range of specialist staff or to assessment staff in other agencies. The priority requirement for assessment staff will be an **indepth understanding of the needs** associated with particular user groups and a **knowledge**

**Managers' Guide—Levels of assessment**

| Assessment | Needs | Services | Agency | Staff | Example of service outcome |
|---|---|---|---|---|---|
| 1 Simple assessment | Simple, defined | Existing universal | Single | Reception or administrative | Bus pass Disabled car badge |
| 2 Limited assessment | Limited, defined, low-risk | Existing, subject to clearly defined criteria | Single | Vocationally qualified | Low-level domiciliary support |
| 3 Multiple assessment | Range of limited, defined, low-risk | Existing in a number of agencies | Multiple | Vocationally qualified or equivalent | Assistance with meals, chiropody and basic nursing |
| 4 Specialist assessment | | | | | |
| (a) simple | Defined, specialist, low-risk | Existing, specialist | Single or multiple | Specialist ancillary | Simple disability equipment |
| (b) complex | Ill-defined, complex, high-risk | Existing and/or new specialist | Single or multiple | Specialist professional | Home adaptation |
| 5 Complex assessment | Ill-defined, inter-related, complex, volatile, high-risk | Existing and/or new individual combinations of service | Single or multiple | Professionally qualified | Speech therapy |
| 6 Comprehensive assessment | Ill-defined, multiple, inter-related, high-risk severe | Existing and/or new individual combinations of service | Multiple | Professionally qualified and/or specialist professional | Family therapy Substitute care or intensive domiciliary support |

**of the range of services and community resources** available to meet those needs. In organisational terms, this is most likely to result in staff specialising in assessment/care management as distinct from service provision. However, alternatively, they may perform both functions but for different users or else rotate between the two roles, at specified intervals.

In order to undertake an assessment of need, staff have to know:
- the needs for which the agency accepts responsibility
- the needs for which other care agencies accept responsibility
- the needs of carers which qualify for assistance
- the agency's priorities in responding to needs
- the financial assessment criteria for determining users' contributions
- the agency's policy on risk to the user and to the community
- the legal requirements.

2.21   It is the responsibility of management to ensure that this information is readily available to staff. It cannot be stressed enough that **assessment of need must be distinguished from the care planning** phase, to promote the needs-led approach. This differentiation should be reinforced by the way in which **revised assessment proformas** are drafted. For example, many existing proformas describe needs in terms of services. Needs are often professionally categorised in a way that fails to capture the desired outcome from the user's and/or carers' perspectives.

2.23   At the conclusion of the assessment and care plannining process authorities are expected to communicate the outcome to the applicant, carers and other involved parties, as outlined in the policy guidance.

2.24   In respect of simple needs, this may be done on a verbal basis, but where an assessment results in the offer of a continuing service, this should normally be communicated in writing in the form of an individual care plan. The content of such plans are set out in the Practioners' Guide (Stage 4, page 67). It should be noted that an assessment of users' financial means will have to be synchronised with the care planning process so that users are not asked to agree a care plan before knowing the financial cost to themselves.

2.31   Reviews have, in the past, been afforded low priority, so have either not taken place or been subject to considerable delay. Fragmentation has resulted from separate reviews for different services and findings have not been fed back into the service planning system. The policy guidance reaffirms the importance of reviews in adapting services to the changing needs of the user and their carers. **The primary focus of a review should be needs** with secondary attention paid to the impact of services on those needs.

## D.  Practitioners' Guide

### Summary of Practice Guidance

### Care management and assessment: the process

1   Community care policies challenge all those in the caring services to re-think their approach to arranging and providing care.

2   Care management and assessment lie at the heart of this new approach—'the cornerstones of quality care' in the words of the White Paper Caring for People.

3   Care management and assessment constitute one integrated process for identifying and addressing the needs of individuals within available resources, recognising that those needs are unique to the individuals concerned. For this reason, care management and assessment emphasise adapting services to needs rather than fitting people into existing services, and dealing with the needs of individuals as a whole rather than assessing needs separately for different services.

4   As is evidenced by recent research (see SSI (1991) Assessment Systems and Community Care), this represents a significant advance on current practice in which service-linked procedures predetermine assessment outcomes, for example, assessing **for** domiciliary day or residential care.

5   If services are to be made more responsive, it is necessary to identify the disparity between assessed needs and currently available services. This is most effectively achieved where the responsibility for assessing need is separated from that of delivering or managing services. This will entail a progressive revision of organisational structures and procedures, but, above all, a change in attitude and approach by managers and practitioners at every level that amounts to creating a new organisational culture.

6   The rationale for this reorganisation is the empowerment of users and carers. Instead of users and carers being subordinate to the wishes of service-providers, the roles will be progressively adjusted. In this way, users and carers will be enabled to exercise the same power as consumers of other services. This redressing of the balance of power is the best guarantee of a continuing improvement in the quality of service.

### What is care management ?

7   Care management is the process of tailoring services to individual needs. Assessment is an integral part of care management but it is only one of seven core tasks that make up the whole process:

| | | |
|---|---|---|
| **Stage 1** | **Publishing information** | Making public the needs for which assistance is offered and the arrangements and resources for meeting those needs. |
| **Stage 2** | **Determining the level of assessment** | Making an initial identification of need and matching the appropriate level of assessment to that need. |
| **Stage 3** | **Assessing need** | Understanding individual needs, relating them to agency policies and priorities, and agreeing the objectives for any intervention. |
| **Stage 4** | **Care planning** | Negotiating the most appropriate ways of achieving the objectives identified by the assessment of need and incorporating them into an individual care plan. |
| **Stage 5** | **Implementing the care plan** | Securing the necessary resources or services. |

| Stage 6 | **Monitoring**   Supporting and controlling the delivery of the care plan on a continuing basis. |
| Stage 7 | **Reviewing**   Reassessing needs and the service outcomes with a view to revising the care plan at specified intervals. |

## What does care management mean in practice ?

8   These core tasks are considered in detail in the Practitioners' Guide, but are outlined briefly below. All or most of these tasks may be undertaken by a single practitioner, known as a care manager; or they may be performed by different practitioners. The implications of adopting different organisational arrangements are examined in the Managers' Guide.

| Stage 1 | Prospective users and carers receive information about the needs for which care agencies accept responsibility to offer assistance, and the range of services currently available. |
| Stage 2 | If an enquirer requests more than information or advice, basic information is taken about the needs in question, sufficient to determine the type of assessment required. |
| Stage 3 | A practitioner is allocated to assess the needs of the individual and of any carers, in a way that also recognises their strengths and aspirations. In order to take account of all relevant needs, assessment may bring together contributions from a number of other specialists or agencies. The purpose of the assessment is to define the individual's needs in the context of local policies and priorities and agree on the desired outcome of any involvement. |
| Stage 4 | The next step is to consider the resources available from statutory, voluntary, private or community sources that best meet the individual's requirements. The role of the practitioner is to assist the user in making choices from these resources, and to put together an individual care plan. |
| Stage 5 | The implementation of that plan means securing the necessary finance or other identified resources. It may involve negotiation with a variety of service providers, specifying the type and quality of service required, and ensuring that services are co-ordinated with one another. The responsibility of practitioners at this stage will vary according to the level of their delegated budgetary authority. |
| Stage 6 | Because circumstances change, the implementation of the care plan has to be continuously monitored, making adjustments, as necessary, to the services provided and supporting the users, carers and service providers in achieving the desired outcomes. |
| Stage 7 | At specified intervals, the progress of the care plan has to be formally reviewed with the user, carers and service providers, firstly to ensure that services remain relevant to needs and, secondly, to evaluate services as part of the continuing quest for improvement. |

9   At every stage of care management, it is the task of the responsible practitioner to identify and report back any deficiencies in the services available.

## What is need ?

10   Because care management begins with needs rather than with services, it is essential that all care agencies and practitioners share a common understanding of the term 'need'.

11   Need is a complex concept which has been analysed in a variety of different ways. In this guidance, the term is used as a shorthand for **the requirements of individuals to enable them to achieve, maintain or restore an acceptable level of social independence or quality of life, as defined by the particular care agency or authority.**

12   Need is a dynamic concept, the definition of which will vary over time in accordance with:
•   changes in national legislation
•   changes in local policy
•   the availability of resources
•   the patterns of local demand.

13   Need is thus a relative concept. In the context of community care, need has to be defined at the local level. That definition sets limits to the discretion of practitioners in accessing resources.

14   Consequently, there is an onus on elected members and board members to revise the policy framework within which managers and practitioners are asked to operate. A needs-led approach requires needs to be explicitly defined and prioritised in policy statements. Elected members/board members have to ensure on a continuing basis that they are able to resource the response to the needs for which they accept any responsibility.

15.   This definition of needs should be incorporated into publicity material which clearly distinguishes between needs that are a mandatory, legislative responsibility and those that are a discretionary duty under the law, assumed as a matter of local policy. The more explicit the definition of need, the clearer users and carers will be about their access to services. By and large, local authorities have wider scope for interpreting their responsibilities in law in relation to the care of adults than to the care of children.

16   In order to have an impact on practice, policy statements must then be translated into operational guidelines that cover all aspects of need. Need is a multi-faceted concept which, for the purpose of this guidance, is sub-divided into six broad categories, each of which should be covered in a comprehensive assessment of need:
•   personal/social care
•   health care
•   accommodation
•   finance
•   education/employment/leisure
•   transport/access.

17   However, need is also a personal concept. No two individuals will perceive or define their needs in exactly the same way. Care management seeks to recognise the individuality of need by challenging practitioners to identify the unique characteristics of each individual's needs and to develop individualised, rather than stereotyped, responses to those need within the constraints of local policy and resources.

Introducing care management should bring major benefits to service users and carers.

## 1: Tailoring services to needs

19   Care management makes the needs and wishes of users and carers central to the caring process. This needs-led approach aims to tailor services to individual requirements.

20   Where there are separate assessment procedures for different services, this makes for a fragmented approach to people's needs. Furthermore, assumptions can be made about the services people require, and these are what they then receive, without the full range of alternatives having been explored.

21   The aim in future is that assessment procedures will be combined into one integrated process bringing together the contributions from all relevant care agencies, so that the needs of the individual are considered as a whole.

22   It is easy to slip out of thinking 'what does this person need ?' into 'what have we got that he/she could have ?'. The focus on need is most clearly achieved where practitioners responsible for assessment do not also carry responsibility for the delivery or management of services arising from that assessment.

23   This means that assessment should be established progressively as a separate organisational function that is not tied to any service or set of services. However, this separatation has to be done in such a way as to recognise the interdependence of assessment and service provision. Assessment must remain rooted in an appreciation of the realities of service provision, and services must be sensitive to the changing needs of recipients. This calls for a high level of mutual understanding and respect between assessors and service providers.

24   The emphasis on need is further reinforced within the assessment process itself by separating the identification of need from the determination of the service response. The new procedure should thus have two clear stages:
- assessment of need—the needs of the individual are assessed in the context of the agency's policies and priorities
- care planning—assessed needs are related to resources.

## 2: Developing commitment to individual care planning

26   The two stages of assessment should come together in the writing of an individual care plan, a copy of which will be given to the user and to other contributors. This will specify:
- the needs to be met
- the services to be provided
- the outcomes to be achieved
- the means of measuring outcomes

\*     \*     \*     \*     \*

## 6: Enabling partnership with users and carers

37   The fundamental aim of community care is to promote the independence of individuals, so that they are able to live as normal lives as possible.Care management, as the process through which users gain access to services, should reinforce, not undermine, that aim.

38   Because practitioners and their managers control access to resources, the relationship will never be totally equal—but the present imbalance can be corrected by sharing information more openly and by encouraging users and carers, or their representatives, to take a full part in decision-making.

39   The contribution of carers should be formally recognised in new procedures for care management and assessment. Because the interests of users and carers may not coincide, both parties should be given the opportunity of separate consultation with an assessing practitioner. If necessary, carers should be offered a separate assessment of their own needs.

## 7:   Improvising opportunities for representation and advocacy

40   The NHS and Community Care Act 1990 requires local authorities to publish complaints procedures. Users will be able to make representations about either the process or the outcome of an assessment.

41   In addition, the associated policy guidance sets out the expectation that local authorities publish information about:
- the types of services available across the statutory and independent sectors
- the criteria for providing services
- the referral, assessment and review procedures within and between agencies
- the standards against which care management and assessment will be measured.

42   The introduction of care management will thus create improved opportunities for representation and advocacy:
- users and carers will be better informed about available services
- practitioners, freed of the responsibility for service delivery, can better identify and argue for users' needs
- services can be judged against explicit standards.

43   By separating the interests of service users and service providers, care management establishes a climate in which representation and advocacy can flourish. Local authorities are positively encouraged to promote the development of local advocacy schemes within available resources, giving priority to individuals from previously disadvantaged groups, such as those from black and minority ethnic communities.

*     *     *     *     *

## 9:   Providing greater continuity of care and accountability

46   In their organisational arrangements, care agencies have to balance the requirements of those with short and long-term needs. Care management is a process that is appropriate to both sets of needs but it will have its greatest impact on the care of individuals with long-term needs.

47   Care management stresses the importance of continuity, giving new weight to the monitoring and reviewing of needs so that services can be adjusted to changing circumstances.

48   Although it will not always be possible for the same practitioner to retain responsibility throughout, care management underlines the importance of one practitioner carrying the coordinating accountability to the user at each stage of the process.

*     *     *     *     *

## Assessment arrangements

60 The specific changes expected of local authorities and health authorities/boards are set out in the third chapter of the policy guidance, Community Care in the Next Decade and Beyond and in the Scottish Office Circular SW11/1991. These involve ensuring that:

- information is published about the services available and the means of accessing them, including a complaints procedure
- all relevant care agencies agree how to refer to one another and to co-operate in the assessment of needs that are the responsibility of more than one agency
- the individual care plans resulting from assessment are shared with users, carers and other contributors
- all users in receipt of a continuing service have the benefit of a regular review
- feedback systems exist to identify deficiencies in type, volume or quality of service.

61 However, the major challenge lies in progressively establishing assessment as a separate function within each care agency, distinct from its service-providing arm.

## Inter-agency arrangements

*Developing shared values*

81 One of the most promising features in recent years has been the emergence of a growing consensus among all care agencies on the values that underpin community care:

---

- A commitment to ensure that all users and carers enjoy the same **rights of citizenship** as everyone else in the community, offering an equal access to service provision, irrespective of gender, race or disability.
- A respect for the **independence** of individuals and their right to self-determination and to take risks, minimising any restraint upon that freedom of action.
- A regard for the **privacy** of the individual, intruding no more than necessary to achieve the agreed purpose and guaranteeing confidentiality.
- An understanding of the **dignity** and **individuality** of every user and carer.
- A quest, within the available resources, to maximise **individual choice** in the type of services on offer and the way in which those services are delivered.
- A responsibility to provide services in a way that promotes the realisation of an **individual's aspirations and abilities** in all aspects of daily life.

---

\* \* \* \* \*

*Valuing the contributions of different agencies*

90 As local authority social services/work departments have the lead responsibility for community care, social workers and social services staff will carry the major responsibility for performing care management tasks but they will be heavily reliant on the support of other agencies. Some of the key issues for different agencies, discussed in detail in the Managers' Guide, are summarised below.

*Community nursing and therapy staff*

91   Community nurses, by reason of their role and expertise, will also have a crucial role to play. Particularly where health care needs predominate, they may be the most appropriate practitioners to assume the responsibility for care management, or it may be shared with other community health professionals on similar grounds.

92   The aim should be that the practitioner concerned is identified with assessment rather than service provision. Practitioners who retain responsibility for both functions (for example, some therapy staff) may not readily assume care management responsibilities.

*General practitioners*

94   General practitioners will have a key role in identifying social care needs and assessing and responding to health care needs. This applies particularly to their surveillance role in respect of people aged over 75 years, but also to two other areas which lie at the interface between health and social services—hospital discharge, and the provision of publicly funded residential and nursing home care. It will be vital that local authorities and health authorities reach agreement on the criteria governing the allocation of resources in these areas.

*Hospital-based practitioners*

95   The transfer of funding responsibility will place new duties on hospital social workers in terms of accessing the resources necessary to facilitate discharges. By the same token, health professionals will have to come to terms with the fact that, in future, these resources will be cash-limited. All disciplines will have to work together to make best use of the available resources.

*Housing*

96   While health and social services have traditionally been associated with community care, less recognition has been afforded to the role of housing agencies. Housing has a major bearing on many social and health care needs, so it is essential that housing authorities and housing associations are now made full partners in the assessment process.

*Other local authority departments*

97   If the needs of the individual are to be considered as a whole, all departments of local authorities must share in that corporate responsibility for community care. This means that service departments such as education, economic development, environmental health, and recreation and leisure, should all be prepared to offer assistance with community care needs.

98   The support of central departments, such as finance and personnel, will also be needed.

*Other statutory agencies*

99   Local authorities will have to work closely with other statutory agencies, such as police, fire, and criminal justice services, to identify the needs that arise from retaining more dependent and vulnerable people in the community. The way that these agencies collaborate in addressing such needs will be a major factor in establishing public confidence in community care.

*Social security*

100 As local authorities assume a greater funding responsibility for community care after April 1993, effective working arrangements with local Social Security offices will take on added significance. Co-operation will help to minimise both delay and duplication in assessing users' financial means.

*Independent care agencies*

101 Local authorities' funding responsibility will also have an impact on the nature of their relationship with agencies in the private and voluntary sector. Local authorities are expected to adopt an enabling role towards independent care agencies, but increasingly hold them to account on a contractual basis for delivering services to a specified quality and volume. This clarification of responsibilities is intended to safeguard the interests not only of the local authorities and independent agencies, but also of users and carers.

102 Voluntary agencies will not only be expanding the range of service options available to users and carers: they will also be needed to perform an advocacy function in support of users and carers. Where practitioners have delegated authority both to assess need and allocate resources, users' access to independent representation and advocacy is particularly important.

## THE PRACTITIONERS' GUIDE—MAIN TEXT

### Stage 1—Publishing Information

1.1 As was emphasised in the Summary, care management is about empowering users and carers, enabling them not only to make choices about the services they receive but also to be more in control of the process through which they gain access to services.

1.2 If this objective is to be achieved, an essential feature of the new arrangements will be a greatly increased emphasis on the sharing of information. In this context, information is power. All care agencies will, therefore, need to examine the information they currently publish on:
- the resources/services available
- the assessment and review procedures

1.3 It is the responsibility of the practitioner to ensure that this published information reaches potential users and carers who are considering seeking assistance. The availability of such material should help practitioners in their tasks but it will also mean that they will be more open to a public challenge on the quality of service they provide. Where practitioners identify deficiencies in the published information available, these should be drawn to the attention of management.

### Fulfil the requirements of statute and policy guidance

1.6 Under the terms of the NHS and Community Care Act 1990 local authorities are required to publish:
- community care plans
- complaints procedures.

1.7 This information sets out the general context of service provision and the statutory means of seeking redress if the individual is dissatisfied with the service provided.

1.8 In addition, the associated policy guidance defines the **information that local authorities are expected to publish in relation to their care management and assessment arrangements.** These are:

- the types of services available across the statutory and independent sectors
- the criteria for providing services
- the referral, assessment and review procedures within and between agencies
- the standards by which the care management system (including assessment) will be measured

1.9 This information should be **presented in a readily accessible form** that takes account of potential users who have:

- a language other than English
- a different cultural background
- a sensory impairment
- a communication difficulty (illiteracy or learning disability).

## The public

1.12 It is central to the care management philosophy that potential users and their carers should be advised of their entitlements including the quantity and quality of the services they may receive. Many authorities have already begun to develop such publicity, for example, by publishing charters of rights for users and carers. Considerable importance is attached to the publication of this information because it should:

- clarify entitlement and allow the public to make an informed choice about whether or not to seek assistance
- spell out where and how people can seek help
- define access to a common assessment process

1.13 Through the published complaints procedure, users and carers are also informed of their entitlement to make representations under the complaints procedure against either the process or the outcome of an assessment. It is recognised, however, that many users and carers will require considerable support to exercise these entitlements, either because of their incapacity or a reluctance born of a sense of dependence and/or powerlessness. As a point of good practice, local authorities should, therefore, promote, within their available resources, **opportunities for independent representation and advocacy.** Details of such services should be included in the published information.

## Elected members

1.17 Increased publicity is likely to stimulate more demand so it is vital that **eligible needs are set in priority order.** In this way, managers and practitioners have a clear mandate for determining the allocation of resources. This definition and prioritisation of needs should take full account of the public consultation with users and carers linked to the process of community care planning.

1.18 Where the local authority has defined the needs which it is prepared to meet this will make it more possible to **devolve responsibility to managers and practitioners** for developing innovative ways of meeting them. Elected members will then hold managers to account for satisfying the identified needs rather than for any particular set of services.

## Care agencies

1.19 Although the legal requirement to publish information is confined to local authorities, it is expected that other care agencies will follow suit as a matter of good practice. Indeed, for the benefit of the general public, the advantages of pooling information about resources, in the statutory and independent sectors, will be considerable. It will also assist practitioners to have collated directories of information about resources.

## Adopt common principles for the sharing of information

1.20 As local authorities, health authorities/boards and other care agencies seek to integrate the way they deliver services, there will be an increasing pressure to develop **shared databases** not only of services but of service users.

1.21 In progressing down this path, it will be vital that **basis principles of confidentiality are observed** and that these are held in common by all agencies.

## Principles of confidentiality

- Information should be used only for the purposes for which it was given.
- Information about a user/patient should normally be shared only with the consent of that person.
- Information should be shared on a 'need to know' basis.
- Users and carers should be advised why and with whom information concerning them has been shared.
- All confidential information should be rigorously safeguarded.

### Stage 2: Determining the Level of Assessment

## Process

2.1 The responsibility for allocating the appropriate assessment in response to a presenting need is shared between:
- the reception staff, administrative and/or professional, who collect the initial information
- the senior or managerial staff who allocate the referral for assessment on the basis of this information.

2.2 Between them they have to perform a number of interrelated functions:
- receive enquiries
- give and gather information
- encourage the full participation of the appropriate people
- develop triggers for identifying other significant needs
- designate responsibility for the allocation of the assessment response
- set criteria for decision making
- identify levels of assessment
- agree priorities for allocation

---

**Example of a standardised referral form**

- Name, address, telephone number and age of potential user.
- Name, address, telephone number of enquirer (if different) and their status.
- Name, address and telephone number of GP (NHS number where known).
- The nature of the presenting problem.
- Whether the enquiry is with the consent and knowledge of the potential user (this should be the norm except for the incapacity of the potential user).
- The purpose to be served by any intervention.
- The urgency or risk as perceived by the enquirer.
- The preferred solution (if any volunteered).
- Any special requirements, for example, difference of language or culture, or communication difficulty.
- Any care services that are currently being received.

---

2.10    The aim of this initial information gathering is to establish as quickly and as sensitively as possible, **the urgency, level and complexity of needs** to inform the allocation decision. This will determine the speed and type of assessment response, including whether assessment by any other care agency is required.

*     *     *     *     *

### Set criteria for decision-making

2.14    Allocation decisions should **consistently apply the same criteria** which should:
- reflect the policies and priorities set out in the published information on assessment practice
- judge the urgency of the required response
- take account of the assessment resources available in terms of the number of administrative, vocationally or prfessionally qualified staff relative to demand
- weigh the options available to meet specific needs which will affect the level and complexity of the assessment required
- use the assessment to make cost-effective use of the available resources.

2.15    As a point of good practice, local authorities should publish their guidelines on timescales for responding to referrals. These guidelines should be monitored and adjusted to keep waiting lists for assessment to a minimum. To avoid unacceptable delays in response where specialist assessment skills are in short supply, it may be necessary for trained ancillary staff to undertake assessments under the supervision of qualified staff. **A designated manager should be held accountable for overseeing any waiting list for assessment.**

2.16    Because allocation decisions sometimes have to be made on the basis of incomplete information, or subsequent experience reveals other needs, **there should be sufficient flexibility for a more comprehensive assessment to be available,** if required. Such instances should be monitored for any lessons that may be learned.

### Identify levels of assessment

2.17    Agencies will want to determine their own levels of assessment according to their policies, priorities and available personnel, but as an example, it is possible to distinguish six levels of assessment.

## Assessment of disabled persons

2.19   The type of assessment response will normally be **related as closely as possible to the presenting need.** However, there is one legally prescribed exception. Where a person appears to be 'disabled' under the terms of the Disabled Persons (SCR) Act 1986, the local authority is required to offer a comprehensive assessment, irrespective of the scale of need that is initially present.

---

**Disabled persons are legally defined as:**
- in England—Persons aged 18 or over who are blind, deaf or dumb or who suffer from mental disorder of any description, and other persons aged 18 or over who are substantially and permanently handicapped by illness, injury or congenital deformity.

Section 29(1) of the National Assistance Act 1948 as amended.

---

2.20   The manager, responsible for allocation, must, therefore, have a clear understanding of the local authority's interpretation of a 'disabled person' and ensure that staff implement the requirement for a comprehensive assessment consistently.

## Allocating a care manager

2.21   Depending upon the model or models of care management adopted by an authority or agency, it may be that only a minority of users with complex needs will be allocated care managers, whereas those with lesser needs will be allocated a practitioner only for the assessment of need with subsequent stages undertaken by different personnel. The basic judgment will hinge on the assessment of the likely duration, changeability and complexity of need, including an assessment of whether an ongoing relationship between the practitioner and user will be of key importance to the effectiveness of the intervention.

## Agree priorities for allocation

2.22   In broad terms, most referrals for assessment will fall into four categories that can be related to the basic objectives of community care. There are those:
- for whom community living is no longer a possibility or who are at risk, for example, people with intensive personal care needs
- reliant on others for survival, requiring help with, for example, feeding, toileting
- reliant on others for support, requiring help with, for example, cleaning, shopping
- whose functioning or morale is reduced, for example, as a consequence of a depressive illness.

2.23   Most cases requiring statutory or crisis intervention are likely to fall in the first two categories. In **each** of the four categories, people may be rated as having a low, medium or high level of need.

2.24   Any judgment of the appropriate assessment and level of priority will have to take account of such factors as:
- the severity or complexity of needs
- the degree of risk or vulnerability of user or carers

- the level and duration of the projected resources required (whether immediately or in the future)
- the degree of stress experienced by user, carers or other agencies
- the necessity for co-ordination with other care agencies, for example, about hospital discharge or housing transfer
- the length of time already spent on a waiting list, for instance, a higher priority response should be triggered after a specified period on a waiting list.

2.25 The majority of adults who appear to have community care needs are affected by some form of disability but there are some who may be suffering disadvantage (homeless persons, travellers) or other difficulties (drug/alcohol misuse). However, it would be **inappropriate to prioritise purely on the basis of disability** since this would reinforce handicapping social stereotypes. It is not the disability itself which should determine priority but the:

- attitude and aspirations of the individual in relation to his/her disability/ disadvantage
- capacity of the individual
- capacity of the individual's carers
- capacity of other services
- suitability of their living environment.

} to deal with identified needs

2.26 It is the interaction of these five elements which determines an individual's level of functioning. Because they are the least tangible of the elements, **attitude and aspiration** are the factors most easily overlooked.

## Stage 3: Assessing Need

To understand an individual's needs; to relate them to agency policies and priorities, and to agree the objectives for any intervention.

3.1 As has been seen, the assessment of need will require a significant change in attitude and approach by most practitioners. They will have to make conscious efforts to treat the assessment of need as a separate exercise from consideration of the service response. As is indicated by the work commissioned by the Department of Health, few practitioners currently make that distinction, nor are they encouraged to do so by the assessment procedures they are required to operate.

## Process

3.2 The assessment of need should broadly follow this sequence:

- negotiate scope of assessment
- choose setting
- clarify expectations
- promote participation
- establish relationship of trust
- assess need
- determine eligibility
- set priorities
- agree objectives
- record the assessment.

## Negotiate scope of assessment

3.3   The scope of an assessment should be related to its purpose. Simple needs will require less investigation than more complex ones. In the interests of both efficiency and consumer satisfaction, **the assessment process should be as simple, speedy and informal as possible.** This means that procedures should be based on the principle of what is the **least** that it is necessary to know:
   •   to understand the needs being presented
   •   to justify the investment of public resources

3.4   It follows, therefore, that staff with any responsibility for assessment have to be trained to use their discretion and to target the assessment on the relevant areas of need.

3.5   **The scope of an assessment has to be individually negotiated.** Both the assessing practitioner and the user have to learn what resources the other brings to the assessment process. These will set the limits to the practitioner's investigation, defining which other individuals should be asked to contribute to the assessment, if the individual's needs are to be seen in their proper social context.

3.6   The practitioner has also to decide whether, subject to the consent of the individual, **there are needs which should be referred to other people or other care agencies** for assessment. At any stage of an assessment an assessing practitioner must be able to identify when he/she does not possess the necessary knowledge and skills and to know how to access them.

\*   \*   \*   \*   \*

3.9   Comprehensive assessments, usually requiring the greatest investments of resources, will be reserved for the minority of users who have complex or severe needs or, once the provision comes into force, are considered disabled . . . Where these are disabled children approaching adulthood, the assessments of social services/social work, health and education professionals should be brought together to provide the foundation for planning care into adult life.

\*   \*   \*   \*   \*

## Choose setting

3.12   The assessing practitioner has to decide the **appropriate location** for an assessment. This may have a material effect on the outcome. Office interviews may be administratively convenient but they may also give false results if the interviewee is not at ease. Interviewees are more likely to relax in their home setting. However, the advantages of domiciliary assessments have to be weighed against their cost.

3.13   Where the assessment is concerned with the maintenance of a person at home, the assessment should take place in that setting. If users are considering admission to residential or nursing home care, involving the irreversible loss of their home, they should always be given the opportunity of experiencing that setting before making their final decision.

3.14   There may be advantages to some part of the assessment being undertaken in settings external to the home, for example, day or residential care settings so that staff have longer contact with the individual. In such circumstances, assessors will be working in close collaboration with service providers.

\*   \*   \*   \*   \*

### Representation and advocacy

3.25  Users and carers should be given every assistance and opportunity to represent their own interests. Where it is clear, however, that a user or carer would benefit from independent advocacy, **they should be given information about any schemes funded by the authority or run locally.** Consideration should also be given to training in self-advocacy skills.

### Assess need

3.34  Need is unlikely to be perceived in the same way by users, their carers and any other care agencies involved. The practitioner must, therefore, aim for a degree of consensus but, so long as they are competent, the users' views should carry the most weight. Where it is impossible to reconcile different perceptions, these **differences should be acknowledged and recorded,** as they may contribute to the evolving understanding of an individual's needs over time. Where there is significant disagreement between users and carers, it may be appropriate to offer the carers the opportunity of a separate assessment of their needs.

3.35  Ultimately, however, having weighed the views of all parties, including his/her own observation, the assessing practitioner is responsible for defining the user's needs. That definition should be recorded and openly shared with the user and other contributors to the assessment, subject to the constraints of confidentiality. The recording of that definition should clearly distinguish between **facts** and the practitioner's **interpretation** of those facts.

\*    \*    \*    \*    \*

### Record the assessment

3.53  If users and carers are to play a more active part in their own assessment, there is no reason why many of them should not complete all, or most, of their own proformas. The design of proformas should allow for such participation. The challenge lies in drafting proformas that are friendly to both users and computers, combining narrative recording with appropriate codings. Proformas should distinguish between fact and opinion and between data that is essential for service monitoring or planning and that which is discretionary as an aid to understanding individuals' needs. **Existing proformas should be reviewed in order to confirm that they focus the assessment on needs,** without categorising those needs in terms of services, for example, listing domiciliary support as home care. Such **a review will usefully bring together the views of practitioners, users and carers** so that there is a common sense of ownership of the outcome. This revision of assessment tools will make a powerful contribution to the consolidation of a needs-led approach.

3.54  A copy of the assessment of needs should normally be shared with the potential user, any representative of that user and all the people who have agreed to provide a service. Except where no intervention is deemed necessary, this record will normally be combined with a written care plan (the next stage of the care management process) setting out how the needs are to be addressed. Where other agencies are involved, they should also have a copy of these plans.

\*    \*    \*    \*    \*

## Stage 4: Care Planning

### Determine the type of plan

4.3 Care plans will vary according to the complexity of need. If it is a simple need which can be met by a single service, the planning can be very swiftly accomplished. **All users in receipt of a continuing service should have a care plan,** even if only a very brief one, which defines the user's needs and the objectives to be met by any service provided.

4.4 At the other extreme, care plans may be very complex, involving the co-ordination of services from a number of different agencies. The earlier that practitioners responsible for care planning are able to identify the contributing agencies and individuals the better they will be able to effect this co-ordination.

### Set priorities

4.5 The assessment should have prioritised the user's needs so they should be tackled in that priority order. Although, ideally, all needs should be assessed before progressing to the care planning stage, in practice, because of urgent needs, some services will have to be planned and arranged while other needs are still being assessed.

4.6 Care planning also has to be sufficiently flexible to adjust priorities as the needs of the user change.

### Complete definition of service requirements

4.7 The needs should have been defined at the assessment stage but more detail may be required to specify the service requirements. The aim of the care planning stage is to target any intervention as precisely as possible on the identified needs. To do this and work out how any intervention may cause as little disruption as possible, the practitioner will require an understanding of the individual's daily pattern of living.

\* \* \* \* \*

4.12 **Care planning should not be seen as matching needs with services 'off the shelf' but as an opportunity to rethink service provision for a particular individual.** Within resource constraints, practitioners should give full rein to their creativity in devising new ways of meeting needs, picking up clues from users and carers about what might be most relevant and effective. Clearly, those who have some or all of the budget delegated to them, will have greater scope to create alternatives or to press service providers into arranging different forms of service.

### Discuss options

4.13 Once identified, these **options should be fully discussed with the user and any relevant carers.** This may involve service providers being invited to discuss the detail of their services directly with users, or users being taken on observation visits. For those users who have limited knowledge of what services provide or have difficulty with the concept of choice, for example, those with learning disabilities, this exploration of options has to be as practical as possible so that they can begin to understand what it will mean for them personally.

### Establish preferences

4.14   Wherever possible, **users should be offered a genuine choice of service options,** appropriate to their ethnic and cultural background. This enables them to feel that they have some control over what is happening to them and reinforces their sense of independence. The degree of choice available will be affected by the level of devolved responsibility held by the care planner.

*     *     *     *     *

### Assess financial means

4.18   If charges are to be levied in respect of any services, then care planning will involve an assessment of the user's financial means and ability to pay. As a point of good practice, **no user should agree a care plan before they have been advised in writing of any charges involved.**

4.19   Local authorities cannot charge for care management and assessment but, within their discretion, are encouraged to levy charges on other services, subject to the user's ability to pay.

*     *     *     *     *

### Fix review

4.30   The user should be told the name of the practitioner responsible for the implementation, monitoring and review of the care plan. This applies particularly where this responsibility is shared between a number of workers. In addition, **a date should be set for the first review** of the care plans. This is a simultaneous review of all the inputs so that their combined impact on the user's needs can be reassessed.

### Identify unmet need

4.32   Having completed the care plan, the practitioner should identify any assessed need which it has not been possible to address and for what reason. This information should be fed back for service planning and quality assurance. It needs to be recorded and collated in a systematic way.

4.33   There may be benefit in differentiating between types of unmet need. This will include those that are:

- statutory obligations, for example, those included in the Disabled Persons' (SCR) Act.
- defined as entitlements under local policies, for example, failure to provide services within defined timescales.
- new needs, identified by assessing staff but falling outside current policies or criteria, for example, the emerging needs of those with HIV/AIDS.

4.34   There should also be a **ready means of prioritising these unmet needs.**

4.35   Needs may remain unmet for a number of reasons:

- resources are unable to meet demand.
- the quality and type of service is irrelevant to need, or unacceptable to users
- the conditions of service are inappropriate to need, for example, no weekend cover.

*     *     *     *     *

## Record the care plan

4.37   Care plans should be set out in concise written form, linked with the assessment of need. The document should be accessible to the user, for example, in braille or translated into the user's own language. A copy should be given to the user but it should also, subject to constraints of confidentiality, be shared with other contributors to the plan. The compilation and distribution of such records has implications for the necessary levels of administrative support.

---

**A care plan should contain the following:**
- the overall objectives
- the specific objectives of:
  — users
  — carers
  — service providers
- the criteria for measuring the achievement of these objectives
- the services to be provided by which personnel/agency
- the cost to the user and the contributing agencies
- the other options considered
- any point of difference between the user, carer, care planning practitioner or other agency
- any unmet needs with reasons—to be separately notified to the service planning system
- the named person(s) responsible for implementing, monitoring and reviewing the care plan
- the date of the first planned review

---

\*    \*    \*    \*    \*

## Monitoring

To support and control the delivery of the care plan on a continuing basis

6.1   The monitoring function has tended to be neglected in the past as a passive or reactive form of surveillance. Care management stresses the proactive role of monitoring in **supporting the achievement of set objectives over time and adapting the care plan to the changing needs of the user.**

6.2   The type and level of monitoring should relate to the **scale of intervention and the complexity of the needs** that are being addressed. Monitoring may be performed in a number of ways:
- home visits
- telephone calls
- letters
- questionnaires
- inter-staff/agency consultation
- observation.

\*    \*    \*    \*    \*

6.3   All users who are in receipt of continuing services should have the benefit of some form of monitoring to ensure the appropriateness of that provision. However, the form of monitoring should be designed to cause as little disruption as possible to the users' daily pattern of living.

\*    \*    \*    \*    \*

## Monitor the care plan objectives

6.10   The aim of monitoring is **to facilitate the achievement of the objectives set in the care plan.** The monitoring practitioner has to keep each contributor on track in terms of delivering their specific objectives. Progress should be measured on a regular basis against the criteria or indicators defined in the care plan.

\*   \*   \*   \*   \*

## Stage 7: Reviewing

To reassess, at specific intervals, needs and service outcomes with a view to revising the care plan.

7.1   Like monitoring, reviewing has traditionally been afforded a low priority. Where reviews have taken place, they have often been subject to lengthy delays. Care management gives reviewing a higher profile. **It is the mechanism by which changing needs are identified and services adapted accordingly.**

7.2   Like assessment, **reviewing should be needs-based.** The prime focus of a review should not be the services provided but the needs, views and preferences of users and carers and the effectiveness of services in addressing those needs. Wherever possible, one review should consider altogether the services that are being received by a user. There should be a standard expectation that the needs of all users in receipt of a continuing service or services will be reviewed at periodic intervals. It is the only way of ensuring that any intervention remains effective.

## Process

7.3   The **scope** of a review will depend upon the complexity of need and the level of invested resources. The **frequency** will be governed by how much the needs are subject to change.

\*   \*   \*   \*   \*

7.6   All those involved in the original care planning or last review should be consulted. All participants to the review should be given sufficient notice to prepare their contribution. This applies particularly to the users and carers themselves to whom the purpose and content of a review should be fully explained together with their entitlement to have a representative present, if they wish.

\*   \*   \*   \*   \*

7.13   A review fulfils a number of different purposes which are to:
- review the achievement of care plan objectives
- examine the reasons for success or failure
- evaluate the quality and cost of the care provided
- reassess current needs
- reappraise eligibility for assistance
- revise the care plan objectives
- redefine the service requirements
- recalculate the cost
- notify quality assurance/service planning of any service deficiencies or unmet needs
- set the date for the next review
- record the findings of the review

## Reassess current needs

7.17 The review will not repeat the original assessment but it should not so concentrate on past needs that it remains blind to new or changed needs that warrant some form of assessment. The assumption should be that needs and the user's preferences in relation to those needs are in a constant state of change and that services should change as a consequence.

\* \* \* \* \*

## Set the date of the next review

7.23 Agencies may wish to set guidelines for the minimum frequency of reviews, for example, not less than once a year. However, the interval of reviews should be related to the pace of change in the user's needs as this determines the need to revise the care plans. Whatever the frequency, there should always be the contingency of an earlier review, if circumstances dictate. However, **each review should set the date for the next** because that sets the deadline for achieving the next set of objectives. Such a discipline will also counter the danger of reviews being delayed. The practitioner who holds the monitoring responsibility for the next review period should be identified at the same time.

## Record the findings of the review

7.24 A copy of the review report should be given to the user and, subject to the constraints of confidentiality, it should also be shared with all other contributors to the review.

---

**A standard schedule for the recording of reviews would include:**
- an evaluation of the achievement of objectives with reasons for success or failure
- an evaluation of the quality and cost of the services provided
- a reassessment of current needs
- a reappraisal of eligibility for assistance with reasons for any changes
- a revision of the care plan objectives
- any required changes in service provision
- a revised costing of the care plan
- any points of difference between parties to the reviews
- identification of any unmet need and any continuing or new service deficiencies
- the date of the next planned review and confirmation of the practitioner and monitoring responsibility for the next review period.

---

## E.  Right to Complain

### Chapter 4: The Procedure Itself

*(refers to the NHS and Community Care Act 1990 unless otherwise stated)*

### The details of the procedure

4.1   There will be three stages to the procedure:
1—The Informal or Problem-Solving Stage;
2—The Formal or Registration Stage;
3—The Review Stage.

### 1—The informal or problem-solving stage

4.2   Normal good practice should sort out, to the user's satisfaction, the queries and grumbles which are part of a social services department's daily workload. Stage 1 then alerts the relevant worker, supervisor or manager to the fact that there is a more fundamental problem, as perceived by the user or her or his representative. It gives users the right to decide whether or not to pursue the issue and ensures that it is taken seriously and not dismissed by busy staff.

4.3   The fact that this stage is not 'formal' does not mean that it is 'casual'. It may well be necessary to involve someone who is not connected with the immediate problem to help resolve it. This is where Clients' Relations Officers can be valuable (see also Chapter 6).

\*     \*     \*     \*     \*

4.5   This is a means by which complaints can be sorted out without recourse to the more formal system. It should not be used as a device to prevent or dissuade users from making a formal complaint.

\*     \*     \*     \*     \*

4.8   **It is recommended that it is made clear to all concerned that the purpose is to solve problems at the earliest possible stage. To pursue every case to the final stage would undermine this concept.**

### 2—The formal or registration stage

4.9   Stage 2 does not imply that problem-solving activities will be abandoned. It may involve investigation, adjudication and a decision or solution. If the complainant wishes, for any reason, to go straight to Stage 2 of the procedure s/he should be helped to do so.

4.10   To 'register' a formal complaint, it will need to be put in writing either by the individual concerned or someone else on their behalf to the Designated Complaints Officer. Many people will need support and advice from someone they trust either from within or outside the department. Some people will need help in writing and sometimes in formulating a complaint. Those who give help in writing down the complaint must ensure that it fully reflects what the complainant wishes to say and ask the complainant to sign it.

\*     \*     \*     \*     \*

4.13 When the report is received by the DCO, the manager or member responsible for the original decision should be given the opportunity to see it and take action on it. If, however, this cannot be done or agreement is not possible, senior management with the responsibility for the service concerned should take the decision about the department's response and the DCO will inform the complainant of the outcome and the department's decision. In relation to the children's complaints procedures, an independent person will be involved at Stage 2 (ie after the problem-solving stage), and may see appropriate papers and interview the people involved.

\* \* \* \* \*

## Membership of the panel

4.22 Some local authorities have used local voluntary organisations to help form the independent element of the panel eg Coventry SSD has approached Age Concern, MIND, and other local groups. Some authorities are considering the formation of consortia of suitable people drawn from a number of local authorities. In contrast, East Sussex have decided not to use former officers or members or people from other local authorities as members of the panel.

4.23 As stated in the policy guidance, it will be useful for the members of the panel to reflect the cultural diversity of the area and to have appropriate expertise or experience of the subject matter of the complaint. For example, if a particular disability or minority group is involved, the panel should be convened so that the complainant's concerns are responded to sensitively and appropriately.

4.24 Some SSDs have decided that all members of the review panel are to be 'independent' as defined in the policy guidance. Others have envisaged the panel with one elected member, one senior officer with management responsibility in the SSD and one independent member, who may be drawn from a range of voluntary organisations, depending on the type of complaint.

4.25 It is important to distinguish between the role of the 'independent person' in the complaints procedure from the task of those who help users and carers to pursue their complaint and are there specifically to support, advise and befriend and may well be from the voluntary sector.

4.26 The Children Act Representations Procedure (Children) Regulations 1991 allow the same independent person to be involved in the consideration of a complaint at both the formal and review stages of the procedure. However, it will be for the local authorities to consider whether the panel will be able to take a fresh look at the complaint if the same independent person is involved at both stages.

\* \* \* \* \*

## Appendix A: Good Practice for Investigators

*Compiled with the help of the Office of the Commission for Local Administration (the local government ombudsman)*

1 Check if there are any previous recorded formal complaints from this person;
2 Contact the complainant to:
    (*a*) clarify the complaint;
    (*b*) ask what is expected in terms of solution or outcome;
    (*c*) check whether s/he needs support of any kind

whether s/he has poor sight or hearing, or a language difficulty;

what s/he needs to understand the discussion properly (and try to ensure that this is provided);

(*d*) explain the investigation procedure;

3   Read about the background and the relevant legal and administrative policies and procedures;

4   Assess whether the complaints procedure is the most appropriate way of handling this complaint. Consider alternative possible procedures, for example appeals to tribunals, legal action, police involvement. If the complaints procedure is not appropriate, discuss the alternatives with the complainant;

5   Consider whether the complaint could be resolved without further investigation;

6   Be aware of the timescale and the importance of speed;

7   If the complaint is about a proposed action by the department, see if the action can be deferred whilst the complaint is investigated;

8   Obtain, and if necessary secure, the relevant documents, such as files, log books and timesheets, and insist on seeing the originals, not copies, and get copies of all the documents needed;

9   Establish the relevant sequence of events from the files and also the names of the officers/Members most directly involved in the content of the complaint;

10   Analyse the complaint into its different elements for further action or decision;

11   Prepare the line of questioning for each officer;

— use open not leading questions

— do not express opinions in words or attitude

— ask single not multiple questions, ie one question at a time;

12   Arrange the order of interviews so that normally followed procedures and practices are established first from more senior officers and end with those officers most directly involved in the complaint;

13   Inform all those to be interviewed that they may be accompanied by a friend or trades union representative, provided that the friend is not in a supervisory position over the interviewee. Explain the complaint clearly to them;

14   Consider whether a witness of a particularly difficult interview is needed—this is also a good way of training new investigators;

15   Interviews should be conducted in as informal and relaxed a manner as possible, but persist with questions if necessary. Do not be afraid to ask the same question twice. Make notes of each answer given;

16   Try to separate hearsay evidence from fact by asking interviewees how they know a particular fact;

17   Deal with conflicts of evidence by seeking corroborative evidence. If this is not available, consider organising a confrontation between the conflicting witnesses;

18   At the end of the interview, summarise the main points covered by the interviewee and ask if s/he has anything to add;

19   Make a formal record of the interview from the written notes as soon as possible after the interview while the memory is fresh. Never leave it longer than the next day;

20   If appropriate, visit the establishment complained about unannounced to check normal practices;

21   Draft a report setting out the evidence obtained, preferably without including opinions, and circulate this for comment to all those interviewed, including the complainant, unless there are special reasons not to do so;

22   Consider comments and amend the report as necessary, adding conclusions and, if appropriate, a suggested remedy for the complainant;

23   Send the report with the recommendations to the DCO who will decide on further distribution as necessary.

## F.  Hospital Discharge Workbook (1994) Department of Health, London

*(Note that this is informal guidance and not issued under s 7 LASSA, rather as good practice guidance.)*

### A message to senior managers

The decision that a patient is medically fit for discharge can only be made by a consultant (or by someone to whom the consultant has delegated this authority), or by another doctor who is responsible for the care of individual patient (such as a general practitioner responsible for GP beds). However, the decision to discharge a patient should be the result of a jointly agreed multidisciplinary process in which social services are responsible for assessing the needs of people for social care.

### Introducing the Workbook

Policy on hospital discharge arrangements remains as set out in earlier Circulars. However, the implementation of the 1990 NHS & Community Care Act means that hospital discharge policies and procedures must also take full account of the new requirements for local authorities to undertake needs based assessment for community care. These arrangements are designed to ensure that all patients leaving hospital either return home with the necessary support, or move to other appropriate care.

A good discharge depends not only on adequate communication with the individual patient and their carers, but also on effective liaison between a variety of health and social care managers and practitioners (including those in the voluntary and private sectors) both in the hospital and the community.

### Outcomes for users and carers

The Patients' Charter includes the discharge of patients from hospital as one of its national charter standards. It states that:—

> The Charter Standard is that before you are discharged from hospital a decision should be made about any continuing health or social care needs you may have. Your hospital will agree arrangements for meeting these needs with agencies such as community nursing services and local authority social services departments before you are discharged. You and, with your agreement, your carers will be consulted and informed at all stages.

This Standard covers the major issues which need to be addressed in ensuring high quality discharges for individuals. However, it can be broken down into stages which examine what an individual patient, and their carer, should be able to expect, that is:—

- to be admitted to hospital only when their needs cannot be appropriately met in the community.
- a written or verbal explanation before, or at the time of admission, about what they can expect to happen during their hospital stay.
- to be asked only once for all basic personal details, and to be given appropriate opportunities to share further information at all stages of their admission and hospital episode.

- to be taken seriously and listened to.
- that all relevant medical and social information should be available at the time of admission or ideally within 48 hours at the outside.
- to receive appropriate assessment of health and social care needs.
- to receive appropriate investigation, treatment and rehabilitation.
- to have an agreed discharge plan and their own copy of it.
- to experience no unnecessary delays in discharge, but to be given sufficient time and support to make important decisions.
- to experience no big surprises in what happens to them, and that discharge happens according to plan.
- that everyone involved in their care will receive any information they need within 24 hours of discharge.
- that continuing health and social care needs will be met as planned.
- that wherever practicable individuals would be enabled to return to their own homes.

## Admission and referral—screening and referral

An initial hospital assessment of newly admitted patients should include both diagnosis and treatment plan, but also early attention to discharge planning and any likely needs for continuing care. The interplay of medical and social needs of any individual patient will have an impact on the length of hospital stay, and those with social care needs should be identified at an early stage. The use of a triage system which classifies patients in relation to discharge according to flow, medium and fast track, may be helpful in distinguishing priorities for discharge planning.

Such a process will identify those individuals who should be referred for community care assessments, and those who would benefit from some social worker or therapist input but who do not require a full community care assessment.

## Community care assessments and care plans

Community care assessments will be triggered for those individuals who have been identified as having continuing social care needs. Social Services authorities will have eligibility criteria for different levels of assessment with which key hospital staff will need to be familiar.

Systems need to be in place which ensure that individuals are appropriately assessed and are aware of the purpose of the assessment, and that a named individual is responsible for managing and coordinating the process. This individual will often be a social worker, but not necessarily so. Multidisciplinary working is essential to successful community care assessments, but should not be heavily reliant on time consuming case conferences for all individuals.

Following assessment, decisions will need to be made about what services can be provided to meet an individual's identified needs, allowing a care plan to be put together and implemented. Key frontline hospital staff should be familiar with what arrangements are in place. It is essential that patients and their carers have good information about assessment, care planning and service provision if they are to make informed choices.

The 'Caring for People' policy places emphasis on supporting people, wherever practical, at home, and the policy should lead to an increase in the number of people returning home who previously may have entered nursing or residential care homes.

Some individuals may require continuing long-term care from the NHS, and there should be explicit eligibility criteria for any NHS continuing care beds, or for NHS purchase beds in independent sector nursing homes. These criteria should reflect the agreements reached between local and health authorities about their respective responsibilities for securing continuing care.

Materials 4

# Specific Guidance

Contents

## A.  Community Care Plans

**Cross references**

1 Community Care Plans Direction 1991.
2 LAC (91) 6—Secretary of State's Direction—Section 46 of the National Health Service and Community Care Act 1990: Community Care Plans.
3 LAC (93) 4—Community Care Plans (Consultation) Directions 1993.
4 LAC (94) 12—Community Care Plans (Independent Sector Non-Residential Care) Direction 1994.
5 LAC (94) 24/HSG (94) 47—Community Care Planning process needs to be linked with the development of local Community Care Charters (joint circular with Department of Health).
6 A framework for Community Care Charters in England (1994), Department of Health and Department of the Environment.
7. LASSL(95)5—Social Services: maintaining standards in a changing world.

## B. Services under Part III National Assistance Act 1948

### LAC(93)10—APPROVALS AND DIRECTIONS FOR ARRANGEMENTS FROM 1 APRIL 1993 MADE UNDER SCHEDULE 8 TO THE NATIONAL HEALTH SERVICE ACT 1977 AND SECTIONS 21 AND 29 OF THE NATIONAL ASSISTANCE ACT 1948

### Summary

This circular contains guidance on the consolidated approvals and directions made by the Secretary of State for Health on local authorities continuing responsibilities from 1 April 1993, to provide residential accommodation and welfare services, in so far as they are provided under Sections 21 and 29 of the National Assistance Act, 1948 and paragraphs 1 and 2 of Schedule 8 of the NHS Act, 1977.

### Action

1   This circular contains approvals and directions made by the Secretary of State in exercise of the powers conferred by Sections 21(1) and 29(1) of the National Assistance Act 1948 and paragraphs 1 and 2 of Schedule 8 to the National Health Service Act 1977.

2   It consolidates the existing approvals and directions contained in LAC13/74, LAC19/74, LAC(74)28 and Annexes 1 and 2 of LAC(91)12. This circular does not of itself create any additional responsibilities which have not previously been expected of local social services authorities. This circular also updates existing guidance on registration practice and related statistics.

### Background

3   Social services authorities' powers under Sections 21 and 29 of the 1948 Act and under Schedule 8 to the 1977 Act are subject to the requirement to act with the approval and under the direction of the Secretary of State. The relevant information is at:

— Appendix 1 = Approvals and Directions under Section 21(1) of the 1948 Act.
— Appendix 2 = Approvals and Directions under Section 29(1) of the 1948 Act.
— Appendix 3 = Approvals and Directions under paras 1 and 2 of Schedule 8 of the 1977 Act.

4   The approvals and directions contained in this circular take account of the amendments made to Part III of the 1948 Act and Schedule 8 of the 1977 Act by the Mental Health Act 1983, the Children Act 1989, the National Health Service and Community Care Act 1990 and the Community Care (Residential Accommodation) Act 1992.

It is the view of the Department that the amendments introduced into the 1948 Act by Section 1 of the Community Care (Residential Accommodation) Act 1992 will require authorities to make some direct provision for residential care under Part III of the 1948 Act.

\*   \*   \*   \*   \*

### White Paper and Policy Guidance

8   It will be the responsibility of Social Services Departments to make maximum possible use of private and voluntary providers and so increase the available range of options and widen consumer choice (paragraph 1.11 of the White Paper 'Caring for People' (Cm 849)). The Government welcomes the action being taken by

authorities to review the range of services they are currently providing, as part of a comprehensive review of the needs and services available in their area. Social services authorities will continue to play a valuable role in the provision of services, but in those cases where they are currently the main or sole providers of services, they will be expected to take all reasonable steps to secure diversity of provision (paragraph 3.4.1). Regarding the circumstances in which direct provision may be needed the White Paper said (paragraph 3.4.11) that the Government will expect local authorities to retain the ability to act as direct service providers, if other forms of service provision are unforthcoming or unsuitable. This is likely to be particularly important in services for people with high levels of dependency, or particularly challenging patterns of behaviour, whose care it is essential to safeguard.

9    The role of housing and social services authorities in relation to housing and community care is set out in the joint circular from the Departments of Health (LAC(92)12) and the Environment (10/92). This circular has also been issued to housing associations by the Housing Corporation.

10    By virtue of Section 2 of the Chronically Sick and Disabled Persons Act 1970 the matters dealt with in sub section (1) of that Section do not need to be included in the arrangements contained in Appendix 2.

11    It is not necessary for the arrangements contained in this circular to cover the provision by local authorities of sheltered employment as this is provided under powers deriving from the Disabled Persons (Employment) Acts 1944 and 1958.

12    The Secretary of State hopes that authorities will keep in mind the needs of individuals, families and groups to ensure that the services provided are administered flexibly and in accordance with changing needs. For the purpose of any of these arrangements, where no express statutory power exists for authorities to use outside service providers, the Secretary of State has also approved the use by authorities of suitable accommodation, services or facilities made available by another authority, voluntary body or person on such conditions as may be agreed. Thus, for example, authorities may continue to make use on a repayment basis of suitable residential or training places made available by other authorities, though they are asked nevertheless to bear in mind the importance of such services being provided as near to the person's home place as is practicable.

13    Social Services authorities' powers to prevent mental disorder or provide care for those who are or have been suffering from mental disorder are embraced in their wider powers under paragraph 2 of Schedule 8 to the 1977 Act to prevent illness and provide care for those who are or have been suffering from it. In addition, if authorities wish to provide services other than accommodation specifically for persons who are alcoholic or drug-dependent, the Secretary of State has approved them so doing. Because authorities' powers to provide accommodation under paragraph 2 of Schedule 8 are being repealed, the approvals and directions in relation to the provision of accommodation for the prevention of mental disorder or for persons who are or who have been suffering from mental disorder, or specifically for persons who are alcoholic or drug-dependent, have all been transferred to Section 21(1) of the 1948 Act. Further guidance on the provision of alcohol and drug services within community care is contained in LAC(93)2.

## Effective date

14    The Approvals and Directions are effective from 1 April 1993.

*    *    *    *    *

# Appendix 1

## Secretary of State's Approvals and Directions under Section 21(1) of the National Assistance Act 1948

The Secretary of State for Health, in exercise of the powers conferred on her by Section 21(1) of the National Assistance Act 1948, hereby makes the following Approvals and Directions:

### Commencement, interpretation and extent

1.—(1) These Approvals and Directions shall come into force on 1st April 1993.

(2) In these Approvals and Directions, unless the context otherwise requires, 'the Act' means the National Assistance Act 1948.

(3) The Interpretation Act 1978 applies to these Approvals and Directions as it applies to an Act of Parliament.

(4) These Approvals and Directions shall apply only to England and Wales.

### Residential accommodation for persons in need of care and attention

2.—(1) The Secretary of State hereby—

(a) approves the making by local authorities of arrangements under section 21(1)(a) of the Act in relation to persons with no settled residence and, to such extent as the authority may consider desirable, in relation to persons who are ordinarily resident in the area of another local authority, with the consent of that other authority; and

(b) directs local authorities to make arrangements under section 21(1)(a) of the Act in relation to persons who are ordinarily resident in their area and other persons who are in urgent need thereof,

to provide residential accommodation for persons aged 18 or over who by reason of age, illness, disability or any other circumstance are in need of care and attention not otherwise available to them.

(2) Without prejudice to the generality of sub-paragraph (1), the Secretary of State hereby directs local authorities to make arrangements under section 21(1)(a) of the Act to provide temporary accommodation for persons who are in urgent need thereof in circumstances where the need for that accommodation could not reasonably have been foreseen.

(3) Without prejudice to the generality of sub-paragraph (1), the Secretary of State hereby directs local authorities to make arrangements under section 21(1)(a) of the Act to provide accommodation—

(a) in relation to persons who are or have been suffering from mental disorder, or

(b) for the purposes of the prevention of mental disorder,

for persons who are ordinarily resident in their area and for persons with no settled residence who are in the authority's area.

(4) Without prejudice to the generality of sub-paragraph (1), and subject to section 24(4) of the Act, the Secretary of State hereby approves the making by local authorities of arrangements under section 21(1)(a) of the Act to provide residential accommodation—

(a) in relation to persons who are or have been suffering from mental disorder; or

(b) for the purposes of the prevention of mental disorder,

for persons who are ordinarily resident in the area of another local authority but who following discharge from hospital have become resident in the authority's area;

(5) Without prejudice to the generality of sub-paragraph (1), the Secretary of State hereby approves the making by local authorities of arrangements under section 21(1)(*a*) of the Act to provide accommodation to meet the needs of persons for—

   (*a*)   the prevention of illness;
   (*b*)   the care of those suffering from illness; and
   (*c*)   the aftercare of those so suffering.

(6) Without prejudice to the generality of sub-paragraph (1), the Secretary of State hereby approves the making by local authorities of arrangements under section 21(1)(*a*) of the Act specifically for persons who are alcoholic or drug-dependent.

**Residential accommodation for expectant and nursing mothers**

**3.** The Secretary of State hereby approves the making by local authorities of arrangements under section 21(1)(*aa*) of the Act to provide residential accommodation (in particular mother and baby homes) for expectant and nursing mothers (of any age) who are in need of care and attention which is not otherwise available to them.

**Arrangements to provide services for residents**

**4.** The Secretary of State hereby directs local authorities to make arrangements in relation to persons provided with accommodation under section 21(1) of the Act for all or any of the following purposes—

   (*a*)   for the welfare of all persons for whom accommodation is provided;
   (*b*)   for the supervision of the hygiene of the accommodation so provided;
   (*c*)   to enable persons for whom accommodation is provided to obtain—
      (i)   medical attention,
      (ii)  nursing attention during illnesses of a kind which are ordinarily nursed at home, and
      (iii) the benefit of any services provided by the National Health Service of which they may from time to time be in need, but nothing in this paragraph shall require a local authority to make any provision authorised or required to be provided under the National Health Service Act 1977;
   (*d*)   for the provision of board and such other services, amenities and requisites provided in connection with the accommodation, except where in the opinion of the authority managing the premises their provision is unnecessary;
   (*e*)   to review regularly the provision made under the arrangements and to make such improvements as the authority considers necessary.

**Arrangements for the conveyance of residents**

**5.** The Secretary of State hereby approves the making by local authorities of arrangements under section 21(1) of the Act to provide, in such cases as the authority considers appropriate, for the conveyance of persons to and from premises in which accommodation is provided for them under Part III of the Act.

**Duties in respect of residents in transferred accommodation**

**6.**—(1) Where a person is provided with accommodation pursuant to section 21(1) of the Act, and—

(a) the residential accommodation is local authority accommodation provided pursuant to Section 21(4) of the 1948 Act;

(b) the local authority transfer the management of the residential accommodation to a voluntary organisation who—

    (i) manages it as a residential care home within the meaning of Part I of the Registered Homes Act 1984, and

    (ii) is registered under that Part or is not required to be so registered by virtue of being an exempt body; and

(c) the person is accommodated in the residential accommodation immediately before and after the transfer,

while that person remains accommodated in that residential accommodation, the local authority shall remain under a duty to make arrangements to provide accommodation for him after any transfer to which paragraph (b) of this sub-paragraph refers.

(2) For the purposes of paragraph (c) of sub-paragraph (1), a person shall be regarded as accommodated in residential accommodation if—

(a) he is temporarily absent from such accommodation (including circumstances in which he is in hospital or on holiday);

(b) before 1st April 1993, that accommodation was provided under paragraph 2(1) of Schedule 8 to the National Health Service Act 1977.

(3) Where immediately before these Approvals and Directions come into force a local authority was under a duty to provide a person with accommodation by virtue of—

(a) the Secretary of State's former Directions under section 21(1) of the National Assistance Act 1948 contained in Annex 1 of Department of Health Circular LAC(91)12; or

(b) the Secretary of State's former Directions under paragraph 2 of Schedule 8 to the National Health Service Act 1977 contained in Annex 2 of Department of Health Circular LAC(91)12,

while that person remains accommodated in that residential accommodation, the local authority shall remain under a duty to make arrangements to provide that person with accommodation from the date on which these Directions come into force.

### Powers to make arrangements with other local authorities and voluntary organisations etc.

**7.** For the avoidance of doubt, these Approvals and Directions are without prejudice to any of the powers conferred on local authorities by section 21(4) and section 26(1) of the Act (arrangements with voluntary organisations etc.).

ANN DE PEYER

Signed on behalf of the

Dated 17/3/1993 Secretary of State for Health

## Appendix 2

### Secretary of State's Approvals and Directions under section 29(1) of the National Assistance Act 1948

The Secretary of State for Health, in exercise of the powers conferred on her by section 29(1) of the National Assistance Act 1948, hereby makes the following Approvals and Directions:—

### Commencement, interpretation and extent

**1.**—(1) These Approvals and Directions shall come into force on 1st April 1993.

(2) In these Approvals and Directions, unless the context otherwise requires, 'the Act' means the National Assistance Act 1948.

(3) The Interpretation Act 1978 applies to these Approvals and Direction as it applies to an Act of Parliament.

(4) These Approvals and Directions shall apply only to England and Wales.

### Powers and duties to make welfare arrangements

**2.**—(1) The Secretary of State hereby approves the making by local authorities of arrangements under section 29(1) of the Act for all persons to whom that subsection applies and directs local authorities to make arrangements under section 29(1) of the Act in relation to persons who are ordinarily resident in their area for all or any of the following purposes—

    (a)  to provide a social work service and such advice and support as may be needed for people in their own homes or elsewhere;

    (b)  to provide, whether at centres or elsewhere, facilities for social rehabilitation and adjustment to disability including assistance in overcoming limitations of mobility or communication;

    (c)  to provide, whether at centres or elsewhere, facilities for occupational, social, cultural and recreational activities and, where appropriate, the making of payments to persons for work undertaken by them;

(2) The Secretary of State hereby directs local authorities to make the arrangements referred to in section 29(4)(g) of the Act (compiling and maintaining registers) in relation to persons who are ordinarily resident in their area.

(3) The Secretary of State hereby approves the making by local authorities of arrangements under section 29(1) of the Act for all persons to whom that subsection applies for the following purposes—

    (a)  to provide holiday homes;

    (b)  to provide free or subsidised travel for all or any persons who do not otherwise qualify for travel concessions, but only in respect of travel arrangements for which concessions are available;

    (c)  to assist a person in finding accommodation which will enable him to take advantage of any arrangements made under section 29(1) of the Act;

    (d)  to contribute to the cost of employing a warden on welfare functions in warden assisted housing schemes;

    (e)  to provide warden services for occupiers of private housing.

(4) Save as is otherwise provided for under this paragraph, the Secretary of State hereby approves the making by local authorities of all or any of the arrangements referred to in section 29(4) of the Act (welfare arrangements etc.) for all persons to whom section 29(1) applies.

### Welfare arrangements with another local authority

**3.** The Secretary of State hereby approves the making by local authorities of arrangements under section 29(1) of the Act, where appropriate, with another local authority for the provision of any of the services referred to in these Approvals and Directions.

### Welfare arrangements with voluntary organisations and otherwise

**4.** For the avoidance of doubt, these Approvals and Directions are without prejudice to the powers conferred on local authorities by section 30(1) of the Act (voluntary organisations for disabled persons welfare).

ANN DE PEYER

Signed on behalf of the
Dated 17/3/1993                           Secretary of State for Health

## Appendix 3

## Secretary of State's Approvals and Directions under paragraphs 1 and 2 of Schedule 8 to the National Health Service Act 1977

The Secretary of State for Health, in exercise of the powers conferred on her by paragraphs 1(1) and 2(1) of Schedule 8 to the National Health Service Act 1977, hereby makes the following Approvals and Directions:—

### Commencement, interpretation and extent

**1.**—(1) These Approvals and Directions shall come into force on 1st April 1993.

(2) In these Approvals and Directions, unless the context otherwise requires, 'the Act' means the National Health Service Act 1977.

(3) The Interpretation Act 1978 applies to these Approvals and Directions as it applies to an Act of Parliament.

(4) For the avoidance of doubt, these Approvals and Directions shall apply only to England and Wales.

### Services for expectant and nursing mothers

**2.** The Secretary of State hereby approves the making of arrangements under paragraph 1(1) of Schedule 8 to the Act for the care of expectant and nursing mothers (of any age) other than the provision of residential accommodation for them.

### Services for the purpose of the prevention of illness etc.

**3.**—(1) The Secretary of State hereby approves the making by local authorities of arrangements under paragraph 2(1) of Schedule 8 to the Act for the purpose of the prevention of illness, and the care of persons suffering from illness and for the aftercare of persons who have been so suffering and in particular for—

(*a*) the provision, for persons whose care is undertaken with a view to preventing them becoming ill, persons suffering from illness and persons who have been so suffering, of centres or other facilities for training them or keeping them suitably occupied and the equipment and maintenance of such centres;

(*b*) the provision, for the benefit of such persons as are mentioned in paragraph (*a*) above, of ancillary or supplemental services.

(2) The Secretary of State hereby directs local authorities to make arrangements under paragraph 2(1) of Schedule 8 to the Act for the purposes of the prevention of mental disorder, or in relation to persons who are or who have been suffering from mental disorder—

(*a*) for the provision of centres (including training centres and day centres) or other facilities (including domiciliary facilities), whether in premises managed by the local authority or otherwise, for training or occupation of such persons;

(b) for the appointment of sufficient social workers in their area to act as approved social workers for the purposes of the Mental Health Act 1983;

(c) for the exercise of the functions of the authority in respect of persons suffering from mental disorder who are received into guardianship under Part II or III of the Mental Health Act 1983 (whether the guardianship of the local social services authority or of other persons);

(d) for the provision of social work and related services to help in the identification, diagnosis, assessment and social treatment of mental disorder and to provide social work support and other domiciliary and care services to people living in their homes and elsewhere.

(3) Without prejudice to the generality of sub-paragraph (1), the Secretary of State hereby approves the making by local authorities of arrangements under paragraph 2(1) of Schedule 8 to the Act for the provision of—

(a) meals to be served at the centres or other facilities referred to in sub-paragraphs (1)(a) and (2)(a) above and meals-on-wheels for house-bound people not provided for—

    (i) under section 45(1) of the Health Services and Public Health Act 1968, or

    (ii) by a district council under paragraph 1 of Part II of Schedule 9 to the Health and Social Services and Social Security Adjudications Act 1983;

(b) remuneration for persons engaged in suitable work at the centres or other facilities referred to in sub-paragraphs (1)(a) and (2)(a) above, subject to paragraph 2(2)(a) of Schedule 8 to the Act;

(c) social services (including advice and support) for the purposes of preventing the impairment of physical or mental health of adults in families where such impairment is likely, and for the purposes of preventing the break-up of such families, or for assisting in their rehabilitation;

(d) night-sitter services;

(e) recuperative holidays;

(f) facilities for social and recreational activities;

(g) services specifically for persons who are alcoholic or drug-dependent.

**Services made available by another local authority etc.**

**4.** For the purposes of any arrangements made under these Approvals and Directions, the Secretary of State hereby approves the use by local authorities of services or facilities made available by another authority, voluntary body or person on such conditions as may be agreed, but in making such arrangements, a local authority shall have regard to the importance of services being provided as near to a person's home as is practicable.

ANN DE PEYER

Signed on behalf of the
Secretary of State for Health

Dated 17/3/1993

## C.   Services under Health Services and Public Health Act 1968

### CIRCULAR NO 19/71, 'WELFARE OF THE ELDERLY', IMPLEMENTATION OF SECTION 45 OF THE HEALTH SERVICES AND PUBLIC HEALTH ACT 1968

\*   \*   \*   \*   \*

2   At the present time the powers (or duties) of authorities to provide social services for the elderly are limited to certain specific activities, ie: the provision of home help (section 29 of the National Health Service Act 1946); the provision of meals and recreation (section 31 (amended) of the National Assistance Act 1948); the provision of residential accommodation for those in need of care and attention, whether directly (section 21 of the 1948 Act) or through voluntary organisations or in private homes (section 44 of the 1968 Act); and the assistance of voluntary organisations to provide services (section 65 of the 1968 Act) . . . But the purpose of section 45 is to enable authorities to make other approved arrangements for services to the elderly who are not substantially and permanently handicapped, and thus to promote the welfare of the elderly generally and so far as possible to prevent or postpone personal or social deterioration or breakdown. . . .

\*   \*   \*   \*   \*

4   The Secretary of State accordingly hereby approves the making by authorities of arrangements under Section 45 of the Health Services and Public Health Act 1968 for any of the following purposes to meet the needs of the elderly:
  (*a*)  to provide meals and recreation in the home and elsewhere;
  (*b*)  to inform the elderly of services available to them and to identify elderly people in need of services;
  (*c*)  to provide facilities or assistance in travelling to and from the home for the purpose of participating in services provided by the authority or similar services;
  (*d*)  to assist in finding suitable households for boarding elderly persons;
  (*e*)  to provide visiting and advisory services and social work support;
  (*f*)  to provide practical assistance in the home, including assistance in the carrying out of works of adaption or the provision of any additional facilities designed to secure greater safety, comfort or convenience;
  (*g*)  to contribute to the cost of employing a warden on welfare functions in warden assisted housing schemes;
  (*h*)  to provide warden services for occupiers of private housing. . . .

\*   \*   \*   \*   \*

5.   The following points should be noted in connection with the making of any arrangements approved in the preceding paragraph:
  (*a*)   Charges may be made and recovered (section 45(2)) . . .

\*   \*   \*   \*   \*

### Development of services for the elderly

6   . . . The first task is that of finding out which of the elderly need help and what kind of help they need, bearing in mind that the concept of 'need' is constantly changing and is complicated because it can involve a mixture of environmental and

health aspects. . . . In undertaking this task authorities are recommended to bear in mind these points:

\* \* \* \* \*

(b) Good services together with wide and continuing publicity about them are a pre-requisite of any scheme for finding out needs. . . .

(c) The identification of need on the part of individuals and the provision of services for them must march together since there will be great disillusion and disappointment if enquiries reveal needs which are then left unmet . . .

(d) It will be essential to secure the closest possible operational integration between the existing and new services provided by the social services departments and those provided by health departments, general practitioners and hospitals, in order to take full advantage of their contribution to the earlier identification and treatment of need . . .If encouraged to do so, and as the attachment of local authority staff becomes more wide-spread, the family doctor is likely increasingly to refer to the social services those of his patients who appear to have a social need. . . .

\* \* \* \* \*

7.   In practical terms the ability to provide a wide range of services in the domiciliary field will require the closest cooperation between those who are responsible for the various elements that make up the community health and social services. . . . The object should be (1) to improve the detection of those in need; (2) to develop improved or new methods of making a wider range of help available (and this will include advice and support for the elderly and their families); (3) to improve arrangements for acquiring and exchanging information to provide for increasingly earlier intervention by the health and social services to reduce breakdown and crisis. Resources of all kinds will be limited, however, and therefore it may well prove desirable to start by identifying the needs of certain groups of the elderly who seem likely to be particularly vulnerable, eg: (a) elderly people, especially the more elderly, who are housebound or living alone or recently bereaved or about to be discharged from hospital, and (b) other persons over, say 75, living in the community, particularly where there are high concentrations of very elderly people in particular districts....

\* \* \* \* \*

10   . . . The most important early need may be that of skilled advice and support in seeking the best solutions available to the problems which face individuals or families. *Home-help*, including laundry services and other aids to independent living, should probably be high on any priority list. . . . Many of the elderly who are mobile or who can be transported will require *social centres* providing meals and opportunities for occupation as well as companionship and recreation. For the housebound and the frailer elderly *meals on wheels* will also need to be developed.

## D.   Services under the National Health Service Act 1977

**LAC(93)10—APPROVAL AND DIRECTIONS FOR ARRANGEMENTS FROM 1 APRIL 1983 MADE UNDER SCHEDULE 8 TO THE NHSA 1977 AND SECTIONS 21 AND 29 OF THE NATIONAL ASSISTANCE ACT 1948(1993) (*Referred to above*).**

## E. Services under the Mental Health Act 1983 and Relating to Discharge of Mentally Disordered Persons in General

### (1) CIRCULAR HC(90)23/LASSL(90)11—THE CARE PROGRAMME APPROACH

JOINT HEALTH/SOCIAL SERVICES CIRCULAR

HEALTH AND SOCIAL SERVICES DEVELOPMENT
'CARING FOR PEOPLE'
THE CARE PROGRAMME APPROACH FOR PEOPLE WITH A MENTAL
ILLNESS REFERRED TO THE SPECIALIST PSYCHIATRIC SERVICES

This Circular will be cancelled on 10 September 1995 *(extended)*

### Summary

This circular:
  i) requires district health authorities, the Bethlem and Maudsley Special Health Authority and the Special Hospitals Service Authority to implement the care programme approach envisaged in HC(88)43 (Appendix 4, paragraph 3) for people with a mental illness, including dementia, whatever its cause, referred to the specialist psychiatric services;
  ii) asks social services authorities to collaborate with health authorities in introducing this approach and, as resources allow, to continue to expand social care services to patients being treated in the community.
It builds on the general circular on hospital discharges (HC(89)5). The Annex to this circular sets out:—
  i) the policy background to the care programme approach;
  ii) how the care programme approach works;
and draws attention to some specific matters which will need to be addressed in establishing care programmes.

* * * * *

### Resources

1   Health authorities are expected to meet any health service costs arising from the introduction of more systematic *procedures* from existing resources. Introducing the care programme approach places no new requirement to provide *services* on either health or social services authorities.

### Annex

#### The care programme approach for people with a mental illness referred to the specialist psychiatric services

*Introduction*
1   This Annex sets out:
  a.   the policy background to the care programme approach;

b.   how the care programme approach works;
and gives guidance on some key issues to be addressed in implementation.

*Policy background*

2   The 1975 White Paper 'Better Services for the Mentally Ill' (Cmnd 6233) first set the general policy within which care programmes should be introduced: this general policy has been endorsed by the Government in the 1989 White Paper 'Caring for People' (Cm 849), paragraph 7.4. Locally-based hospital and community health services, co-ordinated with services provided by social services authorities, voluntary and private sectors, and carers, can provide better care and treatment for many people with a mental illness than traditional specialist psychiatric hospitals.

3   Community based services are only an improvement when the patients who would otherwise have been hospital in-patients get satisfactory health care, and, where appropriate, social care. 'Caring for People' acknowledged that providing adequate arrangements for the community care and treatment of some patients had proved more difficult and resource intensive than expected. In practice adequate arrangements have not always been achieved.

4   The care programme approach is being developed to seek to ensure that in future patients treated in the community receive the health and social care they need, by:

i.    introducing more systematic arrangements for deciding whether a patient referred to the specialist psychiatric services can, in the light of available resources and the views of the patient and, where appropriate, his/her carers, realistically be treated in the community;

ii.   ensuring proper arrangements are then made, and continue to be made, for the continuing health and social care of those patients who can be treated in the community.

*How the care programme approach works*

5   Individual health authorities, in discussion with relevant social services authorities, will agree the exact form the care programme approach will take locally. All care programmes should, however, include the following key elements:

i.    systematic arrangements for assessing the health care needs of patients who could, potentially, be treated in the community, and for regularly reviewing the health care needs of those being treated in the community;

ii.   systematic arrangements, agreed with appropriate social services authorities, for assessing and regularly reviewing what social care such patients need to give them the opportunity of benefiting from treatment in the community;

iii.  effective systems for ensuring that agreed health and, where necessary, social care services are provided to those patients who can be treated in the community.

6   It will be for relevant health and social services staff to decide whether the resources available to them can enable acceptable arrangements to be made for treating specific patients in the community. If a patient's minimum needs for treatment in the community—both in terms of continuing health care and any necessary social care—cannot be met, in-patient treatment should be offered or continued, although (except for patients detained under the Mental Health Act) it is for individual patients to decide whether to accept treatment as an in-

patient. Health authorities will need to ensure that any reduction in the number of hospital beds does not outpace the development of alternative community services.

## Implementation

7   Within the broad framework described it is for health authorities, in discussion with consultant psychiatrists, nurses, social workers and other professional staff, and social services authorities to seek to establish suitable local arrangements, and to see that they are maintained in the context of purchase/provider arrangements post 1 April 1991.

8   There are some specific issues which all authorities will however need to address in determining their local arrangements. These relate to:

- Inter-professional working;
- Involving patients and carers;
- Keeping in touch with patients and ensuring agreed services are provided;
- the role of key workers

## Inter-professional working

9   Although all the patients concerned will be patients of a consultant psychiatrist, modern psychiatric practice calls for effective inter-professional collaboration between psychiatrists, nurses, psychologists, occupational therapists and other health service professional staff; social workers employed by social services authorities, and general practitioners and the primary care team, and proper consultation with patients and their carers.

10   Where it is clear to a consultant and professional colleagues that continuing health and/or social care is necessary for a patient whom they propose to treat in the community, there must be proper arrangements for determining whether the services assessed as necessary can, within available resources, be provided. It is essential to obtain the agreement of all professional staff and carers (see paragraphs 12 and 13 below) expected to contribute to a patient's care programme that they are able to participate as planned.

## Involving patients

11   It is important that proper opportunities are provided for patients themselves to take part in discussions about their proposed care programmes, so that they have the chance to discuss different treatment possibilities and agree the programme to be implemented.

## Involving carers

12   Relatives and other carers often know a great deal about the patient's earlier life, previous interests, abilities and contacts and may have personal experience of the course of his/her illness spanning many years. Wherever consistent with the patient's wishes, professional staff should seek to involve them in the planning and subsequent oversight of community care and treatment.

13   Carers often make a major and valued contribution to the support received by many people with a mental illness being treated in the community. Where a care programme depends on such a contribution, it should be agreed in advance with the carer who should be properly advised both about such aspects of the patient's condition as is necessary for the support to be given, and how to secure professional advice and support, both in emergencies and on a day-to-day basis. In addition,

professional staff may be able to offer the carer help in coming to terms with his/her role vis-à-vis the patient.

*Arrangements for keeping in touch with patients and making sure the services agreed as part of the programme are provided*

14    Once an assessment has been made of the continuing health and social care needs to be met if a patient is to be treated in the community, and all the professional staff expected to contribute to its implementation have agreed that it is realistic for them to make the required contributions, it is necessary to have effective arrangements both for monitoring that the agreed services are, indeed, provided, and for keeping in contact with the patient and drawing attention to changes in his or her condition. This is a narrower concept than that of case management as envisaged in the White Paper 'Caring for People' and upon which specific guidance will shortly be given to local authorities. In the Department's view the most effective means of undertaking this work is through named individuals, often called key workers, identified to carry the responsibilities outlined above in respect of individual patients.

15    *Key workers.* Where this can be agreed between a health authority and the relevant social services authority, the ideal is for one named person to be appointed as key worker to keep in close touch with the patient and to monitor that the agreed health and social care is given. The key worker can come from any discipline but should be sufficiently experienced to command the confidence of colleagues from other disciplines. When the key worker is unavailable, proper arrangements should be made for an alternative point of contact for the patient and any carer(s).

16    A particular responsibility of the key worker is to maintain sufficient contact with the patient to advise professional colleagues of changes in circumstances which might require review and modification of the care programme.

\* \* \* \* \*

18    Sometimes patients being treated in the community will decline to co-operate with the agreed care programmes, for example by missing out-patient appointments. An informal patient is free to discharge himself/herself from patient status at any time, but often treatment may be missed due to the effects of the illness itself, and with limited understanding of the likely consequence.

19    Every reasonable effort should be made to maintain contact with the patient and, where appropriate, his/her carers, to find out what is happening, to seek to sustain the therapeutic relationship and, if this is not possible, to try to ensure that the patient and carer knows how to make contact with his/her key worker or the other professional staff involved. It is particularly important that the patient's general practitioner is kept fully informed of a patient's situation and especially of his or her withdrawal (partial or complete, see paragraph 20 below) from a care programme. The general practitioner will continue to have responsibility for the patient's general medical care if she/he withdraws from the care programme.

20    Often patients only wish to withdraw from part of a care programme and the programme should be sufficiently flexible to accept such a partial rather than complete withdrawal. It is important that, within proper limits of confidentiality, social services day care, residential and domiciliary staff (including those from the voluntary and private sectors) are given sufficient information about the situation to enable them to fulfil completely their responsibility of care to the patient. Similarly, relatives and carers should also be kept properly informed.

## (2) CIRCULAR HSG(94)5—INTRODUCTION OF SUPERVISION REGISTERS FOR MENTALLY ILL PEOPLE FROM 1 APRIL 1994

### Executive summary

The Secretary of State for Health announced in December 1993 a requirement on all health authorities to ensure that mental health service providers establish and maintain supervision registers which identify those people with a severe mental illness who may be a significant risk to themselves or to others. This requirement builds upon guidance set out in HC(90)23/LASSL(90)11 on the introduction of the Care Programme Approach and focuses on the first stage of the development of comprehensive mental health information systems as set out in the *Health of the Nation*, which required all mental health provider units to have effective information systems in place by 1995. It aims to ensure that people with a severe mental illness receive appropriate and effective care in the community.

The annex to this guidance sets out the administrative arrangements required to identify those people significantly at risk and to maintain the register.

### Action

Health Authorities are required to have in place by 1 April 1994 contracts which ensure that:

- All provider units providing mental health care set up registers which identify and provide information on patients who are, or are liable to be, at risk of committing serious violence or suicide, or of serious self neglect, whether existing patients or newly accepted by the secondary psychiatric services;
- All initial assessment and follow up reviews of patients under the Care Programme Approach consider the question of whether the patient should be registered;
- All provider units incorporate the supervision register in the development of mental health information systems to support the full implementation of the Care Programme Approach.

It is envisaged that existing systems set up in connection with Care Programme Approach will require only simple modifications to comply. The Supervision Register need and should not be separate from such systems as long as the information described below is recorded and the procedures outlined are in place.

### Administrative arrangements required for supervision registers

#### Background

1   This guidance takes forward the policy of ensuring those patients subject to the Care Programme Approach who pose most risk to themselves or others receive adequate care, support and supervision in the community to assist in preventing them from falling through the care network. The establishment and maintenance of these records (referred to in this guidance as supervision registers) develops existing policy in the area of mental health information systems. The supervision register should form part of the wider information systems being developed by Health Authorities/provider units under the initiatives detailed below:

### The care programme approach

a.   The White Paper *Caring for People* proposed the development of a *Care Programme Approach* and suggested the maintenance of registers as a component (para 7.7). This was subsequently set out in a Health Circular ('Caring for People': The Care Programme Approach for people with a mental illness referred to the specialist psychiatric services, HC(90)23/LASSL(90) 11). The Care Programme Approach should have been introduced by all Health Authorities in co-operation with Social Services Departments, in April 1991. It involves the development of personalised care packages for all patients accepted by the specialist psychiatric services to ensure that they receive the care they need. A key worker is appointed to keep in close contact with the patient. The present guidance does not alter the general principles of the Care Programme Approach, nor does it affect arrangements for aftercare under the Mental Health Act 1983, section 117, or local authorities' duties in relation to care management.

*     *     *     *     *

### The ten point plan

c.   The Ten Point Plan, announced by the Secretary of State in August 1993 to improve community care for mentally ill people contained a commitment to introduce special supervision registers of patients who are most at risk and need most support, as part of the development of mental health information systems generally.

*     *     *     *     *

19   Withdrawal from the supervision register on the grounds of diminished potential risk must not automatically entail a withdrawal of any services provided for the patient. *All of the responsibilities set out in the Care Programme Approach will continue to apply to such patients as long as they remain under the care of the specialist psychiatric services.*

*     *     *     *     *

## Purpose of the supervision registers

2.   Identifying all individuals who are under the care of an NHS Provider Unit known to be at significant risk or potentially at significant risk of committing serious violence or suicide or of serious self neglect as a result of severe and enduring mental illness is a key element in:

a.   providing a care plan that aims to reduce the risk and ensuring that the patient's care needs are reviewed regularly and that contact by a key worker is maintained;

b.   providing a point of reference for relevant and authorised health and social services staff to enquire whether individuals under the Care Programme Approach are at risk;

c.   planning for the facilities and resources necessary to meet the needs of this group of patients; and,

d.   identifying those patients who should receive the highest priority for care and active follow up.

Mental illness in this context includes people with a diagnosed personality disorder including psychopathic disorders who are receiving treatment from specialist psychiatric services. The register is not intended for young people under 16 years of age.

Complementary guidance on the discharge of mentally disordered patients has been issued for consultation and will be published in definitive form as soon as this is complete.

## Mechanisms for patient inclusion on the supervision register

3 All patients who fall within the scope of the supervision registers should be patients of the specialist psychiatric services. Consideration for inclusion on the supervision register should take place as a normal part of the discussion of the Care Programme before they leave hospital and at Care Programme reviews following discharge, or for new patients at initial assessments. The decision as to whether a patient is included in the register rests with the consultant psychiatrist responsible for the patient's care. This should be made in consultation with the other members of the mental health team (includes the social worker) involved in that patient's care.

4 Patients should be included if a Care Programme review meeting concludes that they are suffering from a severe mental illness and are, or are liable to be, at significant risk of committing serious violence or suicide or of severe self neglect in some foreseeable circumstances which it is felt might well arise in this particular case (eg. ceasing to take medication, loss of a supportive relationship or loss of accommodation). Risk assessment should be of the type described in the discharge guidance circular (circulated in draft to all authorities on 12 January and to be issued substantively following consultation). Patients subject to supervised discharge, when the legislation has been enacted, will be among those included on the register.

Patients, and where they wish an advocate, relative, friend or carer, must have an opportunity to state their views and have these taken into account, for example, through attendance at the review meeting or in discussion with the responsible clinician and key worker. Wherever possible the patient's GP should be involved in the decision.

5 Judgements of the risk of serious violence, suicide or severe self neglect should always be based on detailed evidence about the patient's psychiatric and social history and current condition (including the available evidence from any criminal justice agencies with which the patient has been involved). The evidence on which the judgement was made should be recorded in written form and should be available to the relevant professionals for the review meeting.

\*     \*     \*     \*     \*

## Categories of inclusion

9 At the time of inclusion on the register and at each subsequent review at which the patient is left on the register, patients should be assigned to one or more of the following three categories. Assignment to more than one single category should be for specific reasons.

    a.   Significant risk of suicide.
    b.   Significant risk of serious violence to others.
    c.   Significant risk of severe self neglect.

10 Where the risk of committing serious violence, suicide or severe self neglect is considered to be contingent on specific events (eg. ceasing to take medication, or loss of a supportive relationship or home), the identified warning signs should be recorded in line with current best practice.

\*     \*     \*     \*     \*

## Informing the patient of inclusion on the register

12   Patients should be informed orally and in writing when they are put on a supervision register and broadly told why they have been placed on it, how the information on the register will be used, to whom it may be disclosed, and the mechanisms for review. The only exception to this may be for clinical reasons—for example, when informing the patient would probably cause serious harm to his or her physical or mental health. This is very unlikely to arise in a patient suitable for care outside hospital. If it does, the patient should be informed as soon as there is no longer any risk of harm. A decision not to inform the patient immediately should not be taken lightly, and should be agreed by the mental health team including the consultant psychiatrist responsible.

## Criteria for withdrawal

13   A patient's continued inclusion on the supervision register should be considered at every review. Care Programme Approach reviews of patients on the supervision register should occur at least every 6 months and specific consideration must be given to whether registration should continue. The patient, and if he or she wishes an advocate, relative, friend or carer, must have a suitable opportunity to state his or her views and have them fully considered.

14   Any of the agencies or professionals involved in the care programme may request that a special review meeting be held to consider withdrawal of the at risk status of the patient.

15   There may be occasions when a patient requests a review to consider their withdrawal from the supervision register. The supervision register is a health service record. The inclusion of a patient is a matter for the judgement of health care professionals in consultation with social work colleagues. The decision to withdraw a patient from the register is ultimately a matter for the consultant psychiatrist responsible for the patient's care, taking into account the views of other professionals involved in the patient's care and of the patient.

16   The patient, or his or her chosen advocate, should have the right to request, verbally or in writing, his or her removal from the register. It will be for the consultant psychiatrist, in conjunction with professional colleagues, to consider these representations and inform the patient of the outcome and the reasons for the decision. If the patient remains dissatisfied the normal channels for complaint and the right to a clinical second opinion will apply.

17   Withdrawal of a patient from a supervision register will be appropriate if:
   a.   The patient is no longer considered to be at significant risk of serious violence, suicide or severe self neglect. This decision may only be taken at a review meeting.
   b.   The patient's care and records have been transferred to another Provider Unit. Withdrawal by transfer may only occur on the basis of written agreement with the receiving provider unit.
   c.   The patient has died.

18   Provider Units which have lost contact with the patient should not change the at risk status on the patient's personal record, but should designate the patient as out of contact with the unit. Providers should make every reasonable effort to reestablish contact. The patient's GP, social worker and other members of the care team should be urgently notified and asked to advise and a review meeting should be convened to which they should be invited.

**(3)   LASSL(94)4/HSG(94)27—GUIDANCE ON THE DISCHARGE OF MENTALLY DISORDERED PEOPLE AND THEIR CONTINUING CARE IN THE COMMUNITY**

## 1   Background

This circular draws to the attention of purchasers and providers of local authority social services the enclosed guidance, issued to health authorities on 10 May, on good practice in the discharge of mentally disordered patients into the community. This is part of the series of initiatives taken under the Secretary of State for Health's 10 point plan, announced in August 1993, to ensure the safe and successful care of mentally ill people who have been in contact with the specialist mental health services.

## 2   Action

Authorities are asked to note and act upon the guidance as it relates to:
—   their role in multi-disciplinary, multi-agency discharge decisions;
—   the need to work with purchasers of health care to ensure appropriate support and supervision in the community, primarily in the context of the Care Programme Approach and care management;
—   the question of confidentiality of information;
—   the role of professional staff in the assessment of risk;
—   the conduct of management investigations and/or independent inquiries in the case of untoward incidents.

*     *     *     *     *

**Executive summary**

The Secretary of State for Health attaches great importance to the responsible consideration of the discharge of psychiatric patients from hospital and to the effectiveness of the care and supervision provided in the community when they leave. This guidance is part of the Secretary of State's ten point plan announced in August 1993. The plan's other elements, of which the present document takes account, include the introduction of supervision registers (under HSG(94)5) and the proposed new power of supervised discharge.

The guidance sets out good practice which should be followed for all patients who are discharged following referral to the specialist mental health services. It is based on application of the Care Programme Approach, with particular emphasis on the need for risk assessment prior to discharge. The text takes account of the many comments the Department received on the draft which was circulated for consultation on 12 January 1994.

*     *     *     *     *

This guidance seeks to ensure:
—   that psychiatric patients are discharged only when and if they are ready to leave hospital;
—   that any risk to the public or to patients themselves is minimal and is managed effectively;
—   that when patients are discharged they get the support and supervision they need from the responsible agencies.

*     *     *     *     *

1   It is fundamental in considering whether a person should be discharged from in-patient hospital care that full account is taken of his or her assessed needs and capabilities, including:

— whether, with adequate medication, care, and supervision in the community, the patient could still present any serious risk to him or herself or to others;
— whether his or her needs for therapy, supervision, sanctuary, or security require continuing in-patient treatment; and
— whether he or she could be cared for effectively and safely in the community, if necessary in staffed or supported accommodation.

2   Generally speaking, mentally disordered people are much more likely to harm themselves than to harm others. Either eventuality can be devastating for any of those affected. *Those taking individual decisions about discharge have a fundamental duty to consider both the safety of the patient and the protection of other people. No patient should be discharged from hospital unless and until those taking the decision are satisfied that he or she can live safely in the community, and that proper treatment, supervision, support and care are available.* Detailed advice on *risk assessment* is set out in paragraphs 23-32 below.

\*    \*    \*    \*    \*

4   Where after full consideration of all relevant factors, the conclusion is that it is safe to discharge the patient, and that to do so is in his or her best interests, it is essential that arrangements for discharge and continuing community care are, subject to paragraph 6 below on the confidentiality of information, agreed between, communicated to and understood by the patient and all others involved. These may include the patient's carers and, to the extent that they are directly involved in the delivery of care, social workers, community mental health nurses, the patient's general practitioner and other community, residential, and day care staff.

5   In the patients who have committed offences or been involved with the criminal justice agencies, consideration should also be given to whether these agencies (for example the probation service) have a part to play in their further care. In these cases the circumstances of any victim of the offence should be borne in mind when considering placement in the community. For those patients detained under the Act who are subject to restriction orders and are conditionally discharged, reference should also be made to the joint Home Office/Department of Health Guidance Booklets on *'Supervision and After-care of Conditionally Discharged Restricted Patients'*.

\*    \*    \*    \*    \*

## THE CARE PROGRAMME APPROACH

7   The basic principles governing the discharge and continuing care of all mentally ill people, including those with dementia, are embodied in the Care Programme Approach, which authorities were required to introduce in 1991 (Health Circular (90)23/Local Authority Social Services letter (90)11). The same approach should be applied, so far as it is relevant, to the after-care of other mentally disordered patients: see paragraphs 20-21 below.

8   The Care Programme Approach applies whether or not a patient has been detained under the Mental Health Act, but health and local authorities also have a statutory duty under section 117 of the Act to provide after-care services for patients (in all categories of mental disorder) who have been detained in hospital under sections 3, 37 (whether or not with restrictions under section 41), 47 or 48 of the Act. To fulfil this duty authorities will need to ensure that the Care Programme

Approach is fully implemented for mentally ill patients who have been detained, and that its principles are applied so far as they are relevant to the after-care of other detained patients. Authorities will need to establish mechanisms to monitor the application of the Care Programme Approach as a whole and should report on progress at regular intervals to authority members.

9   The purpose of the Care Programme Approach is to ensure the support of mentally ill people in the community thereby minimising the possibility of their losing contact with services and maximising the effect of any therapeutic intervention. It also applies to all mentally ill people who are accepted by the specialist psychiatric services without having been treated in hospital, including those released from prison.

10   The essential elements of an effective care programme are:
  — *systematic assessment* of health and social care needs (including accommodation), bearing in mind both immediate and longer term requirements;
  — a *care plan* agreed between the relevant professional staff, the patient, and his or her carers, and recorded in writing;
  — the allocation of a *key worker* whose job (with multi-disciplinary managerial and professional support) is:
    — to keep in close contact with the patient;
    — to monitor that the agreed programme of care is delivered; and
    — to take immediate action if it is not;
  — *regular review* of the patient's progress and of his or her health and social care needs.

*Those taking the decisions must be satisfied that these conditions are fulfilled before any patient is discharged.*

11   It is essential for the success of a continuing care plan that decisions and actions are systematically recorded and that arrangements for communication between members of the care team are clear. The patient and others involved (including, as necessary, the carer, health and social services staff, and the patient's general practitioner) should be aware of the contents of the plan and should have a common understanding of:
  — its first review date;
  — information relating to any past violence or assessed risk of violence on the part of the patient;
  — the name of the key worker (prominently identified in, eg, clinical notes, computer records and the care plan);
  — how the key worker or other service providers can be contacted if problems arise;
  — what to do if the patient fails to attend for treatment or to meet other requirements or commitments.

12   The Care Programme Approach lays great emphasis on ensuring continuity of care for patients in the community:

Every reasonable effort should be made to maintain contact with the patient and, where appropriate with his/her carers, to find out what is happening, to seek to sustain the therapeutic relationship . . . Often patients only wish to withdraw from part of a care programme and the programme should be sufficiently flexible to accept such a partial rather than a complete withdrawal.

Any such change to the care programme should as far as practicable be agreed with all those involved.

*      *      *      *      *

14 ... The Care Programme Approach, with its emphasis on systematic assessment of health and social care needs, requires close inter-disciplinary and inter-personal working, particularly at critical times such as when discharge from hospital is being considered. The aim should be to ensure that timely and coordinated responses can be made to individual needs. The inter-agency arrangements necessary to ensure continuity of care and to prevent people 'falling through the net' (eg contact points, knowledge of each other's roles, contingency arrangements, needs assessments) should be clear and easily understood by all parties. They should include the police, courts and probation service so far as they are involved in the management of people with a mental disorder and so far as is compatible with obligations on confidentiality (see paragraph 6).

15 There must also be effective links between local agencies and supra-district services such as special hospitals and medium secure units, as well as prisons, so that agencies know for which patients they will eventually have to accept responsibility and can work jointly with the discharging unit to develop effective arrangements for continuing care.

## Care management

16 Social Services Departments have duties under the *NHS and Community Care Act 1990* to assess people's needs for community care services. Multi-disciplinary assessment under the Care Programme Approach, if properly implemented, will fulfil these duties. Health Authorities and Social Services Departments will need to ensure that the Care Programme Approach and care management arrangements are properly coordinated. The detailed arrangements will depend on the type of care management system the Social Services Department has implemented, but in all cases there should be an allocated key worker as required under the Care Programme Approach.

*     *     *     *     *

## Supervised discharge

18 The conditions attached to supervised discharge would reflect the principles of the Care Programme Approach, as well as including some of the key features of Mental Health Act guardianship. These proposals will reinforce the approaches set out in the present guidance. Services for patients subject to supervised discharge, as for all others receiving care from the specialist mental health services in the community, will be organised and provided in accordance with the Care Programme Approach. Supervised discharge will give legal backing and a power of enforcement to arrangements for patients at risk to themselves or to others and help ensure that they do not get lost to care. Legislation to implement supervised discharge will be introduced as soon as possible.

## Mental Health Review Tribunals

19 Patients detained under the Mental Health Act have the right to have their detention reviewed, at specified intervals, by a Mental Health Review Tribunal. The Tribunal must discharge the patient if the statutory criteria specified in section 72(1) of the Act are met, and has discretion to discharge patients in other cases. If the patient is subject to a restriction order the Tribunal may direct that he or she is discharged subject to conditions. Where a patient has applied for a Tribunal it is impor-

tant that the essential elements of the Care Programme Approach (as outlined in paragraph 10) have been considered and can be put into operation if the patient is discharged, and that the key worker is made immediately aware of any conditions imposed.

## People with personality disorders

20 The Care Programme Approach circular applies only to mentally ill people. However the good practices the Care Programme Approach promotes and the guidance contained in the present document are equally relevant to those parties with personality (or psychopathic) disorders who can safely and suitably be looked after by the specialist psychiatric services in the community.

## People with learning disabilities

21 Similar arrangements may also need to be considered for some people with learning disabilities discharged from in-patient care (eg the Special Hospitals Service Authority applies the Care Programme Approach to all its patients, including those with mental/severe mental impairment). General guidance on learning disability services, including the importance of providing for essential needs on a life-long basis, is contained in Health Service Guidelines (92)42 and Local Authority Circular (92)15.

\* \* \* \* \*

## PATIENTS WHO PRESENT SPECIAL RISKS

23 Patients with longer term, more severe disabilities and particularly those known to have a potential for dangerous or risk-taking behaviour need special consideration both at the time of discharge and during follow-up in the community. No decision should be agreed unless those taking the clinical decisions are satisfied that the behaviour can be controlled without serious risk to the patient or to other people. In each case it must be demonstrable that decisions have been taken after full and proper consideration of any evidence about risk the patient presents.

24 *Before discharge* there must be a careful assessment by both the multi-disciplinary team responsible for a patient in hospital and those who will be taking responsibility for his or her care in the community. Those involved must agree the findings of a risk assessment (see below), the content of a care plan, and who deliver it. In accordance with good practice in the delivery of the Care Programme Approach generally, there must be a contemporaneous note of the outcome of any risk assessment and of any management action deemed necessary and taken.

25 Although the progress of many mentally disordered people *after discharge* from hospital can be monitored adequately by attendance at an out-patient clinic to see a psychiatrist and/or by visits by a community mental health nurse, this is unlikely to be sufficient for those patients presenting a complex range of needs. They are likely to need regular and, at times, possibly urgent multi-disciplinary re-assessments by the community based team. Which members of the team need to come together for any particular case will be a matter of judgment, but at least the consultant; the nurse, social worker or care manager; and always the key worker should be involved. The patient's general practitioner should be informed in all cases even if it is not practical to involve him or her in the immediate consideration. Where an urgent problem arises, one responsible person (preferably the key worker

or another professional in consultation with the key worker) should take the necessary immediate action followed by wider consultation as soon as possible.

\* \* \* \* \*

28 It is widely agreed that assessing the risk of a patient acting in an aggressive or violent way at some time in the future is at best an inexact science. But there are some ways in which uncertainty may be reduced:

(a) *making sure relevant information is available*

A proper assessment cannot be made in the absence of information about a patient's background, present mental state and social functioning and also his or her past behaviour. It is essential to take account of all relevant information, whatever its source. As well as the treatment team and the patient, sources may include relatives, carers, friends, the police, probation officers, housing departments, and social workers, and also local press reports and concerns expressed by neighbours. Proper regard must be paid to legal and other obligations relating to confidentiality. However, wherever possible, information that is relevant to forming on overall view of a case should be made available in the interests of the patient. Too often it has proved that information indicating an increased risk existed but had not been communicated and acted upon.

\* \* \* \* \*

**Assessing the risk of suicide**

31 ... The period around discharge from hospital is a time of particularly high risk of suicide, emphasising the need for proper assessment prior to discharge and effective follow-up afterwards.

\* \* \* \* \*

## RESPONSIBILITIES OF DISTRICT HEALTH AUTHORITIES AND OTHER PURCHASERS OF HEALTH CARE

38 Purchasers of mental health services are responsible (in co-operation with local social services, local housing departments, and voluntary organisations) for ensuring that there is an adequate range of community based services to meet local need. Services should meet medical, nursing, social and therapy requirements; supervised accommodation is likely to be an important component of local provision. There must also be services that will meet effectively the varying needs of mentally disordered offenders and similar patients, including discharged prisoners with continuing mental health care needs (see paragraph 41). The *Mental Illness Key Area Handbook* gives further advice on planning community services.

39 Purchasers have a key responsibility to ensure successful local implementation of the Care Programme Approach. The contracts placed with providers should include:

— explicit and clear requirements to implement the Care Programme Approach;

— explicit and clear arrangements for management accountability for the Care Programme Approach;

— explicit and clear requirements for Care Programme Approach information (including the number of people covered by Care Programme Approach, collected at least quarterly);

— explicit and clear processes for monitoring and auditing Care Programme Approach;

— explicit and clear mechanisms to review the facilities necessary for the discharge of patients; which are reflected in subsequent purchasing plans.

40    In addition purchasers must ensure that the following key elements are implemented through contracts:

— the maintenance or development of a mental health information system, including supervision registers;

— staffed adequately trained in the Care Programme Approach and in risk assessment and management;

— suitable arrangements for the management and clinical supervision of staff in community mental health terms;

— audit of suicides (see paragraph 35 above);

— agreed procedures in the event of a homicide or assault by a patient subject to the Care Programme Approach.

Purchasers are responsible for ensuring, through these arrangements, that the necessary priority is given to the most severely mentally ill patients.

41    The essential requirements for services for mentally disordered offenders are set out in The Health of the Nation and in NHS Management Executive Letter (93)54 which requires NHS authorities to work with personal social services and criminal justice agencies to develop strategic and purchasing plans based on the joint Department of Health/Home Office ('Reed') review of services. These must include:

— an effective range of non-secure and secure services (including those patients with special or differing needs, such as people with learning disabilities or psychopathic disorder, ethnic minorities, young people and women);

— arrangements for the multi-agency assessment and, as necessary, diversion of offenders from the criminal justice system;

— meeting the mental health care needs of transferred or discharged prisoners;

— the placement within six months of special hospital patients who no longer require high security.

Arrangements for the placement of special hospital patients must take full account of the requirements of the Care Programme Approach and the guidance in this document.

## (4)    BUILDING BRIDGES—A GUIDE TO ARRANGEMENTS FOR THE INTER-AGENCY WORKING FOR THE CARE AND PROTECTION OF SEVERELY MENTALLY ILL PEOPLE

*(Informal Guidance)*

### Chapter 1—Introduction and Overview

### 1.0    Introduction

*The purpose of the Guide*

**1.0.1**    Agencies which work with severely mentally ill people need to collaborate to ensure that patients receive proper and co-ordinated care in the community. The main purpose of this Guide is to promote close and effective inter-agency working so that well co-ordinated care can be delivered.

*   *   *   *   *

**1.0.3**   It is Government policy that the specialist mental health services target their resources and efforts first and foremost on severely mentally ill people. The focus of the Guide is therefore on ensuring that severely mentally ill people receive the best possible care, although much of the document is also of relevance to the care of those who are less severely ill. This chapter gives a background to government policy on the care and treatment of mentally ill people, including the legislative background, outlines some of the key principles of inter-agency working, and discusses general issues such as confidentiality and information sharing. Nothing in this guidance is intended to, or should be taken to alter existing legal rights, obligations and duties.

*   *   *   *   *

## 1.1   Principles of inter-agency working

**1.1.1**   All agencies involved in the care of severely mentally ill people will have their own sets of principles and priorities which guide their work. There are however certain basic requirements without which joint working can be difficult or even impossible. These include:
- a commitment to joint working at all levels of the agencies involved, including senior management;
- a focus on service-users, including sensitivity to the particular needs of individuals (specifically including people from ethnic minorities) and a commitment to user and carer involvement in the planning and delivery area;
- an agreed and jointly 'owned' strategy for the care of severely mentally ill people;
- agreed and well-understood procedures for accessing services;
- appropriate and effective arrangements for inter-agency information exchange;
- joint commissioning wherever possible to maximise the use of available resources;
- a commitment to training, on a single and multi-agency basis, which underpins effective joint working and encourages a better understanding of other agencies' roles and structures;
- regular review and evaluation of arrangements for inter-agency working.

The Department of Health has identified inter-agency working as a priority area in its mental health research initiative, and is commissioning research into how best to facilitate its development.

*Users and carers*
**1.1.2**   Reference is made throughout the Guide to the need to involve users and carers wherever possible. Users and carers need to be involved in planning care both on an individual basis (ie their own care or that of the person for whom they are caring) and at a strategic level (for example through consultation with user and carer groups).

*   *   *   *   *

## 1.3   An introduction to the Care Programme Approach (CPA)

*Background*

**1.3.1**   When most people with severe mental illness were cared for in the old-style psychiatric hospitals, all the available facilities and services were in one place. Once the shift is made to community-based care and treatment, the patient is faced with a network of services (including health and social services, social security and housing) that are often physically separate and managed by different agencies. The resulting complex pattern of service provision would tax most people; for users of mental health services and their carers accessing care is particularly difficult.

**1.3.2**   All those concerned with the purchasing and provision of mental health services are aware of what can happen when things go wrong. Experience and research has demonstrated that mentally ill people need care which is integrated across the different agencies, and flexible enough to cope with changing needs over time. Such co-ordinated care will only come about when patients receive a detailed needs assessment, a comprehensive care plan, and have their care monitored and reviewed on a regular basis. Patients themselves and, as far as possible, their carers, should be involved in these processes. These elements represent the core of the Care Programme Approach.

\*   \*   \*   \*   \*

*The care programme approach*

**1.3.4**   The CPA was introduced in 1991 to provide a framework for the care of mentally ill people outside hospital. It requires district health authorities (DHAs), in collaboration with local authority social services departments (LASSDSs), to put in place specified arrangements for the care and treatment of mentally ill people in the community.

**1.3.5**   There are four main elements to the CPA:
- systematic arrangements for assessing the health and social needs of people accepted by the specialist psychiatric services;
- the formulation of a care plan which addresses the identified health and social care needs;
- the appointment of a key worker to keep in close touch with the patient and monitor care;
- regular review, and if need be, agreed changes to the care plan.

**1.3.6**   The principles that underlie the CPA can be summed up as follows:
- Specialist psychiatric services are provided by a multi-disciplinary team of individuals each with his or her particular skills and experience. It is this dimension that makes inter-agency working so crucial, particularly for severely mentally ill people. The multi-disciplinary CPA can only function where all those in the team work effectively together, for the good of the patient.
- The CPA can and should be applied to all patients who are accepted by the specialist psychiatric services. The reason for applying the CPA to all patients is simple; it is the only way in which we can hope to ensure that people receive the services they need and that no vulnerable people slip through the net of care.
- **Users and carers must be involved**. Care plans should be agreed with users and their carers, as far as possible. If users disagree with an aspect of the plan, arrangements should be flexible enough to allow as many of their needs as possible to be met in another way.

- Carers often provide the majority of care to mentally ill people. Their contribution to meeting users' needs should be explicitly recognised in the care plan. Help from the mental health services would include meeting the carers' needs for support, periods of respite care and 24-hour access to an emergency mental health service.
- The CPA is just what it says—**an approach.** The NHS Executive has no intention of prescribing precisely what should be done at a local level.

**1.3.7**   The CPA should change the ways in which many professionals work, but it is not designed to be a bureaucratic exercise. In particular, whilst teams should operate in a multi-disciplinary way, by no means all patients will need to receive care and treatment from the whole multi-disciplinary team. The 'tiered CPA' is covered in more detail below (see 3.2.1-3.2.6).

*The care programme approach, care management and Section 117 after-care*

**1.3.8**   Although Social Services Departments have responsibility for care management, and health authorities for the CPA, the principles underlying the two processes are the same. It is therefore essential that health and social services departments co-ordinate the implementation of the two processes to avoid duplication, and the waste of precious resources. If properly implemented, multi-disciplinary assessment will ensure that the duty to make a community care assessment is fully discharged as part of the CPA, and there should not be a need for separate assessments. The relationship between the two processes is discussed further at 3.2.7-3.2.19.

**1.3.9**   Section 117 of the Mental Health Act 1983 requires health authorities and local authorities, in conjunction with voluntary agencies, to provide after-care for certain categories of detained patients (see paragraph 1.4.9 below). Proper implementation of the CPA will ensure that these legal requirements are fully discharged. Authorities will however need a mechanism to identify those patients who are subject to statutory Section 117 after-care.

## 1.4   The legislative framework

*       *       *       *       *

*Mental Health Review Tribunals*

**1.4.5**   Patients detained under the Mental Health Act have the right to have their detention reviewed, at specified intervals, by a Mental Health Review Tribunal, an independent body consisting of individuals who will all have considerable experience in the mental health field. The Tribunal must discharge the patient if the statutory criteria specified in section 72(1) of the Act are met, and has discretion to discharge patients in other cases. If the patient is subject to a restriction order the Tribunal may direct that he or she is discharged subject to conditions. Where a patient has applied for a Tribunal it is important that the essential elements of a care plan have been agreed and can be put into operation if the patient is discharged.

**1.4.6**   Free legal advice in respect of, and representation at, Mental Health Review Tribunals is available under the legal aid scheme to all patients, regardless of their financial status.

*       *       *       *       *

*Discharged patients*

**1.4.8**    The legal requirements relating to services in the community for discharged patients are summarised at appendix 1.2.

**1.4.9**    Health and local authorities have a statutory duty under **Section 117** to provide after-care services for patients (in all categories of mental disorder) who have been detained in hospital under section 3, 37 (whether or not with restrictions under section 41), 47 or 48 of the Act. To fulfil this duty authorities will need to ensure that the CPA, and care management if needed, is fully implemented for mentally ill patients who have been detained, and that its principles are applied so far as they are relevant to the after-care of other detained patients. Authorities will need to establish mechanisms to monitor the application of the Care Programme Approach as a whole and should report on progress at regular intervals to authority members.

*Supervised discharge (after-care under supervision)*

**1.4.10**    The Mental Health (Patients in the Community) Bill will be implemented on 1 April 1996 (subject to parliamentary approval). The main provision of the Bill is the introduction of supervised discharge for certain patients who have been detained under the Mental Health Act 1983. As one of the measures announced in August 1993 under the Secretary of State's Ten Point Plan for mentally ill people in the community, it complements the discharge guidance issued in May 1994 and the introduction of supervision registers.

**1.4.11**    Supervised discharge is designed for so-called 'revolving door' patients who go through a cycle of repeated admission to hospital under the Mental Health Act followed by the breakdown of arrangements for care in the community, often because they have stopped taking medication, or they have lost contact with the after-care services arranged for them.

**1.4.12**    The new provision will be available for detained patients who are not subject to Home Office restrictions on their discharge (mainly section 3 or section 37 patients) and who, while no longer needing treatment in hospital, would present a substantial risk of serious harm to their own health or safety, or to the safety of others, unless their after-care in the community were supervised.

**1.4.13**    A patient subject to supervised discharge will be required to abide by the terms of a care plan, drawn up under the principles of the Care Programme Approach, agreed by all concerned following consultation with the patient. A supervisor—who will in most cases also be the key worker—will be appointed with powers to:

- require the patient to **reside** in a specified place;
- require the patient to **attend** for medical treatment and rehabilitation;
- **convey** a patient to a place where he or she is to attend for treatment.

**1.4.14**    The supervisor may be any member of the multi-disciplinary team involved in delivering the care programme, for example a community mental health nurse, doctor or social worker.

**1.4.15**    If a patient did not comply with the conditions the care team would be required to review the case, including the possible need for compulsory admission to hospital, under the existing powers in the Act. There is no provision for patients to be given treatment against their will in the community.

**1.4.16**    Supervised discharge will apply initially for six months, which could be extended by a further six months and then by periods of a year at a time. Patients will have the right to appeal to a Mental Health Review Tribunal against supervised discharge being imposed.

**1.4.17** An application for supervised discharge will be made by the patient's responsible medical officer in hospital. This will be done while the patient is still detained in hospital but at a point when he or she will soon be ready to leave approaching the time of discharge. Other members of the team who have been involved with the patient's care in hospital must be consulted as well as must those who will be involved—whether professionally or as an informal carer—in his or her after-care.

**1.4.18** Full guidance on the use of supervised discharge will be given in a supplement to the Mental Health Act Code of Practice in early 1996. The existing provisions for guardianship under the 1993 Act will remain in force alongside the new power (see Appendix 1.2).

*     *     *     *     *

## Chapter 2—The Roles of Agencies involved in Caring for Mentally Ill People

*     *     *     *     *

**2.0.1   The key principle underlying good community care for mentally ill people is that caring for this client group is not the job of one agency alone, just as it is not the responsibility for one professional group alone.**

*     *     *     *     *

*Health authorities and housing*

**2.1.11** A particularly important area in which health authorities need to liaise closely with social services and housing departments is over housing for mentally ill people. Housing plays a crucial role in health outcomes for mentally ill people, and interventions which tackle either mental health or housing conditions alone are not sufficient to prevent subsequent services failures. It is essential that Health Authorities understand the need to address housing issues if they are to commission an efficient and effective service response for people with mental illness.

*     *     *     *     *

## 2.2   Local authorities

*Social services departments*

**2.2.1** LASSDs have a wide range of duties and responsibilities to provide services for individuals and families, and to facilitate positive mental health. They provide services to all kinds of people of all ages, in clients' homes and elsewhere in the community. In addition they have a regulatory function with regard to services provided by the voluntary and private sector, and they may work collaboratively with these bodies.

**2.2.2** LASSDS have a lead role in purchasing and providing social care services for mentally ill people living in the community. Only a small part of their responsibilities is directly related to the purchasing and provision of mental health services, but many of their activities have implications for mentally ill people.

Their main responsibilities in this area are as follows:

- to agree a community care plan for the authority to meet the social care needs of the residents. This must be agreed with the relevant DHA(s);
- to assess people in need:
- to design care packages to meet the assessed needs of users and their carers, which are then monitored in the community ('Care Management');

- to provide social work support to people with mental health problems, and their carers;
- to provide/purchase a range of personal social services (eg residential and day services, domiciliary services, etc);
- to register and inspect residential care homes;
- to liaise with DHAs in implementing the CPA;
- to employ enough Approved Social Workers (ASWs) to provide a seven days a week assessment and emergency service under the Mental Health Act 1983;
- to provide Section 117 after-care jointly with DHAs, in co-operation with relevant voluntary organisations;
- to have in place published policies and arrangements for guardianship under the Mental Health Act 1983.

\* \* \* \* \*

## Housing departments

**2.27** Local Authority Housing Departments have a key role to play in effective community care through ensuring that mentally ill people have a secure, suitable home. The Department of the Environment makes clear in its guidance on Housing Strategies that housing authorities should play a full part in community care, working with social services departments and health authorities:

> The housing strategy statement should set out how the authority is approaching its responsibilities under Community Care, and the way in which it is co-operating with other agencies in the planning and delivery of services. The strategy should summarise the needs that are currently served, the needs it anticipates over the timescale covered by the strategy, and the resources available to meet these needs. (Part 3, section 12.9.)

**2.2.8** Specifically, the Guidance calls on housing authorities to take into account in their Housing Strategies additional housing needs which have arisen, or are likely to arise as a result of community care, such as the consequences of the closure of long-stay hospitals and the reprovision of care locally. It states that 'an inter-agency policy should be in place to provide a framework for the establishment of systems and procedures which ensure that the housing content of a Community Care assessment assists the identification of a potential housing need and consequent referral to the housing authority.' (Part 3, section 12.8.)

**2.2.9** It is not enough merely to provide housing. Mentally ill people can sometimes be difficult neighbours. They may be socially isolated. Without a certain level of support they may become seriously ill. Housing, health and social services agencies need to work together to ensure that the right accommodation is made available with the right levels of domiciliary support to ensure that the placement is a success.

\* \* \* \* \*

## The specialist psychiatric services

**2.3.9** The specialist services have a responsibility to provide a comprehensive range of services for mentally ill people. These services should be characterised by several principles:

- services should be provided on a multi-disciplinary team basis (although individual patients may well need only uni-disciplinary input);

- the needs, wishes and convenience of the user (and carers) should be taken into account as far as possible;
- services should respect the individual qualities and social, cultural, linguistic and religious background of patients;
- services should seek to give patients the maximum amount of self-determination possible. The patient should be able to choose the gender of his or her health or social care worker whenever possible.

\*   \*   \*   \*   \*

*Users, relatives and carers*

**2.4.5   A fundamental principle of mental health care is that users of services should be involved as far as possible in the care process.**

Similarly, carers may have a valuable contribution to make and should be involved wherever possible. Carers may also need their own needs assessed.

**2.4.6**   Those closest to a mentally ill person may be able to help the team in a number of ways by, for example:

- identifying particular social care needs;
- helping the team keep in touch;
- encouraging the patient to keep to his or her care plan.

They should receive a copy of the care plan, provided that the patient has given his or her consent.

**2.4.7**   The idea of involving relatives and friends is one of the expectations set out in the Patient's Charter. The Charter states that 'If you agree, you can expect your relatives and friends to be kept up to date with the progress of your treatment'. The key worker will usually be responsible for keeping relatives and friends up to date with a patient's progress.

**2.4.8**   The Department of Health launched a Framework for Local Community Care Charters earlier this year. A key part of the Framework is putting users and carers first. All areas will put in place charters which commit local agencies to:

- **involving** users and carers in the planning and assessment processes;
- **respecting** users' personal beliefs;
- showing **courtesy and respect** at all times;
- **setting standards** for dealing with letters and enquiries;
- **protecting** personal information; and
- calculating any charges fairly and accurately.

\*   \*   \*   \*   \*

## Chapter 3: The Working of the Care Programme Approach

### 3.0   Introduction

**3.0.1**   The purpose of this chapter is to illustrate how the CPA is being successfully applied in practice. It is based on the experience of practitioners in the field, and on examples of how the CPA can be made to work well for mentally ill people. Most importantly, it stresses the adoption of a tiered Care Programme Approach in order to focus the most resource-intensive assessment, care and treatment on the most severely mentally ill people, whilst ensuring that all patients in the care of the specialist psychiatric services receive the basic elements of the CPA.

**3.0.2**   The CPA should not be a form-filling bureaucratic exercise. It is above all a systematic **approach** to the care of mentally ill people, based on a systematic assessment of needs, both health and social, the appointment of a key worker to co-ordinate care, and continuing monitoring in the community. This Guide does not seek to bring about uniformity of operation. It does however attempt to reinforce the key principles of the CPA. How the CPA is then put into practice will be for local professional staff and managers to decide.

**3.0.3**   The CPA is the cornerstone of the Government's mental health policy. It applies to **all** mentally ill patients who are accepted by the specialist mental health services.

## 3.1   Element of the CPA

**3.1.1**   The essential elements of the CPA are:
- systematic **assessment** of health and social care needs;
- an agreed **care plan**;
- allocation of **key worker**;
- regular **review** of the patient's progress.

\*     \*     \*     \*     \*

**3.1.2**   All aspects of the care planning process should involve the user, his or her advocate, carers and/or interested relatives. In particular, the user should be given an opportunity to set out his or her views of what his or her needs are, for health and social care, and for day activities, including employment. The patient and his or her carer(s) should understand and, if possible, agree the care plan.

*Needs assessment*

**3.1.3**   An initial needs assessment, to try to identify the patient's general health and social care needs, will usually be carried out by the professional to whom the patient has been referred. If required, fuller assessments by members of the multi-disciplinary team should ideally take place as soon as possible. An assessment meeting should then be held to discuss the findings, with as many of the multi-disciplinary team present as reasonably need to attend. The CPA assessment will need to cover both health and social needs, including the individual's accommodation and ability to live independently. It is important that the individual concerned, and his or her carer(s), be given as much notice as possible of what is to happen; ideally he or she should be offered access to an independent advocate.

\*     \*     \*     \*     \*

**3.1.5**   The mechanisms for identifying need are for local teams to determine, and should be agreed between health and social services staff, particularly in respect of social care assessments. An arrangement needs to be reached that whoever is responsible for carrying out such assessments they are acceptable to social services as an assessment for care management purposes. Duplication of social care assessments, for CPA and Care Management can and should be avoided, and arrangements made for the same procedures to be initiated regardless of the route by which a patient first contacts the health or social services.

**3.1.6**   **It is important to remember that the CPA only involves the whole multi-disciplinary team for complex assessments.** If a patient is less severely ill, and needs little more than regular outpatient appointments, the assessment and care planning process will be relatively straightforward. In some cases assessment can be done in the initial professional consultation by the psychiatrist alone (or occasionally a psychologist or other professional who receives direct referrals—though a referring GP will retain medical responsibility for a patient referred direct to a non-medical member of the team). We develop this point at 3.2. However, a patient with less complex needs should still receive systematic assessment, be assigned a key worker and receive monitoring and review of a simple care plan.

**3.1.7** A number of services are using the assessment process to identify and record service shortfalls of one sort or another. These might refer to accommodation, employment, social support, or a wide range of other aspects of person's life. Staff need to be reassured that by recording these shortfalls they are not laying themselves open to attack; the purpose of recording shortfalls should be to help in planning more patient-centred services in the future.

\* \* \* \* \*

**3.1.10** In some cases, however well-prepared the team is, and however good the needs assessment, the care plan will have to juggle the availability of resources and the needs of the patient. To do this effectively, the meeting will need a detailed knowledge of available resources in the community, to help develop the most sensitive and imaginative solutions. A database of community resources would be a useful tool. This will be particularly important if the patient rejects a suggested care plan. Service shortfalls should be noted, and fed back to management to help in the planning process.

\* \* \* \* \*

*Patient and carer involvement*

**3.1.13** It is important that the individual concerned and his or her carer(s) are involved as much as possible in the care planning process. If this has been done, there is a better chance that the patient will keep to the care plan.

*Circulating the care plan*

**3.1.14** Copies of the care plan should be sent to all those present at the meeting, and any other **relevant** parties as soon as possible after the meeting, subject to the need to maintain an appropriate level of confidentiality. The patient should be made aware that, in order for effective care to be provided, personal health information will need to pass between the different agencies involved in their care—particularly between health and social services (see 1.5.2). Care should be taken about how this material is transmitted.

*Ensuring that all is ready for discharge*

**3.1.15** If the patient has been an in-patient, the key worker should ensure before discharge that elements of the plan necessary for discharge are carried out. This will include the patient's needs for medication, therapy, supervision and accommodation. In particular, those taking decisions on discharge have a duty to consider both the safety of the patient and the protection of other people. **No individual should be discharged from hospital unless and until those taking the decision are satisfied he or she can live safely in the community and that proper treatment, supervision, support and care are available** (see HSG(94)27/LASSL(94)4, para 2).

*The key worker and delivery of the care plan*

\* \* \* \* \*

**3.1.17** We have recommended that the key worker should be selected at the needs assessment meeting. Since the key worker is vital to the success of the whole process it is important that he or she be identified as soon as possible. This is particularly the case when patients are soon to be discharged from hospital. However, on occasion it may be that not enough information is available at the assessment meeting to make the most appropriate choice of key worker.

### Who should be the key worker ?
**3.1.18** The choice of the key worker should be a formal item on the agenda of a care planning meeting. Decisions about who should be a key worker should be based on considerations of the patient's needs, matched against the staff available. It should not merely be determined by the staff present at the meeting. There should **not** be an assumption that the key worker should always be a mental health nurse, or a social worker, although in practice they often will be. Indeed, occasionally the key worker may not be a mental health specialist, for example where a patient has multiple disabilities and it makes more sense for their care package to be co-ordinated by a specialist in a different field. In these cases, explicit arrangements must be built into the care plan to ensure that there is a mental health professional who can advise the key worker on changes to the patient's mental health condition.

**3.1.19** The decision on who should be the key worker should take into account;

- the **patient's needs**—if ensuring that a patient follows his or her care plan and medication is the chief concern, a mental health nurse is likely to be the most suitable candidate; if housing and financial concerns and family problems are uppermost, a social worker; if the patient has request outpatient appointments then perhaps a consultant psychiatrist; but there may be good reasons for choosing another professional.
- the **patient's wishes**—the patient (and his or her carer(s)) may wish to state a preference. Where a particular individual has been working with a patient for some time there will often be a preference for that member of the team to take on the key working role. The patient may also wish to have a key worker of the same gender, or of a similar cultural background.
- the **workloads** of members of the team. The degree of input that a key worker needs to make will of course vary according to the patient.
- **authority**—the key worker must carry the necessary authority to monitor the care plan being delivered and, if necessary, call for a review. The team must delegate this authority to the key worker, if she or he is to do the job effectively.
- **training**—it is essential that key workers receive training to enable them to carry out this role. This will include training on the working of the Mental Health Act 1983, and on risk assessment (see chapter 6 below).
- alternative **contact points** must be identified for when the key worker is not available.

**3.1.20** The decision of the meeting to select an individual as key worker should be written down, and the agreement of that individual obtained. The key worker must always be aware of his or her key working caseload, and of what the job entails.

**3.1.21** It is important to remember that key workers do not always have to be appointed on a long-term basis, and will not always be drawn from the people who are involved in the initial assessment of the patient. For people who pose little risk and whose needs are likely to remain stable, the key worker role might change once the care plan is established. For example, a day centre worker might inherit the key worker role from the mental health nurse who was involved in the original assessment once the patient is established at the day centre.

**3.1.22**   People with complex health and social needs, however, are likely to require a key worker to be appointed on a long-term basis, particularly where their needs are likely to be unstable, or where they pose a high degree of risk.

*   *   *   *   *

**3.1.29**   The key worker may be the most important member of the team in terms of delivering the care plan. But usually other professionals will be involved. For the key worker to co-ordinate care effectively, he or she and the other members of the team must ensure that channels of formal and informal communication are open. These will range from planned review meetings, when each professional can give an opinion on the patient's condition, to casual conversations between different members of the team. Any serious problems should be given a more formal airing however, and a written record made.

*   *   *   *   *

*Reviewing care plans*

**3.1.33**   In the process of keeping in touch and monitoring the care plan, the key worker will in effect be monitoring the care plan on a regular basis. This may well lead to minor changes in those elements of the plan which he or she delivers, or in other elements which can be easily negotiated with other members of the team, and with the patient. If minor changes are made, it is important that other members of the team, the patient's GP and, if the patient consents, any carers are informed in writing.

**3.1.34**   A formal review, involving the patient and, if appropriate, his or her carer(s), should take place at least every six months. There will however be occasions in between formal reviews when more urgent action is needed. The key worker (or indeed any member of the team) should have the authority to call together the team to discuss the case; the team should be as well-prepared for the review meeting as for the initial care planning meeting. Again, a written care plan should be produced, to be circulated after the meeting to all the relevant members of the team, and to the GP, patient and carer(s).

**3.1.35**   However effective the care planning and follow up in the community, there will be patients who need re-admission. **This is not necessarily a sign of failure.** A measure of the effectiveness of the CPA might in some cases be how quickly a patient is discharged again after admission. If there is effective monitoring in the community the key worker can ensure that a patient is admitted before the real crisis point comes, thereby aiding a more rapid discharge, in comparison with former admissions.

**3.1.36**   When a patient is in hospital, the CPA does not stop. It is important that the key worker remains in touch with the patient whilst he or she is in hospital, to ensure that the therapeutic relationship is maintained.

*   *   *   *   *

## 3.2   Making the CPA work

*The tiered CPA*

**3.2.1**   As has been emphasised at 3.1.6, following the CPA does not entail involving the whole multi-disciplinary team in every assessment or in the delivery and review of every care plan. The principles of the CPA can be applied regardless of the number of professionals involved in a patient's assessment and care.

**3.2.2** The following is intended as a guide to the way in which the CPA can be 'tiered' to meet appropriately different levels of need. It is not prescriptive, and details such as the number of 'tiers' and their definition in terms of levels of need and service involvement are very much at the discretion of local services.

**3.2.3 A minimal CPA** would apply to patients who have limited disability/health care needs arising from their illness and have low support needs which are likely to remain stable. They will often need regular attention from only one practitioner, who will also fulfil the key worker role. The practitioner may not necessarily be one of those who is involved in the assessment. The care plan will be correspondingly very short, merely indicating the regular interventions planned and the review date. Any changes in the patient's condition will be monitored by the key worker. He or she will keep other members of the team informed if there are any major changes in the condition of the patient.

**3.2.4** If the patient needs a medium level of support, a **more complex CPA** would be appropriate. This may be because the person is likely to need more than one type of service, or because their needs are less likely to remain stable. Such patients will require further needs assessment which may involve several members of the team, including (almost certainly) a psychiatrist, social worker and mental health nurse. There will be a discussion over the identity of the key worker; and the care plan will be more complex, requiring interventions from several members of the team, who will need to be aware of what their colleagues are doing.

**3.2.5** Individuals with severe mental illness, suffering from severe social dysfunction, whose needs are likely to be highly volatile, or who represent a significant risk, are likely to require a **full, multi-disciplinary CPA**. Again, there will need to be a discussion about who should be the key-worker (see 3.1.22). If such a patient represents a significant risk to themselves or others, the consultant psychiatrist, together with his or her colleagues, should consider whether inclusion on the supervision register is appropriate. Some services may choose to regard the supervision register as an additional 'top tier' of the CPA.

**3.2.6** The number of professionals involved with a patient's care is of course not the only factor which will vary according to the level of needs. There is also an important qualitative difference between the key worker role for a patient with limited disability and low support needs, and that for an individual who has a severe mental illness with correspondingly extensive/complex needs. In the former case, the key worker will have a relatively non-intensive role as a named contact point with the specialist services, and a co-ordinator of care if other members of the multi-disciplinary team are involved. In the latter case, the key worker's role is far more intensive and time-consuming. He or she will probably spend a significant amount of time developing a relationship with the patient and maintaining contact assertively, as well as co-ordinating multiple care inputs.

\* \* \* \* \*

*CPA and Section 117 registers*

**3.2.22** Patients subject to Section 117 after-care should also be subject to the CPA, although authorities will need to identify separately patients who are receiving care under Section 117 so that they can demonstrate that they are fulfilling their statutory obligations. Given that the principles of the CPA and Section 117 after-care

are the same, it should be possible to avoid creating two completely separate registers, which would be wasteful of administrative time and potentially confusing. Ideally, the Section 117 after-care register should form a subset of the main CPA register.

## Questions and answers

*Should the needs assessment meeting be separate from the care planning meeting?*
It need not be, but it is essential that in a given meeting needs assessment is separated from care planning itself. The former process should focus on a patient's needs, irrespective of the resources available; the latter on what can be provided, given current resources. The gap between the two, the service shortfalls, should be recorded so that they can influence future planning.

*What if the patient's condition is judged to have deteriorated?*
The assessment should be recorded. If the patient's condition deteriorates then the care plan should be reviewed and all options, including hospital admission or continued in-patient treatment, should be considered. The needs assessment process should be repeated in due course.

*     *     *     *     *

*What should be done if not all the requisite professionals can attend the needs assessment/care plan meeting?*
If suitable deputies cannot be found, a new date must be fixed. This is obviously undesirable for patients and staff. The latter should make every effort to attend meetings. At the same time, every effort must be made to ensure that only those professionals who need to be present are invited.

*If no one is available to act as key worker, should the care planning go ahead?*
If indeed no one is available, then there are inadequate community facilities to allow that patient to be cared for in the community. In-patient treatment should be considered or continued, and senior management informed straight away. If the number of beds is insufficient senior management should urgently consider the position in conjunction with purchasers.

*Should someone who is not present at the needs assessment meeting be appointed as key worker?*
The key worker must know that he or she is the key worker, and have agreed to take on this role. In certain circumstances a decision may be confirmed in writing as soon as possible after the meeting.

*If a key worker believes that the care plan is not being properly carried out, but other members of the team disagree, what can she or he do?*
The key worker needs to be given sufficient authority by the team to discuss the problem with the relevant team member's manager, and if necessary, to call a meeting to discuss the matter. If the key worker is still unhappy, the matter should be taken up with senior management. There should be written record of the review meeting, indicating the concerns, and how they were resolved.

**APPENDIX 1.1** Relationships between the Care Programme Approach and Other Key Processes and Provisions

| PROCEDURE/PROVISION | APPLIES TO: |
| --- | --- |
| **Care Programme Approach (CPA)** | All people accepted by the specialist psychiatric services. |
| **Care Management** | All people subject to the CPA who have associated social care needs. |
| **Supervision Registers** | People subject to the CPA who are severely mentally ill and who may be a significant risk to themselves or others. |
| **Section 117 after-care** | Patients discharged following detention under sections 3, 37 (whether or not with restrictions under section 41), 47 or 48 of the Mental Health Act 1983. All will be subject to the CPA, and some may also be on a supervision register. |
| **Guardianship** | Patients subject to a guardianship under sections 7 or 37 of the Mental Health Act 1983. All will be subject to the CPA, some may be on supervision registers and some may be subject to Section 117 after-care. |
| **Supervised Discharge** | Certain patients who have been detained under the Mental Health Act 1983. All will be subject to the CPA and Section 117 after-care, and most will also be on a supervision register. |

\*     \*     \*     \*     \*

## F. Assessment of Disabled Persons, Including those with Learning Difficulties and Persons in Need of Alcohol and Drug Services

### (1) CIRCULAR NO 12(70)—THE CHRONICALLY SICK AND DISABLED PERSONS ACT 1970

\*    \*    \*    \*    \*

### Sections of special interest to health and welfare authorities

7   SECTION 2. The effect of subsection 2(1) (read with subsection 2(2)(*a*)) is to remove from approved schemes under section 29 of the National Assistance Act 1948 any reference to any of the matters set out in subsections 2(1)(*a*) to (*h*) (or any like reference) and to create statutory duties in these matters together with certain additions. The duty requires the authority to assess the requirements of individuals determined by them to be substantially and permanently handicapped as to their needs in these matters. If they are satisfied that an individual is in need in any (or all) of these matters, they are to make arrangements that are appropriate to his or her case. The task of assessment should be undertaken as a normal part of the authority's social work service, ie, it should be an occasion for considering all relevant needs and not merely those to which the Section refers; and a judgment whether these needs are of prior importance should be drawn from a complete and not a partial picture of the situation. Criteria of need are matters for the authorities to determine in the light of resources.

\*    \*    \*    \*    \*

### (2) CIRCULAR NO (87)6—DISABLED PERSONS (SERVICES, CONSULTATION AND REPRESENTATION) ACT 1986— IMPLEMENTATION OF SECTIONS 4, 8(1), 9 AND 10

**Section 4**

### Services under section 2 of the Chronically Sick and Disabled Persons Act 1970, duty to consider needs of disabled persons

2   Section 2(1) of the CSDP Act places a duty on local authorities to 'make arrangements' for all or any of specified matters (practical assistance in the home, recreational facilities, holidays, telephones etc) in the case of any disabled person who is ordinarily resident in their area where they are satisfied that this is necessary in order to meet the needs of that person.

3   However, Section 2(1) does not make it explicit whether a local authority has a duty to determine the needs of a disabled person. It was suggested in the course of debates in Parliament on the Disabled Persons (Services, Consultation and Representation) Bill that as the duty to 'make arrangements' could be interpreted as applying only after the local authority are satisfied that such arrangements are necessary in order to meet particular needs, local authorities arrangements might refuse to come to a view as to what are those needs as a means of avoiding the obligation to make arrangements. It has never been the Government's view that subsection 2(1) should be interpreted in that way, and it is clear that this is shared by the vast majority of local authorities. However, it was agreed that the matter should be put beyond doubt.

4    Section 4 of the 1986 Act accordingly makes it clear that local authorities have a duty to decide whether the needs of a disabled person call for the provision of services under Section 2 of the 1970 Act, if they are requested to do so by a disabled person (Section 4(*a*)) or by anyone who provides care for him or her (Section 4(*c*)) in the circumstances mentioned in Section 8 of the 1986 Act.

## Section 8(1): Duty of the local authority to take into account the ability of the carer

5    Section 8(1) has effect where a disabled person is living at home, and is receiving a substantial amount of care on a regular basis from another person (other than a person employed to provide such care by any body by virtue of its statutory functions). In these circumstances, where it falls to a local authority to decide whether the disabled person's needs call for the provision of them of any services under the 'welfare enactments' (defined in Section 16 of the 1986 Act as Part III of the National Assistance Act 1948, section 2 of the CSDP Act 1970 or Schedule 8 to the National Health Services Act 1977), the authority is required in deciding that question, to have regard to the ability of the 'carer' to continue to provide such care on a regular basis.

6    Although the section places no specific requirement on the local authority to provide services or support for the carer, authorities will no doubt continue as part of normal good practice to have regard to the possible need for such services and to the desirability of enabling the disabled person to continue living at home for as long as possible if this is what he or she wishes to do.

## Section 9: Information about services

7    Section 1(2)(*b*) of the 1970 CSDP Act requires local social services authorities to ensure that a disabled person who uses any welfare services is informed of any other of these services considered by the authority to be relevant to his needs. Section 9 of the 1986 Act extends the provision of the 1970 Act to require authorities to provide information about other services provided by the same authority and about services provided by other organisations which it considers relevant to that person's needs, if the particulars are in the local authority's possession.

## (3)    HSG(92)42—HEALTH SERVICES FOR PEOPLE WITH LEARNING DISABILITIES (MENTAL HANDICAP)

### Executive summary

People with learning disabilities (mental handicap) have the same rights of access to NHS services as everyone else but they may require assistance to use the services. Special care must be taken to ensure that they are not denied health care because of their disability, and that steps are taken to ensure that any barriers to access are minimized. Purchasing authorities should include in their contracts specific provision to enable people with learning disabilities to obtain NHS health care services and to ensure, where necessary, that special provision is made where the health care needs of people with learning disabilities cannot be met through the ordinary range of services.

## Action

Purchasers should:

- ensure that service specifications for health care include appropriate provision for meeting the needs and promoting the health and wellbeing of people with learning disabilities;
- use contracts with provider units to ensure that wherever possible people with learning disabilities are enabled to use ordinary health services;
- consider contracting for additional services for people with learning disabilities, including:
  i.   alternatives to the ordinary services
  ii.  specialist assessment and treatment services
- wherever possible contract to provide continuity of care and contact; taking into consideration the preference of the patient and his carers.

Additionally DHAs should:

- consider contracting for residential and respite care (annex A).
- ensure that during the transition to community-based services, the improvement in the quality of care in specialist mental handicap hospitals at least matches general improvements in health provision.

Family Health Services Authorities should:

- ensure that people with learning disabilities have access to general medical and dental practitioner services and, in collaboration with District Health Authorities, access to the primary health care team and other community health services.

*   *   *   *   *

## Contracts for additional health services

Purchasers should also consider contracting for services to meet the health needs of people with learning disabilities that cannot be met through contracts for the ordinary range of services. Consideration should be given to the following possibilities:

### Alternatives to the ordinary services

- In some cases it may prove impossible for the general health needs of people with learning disabilities to be met by ordinary NHS services. For example, where local NHS dental practitioners are unable to treat patients with severe learning disabilities, district health and family health services authorities should arrange alternative services as described in circular HC (89) 2.

### Specialist mental health provision

- Some people with learning disabilities need treatment for psychiatric illness or severe behaviour disturbance. If it is not possible adequately to meet these patients' needs within the general psychiatric services, specialist assessment and treatment services will be needed in hospital or community settings.

### NHS residential care

- The large majority of people with learning disabilities not living with their families can be cared for in residential accommodation arranged through the relevant social services authority. There are, however, likely to be a small number of people with severe or profound learning disabilities and physical, sensory or psychiatric conditions who need long term residential care in a health setting. Where this seems to be the case a multi-professional assessment and consultation with parents or carers are necessary to determine whether the services they need can only be provided by the NHS or whether other alternatives would be more appropriate and cost effective. Similarly, where such people are ordinarily cared for by their families, there may be a need for some short term respite care arrangements to be provided by the NHS.

DHA and FHSA contracts for service provision should include a requirement on providers to inform general practitioners and other members of the primary health care team what services are available in their locality.

\*   \*   \*   \*   \*

### NHS responsibilities to local authorities

Local authorities will look to health authorities to secure through their contracts the services of professional staff, including psychiatrists, mental handicap nurses, psychologists and therapists, to help assess the needs of individuals with learning disabilities and to provide health services for them. Health services professional staff will also need to be made available to provide training, advice and support to local authority staff.

Health authorities will also need to contribute to the preparation of Community Care Plans and consider with local authorities how resources can jointly best be used to provide care. FHSAs will also need to ensure that the views of all GPs and other members of the primary health care team are properly reflected in these considerations. Additionally GP fundholders will need to be aware of the overall approach to and of the principles underlying Community Care Plans in order that they can take these into account when contracting for health care.

## (4)   CIRCULAR LAC(92)15—SOCIAL CARE FOR ADULTS WITH LEARNING DISABILITIES (MENTAL HANDICAP)

### Summary

This circular gives specific guidance to local authorities on planning services for adults with learning disabilities (mental handicap). It complements and reinforces the general guidance on developing community care set out in 'Community Care— the Next Decade and Beyond'. Guidance on services for children with learning disabilities is contained in 'Children with Disabilities: Volume 6 of the Children Act series of guidance and regulations'. Guidance on the role of the NHS in providing services for this client group is contained in HSG(92)42.

### Action

Local authorities should take account of the guidance in this circular when preparing their community care plans and purchasing specifications, and when designing and developing care management and quality assurance arrangements for adults with learning disabilities.

### Context

1   Over the years since the 1971 White Paper 'Better Services for the Mentally Handicapped', considerable experience has been developed in providing new forms

of home care, day services and accommodation in the community including residential services for people with learning disabilities. There has also been increasing experience of managing the transition from one form of service to another (especially resettling people from long-term hospital care to locally based, smaller scale forms of care). This experience has confirmed that, with appropriate support and opportunities, people with learning disabilities are capable of considerable personal development and of making a positive contribution to society. Few, if any, need to live in hospitals.

2   Over the last twenty years, local authority social services departments have increasingly been seen as the main statutory agency for planning and arranging services, not only for people with mild or moderate learning disabilities but also for those with severe or profound learning disabilities, including some with multiple disabilities or behaviour disturbance. The Government believes this trend is right, and as the changes resulting from the National Health Services and Community Care Act come into force, local authorities will have a clear statutory responsibility for:

- assessing and within available resources, making arrangements for meeting the social needs of people with learning disabilities within a mixed economy of care.
- bringing apparent housing and health care needs to the attention of the appropriate authorities when consulting with them about the local community care plans.

3   Carers and user groups and providers in the independent sector should be consulted. There is also a clear need to plan services in close collaboration with local education authorities, the Further Education Funding Council, the Employment Service, Training and Enterprise Councils, leisure/recreation departments and general community services.

4   Service planning should be responsive to the findings of assessments and other aspects of care management which should inform future decisions about services including new forms of provision.

*   *   *   *   *

## Service principles

8   Authorities should be guided by the general approach to community care set out in the White Paper 'Caring for People' (Cm 849), the subsequent policy guidance 'Community Care in the Next Decade and Beyond', and 'Care Management and Assessment' and by the guidance more specific to the needs of people with learning disabilities set out in this circular.

### Services should be planned on an individual basis

9   In the past people with learning disabilities have often not been treated as individuals with very personal needs and preferences, but rather have been offered predetermined sets of services (and denied others) on the basis of stereotypical notions of what people with learning disabilities need. The individuality of people with learning disabilities should be recognised and the aim in future should be to arrange services on an increasingly *individual* basis, taking account of age, needs, degree of disability, the personal preferences of the individual and his or her parents or carers, culture, race and gender. Where necessary people should be helped to express their views and preferences either through the development of self-advocacy skills or through an independent advocate. Sometimes people with learning disabilities or

their carers will be dissatisfied with the services provided or offered. Where the service is provided by the local authority the complaint should be dealt with under the complaints procedures described in Chapter 6 of 'Community Care—the next Decade and Beyond'. It will be important to consider what support a complainant with learning disabilities may need in pursuing their complaint about local authority services. Similarly local authorities will wish to consider how they can, where necessary, support individuals and their carers in expressing their anxieties and complaints about services provided by other agencies.

### The contribution of parents and carers and resolving conflicts

10   Parents and carers should be fully involved in decisions about the services to be arranged for the individual disabled person as they are usually best placed to know his/her needs and preferences. Sometimes there will be differences of view between people with learning disabilities and their parents/carers over which services are most appropriate. Conciliation and counselling should be offered in such situations, but in general the views of the person with learning disabilities should be respected. There may also be differences of view between parents and professional staff. Every effort should be made to resolve these. Where this cannot be done it is open to the parent to invoke the complaints procedure and seek a formal review.

### Continuity of service provision

11   Many people with severe or profound learning disabilities will need support throughout their lives, though the nature of that support needs regular appraisal so that changing circumstances and needs can be identified and responded to. Parents and carers are often understandably anxious about the continuity of service provision, particularly continuity of caring and service provision as they become aged and infirm, and after their own deaths. Although attitudes are changing some parents and carers are concerned about the closure of the traditional mental handicap hospitals precisely because such hospitals seem to offer more assurance about continuity of caring and support than community based services. Whilst examples of progress in developing community care will help to alleviate these anxieties authorities should recognise these entirely legitimate concerns and aim to give assurance that the essential needs of disabled people, including access to specialist health care, will be met on a life-long basis.

## Planning to meet social care needs

12   The purchasing, provision and commissioning of social care should be seen as an active and responsive process that builds where possible on the expressed wishes and preferences of individuals, recognising their strengths and aiming to meet their needs. Skills in those care management issues specific to people with learning disabilities will need to be developed. Social care refers essentially to the person-to-person support that may be needed in any or all of the following:
- arranging accommodation that ensures privacy, personal space and an appropriate level of personal security thus helping to make it into a home;
- providing personal support for daily living in relation to basic activities of life such as eating, dressing and washing;
- assisting the development of friendships and social relationships;
- teaching and supporting socially competent behaviour;
- creating opportunities for the development of personal and social skills and enhancing and maintaining competencies.

- enabling the use of everyday education, leisure and other facilities in the community;
- helping develop occupational skills, finding employment and helping to support the individual in work;
- facilitating access to health care and other statutory services and entitlements;
- supporting the individual in identifying and expressing his/her own views and choices;
- counselling to enable the individual with learning disability or his family/carers to make best use of available services;
- providing social work help and support to enable individuals and families to deal with emotional and practical stresses;
- arranging appropriate services for the increasing number of older people with learning disabilities including those with additional psychiatric problems.

13  To meet this diverse range of needs, local authorities will need to adopt a co-ordinated approach, involving all relevant departments, agencies, providers and professional inputs (including those of NHS staff who will continue to provide their essential skills), to plan and arrange a wide range of services, where appropriate by contracting them from the voluntary and private sectors. Services should be developed in accordance with the principles referred to in paragraphs 8-11. The following paragraphs and the annex offer specific guidance on planning and assessing home care, day and residential services.

## Home care and support services

14  **Home care and support services have five main elements:**
  (i)  providing reliable help with direct, physical and personal care, and day to day living activities;
  (ii)  teaching skills in their own or family homes to increase the independence of people with learning disabilities. It will also be necessary to extend this teaching into people's places of work, learning or daily occupation, on public transport and in various community settings;
  (iii)  offering 'sitting services' on a routine basis, in and out of office hours and at times of stress and pressing need;
  (iv)  providing information about services and benefits available to people with learning disabilities and their families or carers.
  (v)  providing specialist assessment and advice to carers in conjunction with the health provider unit, in order to help carers cope with behaviour disturbance, mental health problems and profound multiple disabilities.

## Day services

\* \* \* \* \*

18  Local authorities should plan to shift away from services based on attendance at the traditional adult training centre, towards an approach to day services based on individual assessment and programmes, in which skill learning and vocational preparation are prominent. The aim should be to move towards a personally planned programme of day activities—social, educational, vocational and leisure—which make use of ordinary community facilities wherever practicable.

19   There should be a smooth transition between education and social services and social service departments should identify the need for future services before individuals leave school. It is of particular importance that day opportunities should enable the gains of people's school years to continue to be maintained to enable them to achieve even greater independence. They should be planned to build on the programmes that have been provided by local education authorities with input from health authorities during the school years, to try to meet the expectations of individuals and their families.

* * * * *

22   In planning day services, social services departments will need to work closely a) with the education service, particularly in relation to making provision for those leaving full time education as required by the provisions of the Disabled Persons (Services, Consultation and Representation) Act 1986 (as amended by the Further and Higher Education Act 1992) and the Education Act 1981, b) with health authorities and health provider units, and c) with those concerned to provide employment opportunities.

* * * * *

**Accommodation and residential care**

25   Most adults with severe or profound learning disabilities are likely to need to live other than in their family homes at some point. In considering residential needs local authorities will need regularly to assess and review each individual and the capacity and willingness of his or her family and carers to continue to support the individual and, insofar as resources allow, plan a package of services aimed to ensure that he or she receives any supporting services needed in the setting which offers most scope for individual development and well-being.

26   The need is to continue to move towards arrangements in which people with learning disabilities are treated as individuals, in circumstances where they are supported by people respectful of them as individual human beings and able, in a continuing and stable relationship, to understand their needs and respond sensitively and flexibly. This means, in particular, reappraising the form of housing and support preferred by individuals at different stages in their lives. The ability to arrange an appropriate, individually-based service depends largely, though not exclusively, on the number, type, attitude and training of the staff providing support. This may prove very difficult to achieve in settings accommodating large numbers, as large institutions can have their own, negative effects which are independent of the initial disabilities of those being cared for.

27   Authorities will need to consider what resources are available for developing services, and how these are best used to continue to make progress towards a service based around individuals. In the Government's view there is a wide range of acceptable living arrangements, including sharing with non-disabled people, ordinary housing, hostels, homes and residential communities. All need to be outward looking, closely associated with the general community, and limited in size so that problems of institutionalisation on a large scale are avoided. The key issue to be faced locally in planning commissioning and purchasing services is what range of housing and support services can provide greatest scope in moving towards an increasingly individually-based service able to meet the needs of people as outlined in paragraph 12, while being realistic in terms of resources.

*Short-term care*

28 When considering the extent and nature of long-term housing arrangements to be provided, authorities should also consider the need for short-term care accommodation. The Department estimates that more than half of all adults with severe or profound learning disabilities live with their parents or other informal carers. One of the services that is important to people with learning disabilities and upon which many parents and carers rely is short-term care, to provide a break from caring when family circumstances require it. Short-term care can also assist in helping a person with learning disabilities make the transition from life with his or her family to living more independently. Finally, short-term care can offer extra opportunities and experience for people with learning disabilities living in various kinds of long-term residential accommodation.

29 Authorities should look imaginatively at developing forms of short-term care sensitive to the needs both of people with learning disabilities and their carers. In particular the development of short-term care through planned short-term placements with 'link' families, has often provided both practicable and valued, and should be considered. Another important option is providing short-term care in the person's own home, by arranging to substitute for parents or carers, for a few hours or for a longer period.

**Resources**

30 Services for people with learning disabilities provided or arranged by local authority social services departments have increased substantially. Nationally, since 1979 identifiable expenditure on such services has increased every year in real terms, and the Government expects that this will continue. The pace at which services can develop in particular localities is, however, a matter for local determination in the light of assessment of need, available resources and competing pressure on services.

31 In preparing their Community Care Plans local authorities will need to consider with health authorities how resources can jointly be best used to provide care. Full use should be made of the arrangements for joint finance and dowry payments. It may also involve health authorities supporting personal social services and housing expenditure out of their main allocation using the other powers available under Section 28A of the NHS Act 1977. Guidance on joint finance and other payment arrangements between district health authorities and local authorities under Section 28A of the NHS Act 1977 will be issued shortly.

32 While setting out the direction for future service developments, the preparation of community care plans and target setting, this circular places no specific new requirements on local authorities.

## Annex

### The Development of Day Services
### for
### People with Learning Disabilities

*Introduction*

1 This document sets out the direction in which the Government believes local authorities should aim to develop day services for people with learning disabilities

(mental handicap), and gives guidance on some of the issues which will need consideration. It supersedes all previous guidance on day services.

## The individual programme approach to day services

2  It is widely recognised that day services play an essential role in the range of services needed by people with learning disabilities. Historically, most local authority provision has been made through adult training centres. As resources allow, the Government looks to local authorities to develop existing provision, following the principles set out in the general guidance on community care and those set out in paragraphs 8–11 of LAC(92)15. This means that, increasingly, day services should:

— flow from an *assessment* of the needs of each person with learning disabilities;

— take the form of a *programme* of activities specifically geared to meet an individual's needs;

— involve regular *review* and amendment of the programme in the light of experience and changing needs over time.

## Assessment

3  The bed rock of services should be a skilled assessed, and regular re-assessment, of the individual person with learning disabilities, to cover strengths and needs; abilities and potential; physical, sensory and health considerations; particular needs due to race and gender, and the wishes of the individual and his/her family or carer. This will not involve simply administering tests or schedules, but careful observation, discussion and sharing perceptions between staff of all disciplines, family and the individual. Such assessments must of course be recorded so that the information is available both for use in devising a programme and for later cross reference. As a part of the assessment process clear goals should be established and, where necessary, priorities set.

## Programmes

4  The programme produced for any individual should consist of a set of activities providing experiences and/or training opportunities which link coherently to support and reinforce the goals identified in the assessment. Activities may be provided within the adult training centre but increasingly, centres may make use of either general or specially designed activities arranged elsewhere.

## Reviews

5  Regular review is important in any needs-led provision. It is only by reviewing an individual's progress, and judging the effectiveness of the programme in meeting his or her changing needs, that responsible decisions can be taken about the adequacy of current activities. It is important that reviews are carried out regularly and fully recorded. They should involve the user, his/her family and other relevant staff and agencies. This process enables monitoring not only of the progress of the individual but of particular elements of service delivery in terms of both effectiveness and continued value for the individual and the service as a whole.

## Issues for consideration

6  The report of the national inspection of day services by the Social Services Inspectorate, published as 'Individuals, Programmes and Plans' identified certain

issues which service purchasers and providers will wish to take account of in developing the service.

### Policy and planning

7    Day services need to be considered as an element in individual programmes for people with learning disabilities. They should be planned as an integral part of the overall set of social care services on the basis of an adequate information base about the number of such people and their needs. In developing such a base social services departments should liaise with the education services and district health authorities and consider the needs of potential users outside the area eg in residential schools. The period of transition between residential or day school and adult services is particularly important.

8    The aim should be to build on the existing pattern of services in the light of this developing picture of the needs of people with learning disabilities in the area. Information on general service requirements obtained from individual reviews should be fed back into the preparation of community care plans.

### Form of service

9    Access to and use of ordinary facilities is an essential aspect of living in the community; and in the area of activities broadly described as day services, some use of ordinary facilities is likely to be appropriate. Social Services departments will wish to consider various options for the provision and purchase of elements of service. It may, for example, sometimes be appropriate to support a person with learning disabilities in the use of ordinary services, for example, by arranging for a friend or volunteer to accompany the person when s/he attends an adult education class. Alternatively, it may be sometimes more effective to provide a special service within ordinary facilities, for example, a class for people with learning disabilities within a college of further education, offering special teaching but seeking to afford opportunities to use ordinary college facilities and mix with fellow students. Third, it may sometimes be in the best interests of the service user to receive a service within a day centre for people with learning disabilities. Some people can gain from off the job training to develop the personal and other skills needed whilst others may benefit more from training in the work place. Decisions will rest both on individual need and local circumstances.

### Personal and social development

10    Like everyone else, people with learning disabilities need a range of social skills to be able to contribute to a life in the community and relate to other people. They will often need appropriate opportunities and teaching to gain these skills, improve their social competence and enhance their ability to communicate and relate to other people. This help can be given both directly and indirectly. Directly, it involves the structured teaching of new skills and appropriate forms of behaviour. Indirectly, it can be acquired as an element within any day activity even when the primary aim of that activity is vocational, recreational or educational.

11    Social education will need to be concerned with social and personal relationships. People with learning disabilities have the same range of emotional, friendship and companionship needs as other people, but may need help and support in making relationships with other people with learning disabilities, and with their non-handicapped peers. 'One to One', funded by this Department, have produced an interesting resource pack to help in establishing schemes to encourage people with learning disabilities to develop their network of friendships.

12   The sexuality of people with learning disabilities is an issue which needs to be openly addressed by users, carers and staff, clear guidelines should be prepared and appropriate education provided. The aim should be to enable people with learning disabilities to understand and come to terms with their sexuality and be helped to express their needs and feelings in ways which are acceptable to themselves as well as society. To enable them to do this will require guidance, education and sensitive support. This knowledge will help in development towards maturity and assist possibly vulnerable individuals to protect themselves against the risk of exploitation and the threat of problems such as sexual abuse, unplanned pregnancy or exposure to Aids.

*Leisure, sport and recreation*

13   Leisure pursuits, either individual or group, will serve many of the same purposes for people with learning disabilities, in terms of personal satisfaction, relaxation and sense of achievement as they do for anyone else. But involvement in sports and leisure activities can meet more specific purposes such as community integration, educational experience and social development and should be considered as part of an individual programme. Recreational activities such as music, art, dance and drama can also be part of a therapeutic programme. Such programmes aim to use the recreational activity to overcome communication difficulties by enabling a person to find expression through an artistic medium. If an activity is intended to serve a distinct therapeutic need rather than simply to provide recreation, it will require input from specialists, eg therapists.

14   Staff will need to consider, particularly in relation to more physically demanding sport or recreation, the question of risk. People with learning disabilities should, of course, be allowed to take reasonable risks in their recreational and sporting activities. Some strenuous forms of sporting activity will not, however, be suitable for people who have certain physical disabilities or where specific medical conditions such as epilepsy are present. Staff will need to be aware of any circumstance that prevents people from engaging in these, for example, those with Down's Syndrome who have Atlanto-Axial Instability. (Advice is available in the Chief Medical Officer's letter of the 28 May 1986, CMO 86/9.) Full discussions should take place with the individual and his carers in the context of the assessment and include appropriate advice from health professionals.

*Education*

15   People with learning disabilities have, since the transfer of the junior training centres in 1971 benefited from the resources of the education services. Experience has shown that, given appropriate services and a long term teaching input, many are able to achieve a much higher level of competence in educational work, including numeracy and literacy, than was previously considered possible. It is vital that gains made in the education service are built on at the time of transition to adulthood, which is believed to be a period when further development of these achievements and progress from them are of particular importance. Careful arrangements must be made for transition between education and social services provision when pupils leave school and consideration given to their need for continuing educational input.

16   According to individual need, continuing educational input may be provided in a number of ways; by attendance at a further education college or adult education institute, by secondment into day services of education tutors, or by provision of the necessary educational input by the local authority day services staff.

Decisions on the most appropriate provision will be a matter for joint discussion between service users, social services and education departments.

17 Additionally there is a wide range of further education classes for adults which serve the general public. In many cases, day centre staff have accessed a number of these for service users, often with great success. Careful preparation and support of students with learning disabilities themselves and those teaching staff without prior experience of them are important if such opportunities are to be taken successfully.

18 The increasing use of computers and the subsequent development of skills in Information Technology in both schools and day services has led to significant progress. Day services should continue to build on this.

*Involvement in employment*

19 The opportunity for involvement in employment can have many benefits for people with learning disabilities. First, participation in a paid job will help them to achieve greater social independence and self-assurance. If they go out to work and pay their own way in the world, they are likely to see themselves as more valued members of the community making a contribution to that community. Involvement in employment can also help with integration into society by enabling wider contact and a new pattern of social skills. Finally, it is important that the country makes best use of the skills and potential contribution from all its citizens. Whilst gains may be most obvious in the case of full-time paid employment many of them will be obtainable from participation in other employment related activities.

20 It should not be assumed that 'self-reliance' in terms of employment is matched by independence in respect of people's living circumstances. Because there are non-vocational areas of people's lives which are essential to employment—getting up on time, being clean, wearing appropriate clothes, handling money to buy lunch, catching a bus etc—few people with learning disabilities who secure and hold a job do so without reliable assistance from others in the non-vocational areas of their lives.

21 Ideas about the possibility of employment for people with learning disabilities in open settings have changed considerably in recent years. There is now widespread acceptance of the fact that many people previously thought incapable of work can do so provided that the necessary training and support is made available particularly in the early stages of employment. There is a growing body of useful experience both within this country and abroad. People with learning disabilities are increasingly working in open employment, in sheltered workshops and in a range of special supported employment schemes. Opportunities now cover many jobs and industries.

22 Providers and purchasers of day services have an important role to play in training people for employment, by equipping them with both general and social skills. The individual programme plan approach should be used in relation to work activities, which should be clearly related to the assessment of individual needs and potential for further development. In this way someone who might potentially be a candidate for open or sheltered employment could receive training in such areas as interpersonal skills, development of co-ordination, development of appropriate work habits and attitudes, co-operation with fellow workers, response to authority, assumption of responsibility and ability to follow through tasks and adapt to difficult situations, all of which will enable a job, once found, to be satisfactory maintained.

\* \* \* \* \*

*Special needs*

25    In assessing the requirement for day service facilities, account must be taken of those users who have additional needs. These will include people who have profound learning disabilities or who have other disabilities which may preclude them from benefiting from the normal range of day activities provided for other people within or outside a day centre. The number of such people is increasing, as more people with more profound learning disabilities now survive longer and the reduction in hospital admissions has led to more people being cared for in the community.

26    To meet the requirements of this group of users special needs facilities (units) have been developed, with most places being situated within existing day centres. The special needs unit should not been seen simply as a place where people with profound learning disabilities receive passive care. The unit should be a specialised resource centre, offering intensive treatment and support. It could serve as a base for such users from which they could be exposed to increasingly demanding tasks and experience elsewhere. The time spent in the special needs unit should therefore be varied and rewarding, provide stimulus and challenge, and aim at helping the user to develop his or her maximum potential and independence.

27    An individual assessment of a user's needs, followed by the drawing up of a recorded programme of action, is an essential basis for establishing the pattern of activities in a special care unit. The move towards a new pattern of day services for people with learning disabilities, and the changing role of the ATC, will have obvious implications for those within the special care group. The same principles that apply to day services provision for all other people with learning disabilities should apply equally to those with profound disabilities. These require that a person's needs for day services are assessed on an individual basis and that an individual programme plan is developed, taking account of the person's own preferences in so far as these can be ascertained, and those of carers.

\*    \*    \*    \*    \*

29    The involvement of profoundly disabled people in community day services raises the question of transport arrangements. Here, as with the arrangements for the user to go to and from the special care unit, the aim should be to keep travelling time to a minimum.

30    There will be a need for the ATC/special care unit staff—as well as other day services staff—to establish contact with a wide variety of other agencies and professionals to ensure that the necessary facilities are available to all people within the special care group. Profoundly disabled people may have extra special needs, and may require additional input either directly or as advice to staff (eg from a community mental handicap nurse or therapist on feeding techniques). It is important that authorities identify the particular contribution required from the staff of other agencies such as district health authorities and seek to negotiate its provision.

\*    \*    \*    \*    \*

*Links with families*

32    The most important lifelong stable relationship for many people with learning disabilities is the relationship with their families and it is important that this should be maintained. Perhaps 70% of people using day services live with their families, who quite properly expect to have a significant involvement in the user's daily life and will have a particular wealth of knowledge and information about the user.

General policy guidance has stressed the importance of the proper involvement of families when assessing the needs of people for social care, and this applies in relation to day services. In addition, many carers will come to value the day or resource centre as a focal point and as a source of advice, support and respite. There will be an expectation that such support should be available if required, not only for the present centre users but also those who for a range of reasons, for example open employment, transfer to full-time education are now no longer attending. Wherever practicable, provision to meet these demands should be built into staffing establishment. Consideration should be given in the assessment process to whether the necessary help and support can most appropriately be provided by centre staff or other professionals, for instance from a Community Team, involved with the user and his or her family.

\* \* \* \* \*

*Advocacy*

37. The values of choice, self-expression, and achievement of maximum independence have been recognised as of increasing importance for people with learning disabilities. Promoting individual choice is a central message of 'Caring for People' for all client groups. This SSI inspection reported that there is already much encouraging practice on developing advocacy skills from which to learn. Underpinning all activities will be a move towards maximum achievable independence. Work on self-advocacy skills will be a central part of this. People should be supported and helped to speak for themselves and make realistic choices. More able users will be able to exercise and express choice on many matters, but for the most disabled choice will only be possible in limited areas. Nevertheless their views and wishes should be sought, regarded as important, and taken fully into account in the design of the programme. Approaching such as Citizen Advocacy may help in this process.

\* \* \* \* \*

## (5) CIRCULAR LAC(93)2—ALCOHOL AND DRUG SERVICES WITHIN COMMUNITY CARE

### Summary

This circular gives guidance to local authorities (LAs) on the provision within community care of services for adults who misuse alcohol and/or drugs, after the coming into force of Sections 42-50 of the National Health Service and Community Care Act 1990. All these Sections will be in force after 12 April 1993. This circular is not intended as Secretary of State's Directions under Section 47(4) of the National Health Service and Community Care Act 1990.

The statutory basis for local authority assessment of need, provision of services and placement in residential care of people under 18 who misuse alcohol and drugs rests with the Children Act 1989 and associated guidance and Regulations.

### Action

LAs should plan for continuity of services for alcohol and drug misusers under the new community care arrangements, and, as a priority they should ensure that:
— community care plans properly reflect the needs of these user groups;

— the special circumstances of these people are recognised and reflected in appropriate procedures for assessment and care management.

## Context

1   The Government attaches a high priority to tackling the problems associated with the misuse of alcohol and drugs, and expects LAs to attach a high priority to alcohol and drug misusers within community care. Alcohol and drug misuse is a problem both for individuals and for the public health. The White Paper 'The Health of the Nation' indicates that Government, health authorities, local authorities and others need to continue the development of a comprehensive range of services to meet the needs of alcohol and drug misusers.

*   *   *   *   *

## Local authority responsibilities

4   From April 1993, by virtue of the NHS and Community Care Act 1990, LAs' responsibilities for arranging and funding the social care of alcohol and drug misusers will be:
— assessing the needs of the local population for alcohol and drug services;
— including services for alcohol and drug misusers in their community care plans;
— assessing the social care needs of individual alcohol and drug misusers;
— arranging appropriate packages of care, which may include a range of options.
5   Alcohol and drug misusers who are in independent residential care or nursing homes on 31 March 1993 will generally have preserved rights to higher levels of Income Support. LAs will be responsible from April 1993 for assessing needs and making appropriate provision in accordance with the community care arrangements.
6   People who enter independent homes from 1 April 1993 will be eligible to claim ordinary Income Support, including premiums, and a residential allowance. The LA will take account of these payments when assessing the person's ability to contribute to the cost of their care. LAs will be responsible for arranging and funding the social care costs of alcohol and drug misusers with assistance from resources provided by the Special Transitional Grant.

## Health authority responsibilities

7   Health authority responsibilities for funding health care from general allocations and earmarked funding remain unaffected by the new community care arrangements. Treatment may take place in residential or non-residential settings and the new community care arrangements do not affect health authorities' responsibilities for funding the healthcare element of any alcohol and drug service. LAs will need to consider and draw up clear agreements with health authorities covering arrangements for funding treatment and rehabilitation services for people with alcohol and/or drug problems.

## Community care plans

8   LAs' community care plans should address the needs of the local population for alcohol and drug services, and show the local arrangements for delivery of

community care. A strategy for service provision will need to take account of the patterns and prevalence of alcohol and drug misuse within an area, and LAs will need to bear in mind that many alcohol and drug misusers for whom they are responsible will present for services outside their area.

9   Service provision should be a response to the needs of the total population for which the LA has responsibility. This will include people who live within the area but attend services elsewhere, and people who are staying elsewhere but for whom the LA remain responsible. When developing their plans LAs should consult and collaborate with statutory bodies such as health authorities and the Probation Service and with specialist service providers.

*   *   *   *   *

### Special circumstances of alcohol and drug misusers

12   Addressing the needs of people with alcohol and drug problems will present a particular challenge to LAs. The aim must be to respond effectively and to offer a programme of care that will help the misuser make positive changes in his or her life. LAs will need to bear in mind that people who misuse alcohol and drugs may:

— present to LAs with problems other than alcohol and/or drug misuse. LAs will need to ensure that the possibility of alcohol and drug misuse is covered in assessment procedures.

— have particularly complex needs including urgent workplace or family crises or difficulties with childcare, which may not have been revealed to LA services.

— move between areas frequently, and a significant proportion will have no settled residence or be living away from their area of ordinary residence;

— self-refer to agencies which are not in their home area, both because of their transient lifestyle and for therapeutic reasons, and many will need urgent help;

— avoid contact with statutory services; drug misusers in particular may be reluctant to become involved with statutory agencies because of the illegal nature of their drug-related activities;

— need to be provided with services several times before they succeed in controlling their alcohol or drug misuse;

— require residential treatment and rehabilitation as a positive treatment choice;

— sometimes behave unpredictably and may not fit easily into assessment and care management systems designed to meet the needs of other client groups.

13   People with serious and urgent alcohol and/or drugs problems are likely to need a rapid response because of crises and to capture fluctuating motivation. Serious deterioration which may carry social, legal and care implications may ensue if there is delay before assessment or if assessments procedures are prolonged.

### Eligibility for assessment

14   LAs should ensure that any criteria they may develop governing eligibility for assessment are sensitive to the circumstances of alcohol and drug misusers. As with all other user groups, the LA should have criteria for determining the level of assessment that is appropriate to the severity or complexity of the need. LAs should ensure that:

— arrangements have been agreed with all the agencies in their area to which misusers are likely to present for help, which will enable those agencies to initiate assessment procedures where in their view they are indicated;

— arrangements are in place to facilitate the assessment of a person by another authority where that person is ordinarily resident in that other authority's area, for example by agreeing with another LA to undertake an assessment on that authority's behalf;

— individuals who are of no settled residence are not excluded from assessment by means of eligibility criteria which require a duration of residence.

The Department proposes to issue guidance to LAs in 1993 about the resolution of disputes and the procedures to be adopted in the last resort where disputes cannot be resolved between the authorities concerned. Disputes about ordinary residence should not prevent people receiving the care they need.

## Adapting assessment to the special needs of alcohol and drug misusers

15   LAs will need to ensure that their assessment systems take full account of the different ways in which alcohol and drug misusers present for services, their different characteristics and their particular needs;

— standard LA assessment procedures and documentation should include consideration of substance misuse

— LA staff will need to be able to identify the indications of substance misuse so that specialist agencies can be involved where appropriate.

## Rapid assessment procedures ('fast-track' assessment)

16   There are a range of organisations and professionals who deal frequently with alcohol and drug misusers. A great many of the services, including virtually all residential services, are provided by the independent sector. There is, therefore, within the independent sector, a substantial reservoir of experienced professionals with skills to undertake assessment in this field. LAs should consider involving independent sector agencies in the assessment process. Practice guidance issued by the Department of Health Social Services Inspectorate emphasises the importance of training to equip those people within LAs who undertake assessment with the necessary knowledge and skills. Policy guidance issued by the Department 'Community Care in the Next Decade and Beyond' states that where a specialist service—for example a drug and alcohol service—is provided by an independent agency under arrangements with a social services department, it will be possible to include assessment of needs in relation to such services in contract arrangements. In these circumstances LAs will need to ensure that the specialist agency is aware of other potential needs for which LAs have a responsibility.

17   Residential placements should not normally take place without a comprehensive needs assessment. Where assessment is contracted to an independent specialist agency, decisions to commit resources and ultimate responsibility for the assessment remains with the LA.

18   Because many alcohol and drug misusers present or are referred to services outside their area of ordinary residence LAs are encouraged to work together to identify systems so that they can feel confident about committing resources on the basis of an assessment undertaken in another LA. This may be facilitated by the development of standard and agreed assessment procedures and forms and networks of named responsible officers within LAs.

19   The Department is encouraging local authority associations to work with the independent sector to establish rapid assessment procedures for alcohol and drug misusers and good practice guidance in out of area referrals which they can commend to local authorities.

20   Individual LAs and independent service providers should, together, ensure that rapid assessment procedures meet the needs of alcohol and drug misusers. In order to do so LAs and providers may want to determine the pattern of referrals of their residents/clients in order to establish contact and set up appropriate arrangements where regular flows exist. LAs and independent sector service providers will together wish to have regard to the Department's study examining good practice in care management and assessment for alcohol and drug misusers which will be available to local authorities shortly.

## Emergency action

21   LAs need to be aware that alcohol and drug misusers may sometimes be in such urgent need that residential care will need to be provided immediately. 'The Care Management and Assessment' practice guidance issued by the Department of Health covers the arrangements for urgent admission to both residential and nursing home care.

22   LAs may contract with a provider to offer an emergency direct access service for people in urgent need, with assessment and a decision about longer term treatment following as soon as practicable. LAs may wish to contract with a voluntary organisation to provide direct access to residential care without assessment in these circumstances. In such cases of urgent need the area of ordinary residence of the person should not be a consideration (National Assistance Act 1948 Section 24(3)).

## Out of area referrals

23   Because of the transient lifestyles of a significant proportion of alcohol and drug misusers LAs will be involved in negotiations about area of ordinary residence for people with alcohol and drug misuse problems to a greater extent than for others. Where people are ordinarily resident in the area of the LA undertaking the assessment, there may be a therapeutic benefit in referring people to a residential service away from the area in which they are experiencing their alcohol and drug problems. LAs are reminded that the statutory direction on choice of residential accommodation advises that people who are assessed as needing residential care should be able to exercise choice over the place where they receive that care. LAs should ensure that resources can be identified for out of area placements.

24   LAs should ensure that there are arrangements in place for responding to the following types of out of area referral:

— where people who are ordinarily resident outside the area of the LA undertaking the assessment, there will be a need to liaise with the LA in the area of ordinary residence to establish responsibility for funding the care package.

— where people who are ordinarily resident outside the area of the LA but are in urgent need of residential care (Section 24(3)(b) of the National Assistance Act 1948).

— where it is impossible to identify a person's area of ordinary residence; in these circumstances the LA where they present for services should assume responsibility for arranging and providing the necessary services (Sections 24(3)(*a*) and 32 of the National Assistance Act 1948).

## Probation service

25   Some alcohol and/or drug misusing clients of the Probation Service will continue to seek access to residential and non-residential care, and LAs should liaise with probation services to ensure that these needs can be considered within the community care arrangements. Attention should be given to establishing joint assessment or common assessment procedures, such as those LAs have developed with other client groups. LAs will also need to be aware that there may be requests for resources to provide residential and non-residential care for persons whose alcohol or drug misuse comes to light through offending, appearance in court and/or involvement with probation services. LAs are reminded that the Criminal Justice Act 1991 which came into force on 1 October 1992 emphasises that it is preferable for offenders who misuse alcohol or drugs to be dealt with in the community rather than in custody.

## Residential care for homeless people with other needs

26   There may be other vulnerable people who are homeless and who are in need of residential care. Many of the above considerations apply to them as much as to alcohol and drug misusers. Like any other section of the population, homeless people may be in need of care because of frailty, physical disability, mental disorder of any description or a combination of any of these. They may have complex needs which also include alcohol and drug misuse. Their needs may be hard to classify by standard client groups.

27   As with alcohol and drug misusers, LAs should have flexible systems of assessment and care management that allow such people access to the services they need in a way that meets their special circumstances. Their homelessness may in itself mean that an urgent response is called for. LAs will be aware that there are a variety of agencies which specialise in providing residential care for homeless people. As with specialist alcohol and drug providers, these agencies may be in a position to assist in assessment procedures. Some of these homes receive additional support from the Home Office specifically to reserve places for vulnerable offenders and ex-offenders whose care needs require residential support. As above, LAs will need to collaborate with the Probation Service to make best use of these resources.

## G.  Housing and Community Care

### CIRCULAR 10/92 (DEPARTMENT OF ENVIRONMENT) AND LAC(92)12 (DEPARTMENT OF HEALTH)—JOINT CIRCULAR ON HOUSING AND COMMUNITY CARE

### Introduction

1   Adequate housing has a major role to play in community care and is often the key to independent living. The Government wants housing authorities to play a full part, working together with social services departments and health authorities so that each can effectively discharge their responsibilities.

2   This circular gives guidance on the role of housing authorities in implementing the Government's community care policy following:

- (a)  the White Paper 'Caring for People: Community Care in the Next Decade and Beyond' (Cm 849);
- (b)  the National Health Service and Community Care Act 1990 ('the 1990 Act'); and
- (c)  the Department of Health's policy guidance 'Community Care in the Next Decade and Beyond' issued in November 1990.

3   In particular housing authorities and social services authorities should be aware of:

- (a)  chapter 3 section 5 in the White Paper on housing and community care;
- (b)  sections 46 and 47 of the 1990 Act, which require social services authorities to consult and liaise with housing authorities over local community care plans and the assessment of individual needs;
- (c)  paragraphs 1.12 and 1.13 of the Department of Health's policy guidance.

This circular expands on these and complements the Department of Health's policy guidance to social services authorities which was also sent to housing authorities. This circular is being sent to social services authorities as well as to housing authorities. The Housing Corporation will issue guidance to housing associations in due course.

### Community care

4   Community care is about providing care and support to those people who require it, for example because of the effects of ageing, physical or sensory disability; learning disability; mental illness (including dementia), alcohol or drugs misuse, or degenerative diseases such as HIV/AIDS. The aim is to support people in their own homes or in 'homely' surroundings wherever this is feasible and sensible, through the provision of the right level of intervention and support to enable them to achieve maximum independence and control over their own lives.

5   The Government's policy remains that care should be provided to people as far as possible in their existing housing where this is their preference and it is practicable and cost effective to do so. Appropriate health and social services, where necessary in conjunction with suitably designed or adapted housing, will be key components in enabling people to live independently. For those people who cannot remain in their own homes, even with support, there will be a continuing need for other forms of housing, or residential care or nursing homes.

6   From April 1993 social services departments will assume responsibility for assessing the care and support needs of people who approach them for assistance. The planning and assessment processes which they are required to undertake,

together with other agencies, should identify the full range of needs, including housing needs, of those who require care.

7   The implementation of the new community care arrangements will be accompanied by changes in the way social security benefits are paid for people in residential care and nursing homes. For those entering homes from April 1993, the Department of Social Security will no longer pay higher income support levels. Claimants will instead be eligible for normal rates of income support, as if they were living in their own homes, supplemented by a new residential allowance element. The difference between what would have been paid under the existing arrangements and the new will be transferred from the Department of Social Security's budget to local authorities. Social services authorities will therefore become responsible for meeting the costs of residential and nursing home care for people whom they assess as needing such care, whether they enter local authorities' own homes or those run by the independent sector. As now, social services departments will recover all or part of the cost by charging residents according to their means.

## Community care planning

8   Under the 1990 Act, social services authorities have, from April 1992, had to prepare for the provision of community care services in their areas. Section 46 of the Act requires social services authorities to consult local housing authorities in so far as these plans affect or are affected by the availability of housing in their area.

## Assessment

9   The Act also requires a more systematic assessment of the needs of those who may require care. From April 1993 social services authorities will have a statutory duty to assess individuals' need for community care services, with the aim of ensuring that all support needs are identified, not only needs for which the social services authority is responsible. Section 47 of the Act requires social services authorities to notify the local housing authority if there appears to be a housing need, and invite them to assist in the assessment. Housing needs may include adaptations, repairs or improvements to allow people to stay in their existing home. In most cases this package of services will be based on a person's existing home, but in some cases it may mean alternative accommodation.

10   Referral procedures will need to be developed and agreed locally. Both housing and social services authorities should adopt joint arrangements to deal with assessments, and should consider the need to nominate particular officers to be responsible for liaising and agreeing the possible housing options. Authorities should address the training needs of officers involved in liaison and referrals and the need for good practice guidance. Authorities should involve other agencies as appropriate.

Where adaptations or improvements are called for, referral procedures should include local Home Improvement Agencies (see Annex paragraph 10), since these agencies can play a key role in helping people have such work carried out. The process of care management and assessment is explained further in Chapter 3 of the Department of Health's policy guidance 'Community Care in the Next Decade and Beyond'.

## Housing strategies

11   Housing authorities and social services authorities are asked to co-operate fully in the planning and assessment processes, bringing in other housing providers

in both the public and voluntary sectors, especially housing associations, where they may be able to help. Although for many people there will be no need for social rented housing, nor any change in their housing requirements, if additional housing needs are identified they should be taken into account in the local housing strategy.

12    As well as the generality of needs arising from the new community care arrangements to be introduced in 1993, housing strategies will need to reflect other specific needs identified in community care plans. These may include the consequences of the continuing programme of closures of long stay hospitals and the re-provision of services on a comprehensive local basis (see Annex paragraph 14). Discussions should also be held with the Housing Corporation about housing association investment in the authority's area.

13    This should all be brought together in the context of the Housing Investment Programme process, which is the subject of discussion between local housing authorities and the Department of the Environment every year. Housing authorities should draw up a picture of housing supply and need in the area and identify cost-effective and practical objectives. Consultation procedures will need to be developed and agreed locally, to ensure co-ordination.

14    It is obviously important that county social services authorities should liaise effectively with district housing authorities and, where social services and housing authorities are part of a unified authority, that discussions should take place between the respective departments. Consultation should also take place with neighbouring or regional bodies in order to establish a strategic pattern of provision wherever this makes sense. Local housing authorities should, similarly, consult social services authorities so that their area strategies can both draw from and contribute to community care planning and assessment. Housing strategies and community care plans should be consistent.

## Resources

15    Both community care planning and individual assessment and care management must take account of all the costs involved, including housing and other accommodation costs, and of the resources available to the various parties, and of the other claims on such resources. In no case should the resources of any authority be committed without the agreement of that authority. The ideal solution for an individual or group of individuals, based on a systematic assessment of needs, may not be achievable either immediately or in the near future, but it should inform the planning process. Community care in itself creates no new category of entitlement to housing, and housing needs which are identified by community care planning and individual assessments should be considered alongside existing processes and local priorities.

16    Social services authorities and housing authorities should construct an individual's care plan with the objective of preserving or restoring non-institutional living as far as possible, and of securing the most appropriate and cost-effect package of care, housing and other services that meets the person's future needs. For some people the most appropriate package of care will be in a nursing or residential home, but in many cases this will be achieved by bringing in domiciliary support and making any necessary adaptations in the individual's existing home. The balance between these should be considered carefully. For example, where expensive or disruptive adaptations or improvements are being considered it may be more cost-effective to provide domiciliary care and support together with more

minor works. In other cases adaptations or improvements (eg: to help people bathe or cook by themselves) may reduce or obviate the need for domiciliary support.

## Review of plans and housing provision

17   The impact of the new systematic assessment process will be gradual. There is no evidence to suggest that there will be immediate changes or a need for a new range of housing options. Housing authorities and social services authorities should, however, be aware of the range of new developments in housing which are becoming available, particularly in the housing association sector. In assessing the housing needs for their area in future years, housing authorities should take account of the housing needs identified in the planning process and of demographic changes in the local population, for example, the number of severely disabled people and projected increases in their population aged of 85. This should enable future planning to be based on a more comprehensive picture of an area's needs. Both local authorities and the Government will monitor developments carefully.

18   The Department of the Environment has commissioned independent research into the housing needs of elderly and disabled people, which is expected to provide guidance on key indicators for use in assessing the specialised housing needs of elderly populations. The Department expects to produce guidance to housing authorities on methods for establishing the comparative costs of different housing and care options for elderly people when the research is completed.

## Working together

19   The new proposals will require effective relationships to be established and built upon between all parties involved. The aim should be to proceed a seamless service for clients, with a mutual recognition of all authorities' responsibilities. This will require all the relevant agencies, including housing, health and social services authorities, to put an emphasis on discussion, understanding and agreement in the planning of services, rather than unilateral decision making. Joint working will be important to maximise the use of existing resources. Administrative systems will need to be developed, perhaps including existing joint planning structures, in order to monitor and plan the effective use of services. Authorities may wish to set up pilot projects. In taking forward their role in community care, housing authorities in particular should have regard to the points made in the Annex to this circular.

24 September 1992

## H.  Hospital Discharge

### (1)  LAC(95)5 AND HSG(95)8—NHS RESPONSIBILITIES FOR MEETING CONTINUING HEALTHCARE NEEDS

### A  Introduction

1   The arrangement and funding of services to meeting continuing physical and mental health care needs are an integral part of the responsibilities of the NHS. This includes, but is not limited to, the responsibility to arrange and fund an appropriate level of care from the NHS under specialist clinical supervision in hospital or in a nursing home. It also includes equally important responsibilities around rehabilitation, palliative health care, respite health care, community health services support and specialist health care support in different settings. All health authorities and GP Fundholders must arrange and fund a full range of these services to meet the needs of their population.

2   Both the NHS and local authorities have responsibilities for arranging and funding services to meet peoples' needs for continuing care. Collaboration is crucial to ensuring the effective and integrated delivery of care. The introduction of the new community care arrangements in April 1993 strengthened further the need for joint working. In particular health authorities, GP Fundholders and local authorities need to work together to ensure:

    — clear agreements are in place covering their responsibilities for arranging and funding care;

    — effective co-operation between services to ensure a co-ordinated response to the needs of individual patients or users;

    — good quality and sensitive arrangements for transferring responsibility for a person's care between agencies and between different parts of the NHS.

3   In this context this guidance specifically confirms and clarifies the NHS's responsibilities. It addresses a number of concerns raised in the report made last year by the Health Service Commissioner and:

    — gives details of the range of services which all health authorities and GP Fundholders must arrange and fund;

    — describes the arrangements which should apply for discharging people from hospital or hospice with continuing health or social care needs;

    — highlights key areas in which health authorities, GP Fundholders and local authorities must collaborate and consult in agreeing or changing their respective responsibilities for continuing care;

    — sets out the action which health authorities, in conjunction with GP Fundholders and local authorities, must complete to implement this guidance;

    — stresses the requirement for health authorities and GP Fundholders failing currently to arrange and fund a full range of services to make the necessary investment in their 1996/7 contracts to address this.

*GP fundholders*

4   Health authorities are responsible for purchasing the majority of continuing health care services. Health authorities, in conjunction with local authorities and the other parties involved, have the lead responsibility for implementing this guidance. The guidance also applies, however, to the GP Fundholders:

— in respect of the range of community health services they are responsible for purchasing;

— in respect of other aspects of continuing health care for those fundholding practices taking part in total purchasing pilots.

5   The full list of goods and services to be purchased by GP Fundholders from April 1996 will be issued in April 1995.

6   Health authorities are expected to secure the agreement of GP Fundholders to the relevant aspects of local policies and eligibility criteria for continuing care. In their turn GP Fundholders will be expected to take account of local policies in their purchasing intentions and to apply agreed eligibility criteria.

*Needs of specific client groups*

7   This guidance relates most directly to the needs for continuing health care of:

— older people;

— older people suffering from mental illness;

— people with dementia;

— younger adults requiring continuing health care as a result of illness or accidents;

— children.

8   It is relevant to the general continuing health care needs of other client groups but does not affect the requirements set out in previous guidance for other specific client groups, in particular for children, adolescents and adults with mental illness or with learning disabilities. Details are covered:

— for **adult mental health services** in the Health of the Nation—Key Area Handbook;

— for **learning disability services** in circulars HSG(92)42 and LAC(92)15;

— for **children** in the Welfare of Children and Young People in Hospital guide issued under cover of HSG(91)1. In addition, Section 17 of the Children Act (Children in Need), and the Code of Practice on the Identification and Assessment of Special Educational Needs issued under Part III of the Education Act 1993 provide a framework for the arrangement of continuing care for **children with chronic illness and disabilities.**

## Summary of Action

9   In light of this guidance and in consultation with local authorities and other relevant parties:

(*a*)  *Health Authorities* must develop **by 29 September 1995** draft local policies and eligibility criteria for continuing health care. These should be made publicly available for consultation and finalised by **1 April 1996.**

(*b*)  *Health Authorities and GP Fundholders (as appropriate—see para 4)* must review by **29 September 1995** their current arrangements and funding continuing health care. Where they are currently not purchasing a full range of services they must make the necessary investment in their **1996/7** contracts to address this.

(*c*)  *NHS Trusts and other hospitals and social services departments* must **by 29 September 1995** review arrangements to ensure that appropriate information is available to patients, their families and any carers about how procedures for hospital discharge will work and about the local arrangements for continuing health or social care support.

(*d*)   *NHS Trusts and other hospitals* to ensure **by 1 April 1996** that front line staff are fully conversant with procedures for hospital discharge and arranging continuing care, as outlined in this guidance and including the operation of eligibility criteria.

(*e*)   *Health authorities* must have in place as soon as practicable and no later than **1 April 1996** arrangements to handle requests to review decisions on eligibility for NHS continuing care including arrangements for the operation of independent panels.

## B   NHS responsibilities for securing continuing health care

10   The NHS is responsible for arranging and funding a range of services to meet the needs of people who require continuing physical or mental health care. The range of services which all health authorities and GP Fundholders (as appropriate—see para 4) must arrange and fund to meet the needs of their population includes:

— specialist medical and nursing assessment;
— rehabilitation and recovery;
— palliative health care;
— continuing inpatient care under specialist supervision in hospital or in a nursing home;
— respite health care;
— specialist health care support to people in nursing homes or residential care homes or the community;
— community health services to people at home or in residential care homes;
— primary health care;
— specialist transport services;

11   This guidance requires health authorities to develop local policies and eligibility criteria which set out clearly:

— the criteria which will be used as the basis, in individual cases, for decisions about need for NHS funded care;
— the range, type, location and level of services which will be arranged and funded by the NHS to meet continuing health care needs in their area.

12   As for all other areas of NHS care, health authorities and GP Fundholders will need to set priorities for continuing health care within the total resources available to them. While the balance, type and precise level of services may vary between different parts of the country in the light of local circumstances and needs, there are a number of key conditions which all health authorities and GP Fundholders must be able to cover in their local arrangements. These are set out in **Annex A.** These conditions will be the basis on which the NHS Executive will review health authorities' local policies. Health authorities must be prepared to justify the balance and level of services they are proposing to arrange and fund.

13   In drawing up local policies and criteria health authorities must consult and involve fully:

— local authorities (in particular social services departments but also where relevant housing authorities and in relation to the needs of children, education authorities);
— all GPs (including GP Fundholders);
— providers both in the NHS and the independent sector;
— representatives of users and carers.

14    Draft policies and criteria must be completed by **29 September** to inform decisions for the 1996/7 contracting round. They should be made available for consultation as part of the community care planning round and be finalised by **1 April 1996**. Details should be included in local community care charters. Health authorities will be expected to have agreed their final policies and eligibility criteria with local authorities and GP Fundholders.

15    Until the policies and eligibility criteria required by this guidance have been finalised, health authorities or GP Fundholders should not proceed with any plans to reduce continuing health care services or alter hospital discharge criteria unless those plans are clearly covered by existing agreements with local authorities. Where major gaps in provision exist health authorities or GP Fundholders must consider taking action in 1995/6 to address this, anticipating the outcome of work on local policies and eligibility criteria.

## C    Hospital discharge arrangements for people with continuing health or social care needs

*Responsibility for decisions on discharge*

16    All consultants (or in some community hospitals GPs) are responsible for the medical care of their patients. They are responsible in consultation with other key staff working with them, especially nurses, for deciding when a patient no longer needs acute care. The large majority of people, after a stay in hospital, will be able to return to their own homes.

17    A minority of patients may need intensive support including the possibility of continuing NHS inpatient care, nursing home or residential care or an intensive package of support at home. Decisions about the discharge of these patients from NHS care and on how their continuing care needs might best be met should be taken following an appropriate multi-disciplinary assessment of the patient's needs. In many cases this will involve referral to a consultant with specialist responsibility for continuing care (including geriatricians or psycho-geriatricians or other consultants responsible for continuing inpatient care) along with the other specialist staff, including specialist nursing staff working with them. Such consultants, working with other specialist staff, will also be normally responsible for assessing patients referred directly from the community who may require NHS continuing inpatient care.

18    In all such cases social services staff should be involved at the earliest appropriate opportunity. Hospitals and social services staff should work together to ensure the most effective integration between social services assessments and care management procedures and hospital discharge arrangements.

19    The multi-disciplinary assessment should be co-ordinated between key professional staff from health and social services. The assessment process should involve consultation with the patient's GP and where appropriate community health services or social services staff who are familiar with the patient's circumstances. Where a patient has no form of accommodation to go to or where their housing is no longer suitable for their needs, staff from housing authorities and housing providers should be fully involved at an early stage. The assessment should also take account of the views and wishes of the patient, his or her family and any carer.

20    Taking account of the results of the assessment and local eligibility criteria the consultant (or GP in some community hospitals) in consultation with the multi-disciplinary team and in particular with nursing staff, should consider what the most appropriate response to the patient's needs would be.

21    As a result the consultant (or GP in some community hospitals), in consultation with the multi-disciplinary team, will decide whether:
  (*a*)  The patient needs continuing inpatient care arranged and funded by the NHS because:
    — either he or she needs ongoing and regular specialist clinical supervision (in the majority of cases this might be weekly or more frequent) on account of:
    — the complexity, nature or intensity of his or her medical, nursing or other clinical needs;
    — the need for frequent not easily predictable interventions;
    — or because after acute treatment or inpatient palliative care in hospital or hospice his or her prognosis is such that he or she is likely to die in the very near future and discharge from NHS care would be inappropriate;
  (*b*)  the patient needs a period of rehabilitation or recovery arranged and funded by the NHS to prepare for discharge arrangements breaking down;
  (*c*)  the patient can be appropriately discharged from NHS inpatient care with:
    — either a place in a nursing home or residential care home arranged and funded by social services or by the patient and his or her family;
    — or a package of social and health care support to allow the patient to return to his or her own home or to alternatively arranged accommodation.
22    Where a patient meets the eligibility criteria for continuing NHS inpatient care but a bed is not available within the provision which has been contracted for, the agreement of the health authority should be sought for an extra contractual referral to another hospital or nursing home in the NHS or independent sector.
23    Health and local authorities should have in place clear agreements on how they will resolve disputes about responsibility in individual cases for meeting continuing care needs.
24    Health authorities or local authorities should not place younger people inappropriately in inpatient, nursing or residential care intended for older people.

*Information*
25    Patients and their families and carers should be kept fully informed about how procedures for hospital discharge and assessment will work and should receive the relevant information (in writing and in other formats appropriate to their needs) they require to make decisions about continuing care. In particular:
    — **hospitals** should provide simple written information about how hospital discharge procedures will operate and what will happen if patients need continuing care;
    — **hospital and social services staff** should ensure that patients, their families and any carers have the necessary information, where appropriate in writing, to enable them to take key decisions about continuing care.
    — **social services staff** should provide written details of the likely cost to the patient of any option which he or she is asked to consider (including where possible and appropriate the availability of social security benefits);
    — **hospital and social services staff** should ensure that patients receive written details of any continuing care which is arranged for them. This should include a statement of how aspects of care will be arranged and funded by the NHS.

*Direction on choice*

26   Where a patient has been assessed as needing care in a nursing home or residential care home arranged by a local authority, he or she has the right under the Direction on Choice (LAC(92)27 and LAC(93)18) to choose, within limits on cost and assessed needs, which home he or she moves into. Where, however, a place in the particular home chosen by the patient is not currently available and is unlikely to be available in the near future, it may be necessary for the patient to be discharged to another home until a place becomes available.

*Rights to refuse discharged to nursing home or residential care*

27   Where patients have been assessed as not requiring NHS continuing inpatient care, as now, they do not have the right to occupy indefinitely an NHS bed. In all but a very small number of cases where a patient is being placed under Part II of the Mental Health Act 1983, they do however have the right to refuse to be discharged from NHS care into a nursing home or residential care home.

28   In such cases the social services department should work with hospital and community based staff and with the patient, his or her family and any carer to explore alternative options.

29   If these other options have been rejected it may be necessary for the hospital, in consultation with the health authority, social services department and, where necessary housing authority, to implement discharge to the patient's home or alternative accommodation, with a package of health and social care within the options and resources available. A charge may be payable by the person to the social services department for the social care element of the package.

*Arrangements for reviewing decisions*

30   As a final check before such a discharge is implemented, a patient and his or her family and any carer have the right to ask the health authority, in which the patient is normally resident, to review the decision which has been made about eligibility for NHS continuing inpatient care. The health authority should deal urgently with such a request and the patient and his or her family and any carer should expect a response in writing from the health authority, with an explanation of the basis of its decision, within 2 weeks of them making this request.

31   In reaching a decision the normal expectation will be that the health authority will seek advice from an independent panel who will consider the case and make a recommendation to the health authority. The health authority, in consultation with the local authority, does have the right to decide, in any individual case, not to convene a panel, for instance in those cases where a patient's needs fall well outside the eligibility for NHS continuing inpatient care. In those cases the health authority will be required to give the patient, his or her family and any carer a written explanation of the basis of its decision.

32   Further detailed practical guidance on the establishment and operation of panels and on other aspects of these arrangements will be issued by the end of June, following further work with key interested parties.

33   The key features of these arrangements would be:
  — the role of the panel would be advisory. It would not have any legal status;
  — that, while its decision would not be formally binding, the expectation would be that its recommendation would be accepted in all but very exceptional circumstances by the health authority or GP Fundholder concerned;
  — the panel would have an independent chairman;

— the panel would also include a representative of the health authority and the local authority;

— the panel's key task would be to assess whether the health authority's eligibility criteria for NHS continuing care had been correctly applied in individual cases;

— the panel would seek appropriate professional advice from hospital staff, social services, the patient's GP and community health services staff. It could call for independent clinical advice where it deemed this to be necessary;

— the panel would wish to consider evidence from the patient or his or her family or any carer;

— the procedure and the criteria above would apply to the patients of GP Fundholders in respect of services they were responsible for purchasing. The expectation would be that the health authority would organise the panel on behalf of the Fundholder;

— patients' rights under the existing NHS complaints procedures, and their existing right to refer their case to the Health Service Commissioner, would remain unchanged by these arrangements.

### Review of discharge arrangements

34   Health authorities, in consultation with local authorities, GPs and other agencies, should ensure that hospitals and community health services keep discharge procedures under review and should regularly audit performance. General good practice guidance on hospital discharge procedures—'Hospital Discharge Workbook—a manual on hospital discharge procedures' was issued in 1994 to all health authorities, local authorities, GPs, hospital and community health services. Further copies can be obtained from the same address as this guidance.

### D   Collaboration with local authorities

35   In implementing the new community care arrangements health and local authorities have been required to make agreements on their respective responsibilities for continuing care and on arrangements for hospital discharge. These agreements should continue to form the basis for local collaboration. In this context, health authorities acting on behalf of GP Fundholders, and local authorities should confirm jointly on an annual basis:

— their best estimates of the likely numbers of people who will need continuing health or social care during the year;

— their respective commitments in finance and activity on continuing care;

— their agreed contingency arrangements, at the beginning of the year, for managing in year any unexpected variations in the numbers of people likely to require care.

36   Where either health or local authorities are proposing a significant change in the pattern of services which will impact on the resources of the other agencies for providing care, they must seek the agreement of the other agency. This might relate to:

— changes in the number of people who need care at home as a result of the new community care arrangements;

— changes in acute activity and plans to reduce hospital lengths of stay;

— the reprovision of services into the community from long stay hospitals.

37   Discussions should take account of the need for any appropriate and continuing transfer of resources from the health authority to the local authority under Section 28A of the NHS Act 1977. Details of any significant changes in respective

responsibilities should be included in published community care plans. Health authorities and GP Fundholders should also take account of the need for any resource shifts to community and primary health care services as a result of any planned changes in the pattern of services.

## E   Implementation and monitoring

38   The full implementation of this guidance will be a key priority for the NHS. The NHS Executive and Social Services Inspectorate will work closely with authorities and monitor performance to ensure:
— that by **29 September 1995** all health authorities in consultation with local authorities and GPs and other relevant parties, have developed draft local policies and eligibility criteria which reflect the conditions of this guidance;
— that timed and costed plans are in place for implementation by **1 April 1996** including how any necessary investment is managed;
— that by **1 April 1996** policies and eligibility criteria are finalised and agreed with local authorities and GP Fundholders and that the other requirements of this guidance are effectively implemented, including any required investment in services.

39   Starting from **1 April 1996** health authorities will be required to report to the NHS Executive on an annual basis on their planned and achieved level of spending and activity on continuing health care.

40   This guidance expires on 1 March 2000. It replaces existing guidance on hospital discharge HC(89)5 and LAC(89)7.

## Annex A

### Conditions for local policies and eligibility criteria for continuing health care

Health authorities are required, in collaboration with local authorities and GPs to produce local policies and eligibility criteria for continuing health care. Policies must address the following issues:

## A   Assessment of need

Health authorities, in collaboration with GPs are expected to base purchasing decisions on a full assessment of the needs of their population, fully discussed and, if possible, jointly agreed with local authorities. This should be reflected in policies for continuing health care which should cover trends in demography, morbidity, clinical practice and other factors which are likely to impact on the need for continuing health care.

## B   Balance of services and priorities

Health authorities must ensure, within the total resources available to them, that they purchase a full range of services to meet the needs of their population for continuing health care. They can however determine, in consultation with local authorities, the balance and type of services they purchase locally, in the light of local circumstances. For instance, the existence of good rehabilitation services and well developed community health services and social care support may lessen, although not eliminate the need for continuing inpatient care. Local policies should set out the health authority's plans for meeting continuing health care needs, the range, quality and level of services which will be purchased to meet those needs and how they are planned to change over time to meet projected changes in need.

## C   Rehabilitation and recovery

Health authorities and GP Fundholders (as appropriate—see para 4) must take full account of the need for services to promote the most effective recovery and rehabilitation of patients after acute treatment so as to maximise the chances of the successful implementation of long term care plans. This is particularly important for older people who may need a longer period to reach their full potential for recovery and to regain confidence. Local policies should guard against the risk of premature discharge in terms of poorer experiences for patients and increased levels of re-admissions. Health authorities and GP Fundholders should ensure that hospitals have in place mechanisms for routinely monitoring rates and causes of re-admission (in particular amongst older people) and the outcomes of hospital discharge. Monitoring should be shared with social services and performance should also be reviewed through clinical audit. Local policies should include explicit protocols and eligibility criteria for rehabilitation. Health authorities should agree with local authorities the need for any additional social or educational support which may be required as part of an agreed package of rehabilitation.

## D   Palliative health care

Working closely with the voluntary sector the NHS retains responsibility for arranging and funding palliative health care. This includes:
— palliative health care, on an inpatient basis, fully funded by the NHS in hospital, hospice or in a limited number of cases in nursing homes capable of providing this level of care;
— specialist palliative health care to people already in nursing homes;
— palliative health care support to people in their own homes or in residential care.

Local policies should include protocols and eligibility criteria for the provision of palliative health care in different settings.

Detailed guidance on NHS responsibilities for palliative health care is given in EL(93)14 and EL(94)14.

## E   Continuing inpatient care

All health authorities and GP Fundholders should arrange and fund an adequate level of service to meet the needs of people who because of the nature, complexity or intensity of their health care needs will require continuing inpatient care arranged and funded by the NHS in hospital or in a nursing home. In addition to the other areas already set out in this annex the NHS is responsible for arranging and funding continuing inpatient care, on a short or long term basis, for people
— where the complexity or intensity of their medical, nursing care or clinical care or the need for frequent not easily predictable interventions requires the regular (in the majority of cases this might be weekly or more frequent) supervision of a consultant, specialist nurse or other NHS member of the multi-disciplinary team;

— who require routinely the use of specialist health care equipment or treatments which require the supervision of specialist NHS staff;

— have a rapidly degenerating or unstable condition which means that they will require specialist medical or nursing supervision.

In addition patients who have finished acute treatment or inpatient palliative care in a hospital or hospice, but whose prognosis is that they are likely to die in the very near future should be able to choose to remain in NHS funded accommodation, or where practicable and after an appropriate and sensitive assessment of their needs, to return home with the appropriate support. Health authorities should jointly monitor activity in this area with local authorities and use clinical audit to address areas where inappropriate discharges from NHS care appear to be taking place.

Local policies should include details of arrangements and eligibility criteria for people who require continuing inpatient care from the NHS. Policies should set out details of how continuing inpatient care will be purchased and how resources can be assessed, including arrangements for onward referrals to contracted beds and ECR placements in other NHS hospitals or in the independent sector.

## F  Respite health care

For many people local authorities will have the lead responsibility for arranging and funding respite care. The NHS however also has important responsibilities in this area and all health authorities and GP Fundholders (as appropriate—see para 4) must arrange and fund an adequate level of care. In particular however they should address the needs of:

— people who (as described in Section E) have complex or intense health care needs and will require specialist medical or nursing supervision or assessment during a period of respite care;

— people who during a period of respite care require or could benefit from active rehabilitation;

— people who are receiving a package of palliative care in their own homes but where they or their carer need a period of respite carers.

In making arrangements for respite care health authorities and GP Fundholders should pay careful attention to the wishes of patients and their carers.

Local policies should include details of arrangements and eligibility criteria for people who require respite care from the NHS. Health authorities should agree with local authorities their respective responsibilities.

## G  Access to specialist or intensive medical and nursing support for people placed in nursing home, residential care homes or in the community

Some people who will be appropriately placed by social services in nursing homes, as their permanent home, may still require some regular access to specialist medical, nursing or other community health services. This will also apply to people who have arranged and are funding their own care. This may include occasional continuing specialist medical advice or treatment, specialist palliative care, specialist nursing care such as continence advice, stoma care or diabetic advice or community health services such as physiotherapy, speech and language therapy and chiropody. It should also include specialist medical or nursing equipment (for instance specialist feeding equipment) not available on prescription and normally only available through hospitals. It would not cover basic equipment such as incontinence supplies which should be included in the basic price charged by the home to the local authority or the person.

Assessment procedures and arrangements for purchasing care should take account of such needs and details should be identified in individual care plans. In such cases the NHS can either provide such services directly or contract with the home to provide the additional services required. Such additional services should be free at the point of delivery.

Health authorities should draw up, in consultation with local authorities, GPs (including GP Fundholders) and the independent sector, protocols and eligibility criteria for the availability of such support.

Access to specialist medical and nursing services should also be available on the same basis for people who are receiving a package of social care and community health services support in residential care homes or their own homes.

### H   Community health and primary care services for people at home or in residential care homes

Community health services are a crucial part of the provision of continuing care for people at home or in residential care. Health authorities should work closely with local authorities, GPs, hospital and community provider units and the independent sector to agree the likely demand for continuing community health services support, taking account of the impact of:

— changes in the number of people who need care in their own home as a result of the new community care arrangements;
— changes in acute sector practice and provider plans to reduce hospital lengths of stay;
— significant changes in the local pattern of residential or nursing home care (for instance the impact of the development of new homes or extensions of existing facilities in terms of increased demands on local primary care and community health services).

This should be reflected in health authorities' policies on continuing health care, health authority and GP Fundholder purchasing plans and in community care plans. Health authorities and GP Fundholders should take account of the need for any resource shifts to community and primary care services as a result of any planned changes in the pattern of services.

Policies should also indicate how health authorities intend to work with hospital and community providers and GPs to ensure effective integration between specialist and community and primary care services in meeting needs for continuing health care.

### I   Specialist transport

Health authorities and GP Fundholders should include as part of their local policies for continuing health care arrangements for ambulances and other specialist NHS transport. This should include, on the basis of patients' needs:

— transport to and from hospital or hospice;
— transport where an emergency admission is being made to a residential care or nursing homes;
— non-emergency transport for people in residential care and nursing homes or in their own home to and from health care facilities.

**(2) HSG(95)39/LAC(95)17—DISCHARGE FROM NHS INPATIENT CARE OF PEOPLE WITH CONTINUING HEALTH OR SOCIAL CARE NEEDS: ARRANGEMENTS FOR REVIEWING DECISIONS ON ELIGIBILITY FOR NHS CONTINUING INPATIENT CARE**

## Introduction

1   The guidance issued to health authorities, local authorities and other agencies in February 1995 on 'NHS responsibilities for meeting continuing health care needs', HSG(95)8/LAC(95)5, outlined arrangements for reviewing decisions on eligibility for NHS continuing inpatient care. Further guidance was promised for health authorities and other agencies on the details of the procedure and in particular on the establishment and operation of the independent panels.

## Summary of action

2   In the light of this guidance:
  (*a*) **Health authorities** must, in consultation with local authorities, GP Fundholders and other relevant parties
    — ensure a clear action plan is in place for the introduction of the review procedure
    — review arrangements for handling disputes with local authorities about their respective responsibilities for funding care in individual cases (paragraph 10)
    — ensure that the overall process for the review procedure is established and, where necessary, properly reflected in 1996/7 contracts (paragraph 12)
    — put in place the necessary arrangements to secure independent clinical advice (paragraph 30)
    — appoint a designated officer to be responsible for the operation of the review procedure (paragraph 16)
    — select and appoint a Chairman and members of the panel including, on the nomination of the relevant authority/ies, the LA representative (paragraphs 20–24)
    — ensure other arrangements are in place to enable a smooth start to full operation of the panels from 1 April 1996.
  (*b*) **NHS Trusts and other hospitals and social services departments** must:
    — review arrangements for discharge of patients with continuing health or social care needs (paragraph 3)
    — review procedures for supplying appropriate information to patients and their families and any carers (paragraphs 3, 9, Appendix 2)
    — ensure appropriate front line staff are fully conversant with the review procedure as outlined in this guidance, and with eligibility criteria.

## Scope and purpose of the review procedure

3   It is of crucial importance that the review procedure is seen in the context of high quality discharge policies as outlined in our Hospital Discharge Workbook (A Manual on Hospital Discharge Practice) and in Section C of HSG(95)8. The main stages leading to decisions on discharge are:

— a decision has been taken that a patient no longer needs NHS inpatient care;
— a patient who is likely to have continuing health or social care needs has received an appropriate multi-disciplinary assessment which has included, where necessary, specialists with expertise in continuing care;
— in making decisions on the need for NHS continuing inpatient care those responsible have had regard to all aspects of the criteria, including whether the patient is likely to die in the very near future and discharge from NHS care would be inappropriate;
— the need for rehabilitation and/or time for recovery have been considered, with adequate allowance for the special needs of older poeple who may need a longer period to reach their full potential for recovery;
— where appropriate, the different options for care in the future have been explained and discussed with the patient, his or her family and any carer, and the potential impact of these on family members and carers have been acknowledged;
— the patient and his or her family and any relevant carer have been consulted and kept fully informed at all stages, and have received a written continuing care plan clearly setting out the care and services to be provided following discharge from NHS inpatient care.

4   The review procedure is intended as an additional safeguard for patients assessed as ready for discharge from NHS inpatient care who require ongoing continuing support from health and/or social services, and who consider that the health authority's eligibility criteria for NHS continuing inpatient care (whether in a hospital or in some other setting such as a nursing home) have not been correctly applied in their case.

5   The review procedure applies to all patients who have been receiving NHS inpatient care, whether in hospital, or arranged and funded by the NHS in a hospice, nursing home, or elsewhere, and to all client groups covered in local eligibility criteria.

6   The scope of the review procedure is therefore:
— to check that proper procedures have been followed in reaching decisions about the need for NHS continuing inpatient care;
— to ensure that the health authority's eligibility criteria for NHS continuing inpatient care are properly and consistently applied.

7   It is important that all concerned should appreciate that the review procedure is **not** a formal appeals mechanism or a complaints procedure, and does not affect patients' rights under existing NHS and local authority complaints procedures.

8   The review procedure does **not** apply where patients or their families and any carer wish to challenge:
— the content, rather than the application, of the health authority's eligibility criteria;
— the type and location of any offer of NHS-funded continuing inpatient care;
— the content of any alternative care package which they have been offered;
— their treatment or any other aspect of their stay in hospital.

9   Such patients should be advised of the appropriate route by which to pursue their grievance. In particular, information on NHS and local authority complaints procedures, and any other relevant information, should be made freely available.

10   The review procedure should **not** be used to resolve disputes between health and local authorities about their responsibility for funding care in individual cases, and should be clearly separate from agreements which health and local authorities must have in place for resolving disputes about responsibility for meeting continu-

ing care needs in individual cases. Authorities should ensure that appropriate arrangements are in place for handing disputes of this kind.

11   The procedure applies to patients of those GP Fundholders who are participating in total purchasing pilots. Health authorities are expected to administer the review procedure on behalf of total purchasers. The outcome of reviews may impact upon GPs and GP Fundholders and it is therefore important to ensure that all GPs are consulted fully from the outset on the operation of the procedure. Consultation should of course have taken place at an earlier stage on the health authority's continuing care policies and eligibility criteria, as required in HSG(95)8.

## Review procedure

12   **Appendix 1** describes the various stages of the review procedure. It will be clear from this that both the health authority and the relevant provider unit have important responsibilities in their respective areas. These should be underpinned by contractual arrangements and backed up by effective liaison in order for the process to run smoothly.

13   Patients should be given a written continuing care plan which includes the name of somebody, usually a member of the multi-disciplinary team, who they can talk to if they or their family or any carer wish to discuss the result of the assessment or are unhappy with the arrangements for their discharge from NHS inpatient care. The person identified should be someone who can discuss the relevant decisions clearly and impartially while being sensitive to the concerns of patients, their families and any carers.

14   Patients should be given clear information about the review procedure, the situations it does and does not cover and how it operates locally. It may be helpful to have a standard leaflet for this purpose. The possibility that a patient may require an advocate should be kept in view, and the nominated individual should confirm that a patient who needs this help has had the opportunity and assistance they may need to secure someone suitable. Sources of such help will be well known locally and will normally include the Community Health Council and Citizens Advice Bureau in addition to local advocacy schemes.

15   Every effort should be made to address the concerns of patients and their families at this initial stage. The checklist of the issues which should be properly examined is given at **Appendix 2**. If, after all reasonable efforts, agreement cannot be reached, the patient, his or her family or any carer is entitled to ask the health authority where the patient is normally resident to review the decision that the patient's needs do not meet the eligibility criteria for NHS continuing inpatient care. The normal expectation is that a health authority in reaching a view will seek advice from an independent panel. Before doing so it should ensure that:

—  on the basis of the checklist (Appendix 2) all reasonable action has been taken to resolve the case informally;

—  the issues raised by the patient relate to the application of the eligibility criteria.

16   Within each health authority there should be a designated officer who is responsible for the review procedure. He or she will be responsible for:

—  the efficient operation of the procedure;

—  checking, in liaison with the provider, that all appropriate steps have been taken to resolve the case informally;

—  collection of information for the panel including interviewing patients, family members and any relevant carer(s).

17   Once it has received a request from a patient, his or her family or any relevant carer the health authority should aim to ensure that the review procedure is completed within two weeks. This period starts once any action to resolve the case informally has been completed. It may be extended if there are exceptional circumstances—for example, if unforeseen difficulties arise over the provision of clinical advice or in convening the panel, or public holidays have made adherence to this timescale impossible.

18   While the review procedure is being conducted patients should remain in NHS funded accommodation.

19   The health authority does have the right to decide in any individual case not to convene a panel. It is expected that such decisions will be confined to those cases where the patient falls well outside the eligibility criteria, or where the case is very clearly not appropriate for the panel to consider (see para 8). Before taking a decision the authority should seek the advice of the chairman of the panel. In all cases where a decision not to convene a panel is made, the health authority should give the patient, his or her family or carer a full written explanation of the basis of its decision, together with a reminder of their rights under the NHS complaints procedure.

## Establishment and operation of review panels

20   To ensure consistency of approach and to develop knowledge and expertise the health authority should maintain a standing panel. The panel should comprise an independent chairman and single representatives from the health authority and local authority/ies.

21   The independent chairman should be selected following an open advertisement and his or her appointment should be made by the health authority. The person selected must:

   — have a sound grasp of the remit of the panel and of the pivotal role of the chairman,
   — be seen to be free of bias towards either party,
   — have the capacity to determine, on the basis of appropriate advice, whether eligibility criteria have been properly applied in individual cases,
   — be capable of applying impartial judgement, while taking a sympathetic view of the concerns of patients and their families.
   — have the personal confidence to make difficult decisions in this highly sensitive area without being swayed by the inevitable pressures the role will entail.

22   Selection of the right person as Chairman, who is capable of securing the confidence of all parties, will be a crucial factor in the success of the procedure. Current non-executive Directors of health authorities or LA members should not be considered, but people who have formerly held such a position are eligible for consideration. Health authorities are strongly advised to involve lay people (for example, representatives of CHCs) in the selection process.

23   The appointment of representatives of the health authority and appropriate local authority will be on the basis of the nomination of those authorities. They should take account of the professional and other skills which will be relevant to the work of the panel.

24   Authorities may wish to appoint an alternative Chairman and members to cover absences, or to make a reciprocal arrangement for cover with a neighbouring authority. It is open to authorities with the same eligibility criteria to operate a single panel.

25   The chairman and members should receive reasonable expenses.

26   All members of panels must receive appropriate training for their role. The Department of Health intends to issue training material in the autumn.

27   The designated health authority officer (paragraph 16) is responsible for preparing information for the panel. The panel should have access to any existing documentation which is relevant, including the record of assessment. They should also have access to the views of the key parties involved in the case including the patient, his or her family and, if appropriate, carer, health and social services staff, and any other relevant bodies or individuals. It will be open to the key parties to put their views in writing or to request an interview with the health authority officer, or in exceptional circumstances with another person nominated by the panel.

28   The panel must retain patient confidentiality at all times.

29   When interviewed by the health authority's officer, or other person nominated by the panel, a patient may have a representative present to speak on his or her behalf where they wish, or are unable to present their own views. The health authority must aim to ensure that the views of patients who are unable to speak for themselves, for whatever reason, are appropriately represented. This may be done by a relative or carer, but the health authority will need to ensure that it is not any person whose interests or wishes might conflict with those of the patient.

30   The panel will require access to independent clinical advice which should take account of the range of medical, nursing and therapy needs involved in each case. There should be standing arrangements to provide this, which are reflected in contracts between the provider unit which employs the adviser(s) and the appropriate authority, to ensure consistency of advice. Such arrangements should not involve any providers with whom the authority most commonly contracts for services.

31   The role of the clinical advisers is to advise the panel on the original clinical judgements and on how those judgements relate to the health authority's eligibility criteria. It is **not** to provide a second opinion on the clinical diagnosis, management or prognosis of the patient.

32   The members of the panel should meet to consider individual cases. They may wish to invite the clinical adviser(s) and the health authority officer, or if appropriate the person they have nominated to take the views of the parties concerned, to attend their meetings. This should ensure that the panel has access to all the information it will require and to the views of all parties. It is not proposed that anyone else should attend the panel's meetings.

33   The role of the panel is advisory. However, while its decisions will not be formally binding, the expectation is that its recommendations will be accepted in all but very exceptional circumstances. If a health authority decides to reject a panel's recommendation in an individual case it must put in writing to the patient and to the chairman of the panel its reasons for doing so.

34   In all cases the health authority must communicate in writing to the patient the outcome of the review, with reasons. The relevant hospital, consultant or GP should also receive this information.

## Public information

35   Information on the review procedure should be made publicly available on an annual basis in a report to the health authority. The information likely to be required is:
— number of patients requesting a review;
— number of cases referred to the panel;
— number of cases upheld;
— number of cases upheld by the panel but rejected by the health authority.

36   At a national level the NHS Executive will monitor the numbers and results of the panels held by individual authorities, and will review the operation of the review procedure in the light of this information.

**Appendix 1**

**Overall process for review procedure**

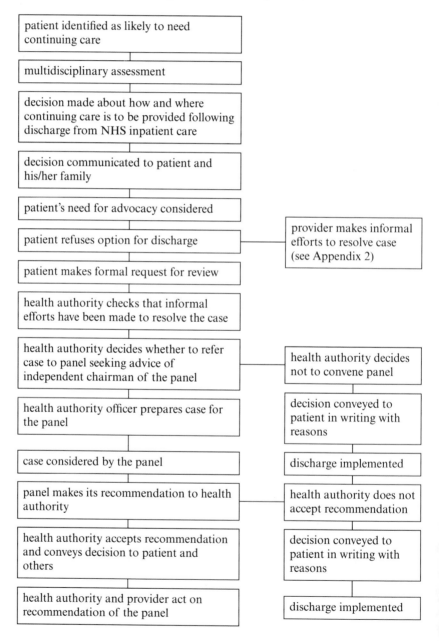

## Appendix 2

## Checklist of issues to be considered before referring a case to a panel

### Assessment of need

1  Has there been an appropriate assessment of the patient's needs? Has this included appropriate specialists with expertise in continuing care needs? Has the need for a second clinical opinion been considered?

2  Have all the criteria in the health authority's published eligibility criteria been considered by the multi-disciplinary team?

3  Has proper account been taken of the patient's clinical prognosis—is the patient likely to die in the very near future so that discharge from NHS care may be inappropriate?

4  Were the patient's needs for a period of rehabilitation or recovery properly considered, bearing in mind that older people may need longer to reach their full potential for recovery?

5  Does the multi-disciplinary team agree that the patient does not meet the eligibility criteria for NHS continuing inpatient care?

6  Has the multi-disciplinary team reviewed its decision?

### Information for the patient, his or her family and any carer

7  Have the patient, his or her family and any carer been made fully aware of the eligibility criteria?

8  Have the patient, his/her family or carer received the following:
— clear written information about how hospital discharge procedures will operate, and what will happen if continuing care is needed?
— the necessary information, where appropriate in writing, to enable them to take any decisions about continuing care?
— written details of the likely cost of any option which they have been asked to consider by social services (including where possible and appropriate the availability of social security benefits and financial assistance from LA social services)?
— a written continuing care plan including a clear statement of which aspects of care will be arranged and funded by the NHS?

9  Have the views of the patient, his or her family and any carer been taken into consideration as part of the assessment process? Has the possibility that the patient might need an advocate been considered?

### Alternative care options

10  Has the possibility of an ECR been considered if the patient met the eligibility criteria but contracted provision for NHS continuing inpatient care was full?

11  Have alternative options for care (eg: a package at home) been discussed with the patient and his or her family?

\* \* \* \* \*

## (3) LAC(92)17 HEALTH AUTHORITY PAYMENTS IN RESPECT OF SOCIAL SERVICES FUNCTIONS

### Summary

Health authorities (HAs) have statutory powers under Section 28A of the NHS Act 1977 to make payments to local authorities (LAs) and other agencies for the purchase of personal social services, education for disabled people and housing. This includes arrangements made under 'joint finance' schemes. This circular sets out the principles and directions governing payments by HAs in respect of social services functions under s 28A.

### Action

1    Authorities are asked to note and follow the guidance in Annexes A and B and comply with the directions in Annex C and, in particular, to note:
   (i)   the importance that the Government places on the use of health service funds to help pay for social services for people who have traditionally been cared for in hospitals, and especially the importance of securing adequate dowries for people leaving long-stay hospitals;
   (ii)  that joint finance expenditure should be linked with the priorities and objectives set out in Community Care Plans;
   (iii) that when a dowry has not been paid in respect of a person who has been discharged from a long-stay hospital, and care arrangements in the community break down, the LA where the person is living should look to the District Health Authority (DHA) responsible for the person before discharge to assist in resecuring those arrangements;
   (iv)  that if LAs assume prime responsibility for arranging care for particular groups, any transfer of responsibility should be reflected in a transfer of funds.
2    Similar guidance is being issued to HAs (HSG(92)43).

*    *    *    *    *

### Annex A

#### Health authority payments in respect of social services functions

### Introduction

1    The White Paper 'Caring for People' puts an increased emphasis on health authorities (HAs) and local authorities (LAs) working together to provide community care services. LAs are required to produce annual community care plans which must be at least complementary and if possible joint with HAs' own plans. These plans should form the basis upon which services for the client groups are commissioned. Innovative and developing services, with for example joint commissioning, require flexible financial arrangements locally, with HAs' budgets sometimes being used to finance social services provision. Such funds continue to be part of health finance for allocation and accountability purposes but by finding social rather than health services, they may more appropriately meet the needs of users and carers.
2    For example, it is well recognised that many people (eg people with learning disabilities) traditionally cared for in long-stay hospitals are predominantly in need of

social care, and should be cared for in the community. In order to support in the community ex long-stay hospital patients and people who might in earlier times have been cared for in long-stay hospitals, health finance may be spent on social services rather than on health services.

## Statutory powers

3   District Health Authorities (DHAs) and Special Health Authorities (SHAs) for London Postgraduate Teaching Hospitals have powers under Section 28A of the NHS Act 1977 to make payments to LAs, housing associations and certain other bodies, and voluntary organisations in respect of personal social services, education for disabled people and housing. These have most usually been used in respect of 'joint finance' projects (ie those funded from the special joint finance allocations made to DHAs by the Government via Regional Health Authorities (RHAs)) and in making 'dowry' payments associated with the discharge of long-stay patients. However, the powers available under Section 28A apply to all cases where a HA proposes to fund personal social services activity, including those cases where locally it has been decided that a service, or a major part of it, could be more appropriately provided by a social services department, for example, services for people with learning disabilities. In all cases, the payments must be recommended by the appropriate Joint Consultative Committee (JCC) and the conditions attached to them must accord with the conditions prescribed in directions by the Secretary of State (see Annex C). The ultimate decision to make the payment rests with the HA and the HA remains accountable for the expenditure. Neither Family Health Services Authorities (FHSAs) nor NHS Trusts have the power to make S28A payments. However, FHSAs and relevant provider units should be involved in planning service charges intended to result from such payments.

4   This circular distinguished between (i) 'joint finance' (ie the special top-sliced allocation); (ii) dowries, which are concerned with funding the discharge of patients from long-stay care and which often relate to individuals; and (iii) other arrangements for the development of services by a LA or voluntary agency as part of a strategy agreed with a HA and to which the latter contributes using the powers available under S28A. More detailed guidance about payments in these categories is at Annexes B and C.

### Joint finance

5   Ministers have reviewed the joint finance scheme in the light of 'Caring for People' and have concluded that, for the moment, special allocations should continue to be made with minor changes to the conditions attached to their spending. However, the success of community care policies depends much more on the use of funding from general allocations than on the joint finance allocations. The emphasis must be on using joint finance to add value to these main programmes. HAs and LAs' joint finance expenditure and plans must be shown in the Community Care Plans or other relevant plans (eg for children's services) and *must be clearly linked with their priorities and objectives as set out in those plans.* Ministers consider that a current important use of joint finance expenditure is to provide new and innovative day, domiciliary and respite services in order to support the general development of community care.

6   Many of the rules governing joint finance have applied to all schemes under Section 28A regardless of whether they were supported by the special top sliced

allocations. These conditions have governed the length of time for which a HA may support a project and the tapering of their contribution. Some of the conditions (which are set out at Annex C) will now apply only where a project is being funded from the special allocation, ie there will be more flexibility when main allocations are to be used to fund S28A payments.

7    Following consultation on the draft guidance it has been decided not to extend the period over which joint finance payments might be made. Commentators were mostly in favour of ensuring that joint finance allocation should continue to be used primarily for pump-priming projects.

### Dowry payments

8    Dowry payments are made in respect of people who have been cared for in long-stay hospitals, which have been providing them with the social care which is now considered more appropriately provided in the community. HAs have been funded to care for these people, and it is therefore for them to fund their transfer into the community.

9    Dowry payments have enabled significant progress to be made in discharging patients from long-stay hospitals into the community, particularly people with learning disabilities where the primary need is for social care. Ministers consider that dowries will continue to have an important part to play in achieving policy objectives. When an individual patient is discharged from a long-stay hospital, the DHA responsible for his hospital care must agree with the receiving local authority the care to be provided and any financial arrangements so that current and future responsibility for providing and meeting or contributing to the cost of that care is clear. Dowry payments should be set at a realistic level to meet the total continuing costs of care, taking account of ex-patients' own resources, including available Social Security Benefits, and the contribution that LAs may be expected to make, bearing in mind the new arrangements and the transfer of funds from DSS in April 1993. It is for the two authorities to agree upon the terms of the dowry unless it is funded from the special joint finance allocation when the rules of that fund relating to limits on the duration of payments apply. Existing dowry agreements are not affected by these changes.

10    Where residential care arrangements in the community for a person who was formerly a patient in a long-stay hospital appear to be breaking down (for example because of changing care needs) then the LA authority where the ex-patient currently resides, as the prime community care authority, should take the lead in seeing that the appropriate arrangements are secured (for example, by helping to arrange a move to another home or by securing additional funds). Where agreement had been reached between the responsible HA and LA on discharge on the contribution which the HA should make to the costs of care, there is no expectation that such an agreement should be re-opened. However, where no agreement had been made between the DHA responsible for hospital care before discharge and the LA about respective responsibilities, the HA should assist the LA eg in arranging a joint assessment of need and, if the resecuring or reprovisioning of care leads the LA to incur additional expenditure, the HA will be expected to use its powers under S28A to assist the LA to fund the care. (The HA will however want to satisfy itself that any cost incurred by the LA is reasonable and necessary in the circumstances.) The LA may also, where appropriate, wish to approach, or ask the responsible DHA to approach, the LA of residence before hospitalisation for a contribution.

11    In summary, DHAs are expected in such circumstances to work with LAs so

as to see that future care arrangements are secure and cost-effective, just as they would for patients for whom arrangements were agreed at the time of discharge. It is recognised that expecting HAs to have some responsibility for long-stay patients who were discharged some years ago may represent an additional burden for some. However, Ministers consider that such agreements should have been made and that it would be wrong to expect LAs to take total responsibility now when no such agreement was negotiated on discharge.

### Other payments by health authorities

12   Ministers expect that in preparing Community Care Plans HAs and LAs will consider how resources can jointly best be used to provide care. This may mean HAs supporting personal social services and housing expenditure, beyond joint finance and dowry payments, using the powers available under Section28A. It may also mean LAs assuming prime responsibility for arranging care for particular client groups. Where this is judged sensible and cost-effective locally, any change in responsibility for arranging such care should be reflected in an agreement about financing. The terms of such agreements will need to be determined locally. However, they must conform to the overall conditions under Section 28A as set out in this guidance. Principal amongst these are the conditions that the expenditure must be recommended by the JCC, that the HA remains accountable for the way in which the funds are spent, and that the NHS retains an interest in any capital developments purchased using such funds. Further details are set out in Annexes B and C.

### Joint consultative committees

13   There are currently no plans to change the role or structure of JCCs. The up-to-date primary and secondary legislation concerning them is attached at Annex D [not reproduced], for information.

## Annex B

## Detailed guidance on section 28A powers

\*   \*   \*   \*   \*

## Dowry payments

11   For dowry payments to be made, HAs must be satisfied that the move to the proposed alternative form of care will benefit the people to be transferred. They must also be satisfied that the responsibility for the care of people which is to be transferred to the LA is commensurate with the payment to be made and that the arrangements will be cost-effective.

12   There should be a joint assessment of a person's needs and of the most appropriate form of care for them. Arrangements for moving people into community care should have regard to the possible need for a continuing programme of rehabilitation both before and after discharge, the training or re-training of staff and the strengthening of the community care services.

13   A project may involve a lump-sum payment or annual payments to a LA taking over the care of any person or group of people. The amount of the lump-sum payments and the length of time for which annual payments will be made will be for negotiation between the DHA and the LA. If the services provided by the LA are reduced the grant must be reduced accordingly. Annual dowry payments should be fixed to take account of likely cost increases.

14  Voluntary organisations may be included in such arrangements and grants may be made to them. HAs and LAs are encouraged to consider in consultation with relevant voluntary organisations the contribution they may be able to make, and to involve relevant organisation closely in planning.

15  It will be advisable to consult with the DSS Benefits Agency District Manager at an early stage in the development of a project regarding benefits payable to people transferred from NHS hospital to LA/voluntary sector community care.

\* \* \* \* \*

## Annex C

### National Health Service Act 1977:
### Directions by the Secretary of State as to the conditions governing payments by health authorities to local authorities and other bodies under section 28A

The Secretary of State for Health, in exercise of powers conferred by section 28A(5), (6) and (7) of the National Health Service Act 1977, hereby gives the following Directions:

**1.**—(1) These Directions shall come into force on 10th December 1992 and shall, subject to sub-paragraph (3) below, have effect in relation to any payment made, or proposed to be made, under section 28A of the National Health Service Act 1977 by a health authority in England on or after that date.

(2) Subject to sub-paragraph (3) below, all Directions previously given under section 28A of the National Health Service Act 1977 in relation to health authorities in England are revoked with effect from 10th December 1992.

(3) Where, prior to 10th December 1992, a health authority has determined that a payment under section 28A should be made in respect of any project, the Directions in force in England under that section immediately before that date shall continue to have effect in relation to any such payment made or to be made after that date in respect of that project.

(4) In these Directions—

'the Act' means the National Health Service Act 1977;

'capital costs' means expenditure of a capital nature incurred by a recipient;

'disposal' includes a disposal by way of a sale, an assignment, the creation of any lease or tenancy, a surrender or a merger; and 'disposes' shall be construed accordingly;

'health authority' means a District Health Authority, or a special health authority established for a London Post-Graduate Teaching Hospital;

'joint finance funds' means funds allotted to a health authority for expenditure only—

　　(*a*)  in accordance with section 28A; or

　　(*b*)  on purposes which are incidental or ancillary to any project in respect of which the health authority makes a payment under that section;

'recipient' means a body specified in paragraph (2) of section 28A, or a voluntary organisation, which has received, or is to receive, a payment under that section;

'revenue costs' means expenditure of a revenue nature incurred by a recipient;

'section 28A' means section 28A of the Act, as substituted by the Health and Social Services and Social Security Adjudications Act 1983.

**2.**—(1) This paragraph applies to any payment made by a health authority under section 28A of the Act, other than one to which paragraph 3 below applies; and such a payment shall be made subject to and in accordance with the conditions specified in the following sub-paragraphs.

(2) Before making a payment under section 28A, the health authority shall be satisfied that the payment is likely to secure a more effective use of public funds than the deployment of an equivalent amount on the provision of services under section 3(1) of the Act.

(3) Where a payment is made under section 28A to meet part or all of the capital costs of any project, the amount of the payment shall be determined before the project begins.

(4) Subject to sub-paragraphs (5), (6) and (7) of this paragraph, where more than one amount is to be paid under section 28A in respect of the revenue costs of any project—

    (*a*)  the period over which such amounts are to be paid shall be determined before the project begins; and

    (*b*)  that period shall not exceed—

        (i)  where the payments are intended to meet the full revenue costs of the project, 3 years, or

        (ii)  in any other case, 7 years.

(5) Sub-paragraph (4) above shall not apply where the payment under section 28A is to be made by the health authority otherwise than out of joint finance funds.

(6) Where, in a case to which sub-paragraph (4) above applies, the health authority and the recipient, at some time after the project has begun, agree that it is reasonable in all the circumstances to revise the period determined under sub-paragraph (4)(*a*), that period may be revised, provided that the revised period does not, subject to sub-paragraph (7) below, exceed whichever of the maximum periods mentioned in sub-paragraph (4)(*b*) above is applicable.

(7) Either of the periods specified in sub-paragraph (4)(*b*) above may, by agreement between the health authority and the recipient, be extended in relation to any project by a further period of not more than 2 years.

(8) Before making any payment to which this paragraph applies in respect of any project, the health authority shall be satisfied that the recipient intends to meet the cost of the project—

    (*a*)  to the extent that it is not funded by payments under section 28A; and

    (*b*)  for so long as the project is considered by the health authority and the recipient to be necessary or desirable.

(9) Where a recipient of a payment which has been made under section 28A in respect of a project reduces the level of services it provides in connection with the project below the level of services which it undertook to provide at the time the payment was agreed, the health authority shall reduce accordingly the amount of any further payments made under section 28A in respect of that project.

**3.**—(1) This paragraph applies to any payment made by a health authority under section 28A in respect of accommodation or services to be provided by the recipient—

    (*a*)  for any person previously accommodated in a hospital as mentioned in sub-paragraph (2) below; or

    (*b*)  for any person who, in the opinion of the recipient, is experiencing problems of a social, psychological , physical or legal nature in consequence of his misuse of drugs or other substances;

and such a payment shall be made subject to and in accordance with the conditions specified in the following sub-paragraphs.

(2) Before making a payment to which this paragraph applies by virtue of sub-paragraph (1)(*a*) above, the health authority shall be satisfied that the payment is to be used by the recipient for the purpose of securing, otherwise than in a hospital, the accommodation or care of a person who was, at the time of, or immediately before, the health authority's decision to make the payment, accommodated in a hospital under section 3(1)(*a*) of the Act.

(3) Where a payment is made under section 28A to meet part or all of the capital costs of any project, the amount of the payment shall be determined before the project begins.

(4) Subject to sub-paragraphs (5) and (6) of this paragraph, where more than one amount is to be paid under section 28A in respect of the revenue costs of any project—

   (*a*) the period over which such amounts are to be paid shall be determined before the project begins; and
   (*b*) that period shall not exceed—
      (i) where the payments are intended to meet the full revenue costs of the project, 3 years, or
      (ii) in any other case, 7 years.

(5) Sub-paragraph (4) above shall not apply where the payment under section 28A is to be made by the health authority otherwise than out of joint finance funds.

(6) Where the health authority is at any time satisfied that it is reasonable in all the circumstances to extend the period determined under sub-paragraph (4)(*a*) of this paragraph, that period may be extended for such further period as the health authority may allow, provided that the period of the payments as so extended shall not exceed—

   (*a*) where the payment is to meet the full revenue costs of a project, 10 years, or
   (*b*) in any other case, 13 years.

(7) Before making any payment to which this paragraph applies in respect of any project, the health authority shall be satisfied that the recipient intends to meet the cost of the project—

   (*a*) to the extent that it is not funded by payments under section 28A; and
   (*b*) for so long as the project is considered by the health authority and the recipient to be necessary or desirable.

(8) Where a recipient of a payment which has been made under section 28A in respect of a project reduces the level of services it provides in connection with the project below the level of services it undertook to provide at the time the payment was agreed, the health authority shall reduce accordingly the amount of any further payments under section 28A in respect of that project.

   **4.** In the case of any payment made under section 28A—

   (*a*) the health authority making the payment shall, so far as is practicable, ensure that the payment is used by the recipient in such a way as will secure the most efficient and effective use of the amount paid;
   (*b*) the health authority making the payment shall, with the agreement of the recipient, prepare a Memorandum in writing specifying—
      (i) details of the purposes for which the payment is to be expended;
      (ii) in the case of a payment in respect of revenue costs, the services which are to be funded by the payment, and the estimated costs of those services to the body providing them; and

     (iii)  the statistical, financial and other information which is to be provided to the health authority by the recipient, in connection with the use it has made of the payment.

**5.**—(1) Subject to paragraph 6 below, where—

(*a*)  a payment has been made under section 28A towards the cost of acquiring, or of executing works to, land or other property for the purposes of any functions specified in section (2) of that section, and

(*b*)  the recipient—

     (i)  disposes of the whole or part of that land or other property, or

     (ii)  uses it or any of it, without the agreement of the joint consultative committee, for any purpose other than that for which the payment was made.

## I.  Children Guidance

## (1)  THE CHILDREN ACT GUIDANCE AND REGULATIONS: VOLUME 2

### Family Support, Day Care and Educational Provision for Young Children

### Preface

This volume contains guidance on Part III (Local Authority Support for Children and their Families) and Part X (Child Minding and Day Care for Young Children) of the Children Act 1989 (referred to as the Act throughout). It is issued under section 7 of the Local Authority Social Services Act 1970 which requires local authorities in the exercise of their social services functions to act under the general guidance of the Secretary of State.

Throughout the document the phrase 'local authorities' is used. It should be noted that under the provisions of the 1970 Act certain functions are referred to the Social Services Committee of a local authority and, unless otherwise stated, references to a local authority in this document denotes the Social Services Committee and its officers. Certain sections of the document are, however, explicitly addressed to local education authorities. This document treats the Act as if it were in force now and uses the past tense to refer to the legislation which is repealed by the Act.

Chapters 1 to 3 contain guidance on local authority responsibilities for children in need and their families.

\*    \*    \*    \*    \*

### Chapter 1: Introduction

1.1   The guidance is intended to provide a clear statement of the requirements placed on local authorities by the Children Act 1989. This is to help local authorities develop effective strategies and policies and provide practitioners with a robust framework within which to work. This volume aims to identify changes and explain the underlying principles in relation to family support services for families with children in need and day care services for young children. It discusses the implications for policies, procedures and practice. In addition it considers day care services for under fives and educational provision for that age group together because of the particular need for close co-operation in respect of services for under fives.

1.2   The Act brings together most private and public law about children, thereby replacing complex and fragmented legislation with a single statute. Part III together with Schedule 2 sets out the main responsibilities of local authorities for children in their area who are in need and their families and for children in need whom they look after. It also draws together local authorities' functions towards children which existed under the Child Care Act 1980, the National Assistance Act 1948 and Schedule 8 of the National Health Services Act 1977 in relation to children with disabilities and under fives. All these provisions reflect the Act's philosophy that the best place for the child to be brought up is usually in his own family and the child in need (who includes the child with disabilities) can be helped most effectively if the local authority, working in partnership with the parents, provides a range and level of services appropriate to the child's needs. To this end the parents and the child (where he is of sufficient understanding) need to be given the opportunity to make their wishes and feelings known and to participate in decision-making.

1.3 Part III gives local authorities a range of new duties, including identification of children who are in need, support of children's links with their families, provision of day care and setting up of procedures to consider representations about the provision of services. Under Part III children with disabilities are treated first as children and then as persons with a disability. They therefore benefit from safeguards which were unavailable to them under previous legislation unless they were in the care of a local authority. The local authorities' general welfare duty under section 22(3) and their duty to review plans for children provide an additional safeguard to such children's welfare.

\* \* \* \* \*

## Policy issues

1.9 Local authorities will need to review all their existing child care policies, their priorities will need to be re-examined and rethought in the light of the Children Act. Priorities in resource allocation must be identified and related to budgeting strategies; there will be a need to re-evaluate service delivery in liaison with the voluntary and private sector and to work out an information strategy. Paragraph 1(1) of Schedule 2 requires that local authorities take reasonable steps to identify the extent to which there are children in need in their area. Under the provisions of the Act children with disabilities should be given the opportunity to lead lives which are as normal as possible. Therefore services for children with disabilities should be integrated with those provided for other children in need. Part III brings together the two streams of law covering local authority responsibilities to families with children: previous childcare legislation and the health and welfare statutes dealing mainly with children and disabilities. The intention is that local authorities should integrate service provision for all children who are in need, for whatever reason. In order to plan service provision, local authorities should integrate service provision for all children who are in need, for whatever reason. In order to plan service provision, local authorities will have to adapt existing information gathering systems so as to identify the need for services in their area and gaps in provision.

\* \* \* \* \*

## Co-ordination, collaboration and co-operation

1.13 The Act puts the responsibility firmly on local authorities to provide accommodation, advice and assistance for children and young people in certain circumstances where such measures are needed to safeguard and promote their welfare. This may involve a social services department of a local authority requesting help from a local housing authority which, under section 27 of the Act, shall comply with a request for help if it is compatible with their statutory functions and does not unduly prejudice the discharge of those functions. Under the same provision the department will on occasion turn to the education authority for assistance in meeting the duties placed on the social services department in respect of family support. Sections 17(5), 27, 28 and 30 provide duties and powers in relation to co-operation between and consultation with different authorities including social services, education departments and housing authorities, health authorities and independent organisations. In relation to a child who has special educational needs, the social services department is under a duty (section 27(4)) to help the education department in the provision of services, and to consult the education department maintaining a child's statement of special educational needs (made under the Education Act 1981) when placing a child at an establishment providing education (section 28(1)). A corporate policy and clear departmental procedures in respect of interdepartmental collaboration will ensure good co-operation at all levels.

1.14    The local authority carries the principal responsibility for co-ordinating and providing services for children in need. In some cases their services will be supportive of other key agencies. The local authority and other relevant agencies remain responsible for decisions about their own service provision or legal and administrative issues assigned to them. They should, however, seek out and have available the best relevant help from other agencies. Similarly they must be available and prepared to contribute to the work of other key agencies in meeting the legitimate needs of children and their families. New organisational links between local authorities and health authorities will be needed in order to implement the Act fully in relation to chronically sick and disabled children and their parents.

1.15    Policies on community care under the NHS and Community Care Act 1990 and service provision under the Children Act should be considered together in respect of the requirement in each case to assess need and deliver services in accordance with available resources. The more formalised approach in community care to assessment, planning and delivery of services and the greater emphasis on the statutory protective element in children's services may require different relationships with other agencies and different styles of working. However, the essential functions are not different in principle and should not lead to operational difficulties if all concerned have a clear understanding of the approach required in the respective areas of work.

1.16    In the case of day care and education services for young children the importance of co-ordination between different local authority departments—particularly but not exclusively social services and education—has long been recognised. A co-ordinated approach is a means of ensuring that all children, whatever type of service they attend, have access to a good quality curriculum or programme with continuity of experience and smooth transition to other forms of day care or education. There are three levels at which co-ordination is needed: policy making, day-to-day operation of services and between staff working on different settings. A co-ordinated approach helps to create an environment where people with different qualifications and experience can share skills and expertise and ideas in a positive way. It is important for all departments within a local authority to find ways of encouraging staff to work with this in mind, so that all the appropriate skills are available in all settings.

\*    \*    \*    \*    \*

## Chapter 2: Service Provision

2.1    Section 17 of Part III gives local authorities a general duty to safeguard and promote the welfare of children in need and to promote the upbringing of such children by their families, so far as this is consistent with their welfare duty to the child, by providing an appropriate range and level of services. Schedule 2 contains further provisions designed to help children in need continue to live with their families and generally to prevent the breakdown of family relationships. Partnership with parents and consultation with children on the basis of careful joint planning and agreement is the guiding principle for the provision of services within the family home and where children are provided with accommodation under voluntary arrangements. Such arrangements are intended to assist the parent and enhance, not undermine, the parent's authority and control. This new approach should also be developed when a child is in care, provided that it does not jeopardise his welfare.

2.2   Part III also covers the general duty of a local authority towards children being 'looked after'. The term 'looked after' is the new term used in the Act to cover all children accommodated by a local authority, whether by voluntary arrangement or because of a care order. There is more emphasis on the need to make plans for children in partnership with those who are important in the child's life and the child, subject to his understanding, and to involve those people in reviewing such plans.

## In need

2.3   Section 17(10) defines 'children in need' as follows:

'For the purposes of this Part a child shall be taken to be in need if:—

(*a*)   he is unlikely to achieve or maintain, or to have the opportunity of achieving or maintaining, a reasonable standard of health or development without the provision for him of services by a local authority under this Part;

(*b*)   his health or development is likely to be significantly impaired, or further impaired, without the provision for him of such services; or

(*c*)   he is disabled,

and 'family', in relation to such a child, includes any person who has parental responsibility for the child and any other person with whom he has been living. Section 17(11) explains that for the purpose of this Part, a child is disabled if he is blind, deaf or dumb or suffers from mental disorder of any kind or is substantially and permanently handicapped by illness, injury or congenital deformity or such other disability as may be prescribed; and in this Part—

'development' means physical, intellectual, emotional, social or behavioural development; and

'health' means physical or mental health.

2.4   The definition of 'need' in the Act is deliberately wide to reinforce the emphasis on preventive support and services to families. It has three categories: a reasonable standard of health or development; significant impairment of health or development; and disablement. It would not be acceptable for an authority to exclude any of these three—for example, by confining services to children at risk of significant harm which attracts the duty to investigate under section 47. The child's needs will include physical, emotional and educational needs according to his age, sex, race, religion, culture and language and the capacity of the current carer to meet those needs. This guidance does not lay down firm criteria or set general priorities because the Act requires each authority to decide their own level and scale of services appropriate to the children in need in their area. However, because the definition is in the Act, a local authority cannot lawfully substitute any other definition for the purposes of Part III.

2.5   In assessing individual need, authorities must assess the existing strengths and skills of the families concerned and help them overcome identified difficulties and enhance strengths. Sometimes the needs will be found to be intrinsic to the child; at other times however it may be that parenting skills and resources are depleted or under-developed and thus threaten the child's well-being. For example, a chronically sick parent may need continuing practical and emotional support of varying degrees of intensity according to the incidence of acute phases of his illness and the developing needs of the child. At times, a sick parent may seek short periods of local authority accommodation for the child so as to have a period of recuperation and avoid stress for the child; in these cases social workers should consider whether a package of support services provided in the home would be the better form of provision. Children should not necessarily be identified as in need because one or both parents are disabled, although this could of course be a factor. It may be that the provision of services to the parent, either under adult disabled persons legislation or under section 17(3) of the Act may safeguard the welfare of the child sufficiently to enable the parent to continue looking after him at home. In other cases social problems, relationship problems, unemployment or bereavement, for example, may temporarily reduce the quality of care of children in the family. A package of support and prompt use of respite care may sustain the child's longer term wellbeing within the family.

2.6   The Act envisages family support services being offered to members of a family of a child in need where the service is provided with a view to safeguarding and promoting the child's welfare (section 17(3)). Any person who has parental responsibility for the child and any other person with whom the child is living is included so that a local authority may put together a package of services for a family which could include home help, day care provision for a family member other than the child in need (eg another child in the household) or a short-term, temporary placement for the child to relieve the carer. The outcome of any service provision under this power should be evaluated to see whether it has met the primary objective, namely to safeguard or promote the child's welfare.

## Assessment

2.7   Good practice requires that the assessment of need should be undertaken in an open way and should involve those caring for the child, the child and other significant persons. Families with a child in need, whether the need results from family difficulties or the child's circumstances, have the right to receive sympathetic support and sensitive intervention in their family's life. Paragraph 3 of Schedule 2 to the Act provides that 'a local authority may assess a child's needs for the purpose of this Act at the same time as any assessment under:

(*a*)   the Chronically Sick and Disabled Persons Act 1970;

(*b*)   the Education Act 1981;

(*c*)   the Disabled Persons (Services, Consultation and Representation) Act 1986; or

(*d*)   any other enactment.'

2.8   In making an assessment, the local authority should take account of the particular needs of the child—that is in relation to health, development, disability, education, religious persuasion, racial origin, cultural and linguistic background, the degree (if any) to which these needs are being met by existing services to the family or child and which agencies' services are best suited to the child's needs. In the case of a child with disabilities or a child with a parent with communication difficulties provision of a sign language interpreter, large print, tape and braille may need to be made if communication is to be effective. The need for an interpreter should be considered where the family's first language is not English.

2.9   Assessment must identify and find a way to provide as helpful a guide as possible to the child's needs. Necessary experience and expertise should be provided for in staffing of services and through relationships with other professions and services and with the community. In some areas the local community may include too great a variety of ethnic groups to be reflected fully in composition of staff. In others, local authorities may be called on only rarely to provide a service for a child or family from a minority ethnic group. In both these circumstances, local authorities will need to identify sources of advice and help so that the necessary experience, expertise and resources are available when needed. Care is needed to ensure that the terms 'black' and 'black family' are not used in isolation or in such a way as to obscure characteristics and needs.

### Planning a service for the individual child

2.10   Once a need has been identified a plan for the best service provision will be required. This may simply amount to matching the need with an existing service in the community. Where the local authority has to allocate resources to arrange a service—for example, a family aide for the family or a day nursery place for the child—the plan must identify how long the service may be required, what the objective of the service should be and what else others are expected to do. In order to be effective this plan should form the basis of an agreement with the parent or other carer and be reviewed at appropriate intervals. A child, not the subject of a care order, who is provided with a service while living at home is not 'looked after'. However where the local authority is significantly involved with the family good practice means that the requirements in respect of 'looked after' children relating to Arrangements for Placement and Review should also apply to these children.

### Meeting needs

2.11   Section 17 and Part I of Schedule 2 to the Act set out in considerable detail the specific duties and powers of the local authorities in relation to support services for children with families. Under section 17(1) local authorities have a general duty to provide a range and level of services appropriate to the children in their area who are 'in need' so as to safeguard and promote their welfare and, so far as is consistent with that aim, promote their upbringing by their families. Local authorities are not expected to meet every individual need, but they are asked to identify the extent of need and then make decisions on the priorities for service provision in their area in the context of that information and their statutory duties. Local authorities will have to ensure that a range of services is available to meet the extent and nature of need identified within their administrative areas. In addition to day care provision for pre-school and school age children, it is likely that a range of services designed to support and improve the strengths and skills of parents in their own homes and neighbourhoods will be required. It is also likely that a vigorous foster care service will be required, offering a range of placements which reflects the racial, cultural, linguistic and religious needs of children requiring accommodation, and is responsive to the amount of short term, longer term, or permanent placements which the children may need. It remains likely that some children will need special forms of residential care. In many areas these services exist already, provided by statutory, voluntary and independent sources. It is important to recognise the benefits of developing packages of services appropriate to the assessed needs of individual children and their families, rather than directing them to existing services which may not be appropriate. Chapter 3 describes the range of services which are likely to be needed but this is not an exhaustive list; others may need to be provided according to the local authority's assessment of need in their own area.

*   *   *   *   *

## Change of emphasis

2.13 The effect of the provision of services to support families may often be to avoid the need to take the child into long-term compulsory care. Section 1 of the Child Care Act 1980 was formulated in a way that implied that the aim of supportive work is to prevent admission to care. This has contributed to a negative interpretation of local authority interaction with families. The direct link between preventive work and reducing the need for court procedures found in section 1 of the Child Care Act 1980 is reproduced in the Children Act in paragraph 7 of Schedule 2 but only as one of a range of local authority duties and powers. The accommodation of a child by a local authority is now to be viewed as a service providing positive support to a child and his family.

2.14 In general, families have the capacity to cope with their own problems, or to identify and draw upon resources in the community for support. Some families however reach a stage where they are not able to resolve their own difficulties, and are therefore providing inadequate care for their child or are afraid of doing so. They may look to social services for support and assistance. If they do this they should receive a positive response which reduces any fears they may have of stigma or loss of parental responsibility.

*   *   *   *   *

2.16 In putting together packages of services, local authorities should take account of services provided by the voluntary sector and other agencies. Some examples of supportive services provided under section 17 are advice on such matters as local facilities, social security benefits, housing or education, domiciliary support in the form of family aides, befriending schemes, play facilities and specialist services such as counselling, parent-craft training, family centres, respite care and the provision of accommodation for longer periods. In appropriate circumstances assistance given may be in kind or, exceptionally, in cash (section 17(6)).

## Services for children with disabilities

2.17 The definition of a disabled child in section 17(11) of the Act is:

A child is disabled if he is blind, deaf or dumb or suffers from mental disorder of any kind or is substantially and permanently handicapped by illness, injury or congenital deformity or such other disability as may be prescribed.

The definition is that used for adults under the National Assistance Act 1948 and covers children affected by physical disability, chronic sickness, mental disability, sensory disability, communication impairment and mental illness.

2.18 The Act places a clear, positive and separate duty on local authorities to provide services for children with disabilities within their area so as to minimise the effect of their disabilities and give such children the opportunity to lead lives which are as normal as possible (Schedule 2, paragraph 6). These services should help in the identification, diagnosis, assessment and treatment of children with physical and mental handicaps, or suffering from mental disorder and help those children in their adjustment to handicap, and in overcoming limitations of mobility and communication in appropriate ways. This may include the funding and provision of equipment such as communication aids and interpreters. Authorities will need to consider in co-operation with the relevant agencies the child's overall developmental needs—physical, social, intellectual, emotional and behavioural—when considering what sort of services are required.

### Registration of children with disabilities

2.19   The Act also continues but separates out the requirement placed on local authorities to keep registers of children with disabilities in their area (Schedule 2 paragraph 2). This provision, which is designed to help their service planning and monitoring, originated from directions made under the National Assistance Act 1948 in relation to disabled persons; if the register is to be of maximum use and benefit it has to be complete and avoid duplication with other registers. It is suggested that local authorities in conjunction with local education authorities and health authorities draw up a common register to assist collaboration and for use in their respective areas of responsibility. Local authorities should try to establish a system, particularly with local education and health authorities, for identifying the number and needs of children in their areas who are disabled through physical, sensory or mental disablement, mental disorders and chronic illness so that they may jointly plan their services for the short and long term. Registration is voluntary on the part of parents and children and not a precondition of service provision, but local authorities, in collaboration with health authorities, local education authorities and voluntary agencies in their area, need to publicise widely and positively the existence and purpose of registers to relevant professionals, parents and young people. The publicity should stress the usefulness of the register as an aid to planning the right level and mix of local services to help parents with children with disabilities. In the longer term, the register will also assist in planning services for when the children become adults. Registration should be encouraged for these reasons and on the grounds that it may improve access to other agency resources such as those provided in the voluntary sector and financial benefits such as social security benefits, tax relief (if registered blind) or assistance with text telephones (if registered deaf). Efforts made to keep accurate and comprehensive registers and to encourage registration will help to ensure that children with disabilities gain access to the services for which the Act makes provision.

2.20   Apart from the Children Act, the Chronically Sick and Disabled Persons Act 1970 and the Disabled Persons (Services, Consultation and Representation) Act 1986 (as amended by the Children Act) confer additional functions on local authorities in respect of children with disabilities. (The relevant circulars are LAO(87)6 and LAC(88)2). These Acts also apply to adults and deal mainly with matters of wider application to both adults and children such as the type of welfare services to be provided and the assessments of need for such services.

2.21   Under Schedule 2, paragraph 3 of the Act, local authorities have the power to arrange for any assessment of a child with a disability because he may be in need, to be combined with any assessment under the Chronically Sick and Disabled Persons Act 1970, the Education Act 1981 (for special educational needs), the Disabled Persons (Services, Consultation and Representation) Act 1986 or any other enactment. In the past assessments have tended to be undertaken separately by the relevant departments. Health authorities, for example, have a key role in assessment, particularly for children with disabilities. Co-ordination may on occasion have been ineffective between health and local authorities or between different departments of the same authority. This Act makes it possible to bring together in one process assessment for several different services where this is appropriate and in the child's best interests. Such collaboration should in future ensure that all authorities see children 'in the round', whether their particular needs are for educational or health or social care. It should ensure that parents and children are not subject to a confusing variety of assessment procedures. Assessment should be less an administrative process for a single department and more an opportunity for a local authority to co-ordinate all services effectively. More detailed guidance on working with children with disabilities in the context of the Children Act is in a separate volume in this series.

*Integration of services*

2.22   The new emphasis on integration of services for children with disabilities with those provided for other children in need has the effect that, in addition to the duty under Schedule 2, paragraph 6 to provide services, local authorities must offer children with disabilities accommodated by them or by other agencies, the benefit of those powers and duties which they have in respect of all children whom they look after. Requirements such as having to review the case of a child who has been living away from home, having to give paramount consideration to his welfare and to consult him and his parents before decisions are taken, therefore, apply to children with disabilities as well as other children in need prior to implementation of the Children Act. This is a change from the old law where a child with a disability only benefited from the welfare provision if 'received or taken into care' by a local authority.

## Children living with their families

2.23   Paragraph 8 of Schedule 2 requires local authorities to make such provision as they consider appropriate so that the following services are available for children in need in their area.
*   advice, guidance and counselling;
*   occupational, social, cultural and recreational activities;
*   home help (including laundry facilities);
*   facilities or assistance with travelling to and from any services provided under the Act or any similar service;
*   assistance to enable the child and the family to have a holiday.
It is important to have regard to this general duty when planning a service for an individual child.

\*   \*   \*   \*   \*

## Publicising services

2.35   Local authorities have a duty under Schedule 2, paragraph 1(2) to publicise the services available to families with children in need under Part III of the Act and to take such steps as are reasonably practicable to ensure that those who might benefit from the services receive the information. This supplements the duty local authorities have under section 1 of the Chronically Sick and Disabled Persons Act 1970, to inform people with disabilities, on request, of relevant services provided by the local authority or an organisation of which particulars are in the local authority's possession. This means that local authorities should publish information about the services they provide themselves and, where appropriate, those provided by others.

2.36  Any publicity materials produced should take account of ethnic minorities' cultural and linguistic needs and the needs of those with sensory disabilities in the audience to whom the materials are addressed. As far as possible, the relevant publicity should encourage parents to seek help if it is needed. Some potential applicants are likely to be wary of invoking official involvement in their lives. Sensitive publicity material can minimise these concerns.

2.37  This new duty is likely to increase interest in and awareness of the importance of information about services for parents in helping them bring up their children and make informed choices about use of facilities in the area.

## Charging for services

2.38  Local authorities should ensure that their policy on charging for services and requiring contributions towards the cost of accommodating a child is clearly stated and understood by staff, and that information about the policy is made available to all concerned. Services and assistance provided under section 17(7) may be unconditional or subject to conditions as to the repayment of the assistance or its value. In planning service provision and resource allocation the local authority must have regard to sections 17(8) and (9) which state:

> (8)  Before giving any assistance or imposing any conditions, a local authority shall have regard to the means of the child concerned and of each of his parents.
>
> (9)  No person shall be liable to make any repayment of assistance or of its value at any time when he is in receipt of income support or family credit under the Social Security Act 1986.

2.39  Local authorities are given discretion to decide whether or not to impose reasonable charges for services, assistance in kind, or cash provided under Part III of the Act (section 29(1)). This is not new. In deciding whether or not to impose charges, local authorities should bear in mind that in some cases parents may accept the provision of services more readily if they are given the opportunity to contribute to the cost. Others may be deferred from seeking support before a crisis if their liability for repayment is unclear. Information on the local authority's policy should be available to the public.

2.40  A local authority which is looking after a child must consider whether or not to recover contributions towards the cost of the child's maintenance from a parent of the child or, when he is sixteen, the child himself. The only exceptions to this are where a child is looked after under an interim care order, an emergency protection order (or any other provision of Part V) or certain other criminal provisions (Schedule 2, paragraph 21). Contributions may only be recovered when the authority considers it reasonable to do so and not at all from a person who is in receipt of income support or family credit or while the child is allowed to live with a parent of his (Schedule 2, paragraph 21(2)-(4)).

2.41  The procedure for recovery of contributions for services including accommodation has been simplified since the Child Care Act 1980. The local authority which wants to receive contributions must serve a contribution notice on the contributor, specifying a weekly sum not greater than that which the authority would be prepared to pay foster parents for looking after a similar child and which it is reasonable to expect the contributor to pay. The notice must also state the proposed arrangements for payment (Schedule 2, paragraph 22). If the contributor does not agree with the sum and arrangements for payment (as specified in the notice or otherwise proposed by the authority), or if he withdraws his agreement, the authority may apply to Court for a contribution order. This order may not specify a sum greater than that which was in the contribution notice. If the contributor and the local authority agree the terms of a new contribution notice, this will discharge an existing contribution order. Failing agreement, a contribution order may be varied or discharged on the application of the contributor or the local authority (Schedule 2, paragraph 23).

## Chapter 3: Range of Services

3.1   Local authorities are given a general duty under the Act to promote the upbringing of children by their families (section 17(1)). In support of this duty local authorities are given a number of related duties in respect of family support services. They are required to make provision for advice, guidance, counselling, assistance and home help services. They are empowered to provide social, cultural or leisure activities or assistance with holidays (Schedule 2). Local authorities are required, in addition to provide such family centres as they consider appropriate in relation to the children in their area.

\*     \*     \*     \*     \*

3.6   There should be a variety of day care facilities in the area so that there is some choice for children in need and they can attend the one which best meets their needs. Where a local authority decides to offer day care for a child in need, the parents should be involved in the discussion about the type of day care service and their views should be respected. Wherever possible local authorities should arrange for a child in need to go to the day care service which the parents prefer so long as that accords with the child's needs and best interests. They should also, where appropriate, have regard to the views of the child.

3.7   Local authorities may discharge their general duty to provide day care for children in need either through their own provision or by making arrangements to use facilities run by independent providers such as voluntary organisations or private firms or individuals. In some cases it will be better for the children and more cost effective to use an independent service. It may also mean that children attend a facility which is in the area where they live or go to school. They will therefore be with children from their own community or neighbourhood.

\*     \*     \*     \*     \*

## Family centres

3.18   Paragraph 9 of Schedule 2 gives local authorities a general duty 'to provide such family centres as they consider appropriate in relation to children within their area'. The Act defines family centres as places where a child, his parents and anyone who has parental responsibility for or is looking after him may go for occupational, social, cultural or recreational activities or advice, guidance or counselling or the person may be accommodated whilst he is receiving advice, guidance and counselling.

\*     \*     \*     \*     \*

## Accommodation

3.25   Under Section 20(1) local authorities must provide accommodation for a child in need in their area where there is no-one with parental responsibility for him, or he has been lost or abandoned, or the person caring for him is prevented (whether or not permanently and for whatever reason) from providing him with suitable accommodation or care. Section 20(3) gives local authorities a duty to provide accommodation for children aged 16 and 17 if the authority considers their welfare will be seriously prejudiced without such a service. Section 20(4) gives them discretion to provide accommodation for any child if they consider it would safeguard or promote his welfare (even if the person with parental responsibility is prepared to accommodate him). Under Section 20(5) they also have power to accommodate 16-21 year olds in community homes (provided the home takes over 16 year olds) if it will safeguard and promote the young person's welfare. Children who are accommodated are referred to as 'looked after' by the local authority and the duty to 'accommodate' a child replaces the duty in the Child Care Act 1980 (section 2) to receive a child into 'voluntary care'. Accommodation in this context relates to the provision of care and maintenance for the child. Section 23(2) of the Children Act points up the Act's specific meaning of 'accommodation' by setting out ways in which the local authority may meet their duty to accommodate.

3.26   The Act also empowers local authorities to assist an adult deemed to be a risk to a child and who is willing to leave so as to save the child the trauma of removal, to obtain accommodation away from the family home (Schedule 2 Paragraph 5).

*Duty to collaborate*

3.27   It is emphasised that the obligation to fulfil these requirements in the Act rests with the social services department of a local authority. However, section 27 requires co-operation between a local social services authority and other authorities which has implications for housing authorities. Section 27 states:

(1)  Where it appears to a local authority that any authority mentioned in subsection (3) could, by taking any specified action, help in the exercise of any of their functions under this Part, they may request the help of the other authority, specifying the action in question.

(2)  An authority whose help is so requested shall comply with the request if it is compatible with their own statutory or other duties and obligations and does not unduly prejudice the discharge of any of their functions.

(3)  The persons are—
(a)  any local authority;
(b)  any local education authority;
(c)  any local housing authority;
(d)  any health authority; and
(e)  any person authorised by the Secretary of State for the purposes of this section.

\*    \*    \*    \*    \*

# (2)   THE CHILDREN ACT GUIDANCE AND REGULATIONS VOLUME 3

## Family Placements

## Preface

The guidance in this volume is issued under section 7 of the Local Authority Social Services Act 1970. It is one in a series of such books designed to bring to managers and practitioners an understanding of the principles of the Children Act and associated regulations, to identify areas of change and to discuss the implications for policies, procedures and practice. It is not intended that any one handbook should be read as a discrete entity. The Children Act was conceived as a cohesive legal framework for the care and protection of children. Each volume of guidance should therefore be read in conjunction with the others in the series and cross-references are made where appropriate. The need to build on sound practice and the multi-agency, multi-disciplinary co-operation identified in **Working Together** and the **Principles and Practice Guide** is also reinforced throughout the Act.

The guidance is written as if the Children Act is currently in force and refers in the past tense to legislation which is repealed by the Act and guidance which is withdrawn in consequence. A glossary of terms and index will be provided for the guidance as a whole.

## Chapter 1: Introduction

1.1   This volume is about family placements. The Children Act 1989 brings together most private and public law relating to children, replacing complex and fragmented legislation with a single statute. Part III of the Act places a new emphasis on local authorities' duty to provide services to support parents in bringing up children in need in their own home and to work in partnership with parents in looking after children away from home. Reference to 'parents' includes any person with parental responsibility unless otherwise indicated.

1.2   The first provision in Part III is the general duty to safeguard and promote the welfare of children in need (section 17). In addition Part III addresses the general duty of a local authority towards children being looked after by them. 'Looked after' is the new term used in the Act which covers all children accommodated by a local authority, whether this is by voluntary arrangement or because of a care order (references to 'in care' are to children subject to a care order). Emphasis is placed upon the need to make plans for children looked after in partnership with those who are important in the child's life and to involve those people and the child, subject to his understanding in reviewing such plans. This is reinforced by the requirement to provide a representations procedure. The Part III provisions supported by those in Schedule 2 are intended to put beyond doubt the powers and duties of local authorities in assisting families to provide appropriately for the good health, proper care and development of their children.

*     *     *     *     *

## Chapter 2: Arrangements for Placement of Children

### Children who are looked after by the local authority

*Welfare*

2.5   The primary duty of the local authority is to safeguard and promote the welfare of a child who is looked after and to make such use of services available for children cared for by their own parents as appears to the authority to be reasonable in the case of a particular child (section 22(3)(*b*)). Although the Child Care Act 1980 requirement in respect of promotion of a child's welfare, 'throughout his childhood' is not reproduced the intention is still that both the immediate and long-term needs of the child should be considered and provided for in the local authority's planning for the child. In undertaking that planning for a child in care the local authority is required to give the same attention to the wishes and feelings of the child, parents and others as they must when providing accommodation under voluntary arrangements. The local authority should also take into account and consider fully the child's religious persuasion, racial origin and cultural and linguistic background. Children with physical and/or sensory disability or mental handicap will require particular consideration and the accommodation provided for them should not be unsuitable to the needs of the child (section 23(8)).

*   *   *   *   *

## The purpose of planning

2.20   The purpose of planning is to safeguard and promote the child's welfare as required by the general welfare duties in sections 17(1) and 22(3) and 61 and 64 of the Act. The drawing up of an individual plan for each child looked after will prevent drift and help to focus work with the family and child. This will be achieved in broad terms by:

    (*a*)  assessing the child's needs;
    (*b*)  determining what objectives have to be met to safeguard and promote the child's welfare;
    (*c*)  consulting with the parents, the child and others whom the local authority consider are relevant;
    (*d*)  appraising fully the available options to meet those objectives;
    (*e*)  making decisions only after full consultation with the child, his parents and other agencies and individuals with a legitimate interest;
    (*f*)  identifying which individuals are to undertake which tasks; and
    (*g*)  setting a timescale in which tasks must be achieved or reassessed.

## Welfare of the child

2.21   Regulation 4 and Schedules 1-3 of the Arrangements for Placement of Children Regulations list matters to be considered by the responsible authority, so far as is reasonably practicable, when drawing up a plan for a child who is to be looked after or accommodated. The list covers different aspects of the child's welfare, but is not intended to be exclusive and does not repeat matters already covered by the Act. There may well also be other matters for consideration in individual cases. The Act and the Regulations indicate the need to cover the following aspects in relation to the child's welfare:

- the child's needs;
- the ability of the parent to adhere to an agreed plan (relevant except in cases where a child is looked after subject to a court order);
- parental responsibilities and the parents' capacity to provide for the child's needs;
- the wishes and views of the child having regard to his understanding;
- the provision of services under Part III of the Act in respect of children looked after by a local authority;
- what is necessary to fulfil the responsible authority's duty under the Act to safeguard and promote the child's welfare;
- the type of placement best suited to the child's needs (taking into account the duty in relation to children looked after by a local authority to place the child near his home and with siblings if applicable);

- what is necessary to make the appropriate provision for the child's religious persuasion, racial origin and cultural and linguistic background;
- any needs the child may have because of disability. This may include a consideration of the type of accommodation to be provided, the suitability of the carer, the need to arrange any specific assessments (for example, under the Education Act 1981) and for any physical and/or sensory disability or learning difficulty;
- the local authority's duty under section 23(6) to enable the child to live with a parent, other person with parental responsibility for the child, relative or friend. Where the child is in care, a person in whose favour a residence order was in force immediately before the care order was made, or other person with a legitimate interest in the child;
- reunification issues not covered above;
- the arrangements proposed for contact with regard to the duty on the local authority in paragraph 15 of Schedule 2, to promote and maintain contact between the child and his family or contact under directions from the court;
- the requirement in Regulation 6 that a voluntary organisation or the person carrying on a registered child's home should endeavour to promote contact between the child and his parents, other persons with parental responsibility or a relative, friend, or person connected with him; and
- the arrangements to be made for the child's health and education. (Health and education are dealt with more fully below.)

2.22   All factors relevant to the welfare of the individual child must be taken into account in assessing the child's needs and making decisions about the child's welfare. None of the separate factors involved should be abstracted and converted into a general pre-condition which overrides the others or causes any of them to be less than fully considered. The only general policy that is acceptable in making decisions about placing children is that all relevant factors should be considered. Different factors will obviously vary in importance in relation to different children or in relation to the same child at different times. It will be right in those circumstances to weigh different factors differently. But it is not right to define any factor as of such general significance or primary that it overrides or qualifies the duty to consider together all factors bearing on the welfare of the child as an individual.

\*   \*   \*   \*   \*

*Assessment*

2.54   Using the information gathered together in the inquiry process it will be possible to make a full assessment of the child's needs in relation to safeguarding or promoting his welfare, taking into account any services the responsible authority or other agencies may already be providing. The assessment should link in to other assessment processes. The Act provides that a local authority may assess a child's needs for the purpose of the Children Act at the same time as any assessment under:

(*a*)   the Chronically Sick and Disabled Persons Act 1970;
(*b*)   the Education Act 1981;
(*c*)   the Disabled Persons (Services, Consultation and Representation) Act 1986; or
(*d*)   any other enactment.

2.55   Joint assessment in appropriate cases will help to ensure that the child's needs are not addressed in isolation and that the child is looked at 'in the round'. Working in collaboration with other agencies will help to identify how the responsible authority and other agencies can best meet the child's needs.

2.56 In assessing the need for local authority provision of services due account needs to be taken of the particular needs of the child, ie: health, disability, education, religious persuasion, racial origin, cultural and linguistic background, the degree (if any) to which these needs are being met by existing services to the family or child and which agencies' services are best suited to the child's needs.

2.57 Assessment must identify a child's ethnic origins, religion, special needs and family experience to provide as comprehensive a guide as possible to the child's needs. Necessary experience and expertise should be provided for in staffing of services and through relationships with other professions and services and with the community. In some areas the local community may include too great a variety of ethnic groups to be reflected fully in composition of staff. In others, local authorities may be called on only rarely to provide a service for a child or family from a minority ethnic group. In both these circumstances, local authorities will need to identify sources of advice and help so that the necessary experience, expertise and resources are available when needed. Care is needed so that the terms 'black' and 'black family' are not used in isolation in such a way as to obscure characteristics and needs. In assessing the needs of a child with communication difficulties or a child with a parent with communication difficulties, it is important that local authorities are aware that a sign language interpreter, large print, tape and braille may need to be provided if communication is to be effective.

2.58 The Department's publication **Protecting Children: A Guide for Social Workers undertaking a Comprehensive Assessment (HMSO 1988)** contains much useful guidance which is applicable to all assessments of children by social workers.

## Decision-making

2.59 During the process the social worker will be deciding on the best approach to the case by identifying the child's needs, obtaining and taking into account the wishes and feelings of the child, his parents and others involved with the child, seeking the advice of other professionals in the consultation process and will be considering:

- is the best approach the provision of services (including if appropriate) accommodation by voluntary agreement;
- whether or not the child protection action is needed (which may often include provision of accommodation for the child by voluntary agreement); or
- is it compulsory care subject to a court order that is required.

2.60 Decision-making will entail:

- translating the assessed needs into aims and general objectives;
- listing and appraising the specific options available (or which may need to be created) for achieving these objectives;
- deciding on the preferred option, setting out the reasons for the decision.

2.61 The proposed plan will explain in detail how the objectives can be achieved ie if and what sort of accommodation is needed; what other services for the child and services for parents or other members of family or the child's carer need to be provided; services which might be provided by other agencies such as the health authority or a voluntary organisation; likely duration of the placement; and arrangements for sustaining family links, promoting contact and reunification of the family.

*Contents of the plan for the child*

2.62 There is no prescribed format for a child care plan (but see the considerations in Regulation 4 and Schedules 1-4). The plan should be recorded in writing and contain the child's and his family's social history and the following key elements:

- the child's identified needs (including needs arising from race, culture, religion or language, special educational or health needs);
- how these needs might be met;
- aim or plan and timescale;
- proposed placement (type and details);
- other services to be provided to child and or family either by the local authority or other agencies;
- arrangements for contact and reunification;
- support in the placement;
- likely duration of placement in the accommodation;
- contingency plan, if placement breaks down;
- arrangements for ending the placement (if made under voluntary arrangements);
- who is to be responsible for implementing the plan (specific tasks and overall plan);
- specific detail of the parents' role in day to day arrangements;
- the extent to which the wishes and views of the child, his parents and anyone else with a sufficient interest in the child (including representatives of other agencies) have been obtained and acted upon and the reasons supporting this or explanations of why wishes/views have been discounted;
- arrangements for input by parents, the child and others into the ongoing decision-making process;
- arrangements for notifying the responsible authority of disagreements or making representations;
- arrangements for health care (including consent to examination and treatment);
- arrangements for education; and
- dates of reviews.

\* \* \* \* \*

## Aftercare: advice and assistance: Implementation of decisions arising from the plan

2.73 One of the most important aspects of planning is to ensure that the decisions arising from the plan are implemented. This is best done by ensuring that all those involved in the planning and subsequent review process know clearly who is responsible for implementing which decisions and when. The value of the plan will rapidly diminish if objectives are not met in part or in whole because there has been poor communication, lack of clarity about who is responsible for what and the relevant timescales. Therefore the letter notifying the proposed plan should make it clear who is responsible for the implementation of different components of the plan.

### Young people with disabilities: particular needs

9.28 Young people with disabilities are, for the purpose of this guidance, young people who are 'blind, deaf, or dumb or (suffer) from mental disorder of any kind or (are) substantially and permanently handicapped by illness, injury or congenital deformity . . .' (section 17(11) of the Children Act).

9.29 Young people with disabilities may well have particular needs over and above the needs of other young people who are being cared for. It is essential to ensure that these needs are met when preparing these young people for leaving care and subsequently, providing aftercare. At the same time, care must be taken to ensure that these young people do not fail to achieve their full potential as a result of under-expectation on the part of those caring for them.

9.30 The following paragraphs refer specifically to the responsibilities of local authorities (particularly SSDs). However, apart from paragraphs 9.34 to 9.39, they also apply to voluntary organisations and registered children's homes, who have a duty to prepare young people whom they are caring for, for the time when they leave care, and who may also provide aftercare for these young people.

9.31 SSDs should ensure that they have access to information on special resources and services necessary to meet the needs of young people with disabilities who are leaving care. They will also need to liaise closely with education departments and health authorities to ensure that the particular needs of these young people are met at all times. And they will need to take any steps necessary to ensure that the views of these young people about their needs, and the ways in which these can be met, are taken into account. This may necessitate the use of skilled appropriate communications to enable better communication to take place between young people with disabilities and the various agencies.

9.32 Local authorities will need to note, in addition, that they have a duty to assist local education authorities with the provision of services for any young person who is subject to a statement of special educational needs (section 27(4) of the Children Act).

9.33 SSDs will also need to liaise with housing authorities over the housing needs of young people with disabilities. They should ask the relevant housing authority to consider the particular needs of any young person with a disability who is leaving care.

9.34 In discharging these responsibilities, local authorities will need to take account of their powers and duties under other Acts of Parliament, as set out below. These powers and duties are not, of course, limited to young people who are being looked after by local authorities. Voluntary organisations and registered children's homes may therefore consider what help the local authority can give, under these Acts, to young people whom they themselves are preparing for leaving care or providing with aftercare.

9.35 Section 2(1) of the Chronically Sick and Disabled Persons Act 1970 lays on each local authority a duty to provide various welfare services to any person living within its area if this is necessary in order to meet the needs of that person.

9.36 Sections 5 and 6 of the Disabled Persons (Services, Consultation and Representation) Act 1986 are also relevant since they are designed to ensure a smooth transition from full-time education to adult life for a young person who is subject to a 'statement of special educational needs'. Their effect is to require the relevant education department to obtain the view of the SSD as to whether such a young person is disabled. This is done at the first reassessment of the young person's educational needs, following the young person's 14th birthday. If the SSD does consider that the young person is disabled, it must assess his needs, before he leaves full-time education, to decide what welfare services it has a duty to provide him with. (See the relevant sections of the 1986 Act for details).

9.37 Local authorities should, as a matter of good practice, also provide communication support for all young people who require it. This could take the form, for instance, of text telephones or interpreters.

9.38   When a child is being looked after by a local authority and placed in accommodation which provides education on the premises, the local authority is required to inform the appropriate education department when the child leaves that accommodation (section 28(3)).

9.39   In deciding the young person's future needs, the SSD should continue to liaise with the education department, which is responsible for providing 'adequate facilities for further education' and which needs to 'have regard to the requirements of persons over compulsory school age who have learning difficulties' (section 41 of the Education Act 1944 as substituted by section 120(2) of the Education Reform Act 1988).

9.40   More generally, local authorities will wish to note that some disabilities inhibit natural maturity and may delay learning processes and this must be taken account of in preparing a young person for leaving care and in providing aftercare.

9.41   Specific health requirements may also continue into adulthood. The transition from child to adult health services is not always easily made by a young person, who may well require help and support from the local authority, acting as a 'good parent'. In providing this help and support, local authorities should, of course, liaise closely with health authorities.

9.42   The particular needs of young people with disabilities will—as mentioned above—need to be taken into account in preparing them for leaving care and also in providing the necessary aftercare. It is important to note that the needs of young people with disabilities will not suddenly and fundamentally cease when they do leave care. Liaison between the various agencies concerned with a young person's welfare should continue after he has left care.

*   *   *   *   *

## (3)   THE CHILDREN ACT GUIDANCE AND REGULATIONS: VOLUME 6

### Children with Disabilities

### Preface

The guidance in this volume is issued under section 7 of the Local Authority Social Services Act 1970. . . .

### Chapter 1: Introduction

1.1   The Children Act 1989, brings together most public and private law relating to children and establishes a new approach in England and Wales to SSD services for children and their families. This guidance considers the implications of the Act's drawing together the SSD's functions towards children which existed under the Child Care Act 1980, the National Assistance Act 1948 and Schedule 8 of the National Health Service Act 1977 so that apart from the Chronically Sick and Disabled Persons Act 1970 and the Disabled Persons (Services, Consultation and Representation) Act 1986, the SSD's functions in respect of children with disabilities are covered by the Children Act.

1.2   The Children Act provides a legal framework for a new approach to provision of services to a child with disabilities. Unification of all legislation governing the

SSD's provision of services to children seeks to ensure integration of provision of services for children and requires that they must offer children with disabilities looked after by them or by other agencies, the benefit of those powers and duties which they have in respect of all children whom they look after. As with other parts of the Act, provisions in relation to children with disabilities do not stand alone but must be considered within the context of the wider range of provisions under the Act. This separate guidance does not contain any regulations or present requirements that are not contained within the other volumes in the Children Act series. Brief summaries and explanations in the context of working with children with disabilities are provided in this document to make clear the new approach to working with children with disabilities that the Act requires. This is to help local authorities (SSDs and LEAs) and the health service to consider afresh their policies and strategies for the provision of services to children with disabilities.

1.3   The Act provides new safeguards for children with disabilities which they were unable to enjoy previously unless they were in the care of the SSD (as health and welfare legislation generally made no provision for the welfare of individual children provided with services by a SSD). Requirements such as having to review the case of a child who has been living away from home, having to give consideration to his welfare and to consult him and his parents before decisions are taken, therefore, apply to children with disabilities as well as other children in need. This is without any loss of any special provisions that applied to children with disabilities prior to implementation of the Children Act.

1.4   The Children Act contains provisions in respect of services to children with disabilities:

- Section 23(8) requires that 'where a local authority provide accommodation for a child whom they are looking after and who is disabled, they shall, so far as is reasonably practicable, secure that the accommodation is not unsuitable to his particular needs' (see Chapter 11);
- Schedule 2, paragraph 2 separates out the requirement on local authorities to open and maintain a register of children with disabilities in their area (see Chapter 4);
- Schedule 2, paragraph 3 provides that a local authority may assess a child's needs for the purpose of the Children Act at the same time as any assessment under certain other Acts (see Chapter 5);
- Schedule 2, paragraph 9 requires local authorities to provide services for children with disabilities which are designed to minimise the effects of the children's disabilities and to give them the opportunity to lead lives that are as normal as possible (see Chapter 6).

1.5   SSDs have a clear, positive and separate duty to provide services to children with disabilities in their area. SSDs developing policies for children with disabilities within the overall framework of the Children Act should ensure that they have a specific policy on integration of their services which meets their general duties and powers towards children and families under the Children Act. Policies should take account of the wishes and views of the local community including user groups. Every effort should be made to work collaboratively in team and multi-agency structures in order to avoid the creation of separate and segregated services.

1.6   Work with children with disabilities in the context of the Children Act should be based on the following principles:

- The welfare of the child should be safeguarded and promoted by those providing services;

- A primary aim should be to promote access for all children to the same range of services;
- Children with disabilities are children first;
- Recognition of the importance of parents and families in children's lives;
- Partnership between parents and local authorities and other agencies; and
- The views of children and parents should be sought and taken into account.

1.7   In support of these principles, the Act:

- Provides for parents to retain parental responsibility for their children (even when there is a court order committing children to care);
- Imposes new duties on the SSD towards children *in need* and their families. The definition of children *in need* includes children with disabilities;
- Requires SSDs to provide services designed to minimise the effect of a child's disabilities and to give a child with disabilities the opportunity to lead as normal a life as possible.
- Requires SSDs providing services to give due consideration to the child's religious persuasion, racial origin, cultural and linguistic background;
- Provides for a collaborative and inter-agency approach in the provision of services to families and children;
- Gives SSDs new responsibilities for children it is looking after; and
- Provides a range of new court orders to protect children at risk.

1.8   Treating children as children first is of paramount importance. However, there is a need for all staff who may be involved in providing a service to a child with disabilities to be aware of legislation and local arrangements with specific relevance to the provision of services for people with disabilities. Work with many children with disabilities requires particular experience and expertise and SSDs should ensure arrangements provide for the necessary advice, expertise and resources to be available to their staff when needed. The Children Act provides that assessment arrangements for children who may be in need can be carried out simultaneously with assessments under the Chronically Sick and Disabled Persons Act 1970, the Education Act 1981, the Disabled Persons Act 1986 or any other enactment (see Chapter 5). SSDs should discuss with LEAs, DHAs (and where appropriate NHS Trusts) arrangements for joint assessment in appropriate cases and the provision of health services under the collaborative arrangements in the light of the Children Act and the NHS reforms.

### Chapter 3: Children in Need

**Definition**

3.1   The Act defines a category of children *in need* for whom the SSD should provide services, if necessary, to safeguard and promote their welfare. A child is defined by the Act as being *in need* if:

   (*a*)   he is unlikely to achieve or maintain, or to have the opportunity of achieving or maintaining, a reasonable standard of health or development without the provision for him of services by a local authority under this Part [of the Act];

   (*b*)   his health or development is likely to be significantly impaired, or further impaired, without the provision for him of such services; or

   (*c*)   he is disabled.

'development' means physical, intellectual, emotional, social or behavioural development, and

'health' means physical or mental health.

3.2    The Children Act mirrors the National Assistance Act 1948 definition of disability, stating that:

> a child is disabled if he is blind, deaf or dumb or suffers from mental disorder of any kind or is substantially and permanently handicapped by illness, injury or congenital deformity or such other disability as may be prescribed.

Thus a person with a disability qualifies for services before and after the age of 18.

## General duty to provide services

3.3    The Act's definitions of in need and disability provide the basis of a general duty on the SSD to provide an appropriate range and level of services to safeguard and promote the welfare of children in need and '*so far as is consistent with that duty to promote the upbringing of such children by their families*'. This general duty is supported by other specific duties and powers such as facilitation of 'the provision by others, including in particular voluntary organisations of services' (section 17(5) and Schedule 2). These provisions encourage SSDs to provide day and domiciliary services, guidance and counselling, respite care and a range of other services as a means of supporting children in need (including children with disabilities) within their families. The Act recognises that sometimes a child can only be helped by providing services for other members of his family (section 17(3)) 'if it [the service] is provided with a view to safeguarding or promoting the child's welfare'. 'Family' in relation to such a child, includes any person who has parental responsibility for the child and any other person with whom he has been living. The SSD may make such arrangements as they see fit for *any* person to provide services and support 'may include giving assistance in kind, or in exceptional circumstances in cash' (section 17(6)). However, where it is the SSD's view that a child's welfare is adequately provided for and no unmet need exists, they need not act. SSDs now have a general duty to provide day care services and supervise activities for children in need aged five and under and not at school and for school age children outside school hours and in school holidays. Children have common needs in terms of care, affection and a stimulating environment in which to develop. The Children Act's definition of children in need and the range of duties and powers provided in Part III of the Act should therefore be seen as an important opportunity not only to ensure that children with disabilities are treated as children first, but also to ensure access to the range of generic and specialist provision available to support children and families in their own homes and their local communities.
3.4    The SSD is not obliged to provide all the services which may be needed itself. Section 17(5)(a) of the Act states that every SSD shall facilitate the provision by others (including in particular voluntary organisations) of services which the local authority have power to provide by virtue of this section or sections 18, 20, 23 and 24 of the Act. SSDs may also arrange for others to provide services on their behalf (section 17(5)(b)).
3.5    In deciding which services are needed by individual families, SSDs will need to give careful attention not only to families' stated preferences but to the contribution which other statutory and voluntary agencies might make. The potential contributions of the respective agencies in the statutory, voluntary and independent sectors are shown in Annex A. Coordinating packages of services from multiple service providers will require time and resources and the compatibility of services offered should be carefully assessed. Individual children and families will have very different levels of need which may fluctuate throughout the year according to other pressures of family life. The provision of education, respite care and day care will

not be effective unless they are tailored to the needs of the child and family. Arrangements must be such that parents are reassured that the child will receive good quality care and that the child's interests are met. In some instances provision of a discrete service (eg aids and adaptations to a house or transport in order to use a local after school club) may assist the child and his family to lead fulfilling lives without other service provision.

### Identification of need and publicising services

3.6    Paragraph 1 of Schedule 2 to the Act requires SSDs to identify the extent to which there are children in need in their area and to publicise the availability of services. SSDs should build on existing links with community groups, voluntary organisations and ethnic minority groups to involve them in planning services and as a sounding board when formulating policies. The publicity required must include information about services provided both by the SSD and, to the extent they consider it appropriate, about such provision by others (eg voluntary organisations). Publicity should be clearly presented and accessible to all groups in the community, taking account of linguistic and cultural factors and the needs of people with communication difficulties. SSDs should take reasonable steps to ensure that all those who might benefit from such services receive the relevant information.

*   *   *   *   *

## Chapter 4: Co-ordinating Services

### Collaborative working

4.1    New organisational links between SSDs and NHS staff will need to be developed if they are to implement the Act. DHAs may help SSDs to fulfil their duty to take reasonable steps to identify the extent to which there are children in need in their area by identifying the numbers and needs of children in their areas who are disabled through physical, sensory or learning disablement, mental disorders and chronic illness. Such assistance would not require identification of individual children. In respect of an individual child SSDs will need to consider in co-operation with other relevant agencies such as DHAs or LEAs, a child's overall developmental needs—physical, social, intellectual, emotional and behavioural in assessing what sort of services are required. The Children Act requires SSDs, LEAs, local housing authorities, DHAs and NHS Trusts to comply with a request from a SSD for assistance in providing services under Part III of the Act so long as it is compatible with their own legal duty or other duties and does not unduly prejudice the discharge of any of their functions (section 27).

### Register of children with disabilities

4.2    The Act replaces and separates out the previous requirements placed on SSDs to keep registers of children with disabilities in their area. Paragraph 2 of Schedule 2 to the Children Act requires SSDs to keep a register of children with disabilities. This provision, which is designed to help their service planning and monitoring, originated from directions made under the National Assistance Act 1948 in relation to disabled persons. There is no corresponding duty on parents to agree to registration (which is a voluntary procedure) and services are not dependent on registration. Registration can contribute positively to coherent planning of service provision for children with disabilities under the Children Act. However, registration will necessitate clear criteria for definitions of disability. This will be decided best in discussions between SSDs, LEAs and DHAs. As will the fact that registers should be regularly updated.

4.3   SSDs whilst acknowledging the legal definition of disability in the Children Act, will need to liaise with their education and health counterparts to achieve an understanding of disability which permits early identification; which facilitates joint working; which encourages parents to agree to registration and which is meaningful in terms of planning services for the child in question and children in general. The creation of a joint register of children with disabilities between health, education and social services would greatly facilitate collaboration in identification and co-ordinated provision of services under the Act. It is possible for a SSD to arrange for another agency (a DHA for example) to maintain and operate the register on their behalf. In such circumstances responsibility for the register remains with the SSD.

4.4   Whichever agency is the first to identify a child having a disability whether it is the LEA, SSD or child health services they should initiate discussions with the parents about services or procedures which might be beneficial to the child and family. This should include an explanation of what other agencies can provide and information about the register.

\* \* \* \* \*

## Chapter 5: Assessment and Planning Process

5.1   SSDs will need to develop clear assessment procedures for children in need within agreed criteria which take account of the child's and family's needs and preferences, racial and ethnic origins, their culture, religion and any special needs relating to the circumstances of individual families. The assessment procedures are not laid down in primary legislation or regulations, but assessments under the Children Act should be undertaken in the context of Part 3 and Schedule 2 of the Act (as part of the process of recognition of need and the identification of appropriate services). The Children Act empowers SSDs to combine assessments under the Children Act with those under other legislation such as the Education Act 1981; the Disabled Persons Act 1986 and the Chronically Sick and Disabled Persons Act 1970 (paragraph 3 of Schedule 2 to the Children Act). Formal assessment under the Education Act 1981 already involves collaboration between DHAs, LEAs and SSDs and parents. The procedures under the Education Act 1981 are likely to contribute significantly to assessment by SSDs and can be used as a basis for further collaborative decision-making about the wider needs of children and families. The Disabled Persons Act 1986 requires SSDs to assess young people with disabilities at the time they leave school for a range of welfare services as outlined in the Chronically Sick and Disabled Persons Act 1970. At eighteen years of age, young persons who have a continuing need for community care services, or who may require them for the first time, are covered by the provisions of the NHS and Community Care Act 1990, which include an assessment of their need for services.

5.2   In many cases children with disabilities will need continuing services throughout their lives. It will therefore be particularly important that for these children, the assessment process takes a longer perspective than is usual or necessary for children without disabilities, who will usually cease to have a need for services after reaching adulthood.

5.3   The requirements of children with disabilities may need to be met from a number of sources. In conducting assessments and managing the care provided, SSDs will need to ensure that all necessary expertise is marshalled and that all those provided services are involved from both within and beyond the SSD. The outcome of assessment should be a holistic and realistic picture of the individual and family being assessed, which takes into account their strengths and capacities as well as any difficulties and which acknowledges the need to make provision appropriate to the family's cultural background and their expressed views and preferences.

5.4   The SSD's provision of services to children with disabilities should involve an initial assessment of need, a continuing process of reassessment and review of the plan for the child. Continuity should not be broken for reasons which concern organisational or administrative convenience rather than the welfare of the child or young person. A smooth transition, when the young person reaches 18 and comes within the provisions of the NHS and Community Care Act 1990 should be the objective.

## NHS and Community Care Act 1990—Care management

5.5   In the White Paper **'Caring for People'** and subsequent policy guidance issued in November 1990, care management and assessment are key processes in the provision of community care services. This has relevance for SSDs in planning services for children under the Children Act and may provide a useful model for consideration.

5.6   The NHS and Community Care Act 1990 requires the SSD to assess the needs of persons who may require community care services. If during the course of assessment it appears that a person is disabled, the SSD is required if requested to decide upon the need for services under Section 4 of the Disabled Persons Act 1986. Over time, these assessment arrangements will be expected to form part of wider care management systems that cover all arrangements for the care of the service user from the beginning to the end of their contact with the SSD.

5.7   Policy guidance **(Caring for People: Community Care in the Next Decade and Beyond—Policy Guidance: Chapter 3—Care Management and Assessment)** describes 3 distinct processes which characterise care management in its most comprehensive form:

— assessment of the users' circumstances
— design of a 'care package' in agreement with users' carers and relevant agencies to meet the identified needs within the care resources available, including help from willing and able carers
— implementation and monitoring of the agreed package; review of the outcomes for users and carers; and any necessary revision of service provision.

5.8   An important feature of the care management process is that it is based on a needs-led approach within resources available. Responsibility for assessment and care planning should be progressively separated from service provision in order to focus on needs, where possible having the tasks carried out by different staff. The intention is to ensure that people are not fitted into existing services, but that services are adapted to individual needs. This separation enables discrepancies between assessed needs and available service to be identified.

5.9   Care management arrangements also take account of the multiple service providers which will be required to meet the majority of special needs. The approach aims to encourage the identification of the full range of services which may be needed. The SSD will have overall responsibility for the co-ordination of the services required. However, the day to day management and provision of these services may rest elsewhere. Packages of support can be put together using the statutory and the voluntary and independent sectors thereby making use of whatever pattern of provision has been developed within the context of a particular SSD.

## Child care practice

5.10 Good child care practice incorporates many of the features of care management. The procedures of the Education Act 1981, for example, encourages the resolution of a child's special educational needs where necessary by the definition of an educational care package which includes services from the child health service, SSD and LEA concerned. Some SSDs are now developing 'packages of support' for children.

5.11 There is a further similarity between child care practice and care management in that the aim is normally to provide one worker with continuing responsibility for providing and co-ordinating services. This is one means by which care management may be delivered, and may be the means best suited to meet the needs of children with disabilities. It should be emphasised, however, that the appointment of a single care manager is but one way of delivering care management, the responsibility for different aspects of which may be shared by different workers. Moreover it should be emphasised that where responsibility is given to a single care manager, that care manager should be from the agency most relevant to the current needs of the child with a disability, and that this agency may change over time.

5.12 The distinction between the terms 'key worker' and 'care manager' should also be noted. The range of responsibilities carried by care managers and the fact that they are not involved in direct service delivery distinguishes their role from that of key workers.

5.13 Standards of service are agreed between the SSD and service providers and the individual package of care may reflect a very wide diversity of service provision. The parents and children concerned are important contributors to the planning process. But the development of a flexible child care service for children with disabilities will not be possible without the closest liaison between health, education and social services and the use of whatever team approach to special needs is available in the locality. If district handicap, child development or community mental handicap teams are to contribute positively to assessment and planning services to children with disabilities (and to forward planning under the NHS and Community Care Act when the young person makes the transition to adult services), SSD representation on and involvement in the work of the team in question will be crucial. Ensuring an input from a SSD representative into existing teams will often be a cost-effective way of enabling all local resources to be used in the most effective way. Additionally the representative in question will have direct access to team members and to the planning process of the other services.

## The management process

5.14 Many children with disabilities will require support from a very wide range of services. Their need for services will often be a continuing need. An ongoing process of assessment, monitoring and review will therefore be essential in order to ensure appropriateness and effectiveness of service provision. Where a multi-disciplinary team already exists, the appointment of key workers or care manager may pose no problems. Since the development of individual packages of care will necessitate negotiations with service managers and budget holders across a range of agencies, a team base for such an arrangement may be the most effective. But care management will require skilled support, training and regular appraisal. In implementing the new arrangements for children with disabilities under the Children Act, SSDs will need to look carefully at:

- the range of existing assessment arrangements within agencies providing services for children with disabilities within the SSD in question;
- the recording and monitoring systems to be used by the SSD in assessing and planning to meet needs:
- the use of the register with regard to recording and reviewing provision;
- the extent to which existing multi-disciplinary teams can be utilised and developed in creating shared assessment systems;
- how best to involve consumers—parents and children—in the assessment process and to ensure that they have ownership of the outcomes of any assessment process; and
- procedures when the young person reaches the age of 18 and the provisions of the NHS and Community Care Act 1990 and the Children Act 1989 overlap. The aim must be to ensure by early planning that a seamless transition to adult services takes place.

5.15   Policy guidance requires that where community care arrangements are fully implemented SSDs will need to have available published information accessible to all potential service users and carers, including those with any communication difficulty or difference in language or culture. The information should set out the types of community care available, the criteria for provision of services, the assessment procedures to agree needs and ways of addressing them and the standards by which the care management system (including assessment) will be measured.

5.16   SSDs should include in this information care management and assessment arrangements for children with disabilities. Such information could be linked to wider duties to provide information on the full range of local services and could be made available to children and families undergoing assessment through procedures relating to the 1981 Act and other relevant legislation.

5.17   Detailed practice guidance has been prepared by the Department's Social Services Inspectorate on the implementation of care management and assessment arrangements. Many of the principles are also applicable to aspects of child care. SSDs should refer to the community care assessment and care management practice guide.

## Chapter 6: Planning of services in partnership with parents and children

6.1   A key theme in the Children Act is that of partnership with parents and, where the child is of sufficient understanding, with the child. The concept of partnership is not new, but is based on well established beliefs that:

- the family home is the natural and most appropriate place for the majority of children;
- families are already caring for children, and supporting them to do so is, in most cases, in the best interests of the child and best allocation of resources in the SSD;

- children are individuals with their own needs, wishes and feelings;
- the family has a unique and special knowledge of a child and can therefore contribute significantly to that child's health and development—albeit often in partnership with a range of service providers; and
- families provide continuity for children throughout their childhood—and, in the context of the Children Act, families are recognised as being more widely defined than parents and brothers and sisters and other relatives, and often play an important part in the life of a child.

6.2   Parents and children from all backgrounds, ethnic origins and different life-styles, will need clear information and sensitive responses when they seek support. The services needed may be day care; health services and educational provision which all parents and children will use sometime or a targeted service to meet a particular need.

6.3   The Arrangements for Placement of Children (General) Regulations 1991 and the Review of Children Case's Regulations 1991 together with specific placement regulations are the framework for the provision of the service of accommodation to children looked after by SSDs or accommodated by voluntary organisations or in registered children's homes (see Chapter 11). Good practice requires that the same approach is taken to the provision of services other than accommodation. This is implicit in the provision contained in paragraph 6 of Schedule 2 to the Act which requires that:

> every local authority shall provide services designed—
> (a)  to minimise the effect on disabled children within their area of their disabilities; and
> (b)  to give such children the opportunity to lead lives which are as normal as possible.

## Planning a service for the individual child

6.4   Once a need has been identified a plan for the best service provision will be required. This may amount to no more than matching the need with an existing service in the community. Where the SSD has to allocate resources to arrange a service—for example, a family aide for the family or a day nursery place for the child—the plan should estimate how long the service may be required, what the objective of the service should be and what else others are expected to do. In order to be effective this plan should form the basis of an agreement with the child, parent or other carer and be reviewed at appropriate intervals. In planning for the individual child, the SSD should take account of the particular needs of the child—that is in relation to health, development, disability, education, religious persuasion, racial origin, gender, cultural and linguistic background, the degree (if any) to which these needs are being met by existing services to the family or child and which agencies' services are best suited to the child's needs. The needs of brothers and sisters should not be overlooked and they should be provided for as part of a package of services for the child with a disability. They may however be in need in their own right and require separate assessment. SSDs must be sensitive to the needs and requirements of ethnic minority families, and in particular ensure assessments take into account individual circumstances and are not based on a stereotypical view of what may be required. Equally partnership and consultation with parents and children on the basis of careful joint planning and agreement is the guiding principle for the provision of services whether within the family home or where children are provided with accommodation under voluntary arrangements. Such arrangements are intended to assist the parent and enhance, not undermine, the parent's authority and control. This approach should also be developed when a child is in care, provided that it does not jeopardise his welfare.

6.5 Where a child is looked after (accommodated) by the SSD, the Act requires that his views should be sought subject to his understanding (see sections 22(4)(*a*) and (5), 61 and 64 of the Children Act). It is required that the child's views as expressed be discussed, recorded and given due consideration when plans for the welfare of the child are in hand, before a placement decision is made and at every review meeting and at case conferences.

\* \* \* \* \*

## Chapter 7: Working with the Community

7.1 The Children Act requires SSDs to provide services to support families in bringing up children in need. SSDs are also required to facilitate the provision of such services by others, including in particular, voluntary organisations. The Children Act requires SSDs to facilitate the provision of family support services, day care, accommodation and after care by others and to publicise such services provided by others (section 17(5) and paragraph 1(2) of Schedule 2). Family support will require effective coordination, communication and mutual respect between and with professionals and services in the community. It will also necessitate sensitive assessment of parents' and children's preferences in terms of family support and require providing them with full information in order that they can make an informed choice. Some families caring for children with complex or multiple disabilities may have neither the time nor the energy to contribute to assessment and planning unless they are given personal counselling, support and representation. Working with the child and family in the family home may also contribute to realistic assessment of overall needs and preferences and contribute to a realistic partnership in assessment.

7.2 SSDs have a duty to inform parents of the local range of services which can support families with children in need at home. Voluntary organisations, as well as the education service, may provide a range of provision which is flexible and can be adapted to individual family needs. A number of local authorities now work with the voluntary sector in providing advice. However, the OPCS Reports (1989) noted that most parents did not know of relevant local voluntary organisations. All statutory and voluntary services should ensure that information is given to parents.

\* \* \* \* \*

## Chapter 8: Services to children living with their families

### Domiciliary services

8.1 As stated in paragraph 7.1 services for children with disabilities may be appropriately provided in the home. Investing in a package of family support services to assist parents looking after a child with disabilities at home will in most cases be a better alternative than residential care. A home care service can provide valuable day to day support to families.

\* \* \* \* \*

## Family centres

8.5   Every effort should be made to enable families with young children with dis-abilities to use local services generally available to children and their families wher-ever possible. The family centres, which SSDs are now required to provide for children in their area as a community resource (paragraph 9 of Schedule 2), may provide a range of activities ranging from counselling and general support with par-enting to occupational, social, cultural and recreational activities.

*    *    *    *    *

## Chapter 9: Working with Education Services

### LEA involvement with SSDs

9.1   Joint Circular **HN(89)20/HN(FP)(19)/LASSL(89)7/WOC54/89/DES:22/89**. **Assessments and Statements of Special Educational Needs: Procedures within the Education, Health and Social Services** clearly acknowledges that assessment cannot be seen as a single-agency approach, whatever the specific purpose or outcome of the particular assessment procedure. Paragraph 17 of this circular notes that:
'When it is thought that a child may need special educational provision, the posi-tive and constructive approach is to focus on his or her needs rather than on disabil-ities. The feelings and perceptions of the child concerned should be taken into account and older children and young persons should be able to share in discussions on their needs and any proposed provision. The extent to which a learning difficulty hinders a child's development does not depend solely on the nature and severity of that difficulty. Other significant factors include the personal resources and attrib-utes of the child as well as the help and support provided at home and the provision made by the school and the LEA and other statutory and voluntary agencies. A child's special educational needs are thus related both to abilities and disabilities and to the nature and extent of the interaction of these with his or her environment.'
9.2   Circular 22/89 acknowledges the multifactorial nature of assessment and the extent to which a range of factors will encourage or impede a child in his or her development. LEAs are reminded that in carrying out assessments of a child's special *educational* needs, they must make clear distinctions between:
(i)    the child's relevant past and present levels of functioning, emotional states and interests and how these present resources and deficiencies in relation to the educational demands which will be made on the child;
(ii)   the analysis of the child's consequent learning difficulties;
(iii)  the specification of goals for change in the child and environment (includ-ing school, home and the wider community);
(iv)  the specification of the child's requirement for different kinds of approaches, facilities or resources, in order to facilitate access to the National Curriculum, with any modifications that are considered essential;
(v)   the perceptions and wishes of the parent and child;
(vi)  the special educational provision and services required to meet the identi-fied needs.
9.3   The LEA is also reminded that the monitoring and assessment and review of each child's progress should be seen as a continuous process. A process which begins at birth and continues in the family home and with health and social services *before* a child becomes known to the LEA. The 1981 Act, like the Children Act, clearly defines the need for communication between teachers, the school health service and

SSDs as well as between the LEA and SSDs at a senior management level. Assistance before a situation becomes critical will be more effective than formal assessment procedures initiated too late and in isolation. The needs of some children will be first identified while they are living with their family. Statutory assessments under Section 5 of the 1981 Act may sometimes be required for children who are living in provision made by the local authority such as foster placements; residential care homes or whilst placed in an independent school for primarily residential care needs. Circular 22/89 highlights four particular cases when a SSD or health authority may initiate an assessment of a child's potential special *educational* needs or ask for the decisions reached at a previous assessment to be formally reviewed or reassessed because of concern about their appropriateness for the child in question. The four special circumstances envisaged are:

  (i)   if the child has a medical condition likely to affect future learning ability;
  (ii)  if the child has been admitted in connection with a social condition which is likely to affect future learning ability (such as social deprivation, whether negligence, neglect or child abuse);
  (iii) if a child is receiving treatment likely to affect his future learning ability;
  (iv)  if the child has been admitted to a children's or adolescent psychiatric ward.

9.4   Under Education (Special Educational Needs) Regulations 1983, LEAs must seek educational, medical and psychological advice relating to a child with potential special educational needs, together with advice *from any other source* which they consider desirable in making an assessment under Section 5 of the 1981 Act. Advice is interpreted as written advice on any features of the case which are relevant to or which affect the child's special educational needs and on the best way of meeting these needs. Some LEAs have drawn up their own structured forms for the collection of information on particular children. LEAs must provide all professionals with copies of any representations or views submitted by or on behalf of a child's parent. Parents have the legal right to see all advice used in drawing up a statement. The LEA has the final responsibility for collecting and collating such advice (which may include advice from the SSD) and in making decisions about any special educational provision which may be required. In making its decisions, an LEA must have considered:

  (i)   educational, medical and psychological advice;
  (ii)  any evidence from the child's parents;
  (iii) any information or advice provided by a DHA or SSD;
  (iv)  any other relevant advice.

9.5   Where a statement results, copies of all these documents must be appended to it, since the information forms part of the statement. The statement should, therefore, provide a comprehensive picture of the child and his or her needs which extends beyond the specific educational purpose of the assessment process. Where SSDs have parental responsibility for a child, they will have a dual role. Firstly they should play the part of a good parent. Secondly they should ensure that a social services contribution is made to the assessment. Although not all children in need— or indeed children with disabilities—will have special educational needs which cannot be met without a statement some will come within both groups and more effective participation in assessment under the 1981 Act should therefore be a priority for SSDs.

## Notification of SSDs by the LEA

9.6   When the LEA notifies the parent of their decision to assess formally a child's special educational needs, a copy of the notification must be sent to an officer nominated for this purpose by the SSD. This is intended to offer the SSD an opportunity to consider whether they know of any problems affecting the child relevant to that authority and the range of services it might offer and to indicate to the LEA whether the social services has information relevant to the assessment of a child's special educational needs. Any advice provided by the SSD will be attached as an appendix to the statement. Parents have a right to see such advice. The LEA may also seek advice from the SSD of their own accord.

9.7 The notification of SSDs by LEAs may be an important opportunity for the SSD to meet with and inform parents of children in need with disabilities at a very early stage and to provide information about available services. This notification offers one of the few formal bridges between the two authorities and is an opportunity to link educational assessment to the assessment of a wider range of personal, social or health needs.

## Provision of information

9.8 Under Section 10 of the Education Act 1981, DHAs must notify parents of children under five of any relevant voluntary organisation which would be likely to help them. Information provided by SSDs with regard to provision for children in need under the Children Act could usefully be made available to DHAs to give to parents when making such a referral. In any event DHAs and SSDs will frequently be working together in supporting particular children and families and a collaborative approach is likely to be the most helpful.

9.9 Under Section 10 of the 1981 Act, health authorities also have a duty to inform LEAs of any children under five who might have special educational needs. This procedure has resulted in earlier cooperation in meeting special needs. Although *Section 10* of the Act does not refer to social services departments, they will need to work with health and education with reference to this section of the Act, as it will directly relate to the efficiency of registration procedure and the establishment of a joint register.

## Parental involvement

9.10 Parents have greatly enhanced rights to participation in assessment and subsequent special education provision under the 1981 Education Act procedures. They will see all copies of any professional advice made with regard to the assessment; they may contribute their own written comments on their child's special needs and their preferences and they have rights of appeal to a local appeals tribunal if they are unhappy with the outcome of assessment. However, some parents do not participate as fully as they might in assessment without support. In some instances, particularly where the family have a range of needs unrelated to the educational assessment, SSDs or voluntary organisations could support parents in assessment. An important outcome of such partnership could be a strengthened understanding of the needs of child and parents and an opportunity to learn from the wider advice on the child's medical and psychological as well as social and educational needs. When a child is subject to a care order, the local authority should also ensure that firstly, it involves anybody with parental responsibility for the child in any assessment procedure (supporting them in travelling to an assessment if necessary) and secondly, that it also acts as a good parent and contributes positively to assessment and encourages the child or young person to do likewise.

## Review of statements of special educational needs

9.11   Every Statement of Special Educational Needs must be annually reviewed. Although SSDs are not necessarily involved, every effort should be made to ensure that a relevant member of social services (normally the child's social worker) attends the review of a child looked after. This will ensure that the department is informed of the child's progress and of any special difficulties which the school may be encountering. If there is anxiety about the arrangements made for the child, then reassessment may be requested.

## Under fives

9.12   Section 6 of the Education Act 1981 places duties on LEAs with regard to children with special educational needs under the age of 2. Section 4(2) of the 1981 Act gives LEAs special responsibilities towards children with special educational needs from the age of 2 to the end of compulsory school age. The early identification of special educational needs is crucial for the young child with disabilities and/or delayed development as prompt suitable provision right from the start can considerably enhance the child's future progress. Circular 22/89 states that 'LEAs should give priority to children with special educational needs in admitting children to nursery provision' and emphasises the importance of liaison with school health and social services during the process. Precisely because many local authorities now operate Portage or other home based learning programmes or peripatetic teaching service, early referral to the LEA is essential for young children and parents. Additionally many LEAs provide advisory and support services to social services daycare provision (for example through the school psychological services). The Children Act contains important new provisions to help LEAs and SSDs work in a co-ordinated way. The new review duty—section 19 in Part III—requires the two departments to work together in looking at the pattern of day care services in their area, consulting DHAs and others and finally publishing a report. The legislation requires the review to be undertaken every three years, and Volume 2 of the Children Act 1989 Guidance and Regulations makes it clear that the process should involve follow up so that it is not to be treated as a one off exercise. The new legislation on the regulation of independent day care services and childminding—Part X of Schedule 9 to the Act—give SSDs power to ask the LEA for advice if it seems to them it would help them in the exercise of their functions under this Part. These provisions in the Act will make co-ordination and co-operation easier to achieve and thus help to ensure acceptable standards of service for all children.

## Assessment of children in social services settings

9.13   DES has issued a circular and Regulations on the approval of Independent Schools to admit pupils with statements of special educational needs (DES 2/91 and SI 1991 No 449). A child placed in a specific setting with an existing statement of special educational needs will already have considerable information on record about his needs. The identification of an actual or potential learning difficulty when the child is already placed in a care setting requires staff training and should be covered by clear procedures with regard to notification of the appropriate people and agencies.

9.14   If a child's special needs are identified when already using a day care or residential service provided by social services, the LEA may wish to carry out part of the assessment in the setting which is most familiar to the child. Parents may be very anxious and distressed at the potential identification of a disability or learning difficulty and will need counselling and support. Both care staff and parents should have accurate and clear information on the assessment process and should be aware of the possibility of a special need before any formal assessment arrangements are initiated. Social services staff (and those working in voluntary and independent settings) sometimes feel concerned but inadequate at participating in a primarily educational assessment. But parents and staff working with children observe and assess children. They learn from their behaviour, their preferences, their daily routines and they are likely to be able to predict behaviour in certain situations. They can provide invaluable information for assessment if encouraged to do so. As noted elsewhere change in the educational arrangements of a child may produce difficult behaviour and problems at school which may be short-term in the first instance, but predictive of longer term difficulties and failures if not dealt with promptly.

9.15 Since schools are also sources of social networks for children—and may provide consistent and positive role models for very disadvantaged children—every effort should be made not only to sustain a child's educational placement so that there is familiarity with his or her needs, but also to enable SSDs to work with the education services and to share knowledge and expertise in planning the best way forward. Participation by social services or other care staff can extend to a range of activities which an ordinary parent might expect to share. It should also include participation in home/school activities such as paired reading schemes or sharing in school-based social and other activities. Many schools now operate records of achievement for children and every effort should be made to ensure that children and young people with disabilities are enabled to contribute positively to recording their own achievements and progress and planning for the future. When a child is being formally assessed for a possible Statement of Special Educational Needs, staff working closely with a child should be encouraged to make their contribution to the assessment process and should have access to development checklists, local authority guidelines and any material locally developed to help parents carry out a similar exercise.

## Integration

9.16 Both the Children Act 1989 and the Education Act 1981 place emphasis upon the importance of integration within mainstream provision for children with special needs wherever possible. SSDs, in considering placements for a child with a disability, should therefore take account of the educational arrangements which would accompany such a placement and make every effort to ensure that children can attend an ordinary local school or a local special school if this is regarded as the most positive option. The success or otherwise of an integrated placement will in part depend upon positive attitudes and expectations. But such attitudes are insufficient without a clear understanding of the needs of the child and the best way to meet them. The Fish Committee (1985) noted that:

> The concept of integration as a dynamic process is difficult to grasp. It is often confused with physical location and discussed in terms of specific situations rather than the whole life-styles of children. Integration is about planned interaction between a child and his or her environment and is not about changing the concept of special educational needs but about its context.

\*  \*  \*  \*  \*

## Chapter 10: The Role of Child Health Services

10.1    The SSD's role with regard to children with disabilities and their families
under the Children Act cannot be effectively implemented without close partnership with child health services. The role of the SSD cannot be fulfilled unless it is
fully understood by the local health services, and unless there are shared arrangements for the transfer of information about children and joint planning for their
futures. In addition to identification and assessment, children and young people
with disabilities will have a range of other health care needs including health promotion advice which should be considered when planning for the future. All DHAs
have surveillance and prevention programmes agreed with their appropriate
FHSAs, although the arrangements will vary according to local policy and practice.
SSDs now have to consider health and development as part of their assessment of
children in need and they should be aware of local policies and practice on child
health surveillance. The Court Report (1976) described surveillance as including
five main areas of activity, namely:

(a)   the oversight of the health and physical growth of children;

(b)   monitoring the development progress of all children;

(c)   providing advice and support to parents or those caring for the child, and
referral of the child to appropriate services;

(d)   providing an effective immunisation programme against infectious diseases;
and

(e)   encouraging parents to participate in health education and training for par-
enthood programmes.

*     *     *     *     *

## Assessment

10.4    The full benefits of early identification and the register of children with disabilities will only be achieved if there is a genuine partnership between DHAs and,
in some areas, NHS Trusts and SSDs. DHAs already have duties under section 10
of the Education Act 1981 to inform LEAs of any child under five years of age who
might have special educational needs. Anxieties expressed by many parents about
the association between SSD intervention and the diagnosis of potential child abuse
will necessitate open and honest discussion between parents, carers, SSDs and
health service staff about the role of the individual agencies and their agreed procedures for transfer of information, Indeed transfer of information is unlikely to
occur unless the DHA and parents have clear intelligible and relevant information
on the Children Act and unless parents are confident of the purpose and subsequent
use of the register.

10.5    Under the Education Act 1981, DHAs and SSDs are required to contribute
medical and social services advice to the Statement of Special Educational Needs,
under a section 5 assessment. Although the purpose of such an assessment is to
identify the educational special needs of the child, the assessment process will be a
useful additional source of information about the child who receives help both from
the SSD and the DHA. In such cases, joint discussion should take place on the relevance of the information contained in the medical advice for the future planning
of services.

*     *     *     *     *

## Children living in NHS provision

10.9 In some cases, for children with substantial medical, paramedical and nursing needs the health service will still have a continuing role in the provision of respite and longer term residential care. This is ultimately best decided through multi-disciplinary assessment properly involving parents and child. The use of NHS provision should be part of a planned programme of support for the individual child. Every effort should be made to support placements in local community provision with appropriate input from the NHS. It is clear government policy that children with a learning disability should no longer live in long-stay mental handicap hospitals. Instead, where NHS provision is required, the aim should be to provide care in small, homely, locally-based units. The Welfare of Children and Young People in Hospital guide (HMSO 1991) should be made available to staff in social services, educational departments and child health services to ensure that any care provided is appropriate to the needs of children and the general provisions of the Children Act (see also paragraphs 13.7–13.13). Hospital based social workers are well placed to contribute to the continuing assessment of the health and social care needs of children in hospital and to give practical advice and support.

## Chapter 11: Accommodation as a Service

11.1 The Children Act intends accommodation to be provided, wherever possible under voluntary arrangements, as a service to children in need and their families. The Act assumes a high degree of co-operation between parents and SSDs in negotiating and agreeing what form of accommodation can be offered and the use made of it. Where a child with disabilities is provided with accommodation by a SSD, the Act requires that, so far as is reasonably practicable, the accommodation should not be unsuitable to the needs of the child (section 23(8)). For example, the SSD may wish to provide for suitable adaptations to a foster parent's home. By including children with disabilities in the category of children in need, the Children Act requires SSDs looking after children in need to apply the same planning and review arrangements to them as are needed for other children in need.

* * * * *

11.3 As well as stating that accommodation for children with disabilities should not be unsuitable for their needs, the Act says that services should minimise the effects of a child's disability. Planning a placement for a child with a disability who will be living away from home should follow the same principles for placements which would apply to a child without a disability. All children need arrangements which offer them a sense of permanence and security; which whenever possible provide an experience of ordinary family life; ensure that appropriate education is available and encourage the child to develop a positive self-image and to enjoy the same opportunities for personal growth as would be available to other children with a disability. SSDs should not lose sight of the need to establish who exercises parental responsibility for the child on a day to day basis. Every effort should be made to ensure that children are not placed far from their family home and local community. If the use of such provision is essential, family links should be maintained and encouraged. The child and his relatives should be enabled (through financial support if necessary (see 11.5–11.6)) to maintain a good relationship. SSDs should seek to involve parents where they have become peripheral to the child's life. Children with disabilities may be among the most vulnerable children in terms of creating and maintaining family and community links. Their views may not be actively sought because of misconceptions about their level of ability to understand and communicate (see paragraph 6.6–6.8) As for all children, attention should be given to issues relating to racial origin, gender, cultural and linguistic background and religion – and to the child's preferences and personal aspirations and interests.

\*    \*    \*    \*    \*

## Promoting contact

11.5    When a child is looked after by the SSD they must endeavour to promote contact between the child and parents, relatives and friends and anyone else connected with him (paragraph 15 of Schedule 2 to the Act). The SSD also has a duty to promote contact between children in need and their families where the children are not accommodated by the SSD but are living apart from their family, if it is necessary in the opinion of the SSD to safeguard or promote the child's welfare (paragraph 10 of Schedule 2). If parents feel guilty or ambivalent about the residential placement—or if the cost of visiting is high—relationships may also suffer. One important consideration in any foster care or residential placement is reunification of child and family. This is more difficult to achieve if contact with parents and other significant figures in the child's life such as friends, brothers and sisters, relatives from the extended family or other people in the local community is lost.

11.6    Promoting contact should be seen as an integral part of a placement plan. SSDs should assist the family, relatives and child with travelling expenses where they consider that there would be undue financial hardship if assistance was not given and the circumstances warrant it (paragraph 16 of Schedule 2). Families may feel inadequate and uncertain about maintaining links with a child in a residential setting. Encouragement and a positive welcome to visits on a regular basis are therefore extremely important. Similarly residential care and foster family members should be reminded of the importance of their role in reunification by promoting the child's links with home through letters, phone calls, visits and open days. More detailed guidance on contact is contained in Volume 3: Family Placements.

\*    \*    \*    \*    \*

## Planning

11.10    Under the Children Act regulations assessing and planning for a placement will be reinforced and updated by regular reviews which take account of the child or young person's views, with those of parents and others. Parents who retain parental responsibility for the child during a placement, should also be actively encouraged to plan for the child's future. Many families find relationships with carers very difficult to cope with and may perceive a residential or foster placement as family failure. Involvement of parents during the planning stage and subsequent placement is essential to the success of the placement and to any longer term plan for the child's return to his family.

### Short-term or respite care

11.11    Respite care should be provided in the context of a package of care for families. Many children with disabilities are cared for away from home or usual placement on a short-term basis as part of a planned programme of respite care. Respite or short-term care for families with a child with disabilities has developed historically as an emergency service—frequently providing short-term care within a long-stay hospital or other institution in order or meet a family crisis. In the past decade there has been growing concern to provide more appropriate flexible short-term care which offers:

- a local service, where the child can continue to attend school as if still living at home;
- Good quality child care in which parents have confidence and which ensures that the child is treated first as a child and then for any disability which may require special provision;
- Planned availability. Research into different models of respite care has clearly indicated the importance of parents (and older child) choosing patterns of use and being able to use a service flexibly;
- A service which meets the needs of all children. Concern has been expressed about the lack of respite care for children with complex needs. The service should be available to children living with long-term foster carers or adoptive parents;
- Care which is compatible with the child's family background and culture, racial origin, religious persuasion and language;
- Age-appropriate care—so that young children and adolescents are given relevant care and occupation; and
- An integrated programme of family support which sees planned respite care as part of a wider range of professional support services to meet family needs. Escalating use of respite care may indicate a need for other family support services.

11.12 Some children still receive such care in NHS provision. This may be appropriate where the child has substantial medical, paramedical and nursing needs. It is clear government policy that children with a learning disability should no longer live in long stay mental handicap hospitals. Instead if NHS provision is required the aim should be to provide care in small homely, locally-based units. However for most children care provided by SSDs or voluntary organisations will be appropriate with an input from child health services if required. There are examples of community facilities run by DHAs, SSDs and voluntary organisations, sometimes working in partnership, which achieve high standards of respite care.

11.13 A number of evaluations of respite care schemes have shown varied patterns of use by families, with some a few hours a week with occasional overnight stays and others, shared care arrangements in which the child spent regular periods away from home. It is important to acknowledge the stresses associated with the child using respite care for the first time and sensitive introductions are required.

## Application of Regulations

11.14 The Children Act regulations relating to placements makes special provision for short-term placements within schemes which are variously known as respite care, phased care or family link schemes. Under such schemes, a SSD or voluntary agency makes arrangements for a child who normally lives with his family—and whose family continues to exercise full parental responsibility—to spend short or sometimes longer periods of time with either an approved foster parent or in a residential home. These regulations apply to all placements of more than 24 hours. The arrangements for respite care vary greatly and many schemes only make provision for day-time or occasional over-night stay. In these cases, if the provision of services to the family does not include accommodating the child for a period of more than 24 hours then the regulations relating to placements do not apply. However, good practice requires that all such provision is properly planned.

\* \* \* \* \*

11.17 Regulation 13 of the Arrangement for Placement of Children (General) Regulations 1991 allows for a pre-planned respite care arrangement involving a series of placements at the same place to be treated as a single placement. For family placements, all placements should take place with the same carer. For residential placements, all placements should take place at the same establishment. The length and timing of the individual placements within this arrangement need not be specified in advance, but all the placements should occur within a period which does not exceed one year, no single placement should exceed four weeks and the total time spent by a child in respite care should not exceed 90 days. The purpose of this provision is to allow the regulations to be applied once in relation to a series of placements if the conditions above are met.

11.18 Under the Arrangements for Placement Regulations, SSDs or voluntary organisations are required to have a plan for each child setting out the proposed respite care arrangements as required under these regulations. The Foster Placement (Children) Regulations 1991 apply in all other respects for family placements. Children may only be placed with an approved foster parent – but a foster parent may be approved if desired for a respite care scheme only and the chosen name of the scheme and the carers may be used within the agreement. There has been some concern that the new arrangements might over-formalise a service which has been designed to offer highly flexible and consumer-sensitive care reflecting the needs of a particular local community. However, the new regulations and guidance provide flexibility in their application to short-term respite care placements while seeking to ensure a child focused service. Regulations require medical examination of the child at stated intervals, but do not set out the form the examination should take nor whether it should be a child's GP or a consultant who should carry it out. This will be a matter to be decided in the individual case. The matter should be discussed with the parents, the child, the carers, the consultant responsible for the child and the GP if doubt exists about the most appropriate person to carry out the medical examination. It is envisaged that these examinations will be part of the usual health care arrangement for the child.

11.19 The formalisation of previously more informal arrangements is to safeguard the welfare of the child. Some parents perceive regulated foster care arrangements as relating to care proceedings and inadequate or uncaring parenting. Equally some of the families recruited for family-based respite care have never seen themselves as foster parents and may be alarmed at the prospect of a more regulated service. In practice all good family based respite care schemes have always operated upon a firm principle of written agency and parent agreements and planning around the individual needs of children. The recruitment and training procedures for respite carers should now include opportunities to explain the new basis of regulating respite care and the mutual advantages to children, parents and respite carers of having greater accountability for the service provided. Positive publicity should emphasise the advantages of working within a planned framework which supports both parents and carers.

## Chapter 12: Foster Placements

12.1 It is generally agreed that all children benefit from the opportunity to grow up in a family setting. Although finding a suitable foster family placement for a child with a disability may create certain challenges, the past decade has seen a major growth in successful foster placements for children with a range of special needs. While SSDs must take the lead, the contribution of the LEA and the DHA to assessment of needs and support in the placement will be crucial. A number of national voluntary agencies also provide specialist fostering programmes for children with disabilities.

12.2 Under the Children Act, there are three different types of fostering arrangements:

(*a*) Local authority foster parents;

(*b*) Foster parents with whom a child is placed by a voluntary agency: and

(*c*) Private foster parents.

Foster placements under the Children Act are governed by the Foster Placement (Children) Regulations 1991 which apply to foster placements by SSDs and voluntary organisations (see Volume 3: Family Placements for detailed guidance on foster placement). Without special exemption from the SSD, no person may foster more than three children unless the children concerned are all siblings from the same family.

\*   \*   \*   \*   \*

**The foster home**

\*   \*   \*   \*   \*

12.9 SSDs should make every effort to ensure that accommodation for a child with a disability is suitable for his or her needs. Section 23(8) of the Children Act requires that they 'so far as is reasonably practicable, secure that the accommodation is not unsuitable to his particular needs.' The provision of appropriate equipment or adaptations to bathrooms and bedrooms can make accommodation suitable and encourage independence. Where necessary, an occupational therapist can make an assessment of the child's future living environment and ensure that it is as barrier free as possible.

12.10 It is essential that children with disabilities (who may have incontinence or special personal care needs) should have privacy in bathroom and bedroom and that they should not be excluded from the main areas of the home such as living rooms and kitchen (and the social activities which take place in these areas) because of access difficulties. In many instances access problems can be resolved through the use of relatively simple and cheap modifications such as the use of moveable ramps and other aids. It is quite unacceptable for a child to be placed in a setting where he or she is more restricted than would have been the case in the natural home or in a residential setting. Similarly accommodation may be suitable in itself, but the child will be severely limited in his or her use of it if carers lack confidence in the management of a child with, for example, a severe visual handicap or if the child concerned is hyperactive. SSDs should additionally ensure that the accommodation is safe for the child in question that access (and egress) can be easily accomplished in the case of fire. If a child is hyperactive or for some other reason is liable to be at risk if playing outside the house, the safety of any garden gates and fences should also be assessed. It would be inappropriate for a child with a disability to have to be confined unnecessarily to particular rooms because of problems of safety relating to the physical environment of the placement.

*   *   *   *   *

## Chapter 13: Residential Care for Children with disabilities

### Residential care

13.1    Volume 4 in the Children Act series provides regulations guidance on children in residential homes and establishes important ground rules about the quality of the care and environment which should be provided. However, some children with disabilities will have special needs over and above those of their able-bodied peers. The availability of privacy and domestic-style living arrangements for children with disabilities may depend on access arrangements. Children with disabilities should have access to all the accommodation and the same rights to privacy as their able-bodied counterparts. For example, the management of incontinence or other personal care needs in an integrated setting will necessitate suitable bathroom accommodation which offers space, privacy, sufficient hot water and convenient location to other living areas. No child with a disability should be placed where he cannot use the recreation, living or garden areas because he can literally not gain access to them. Homes which accommodate children with a disability are required to provide the necessary equipment, facilities and adaptations. The aim should be to integrate the child in every aspect of life in the home, not merely the physical aspects.

*   *   *   *   *

### Children accommodated by a health authority, NHS trust or local education authority

13.7    Although some children with disabilities or with serious health problems may spend substantial periods of time receiving care or treatment in an NHS facility, it is against government policy that such children should be placed for long-term residential care in a NHS hospital setting. The use of NHS facilities should reflect a child's need for assessment, treatment or other services which cannot be made in SSD provision or at home and should in no way constitute a permanent placement. Close working partnerships between SSDs and DHAs and NHS trusts should be an integral factor in local policies for implementation of the Children Act. Such partnerships will clearly identify the particular health care needs of individual children and the extent to which they should be met in a health setting. It should be emphasised that not all children with disabilities have health care needs. In many instances advice from child health services, with appropriate support, should enable children to continue to be cared for in SSD or voluntary provision.

*   *   *   *   *

### Notification duty

13.9    If a child is provided with accommodation by a health authority, NHS Trust or LEA for more than three months on a consecutive basis or the intention is that this will happen, the health authority, NHS Trust or LEA *must* notify the responsible SSD. The responsible SSD is interpreted as being the SSD for the area in which the child lives or was ordinarily resident immediately before being accommodated or (if there is no such SSD) the SSD in whose area the accommodation for the child is being provided. The accommodating authority must also notify the responsible SSD (section 85(2)) when it is proposed to end the child's placement. The responsible SSD must take all reasonably practicable steps to enable them to decide whether the child's welfare is adequately safeguarded and promoted while he stays in the accommodation and to decide whether it is necessary to exercise any of their functions under the Act.

13.10   The intention of this new notification duty is to ensure that children are not 'forgotten' and that SSDs assess the quality of child care offered. Children with disabilities are more likely than other children to be place in 'out of county' placements, frequently in remote and rural areas. The new arrangements should ensure more coherent planning for children and will necessitate close collaboration with child health services (including the specialist advice available through district handicap, child development and community mental handicap teams).

13.11   Where a child's stay in hospital is prolonged, the hospital social worker may have an important role to play. Chronic illness places enormous strain on a family's emotional and financial reserves. Counselling, practical and financial support (for example for hospital visits, baby-sitting etc) during and immediately after hospitalisation will do much to avoid longer-term problems. SSDs will need to work closely with health services including GPs and health visitors to support families when the child returns home.

*   *   *   *   *

## Chapter 14: Complaints Procedures

14.1   The Act requires SSDs, voluntary organisations and registered children's homes to establish procedures for considering representations (including complaints) about children's services. The procedure should cover all representations or complaints about a SSD's actions in exercising their functions under Part III of the Act (Local Authority Support for Children and their Families). Voluntary organisations and registered children's homes will also be required to set up representations procedures to consider representations or complaints made by or on behalf of children accommodated by them but not looked after by a SSD. The arrangements for such procedures are covered by the Representations Procedure (Children) Regulations 1991 (see Chapter 10 of Volume 3: Family Placements for detailed guidance). Representations and complaints which do not come under the Children Act procedure may be considered under the Local Authority Social Services Act 1970 procedure (section 7B as inserted by section 50 of the National Health Service and Community Care Act 1990 (see Caring for People: Community Care in the next decade and beyond Chapter 6 (HMSO 1990)) or may be more appropriately considered under another agency's procedure.

14.2   The principles behind the representation and complaints procedure are that children and other complainants should have access to a procedure which offers an opportunity to make statements about or to challenge decisions made by service providers and to ensure that the complaints procedure in question is fully understood and accepted by not only service users and their representatives but also by the SSD's or service providing agency's staff and the local authority's own elected members. Implementation plans should reflect the views of local consumer groups and service users and both should be involved wherever possible in setting procedures up so that they are confident that the system arrived at is fair, equitable and usable in the context of local needs.

14.3 Complaints and representations may be made about the way in which the SSD is acting in relation to a child in need, by the child, the child's parent or anyone having parental responsibility for him or her, any SSD foster parent or any other person who could be regarded as having sufficient interest in the child's welfare to warrant representations being considered by them.

14.4 The procedure developed by the SSD must have an *independent* element, which means that at the first stage of the procedure a person who is not a member or an officer of the local authority must take part in the discussion and consideration of such representations or complaints and in determining what action should be taken (section 26(4)). If the complainant is dissatisfied with the action the SSD propose to take after the first stage, the complaint may be referred to a panel with an independent element for further consideration. Local voluntary organisations and consumer groups may be able to provide nominations for panel members and can be a source of independent advice and advocacy for the child or family concerned. Every effort should be made to work with local disability groups to ensure that the procedures are accessible, useable and effective when dealing with issues relating to disabilities.

14.5 Authorities will be expected to give due consideration to the findings of those who carry out the complaints and representation procedure. They are not, however, bound to implement the findings. They will be required to notify in writing the person who made the complaint or representation, the child (if he has sufficient understanding) and anyone else likely to be affected by the SSD's decision, the reasons for it and what action (if any) they propose to take.

14.6 In the case of children with disabilities, complaints and representations are likely to focus around assessment and the delivery of (or failure to deliver) certain services. Because of the multiprofessional support needed by the majority of children with disabilities, the consideration of a complaint made by or on behalf of a child with disabilities should:

(*a*) consider whether there is a need to consult a range of relevant expert opinion, for example from the health authority or education department;

(*b*) ensure that children with disabilities are given appropriate support in making complaints or representations and in participating in decision-making about their own futures; and

(*c*) consider whether the complaint is really about another agency's services and should be directed to a different procedure.

14.7 There will be occasions when children or young people (and indeed many parents) will need help, advice or support from another individual or from an outside agency in framing or pursuing a complaint. Support should be offered or advice given on where support may be obtained, where a complainant is vulnerable or unsupported or where language, cultural diversity or a complex communication disorder or disability may impede communication. Many children and young people with sensory or learning disabilities will have more complex communication needs than can be met by the provision of an interpreter. If a written complaint is made or a verbal complaint recorded, they may not be easily able to verify the nature of the recording. Equally they are most unlikely to have easy access to information on complaints procedures which will be readily available to other potential users in the community. SSDs are required to give information on complaints procedures to children and young people with disabilities, with relevant and useable information about how a complaint may be initiated (particularly in a residential setting where access to a private telephone may be problematic). Schools may be a useful source of information for both children and parents. As noted above, complaints procedures should not be seen as the only way of resolving differences of opinion about services and management. Every effort should be made to use assessment and review in a positive and constructive way in order to negotiate a clearly understood package of services, with accurate information for all concerned about what is being provided.

14.8    In some instances complaints may relate to inappropriate services for children with disabilities, for example where there are poor access facilities, unsuitable furnishings or equipment or where children are unnecessarily excluded from the full range of activities appropriate to their ages, interests and general ability. In these instances expert advice on the particular disability should be identified eg from within the SSD, from a DHA or from a voluntary organisation and the SSD's existing arrangements for placement reassessed to avoid similar difficulties in the future.

14.9    It is essential that complaints procedures are explicit about how such vulnerable people may learn about complaints procedures and how they may use them, particularly if they are receiving services within their own homes. Section 26(8) of the Children Act requires SSDs to publicise their complaints procedures. This might be done in a variety of ways, ensuring that information is available in any relevant minority languages and that the local disability and users groups are part of the publicity process. SSDs might consider holding special meetings for their local voluntary sector to publicise the procedures and to ensure that the SSD and the consumer groups work in tandem in making the procedures work. Written information should also be freely available in SSDs, GP surgeries, hospital out-patients departments, health clinics, schools, libraries, nurseries, citizen advice bureaux and any other appropriate local setting used by the public. Because many people with disabilities have limited access to public buildings where such information is most likely to be prominently displayed, consideration should be given to how information on complaints procedures may be made widely available to parents of and children with disabilities.

*    *    *    *    *

## Chapter 16: Transition to Adulthood

### Background

*    *    *    *    *

*The need for ongoing support*

*    *    *    *    *

16.6    To assist a young person with a disability to make a successful transition from childhood to adulthood requires that SSDs work closely with the youth service, schools and colleges to make certain that the arrangements are understood and also to identify any new needs. The local careers service should be involved in publicising information and also in identifying the full range of local services to which families might require access. It should also be stressed that in some instances the young people and their parents will need independent advice, counselling and advocacy in determining their needs and the most effective way of meeting them. For example, where a youngster has been in a residential school the holiday periods should be used to prepare the family for an eventual return home at the end of full-time education, or to test out alternatives explored as part of the review and planning process.

Sometimes parents' and children's needs may appear to diverge when the young person grows older. Issues like the possibility of a move away from the family home, home adaptations or respite care should be explored in the light of the wishes and feelings of the young person and the family and should be given sensitive consideration. Where the young person comes from a minority ethnic group, efforts should be made to use every opportunity to identify the young person's and family's personal and cultural preferences. No assumption should be made about what the parents or the young person want.

### The Disabled Persons Act 1986—Working with the LEA

16.7    Under the Education Act 1981, there is a statutory requirement that the LEA should reassess all pupils with Statements of Special Educational Needs at the age of thirteen years and six months, providing that they have not been formally assessed under Section 5 of the Act after the age of 12 years 6 months. The purpose of this assessment is not only to determine the pupil's needs during his final years at school but also to begin the plan for post-school provision. It is therefore an important opportunity for the beginning of realistic forward planning for adult life, which should involve the child, the parents, the school, the DHA and the SSD in looking at a range of future options. Section 5 of the Disabled Persons Act 1986 requires LEAs to notify their relevant SSDs at the time of the first annual review of a statement following the child's 14th birthday, or at the time of a reassessment after that birthday, whichever is earlier. This notification is required so that the SSD may consider whether the child will require any future services from the SSD after they have left school. LEAs have a further duty to notify the SSD between twelve months and eight months before the actual date of ceasing full-time education. Section 5 then requires the SSD to carry out an assessment of the young person's needs, normally 3 months before he leaves school. This assessment should cover the whole range of need for social and welfare services, and the SSD are also expected, as far as possible, to give appropriate advice about matters such as employment and further education, and other services which may be available. This assessment and the consequent provision of services is of crucial importance in setting the scene for the young person's transition to adult life.

\*    \*    \*    \*    \*

### Collaborative working

16.9    Planning for post-school provision will require careful assessment and ongoing planning. Parents and young people may have different preferences and views about where and when services should be provided. Realistic assessment should take account of the needs of both and should ensure that assessment takes account of the wider personal and social, health, occupational and vocational and educational abilities and needs of the young person in question. Education providers and their health authority counterparts will need to consider carefully how best to work together and with the young person and parents in planning for young people with disabilities. Patterns of collaborative working will vary across the country, but existing collaborative mechanisms in district handicap or child development teams, community mental handicap or learning disabilities teams and joint consultative committees may need reviewing or strengthening in order to ensure that young people have access to inter-agency expertise and provision.

\*    \*    \*    \*    \*

16.11   The support of the primary health care team is of crucial importance to successful community care. SSDs should therefore ensure that they have precise arrangements for working with DHAs and FHSAs in order to ensure that joint planning is followed by joint service arrangements for young people with disabilities. Joint assessment and review cannot underpin more effective planning and care management if they do not involve all relevant agencies and professionals. GPs are crucial contributors to the assessment process. Their contribution to community care through knowledge of the whole family and the local community and their ability to monitor the individual young person's health and well being—as well as the delivery of general medical services—are essential in terms of support to young people living in their local community. For all young people the maintenance of good health is important. For children with disabilities the prevention of secondary handicaps or deterioration of an existing disability will require regular review.

16.12   The Children Act (section 27) provides for co-operation between housing authorities, SSDs, LEAs, DHAs and NHS Trusts. SSDs will need to liaise with housing authorities over the housing needs of young people with disabilities.

16.13   With regard to young people with disabilities. SSDs should consider their existing duties under the Chronically Sick and Disabled Persons Act 1970 and the Disabled Persons Act 1986. In some instances the ability of a young person with a disability to return home from a residential school or home—or to move into more independent living on his own—will depend not so much on the availability of accommodation but on the aids and adaptations that are provided to make existing accommodation suitable. Many young people with disabilities are severely limited by access problems in their own homes as they get larger and heavier. If the disability is degenerative or is acquired in the adolescent years, there may be major difficulties for all family members for example, because of use of living areas limited by access, and a consequent reduction in quality of life for the whole family. When the child has lived away from home for some years, reunification will be particularly difficult to achieve if the home is unsuitable and heavy burdens of care are suddenly imposed on the family.

\*     \*     \*     \*     \*

16.15   Where a young person has very complex disabilities or where the family feel that they are unable to offer continued care, every effort should be made to find an acceptable local alternative. Residential care should not be regarded as a failure but as a positive option where parents, families and friends have a continuing role. With the cessation of admissions to long-stay hospitals for residential care, SSDs should consider as a matter of urgency how they can work in partnership with their health and education counterparts to develop new patterns of residential services which provided good quality care in the local community. Such care may be provided through SSDs, DHAs, voluntary or independent agencies or by combinations and consortia according to local provision. Wherever the young person is placed, SSDs, DHAs and LEAs will have a continuing role and every effort should be made to ensure that any placement encourages development and offers opportunities for continuing education.

\*     \*     \*     \*     \*

## J.  Ordinary Residence

### LAC(93)7—ORDINARY RESIDENCE

**Summary**

This circular contains guidance on the identification of the ordinary residence of people who require personal social services under the National Assistance Act 1948. The guidance is applicable not only to local authorities' responsibilities for residential and, from 1 April 1993, nursing home care but also for care in other types of residential accommodation provided under Section 21 (and Section 26) of the National Assistance Act, for instance hostels and group homes. It also covers welfare services provided under Section 29 of the National Assistance Act 1948. Reference is also made to the responsibilities of other authorities, the Children Act 1989, and after-care for people who have been detained under the Mental Health Act 1983. It does *not* apply to the provision of residential accommodation or other services in respect of people aged under 18 as such services cannot be provided under the National Assistance Act.

The purpose of the circular is to clarify where possible where responsibility lies between social services authorities, so that the scope for disputes is reduced. Authorities should note in particular that the provision of services for individuals requiring social services should not be delayed because of uncertainty about which authority is responsible, and that when an individual does not appear to have any settled residence, it is the responsibility of the authority of the moment to provide any residential care required to meet their needs. The circular also sets out in Part II the procedure for referring to the Secretary of State for determination any disputes that cannot be resolved between the local authorities concerned.

### Part I

### Background

**The National Assistance Act 1948**

1   Under sections 21 and 29 of the National Assistance Act 1948 ('NA Act') each local authority has a power, and so far as directed by the Secretary of State a duty, to provide residential accommodation and certain other welfare services for people who are 'ordinarily resident' in the authority's area. The current Approvals and Directions relating to social services authorities will be restated in a circular to be issued in the near future.

2   There is no definition of 'ordinarily resident' in the Act and the term should be given its ordinary and natural meaning subject to any interpretation by the Courts. The concept of ordinary residence involves questions of fact and degree, and factors such as time, intention and continuity, each of which may be given different weight according to the context, have to be taken into account. Section 24 of the NA Act makes the following provisions relating to ordinary residence which are summarised below:

    i.    Sec 24(3): Where a person in the area of a local authority is a person with no settled residence, or not being ordinarily resident in the area is in urgent need of residential accommodation, the authority shall have the like power to provide residential accommodation as if he were ordinarily resident in their area.

ii.  Sec 24(4): A local authority has the power to provide residential accommodation for a person ordinarily resident in the area of another authority, providing they have the consent of that authority to do so.

iii.  Sec 24(5): Where a person is provided with residential accommodation he shall be deemed to be ordinarily resident in the area in which he was ordinarily resident immediately before the residential accommodation was provided for him.

iv.  Sec 24(6): A patient in an NHS hospital, including hospitals that are part of an NHS trust, shall be deemed to be ordinarily resident in the area if any in which he was ordinarily resident immediately before he was admitted as a patient to the hospital.

3    If a person comes within the terms of Section 24(3) it is the responsibility of the local authority of the moment to make a care assessment if it appears to the authority that he may be in need of services. For example, an urgent need might arise in the case of someone ordinarily resident elsewhere who is visiting or on holiday. The local authority where the person is ordinarily resident can arrange for the assessment and the provision of services to be carried out on its behalf by the local authority of the moment. A person who arrives in a local authority's area from abroad (including for example a person returning to this country after a period when they have been resident abroad and who had given up their previous home here) who appears to the authority to be in need of social services assistance may come within the terms of Section 24(3). If the person does not come within the terms of Section 24(3) then it is the local authority where he has his settled residence that should carry out the care assessment. If there is a dispute about the ordinary residence of a person in need of services it should be debated after the care assessment and any provision of service.

4    Section 32(3) of the NA Act gives the Secretary of State the responsibility to determine disputes about ordinary residence where such disputes arise between local authorities and the authorities concerned cannot resolve the issue themselves. A determination by the Secretary of State should only be sought as a last resort, and local authorities are expected normally to resolve disputes themselves. Further information about referrals to the Secretary of State for decision is in Part II.

## The NHS Act 1977

5    In addition to the NA Act, until 1 April 1993 local authorities also have the power to provide or arrange for residential accommodation under paragraph 2 of Schedule 8 to the NHS Act 1977. With effect from 1 April 1993 the provision in Schedule 8 relating to residential accommodation is repealed by the NHS and Community Care Act 1990, and will thereafter fall within Section 21 of the NA Act. Residents for whom residential accommodation is provided from 1 April 1993 under the NHS Act will, from that date, be deemed to be in accommodation provided under the NA Act and, consequently, issues concerning their ordinary residence will fall within the ambit of this circular.

## General guidance about procedures

*Responsibility for assessment*

6    Local authorities should note that their duty from 1 April 1993 under Section 47 of the NHS and Community Care Act 1990 is to undertake a care assessment

where it appears to the authority that any person for whom they may provide or arrange community care services may be in need of services. Within that duty a local authority therefore has discretion over who it does and does not assess, and the level of the assessment. In LAC(93)2 (paragraph 14) local authorities were reminded that any criteria they develop governing eligibility for assessment should be sensitive to the circumstances of alcohol and drug misusers. However authorities have a duty under Section 4(a) of the Disabled Persons (Services, Consultation and Representations) Act 1986 to decide on request whether the needs of a disabled person call for the provision of welfare services under Section 2 of the Chronically Sick and Disabled Persons Act 1970.

## People who are placed in accommodation in the area of another local authority

7 Where, following an assessment, a local authority arranges a placement in a private or voluntary home in another authority's area or in a home provided by another local authority the placing authority will normally retain for that person the same responsibility that it has for someone living in its own area. The person so placed will not as a general rule become ordinarily resident in the other local authority's area. If subsequently, by private arrangement, the person moves he may, depending on the specific circumstances, become ordinarily resident in the area of the local authority where he has chosen to live.

8 A local authority should not place a person for whom they are financially responsible in accommodation provided by a private proprietor or a voluntary organisation in the area of another authority without informing the other authority. They should also ensure that satisfactory arrangements are made before placement for any necessary support services, such as day care, and for periodic reviews, and that there are clear agreements about the financing for all aspects of the individual's care. The local authority responsible for the placement may negotiate for these services to be provided by the host authority and reimburse the costs. Similarly, except in an emergency situation, no host local authority should alter the accommodation or services provided for that person to a significant degree without consulting in advance the responsible local authority. It is recognised that there will be some circumstances where an urgent placement is necessary, and prior consultation will not be possible. In such cases the necessary consultation should take place immediately after the placement has been made.

9 Good record keeping will be essential, including recording verbal agreements and confirming these with written agreements. When a care manager has been appointed he should usually be the main link between the responsible and host authorities. All changes should be confirmed and recorded in writing at the regular review of each individual's needs.

## People who move to residential accommodation of their own volition

10 When an individual arranges to go into permanent residential or nursing home care in a new area, without any local authority having taken responsibility for the arrangements, they usually become ordinarily resident in the new area. If subsequently social services help is sought the person will look to the authority where the residential accommodation is situated. The local authority in the original area may become aware of the arrangements the individual is making and, with the permis-

sion of the person concerned, they should inform the local authority for the new area, particularly if it seems possible that social services help may later be required.

## People whose accommodation is partly financed by a health authority

11   Health authorities might negotiate with local authorities to provide finance in respect of people moving from long-stay hospitals to care accommodation in the community (see LAC(92)17). This might take the form of joint financial arrangements between the health authority and the local authority (the local authority of ordinary residence and/or the local authority where the individuals are to be settled) or dowry payments made by health authorities in respect of individuals discharged from hospital. Funding may be provided to a particular local authority for a number of individuals regardless of their original 'ordinary residence'. In entering into such agreements local authorities must be clear about the responsibilities they entail. Such agreements should always be recorded in writing to avoid disputes because of lack of clarity, including a statement recording the ordinary residence of each individual concerned so that the question of future financial responsibility is addressed.

## The meaning of ordinarily resident

*Case law*

12   The meaning of 'ordinarily resident' or 'ordinary residence' has been considered by the Courts, and regard must be had to such cases as:
  i.    *Shah v London Borough of Barnet (1983)* Lord Scarman stated that 'unless . . . it can be shown that the statutory framework or the legal context in which the words are used requires a different meaning I unhesitatingly subscribe to the view that 'ordinarily resident' refers to a man's abode in a particular place or country which he had adopted voluntarily and for settled purposes as part of the regular order of his life for the time being, whether of short or long duration'.
  ii.   *Levene v IRC (1928)* Viscount Care said that 'ordinary residence' connotes residence in a place with some degree of continuity and apart from accidental or temporary absences.

13   In general, an adult with learning disabilities should be regarded as capable of forming his own intention of where he wishes to live. The case of *Regina v Waltham Forest London Borough Council, ex parte Vale* (1985) should be noted. In this case it was held that a person with severe learning disabilities who was totally dependent on his parents was to be treated as ordinarily resident at his parents' address since he was in the same position as a small child who is unable to choose where to live. This case will need to be considered if there is an ordinary residence dispute involving people with severe learning disabilities but its relevance will vary in accordance with the ability of the person with learning difficulties to make choices and the extent to which they rely upon their parents. In some cases some other person(s), or body, may be acting in place of their parents. In a recent decision of the High Court in December 1992 *London Borough of Redbridge ex parte East Sussex County Council* the principles outlined in *Vale* were applied where the parents of young adult twins with learning disabilities who had been ordinarily resident in Redbridge left this country to live in Nigeria and soon after their departure the residential school in East Sussex attended by the twins closed. At this point the twins were held

by the court to have no settled residence. As they were in the area of East Sussex it was held that no duty to provide for them fell on Redbridge as they were not ordinarily resident there, but that there was a duty to make provision under relevant legislation on East Sussex as they were in that county and had no settled residence.

## Discharge from hospital, nursing homes, prison and other similar establishments

14 Section 24(6) of the NA Act provides that a patient in an NHS hospital or NHS trust hospital shall be deemed to be ordinarily resident in the area in which he was ordinarily resident before he was admitted to hospital. If they were not ordinarily resident in any area prior to their admission, then the powers in Section 24(3) are applicable. Local authorities could reasonably apply this approach when considering responsibility for people leaving prisons, resettlement units and other similar establishments without a permanent place to live who will require social services involvement at the time of their discharge. No case law exists however, and any dispute must be resolved in the light of the specific circumstances.

15 A person who, without the involvement of a social services authority, has become a permanent resident in an independent nursing home or residential care home, meeting the costs from private resources (including any Income Support entitlement), is likely to be regarded as ordinarily resident in the area where the establishment is located but this will always depend on the particular circumstances. The extent to which social services help, in the form of residential accommodation, may be made available to such a resident who has preserved rights to the higher levels of Income Support will be affected by the limitations and exceptions set out in LAC(93)6.

## Homelessness legislation

16 The test of 'ordinary residence' is not the same as that of 'local connection' used in the homelessness legislation for establishing which housing authority has the responsibility for securing accommodation for homeless applicants in priority need. When a person states that he has no settled residence or describes himself as NFA (no fixed abode) the social services authority where he presents himself should normally accept responsibility. For a person in urgent need, the social services authority of the moment cannot argue that the possible existence of a 'local connection' elsewhere excuses it from the duty to assess and provide any necessary social services; decisions on where the responsibility for the funding of such services rests, based on ordinary residence, should be decided subsequently. Rules for determining responsibility under Housing Acts should not be used to identify ordinary residence for social services purposes. Any outstanding ordinary residence questions should be clearly recorded in social services records at the time they arise. Failure to do this may prejudice subsequent consideration.

17 'Local connection' for housing purposes (defined in Section 61 of the Housing Act 1985, and discussed further in the statutory Homelessness Code of Guidance for Local Authorities, 3rd edition) may be established by present or past settled residence in an area, by employment in that area, by family connections, or other special circumstances. Where the test of 'local connection' results in the transfer of responsibility for securing accommodation to another housing authority the social services authority will wish to consider where 'ordinary residence' then rests. The homelessness legislation provides that, where a person has no local connection, the

duties to provide accommodation rest with the housing authority to whom he first applies. Even if a housing authority suspects that a person may have a local connection elsewhere, this does not absolve it from an initial duty to provide temporary accommodation if the immediate circumstances require it, pending the transfer of responsibility to another housing authority.

### Responsible health authority for people needing health care

18   The responsible health authority is the one where a person is usually resident. The NHS Functions Regulations 1991 set out the means by which a patient's district of residence should be determined. For the majority of cases the arbiter of the patient's residence is the patient himself. If there is any doubt about where a person is usually resident, he is to be treated as usually resident at the address which he gives as being where he usually resides. If the patient is unable to give an address at which he considers himself resident, then the address at which he was last resident will establish the district of residence. In the very small number of cases where the position is still not clear, the Regulations provide that the patient should be treated as usually resident in the health district in which he is present, which means where he is found to be in need of treatment by the provider. It follows from this that in the majority of cases the area of ordinary residence for social services care and the area where a person needing health care is usually resident will be the same. If there are disputes between District Health Authorities, cases should be referred to the appropriate Region. LAC(93)2 reminded local authorities that they need to draw up clear agreements with health authorities covering arrangements for funding treatment and rehabilitation services for people with alcohol or drug problems.

### Identifying DHA to give consent to LA placement in a nursing home

19   Guidance has been issued in LAC(92)22, and further guidance will be issued shortly.

### Identifying DHA responsible for providing health services to residents in homes

20   In organising a placement in a residential care or nursing home, a LA must liaise with the DHA responsible (or GP Fundholder where applicable) for securing the provision of community health services. This liaison must be with the DHA of usual residence. A LA may place someone in a residential care or nursing home outside the DHA of usual residence. If the move to the residential care or nursing home is permanent, then the DHA for the residential care or nursing home would become the DHA of usual residence for the residents of the home, and responsible for providing the appropriate health services for the residents, ie: the LA should liaise with the 'new' DHA. If people are placed in a home for a temporary period, they remain usually resident in their own DHA. LAC(92)24 (sent to health authorities with HSG(92)54) sets out the community health services that health authorities are expected to secure for residents of residential and nursing homes.

### Young adults

21   In the case of young people who cease to be looked after under the Children Act 1989 on reaching the age of 18 years, authorities could reasonably have regard

to the definition of 'ordinary residence' in that Act in determining where responsibility for the future delivery of services might most appropriately lie. Section 105(6) of the Children Act 1989 provides that for any purpose under that Act any period in which a child lives in any place—

a.   which is a school or other institution;
b.   in accordance with the requirements of a supervision order under Children Act 1989 or an order under section 7(7)(*b*) of the Children and Young Persons Act 1969; or
c.   which he is being provided with accommodation by or on behalf of a local authority

shall be disregarded in determining the 'ordinary residence' of the child.

It should be noted that the responsibility to provide aftercare support, through advice and befriending, to those who have ceased to be looked after under the Children Act 1989, rests with the authority in whose area the young person is living, and continues until he attains the age of 21 in accordance with Section 24 of that Act.

## People who have been detained for treatment under the Mental Health Act 1983

22   Section 117 of the Mental Health Act 1983 places a duty on DHAs and local authorities to provide aftercare for certain individuals who have been discharged from hospitals. The people concerned are those who have been detained for treatment under the Act or admitted under a hospital order made by a court or under a transfer direction by the Home Secretary as provided for in the Act.

23   From 1 April 1991 all district health authorities were required to initiate, in collaboration with local social services departments, explicit individually tailored care programmes for all in-patients about to be discharged from mental illness hospitals and all new patients accepted by the specialist psychiatric services. The care programme approach operationalises good professional practice. The essence of the approach is that the needs of each patient, both for continuing health and social care and for accommodation, are systematically assessed and that the appropriate arrangements are made. These include the appointment of a key worker to keep in close touch with the patient and to monitor that the agreed health and social care is given.

24   The Secretary of State's powers to determine disputes under Section 32(3) of the NA Act do not extend to any disputes regarding residence which may arise under the Mental Health Act 1983. However, guidance issued by the ACC and AMA on 4 October 1989 (ref no 299/89) offers helpful advice on the accommodation and day care needs of discharged patients to whom Section 117 of the 1993 Act applies. For effective application, it is also implicit in the care programme approach that health and social services authorities are able to cooperate and agree an appropriate provision.

## Part II

## Determination of Disputes by Secretary of State

25   Section 32(3) of the National Assistance Act provides that any question arising under Part III of the Act as to the ordinary residence of a person shall be determined by the Secretary of State. This extends to disputes about the local authority

responsible for non-residential services provided under Part III of this Act as well as the provision of accommodation.

26   Nothing contained in Part I of this guidance is to be taken to affect the discretion of the Secretary of State in giving a determination. Each case has to be considered in the light of its own facts. The Secretary of State's decision is final subject only to judicial review.

27   The question of establishing where someone is ordinarily resident for the purposes of the NA Act is essentially a legal one. When local authorities, having taken appropriate legal advice and considered the position in the light of this circular, are still unable to resolve a particular dispute, they may apply for a determination under Section 32(3).

## Procedure for seeking a determination

28   Before the Secretary of State is approached for a determination, one of the local authorities involved in the dispute should have provisionally accepted liability under Part III of the NA Act and be providing services.

29   An agreed written statement of facts, signed by all the authorities involved, must be sent, together with the application for a determination. This agreed statement should be as detailed as possible, including (i) full information about the person to whom the services under Part III have been supplied; (ii) details relating to the prior residence of the person to whom services are provided; (iii) details of the statutory provisions under which services have been provided. Copies of all relevant correspondence between the authorities concerned should be annexed to the agreed statement.

30   Each local authority may additionally provide separate written representations concerning the agreed statement, including for example a legal submission.

31   The agreed statement of facts, with any annexed documentation, and separate written representations should be sent to Community Services Division 1B.

*   *   *   *   *

## K. Charging for Residential and Domiciliary Services

**Cross references**
1 LAC(95)7—CRAG—Charging for Residential Accommodation Guide Amendment No 5.
2 LAC(95)21—CRAG Amendment No 6.
3 LAC(96)6—CRAG Amendment No 7.
4 Discretionary Charges for Adult Social Services—Advice Note for use by the Department of Health Social Services Inspectorate (1994).

*The text of the guidance is not reproduced in this publication but is referred to extensively in Chapter 14 of the text.*

## L. Access to Information

**Cross references**
1 Access to Personal Files Act 1987.
2 Access to Health Records Act 1990.
3 LAC(89)2—Access to Personal Files Held by Social Services and Housing Departments.
4 LAC(91)11—Access to Personal Files (Social Services)(Amendment) Regulations 1991.
5 HSG(91)6—Access to Manually Held Medical Records.
6 LAC(87)10 and LAC(88)16—Access to Information Held under Data Protection Act 1984.
7 LAC(88)17—Personal Social Services—Confidentiality of Personal Information.
8 Access to Personal Files (Social Services) Regulations 1989, SI No. 206, Regulation 2.1.

## M.  Carers

### (1)  CARERS (RECOGNITION AND SERVICES) ACT 1995—
### PRACTICE GUIDE

### Introduction

1   The practice guidance follows the same order as the policy guidance and the Act itself. Recent SSI reports on carers and young carers address a number of issues, including assessment, in more detail than this guidance. These reports are referred to frequently; other useful material is listed at the back.

2   Most carers are adults, many are older people caring for another older person. These carers' lives will be significantly affected by caring for an ill or disabled person. Recent work has drawn attention to the situation of children and young people who take on considerable caring responsibilities within families. There are separate sections on young carers and parents of disabled children. The guidance goes into some detail about assessment of young carers as this has not been dealt with previously in guidance.

### Practice aims and objectives

3   A shift in practice towards:
— greater recognition of carers: paying attention to and taking account of what they say
— an assessment of the 'caring system' which considers the range of support available to users and carers and encourages intervention at the right time without destroying existing informal support networks
— an integrated family based approach which does not see either the user or carer in isolation
— improving practice: not increasing bureaucracy by providing the opportunity for a private conversation without an elaborate procedure. Trying to ensure that carers are not having to repeatedly provide the same information.

### Scope of the Act

4   The provisions of the Act cover
(*a*)  Adults (people aged 18 and over) who provide or intend to provide a substantial amount of care on a regular basis
(*b*)  Children and young people (under 18) who provide or intend to provide a substantial amount of care on a regular basis
(*c*)  Parents who provide or intend to provide a substantial amount of care on a regular basis for disabled children.

5   For the purpose of the Act the term carer includes people who may or may not be a relative and who may or may not be living with the person for whom they are caring.

6   The Act describes local authorities' duties in relation to carers who provide or intend to provide a substantial amount of care on a regular basis. There has been a considerable amount of research undertaken about carers and caring.

Annex 1 provides a precis of some of this research which identifies factors associated with different types of carer and caring. Information about a carer's involvement should be gathered as part of a user's assessment. This will enable the following questions to be answered which may indicate whether somebody is providing substantial and regular care.

- What type of tasks does or will the carer undertake?
- How much time does or will the carer spend providing assistance for the user?
- How much supervision does the user require to manage her/his life?
- Is this (or will it be) a continuing commitment for the carer?

7   The nature of the caring task will vary according to the disability or illness of the user, with some conditions requiring, for example, intensive supervision or emotional support rather than physical or personal care. Some users with mental health or substance misuse problems or with conditions such as neurological disorders, dementia, cancer or HIV/AIDS will have care needs which vary over time but may present regular and substantial burdens for carers.

## Information

8   A common theme emerges from the SSI reports on carers. It was the policy in many of the authorities visited to offer carers an assessment. However, often carers did not know that they could have their needs assessed. Similarly some carers were not clear when their needs had been assessed as this was not made explicit. The process, therefore, needs to be formal insofar as it is

(a)   documented

(b)   mutually understood by user, carer and care manager and the results of the assessment and the care plan confirmed in writing.

A Way Ahead for Carers and Caring Today give examples of local authorities' approaches to providing information for carers and underline the importance of a strategic, targeted approach

---

**Information** should
- be available for carers when they need it
- be accessible to all members of the community, easy to understand and available in a variety of formats
- be part of routine assessment practice
- inform carers who appear to be eligible under the Act, of their right to request an assessment
- be available for users and carers about the local authority social services department's complaints procedure.

---

## The assessment

9   *Some key issues*

9.1   The assessment is not a test for the carer. It should not be prescriptive but recognise carers' knowledge and expertise. The assessment should listen to what they are saying and offer an opportunity for private discussion in which carers can candidly express their views.

9.2   In some cases it may be appropriate to offer a private discussion to both user and carer. Users and carers will need to be assured about confidentiality but it will always be important to reach agreement about how the results of such discussions will be shared with either the user or carer. Carers should be involved in the arrangements for monitoring and in all reviews. Particular aspects of the carer's circumstances may point to the need for regular review. Carers value the co-ordination of services achieved by care management and appreciate having a named person whom they can contact.

9.3    Carers often give most of the assistance needed by the person for whom they care, and may only want a fairly small amount of help to enable them to continue caring. A PSSRU study found that some of the most cost effective care packages were where carers continued to perform caring tasks but were given sufficient support and respite to enhance their well being and maintain their own health. Equally it is important that care managers do not make assumptions about carers' willingness to undertake the range of caring tasks, particularly those related to intimate personal care. This is highlighted in a discussion of spouse carers which emphasises the difficulties faced by some husbands or wives when their ability to cope with changed behaviour or personality and/or tasks involving physical intimacy is taken for granted.

9.4    Carers and users are not a single, homogeneous group. Practitioners need to be sensitive to relationships between users and carers and to some of the stresses and difficulties, as well as benefits of caring. Some situations will require skilful counselling and mediation, using core social work skills.

9.5    Information on charges for services and financial assessment should be clearly explained to the user and carer. A financial assessment is separate from either an assessment under Section 47 of the NHS and Community Care Act or under the Carers (Recognition and Services) Act.

9.6    When undertaking a carer's assessment, it is important to recognise the value of early intervention and ongoing support in preventing deterioration in the carer's and user's welfare. In many instances, early access to advice and practical help can minimise the subsequent need for increased levels of services. A swift response to requests for emergency, short-term care can alleviate carers' anxieties and avoid a possible breakdown in the caring arrangements and need for long term care.

9.7    By including carers who are intending to provide regular or substantial care, the Act provides an opportunity to fully consider the circumstances of carers in employment who are taking on this type of caring commitment.

9.8    In assessing the carer's ability to care or continue to care, care managers should not assume a willingness by the carer to continue caring, or to continue to provide the same level of support. They will wish to bear in mind the distinction between caring *about* someone and caring *for* them. Many carers continue to care deeply *about* a person even though their ability to care for them may change.

10    Carers living in rural areas will be affected by the type of transport available and increased travelling times and so may have extra difficulties in gaining access to services and facilities. Care planning should take account of how best to support carers in such circumstances.

---

What might a carer's assessment cover?
- their perception of the situation
- the nature of their relationship with the user
- the tasks undertaken and consequent impact
- tasks carers would like help with
- their social contacts, and support received from family, friends, and neighbours
- their emotional, mental and physical health
- their willingness and/or ability to continue to provide care; options available to the carer, particularly carers who are in employment

- their undertaking of the illness or disability of the patient, and its likely/possible development
- other responsibilities eg work, education, family/child care commitments
- carers' strengths and ways of coping

any particular stress factors and/or aspects of the caring task which the carer finds particularly difficult.

## 11   Tension and conflict between user and carer

11.1   Illness and disability often create stress in family relationships and may give rise to significant tension and conflict between users and carers. Care managers may be working with complex relationships. Assessment, in such cases, is a skilful process the aim of which is to support family and other caring relationships and to assist individuals in finding their own solutions. Conflict may arise over the user's refusal of services. It can be helpful, particularly if a multi-disciplinary team is already involved, to use two workers to negotiate a resolution.

11.2   If a user refuses an assessment under Section 47 of the NHS and Community Care Act, their carer does not have the right to request an assessment under the Act as one of the triggers for a carer's assessment is that the user is being assessed.

Care managers will need to work closely with the family, user and carer to seek to resolve the situation. In such circumstances it is important that care managers see carers as individuals who may have a need for services and whom they therefore may be able to assist in their own right.

- A carer may appear to have a need for community care services and so be eligible for an assessment under Section 47(1)(a) of the NHS and Community Care Act. Local authorities should have particular regard to their function of prevention of illness under Paragraph 2 of Schedule 8 of the NHS Act 1977.
- Parents of disabled children and young carers may be eligible for services under Section 17 of the Children Act 1989.

Many such situations will be resolved through discussion and negotiation, but it is important that care managers are aware of their functions outside this Act to assist carers in these very difficult circumstances.

11.3   Tension can arise when either the user's or the carer's ability to communicate is affected by a learning, physical or mental disability. This can also be the case where either the user's or carer's first language is not English and one interprets for the other. Care managers need to communicate effectively with both users and carers so that both perspectives are known. A carer, for example, may have a long history of involvement which must be taken seriously. There are ways of overcoming communication difficulties so that all views can be sought.

11.4   Some carers find it difficult to relinquish either the care or the person for whom they are caring. What Next for Carers (Chapter 4) discusses how practitioners (and other carers) might assist carers who are reluctant to accept help. A useful model for understanding intervention is one which aims to maximise the disabled person's independence and support the carer in relinquishing some of the care. Conflict of interest is fully recognised and from the view point of both people.

11.5   The care plan should be a result of careful discussion with the users and carer and where differences arise, these should be recorded. Care should be taken to ensure that when requested by the user or carer, information given remains confidential and where there are conflicts of interest, interviews should be recorded separately on the file. In certain cases some thought might need to be given as to whether the carer and user should have separate records in view of possible conflicts of interest and confidential information each may give.

11.6   Tension and conflict can result in physical or other forms of abuse. Should this occur, No Longer Afraid: The Safeguard of Older People in Domestic Settings (HMSO 1993) provides advice on developing policy and practice to respond to cases of older people.

---

What works in Assessment and Care Management?
- an integrated approach to assessment, which fully involves both user and carer and other agencies
- giving user and carer the opportunity for separate discussion with the worker
- recognising that caring takes place within a context of existing relationships often characterised by strong feelings and mutual obligations and setting assessment sensitively in this framework
- active use of monitoring and review to pick up changing carers' needs
- giving care managers the capacity to arrange flexible services for users and carers
- understanding that carers are most satisfied when services resulting from an assessment are carefully planned and efficiently provided.

---

12   *Equal opportunities*

12.1   All caring situations are unique and, as such, are influenced by personal and family lifestyles, relationships, religions and cultural factors. Assessments should take account of the cultural context and relationship within which caring takes place.

12.2   At the start of the assessment, ascertain whether there are any language, communication and comprehension difficulties and take steps to overcome these. There are a range of communication methods including British Sign Language, Palantype and Deaf, Blind Manual and these and others should be considered.

12.3   Local authorities should have arrangements in place so that care managers can bring in appropriate personnel which may involve the use of interpreters and/or signers when necessary. It is important that interpreters and signers receive appropriate training and understand the nature of their task. It is not appropriate to assume that users and carers should interpret or sign for each other.

12.4   SSI reports document concerns that some groups of carers were less well served than others, this included carers of very elderly people and of people with mental health problems.

12.5   Effective consultation with black and ethnic minority communities can improve assessment and services. Practical examples of some initiatives to consult with black and minority ethnic communities are described in Chapters 3 and 6 of What Next for Carers? and Chapters 6 and 8 of Caring Today.

13   *Inter-agency working*

13.1   Strategic implementation of the Act will need to involve a range of agencies besides social services. Future Community Care Plans; Children Services Plans and Community Care Charters should therefore include reference to the agreed local response to the new legislation.

13.2   Voluntary organisations play an active role in supporting carers. Effective working between statutory and voluntary agencies can assist the implementation of this Act.

13.3 It will be important that local authorities use existing joint planning arrangements with local health agencies to ensure that effective systems are in place to implement the Act as well as to discuss their judgment of what amounts to 'substantial and regular care' with local carers groups.

13.4 Some carers will now have a right to request an assessment in anticipation of a patient's discharge from hospital. This reinforces the need to involve all carers in hospital discharge planning to ensure a smooth transition from hospital to community care and to ask carers their views and include them in discussions once discharge planning has begun and in any planned admissions for elective surgery.

## Young carers

14 This section of the practice guide concentrates on assessments of young carers undertaken within the provisions of the Carers (Recognition and Services) Act. The appropriate legislative framework for the provision of services to children is Part III of the Children Act 1989. SSI, as part of its development programme on young carers, has recently been published Young Carers: Something to Think About, a report of four SSI workshops held between May and July 1995. The report addresses more general questions of policy and practice concerning young carers.

15 *Recognition*

15.1 A young carer's right to request an assessment under the Carers Act occurs at the time of the user's assessment. The community care assessment will, therefore, be the starting point for an assessment of a young carer.

15.2 The provision of community care services should ensure that young carers are not expected to carry inappropriate levels of caring responsibilities. It should not be assumed that children should take on similar levels of caring responsibilities as adults.

15.3 Children and young people are at an earlier and important stage of development. Denial of proper educational and social opportunities may have harmful consequences on their ability to achieve independent adult life.

15.4 Where there are children in the family, the care manager should, by careful exploration, establish how the disabled person is assisted with his/her care needs and parenting responsibilities and whether or how the children might be helping.

15.5 If it appears to the care manager that a child or young person is providing regular and substantial care and the young carer does not request an assessment, the care manager should still consider whether there is a need to assist or relieve the child either through the provision of community care services for the user or through the provision of services to promote the welfare of the child. There may be some young carers who do not provide substantial and regular care but their development is impaired as a result of their caring responsibilities. In such situations local authorities will wish to consider whether they should exercise their existing duties towards children in need.

15.6 The definition of young carer (Section 1(2)(b)) could include siblings of disabled children. Local authorities will wish to ensure that through the assessment, siblings are not expected to carry out a burdensome level of caring responsibilities which impairs their own development.

15.7 Social Services Departments should ensure that any young carers known to them have information on local arrangements for community care and children's services and that they are encouraged to discuss any concerns informally with social services.

---

**Assessment**

When doing an assessment of a young carer:

* listen to the child or young person and respect their views
* give time and privacy to children who may need this in order to talk about their situation
* acknowledge that this is the way the family copes with the disability or illness of a family member
* acknowledge parents' strengths
* beware of undermining parenting capacity
* consider what is needed to assist the parent in her/his parenting role
* what needs does the child(ren) have arising from caring responsibilities?
* consider whether the caring responsibilities are restricting the child's ability to benefit from his/her education
* consider whether the child's emotional and social development are being impaired
* **REMEMBER** children must be allowed to be children
* provide information on the full range of relevant support services; any young carers' groups and contact points for further advice or information on specific issues.

---

16   There may be differences of views between young carers and their parents which have not been expressed. Care managers will need to be alert to the possibility that children's worlds are largely determined by their parents and that children may feel that their views have no weight. Equally they may be afraid that any admission of the difficulties may lead to a break up of the family. Such potential conflicts of views and interests may be very difficult to recognise and manage, especially for staff who have no experience of working with children. Arrangements may have to be made to ensure that the necessary range of skills and knowledge is made available to the whole family.

17   Staff will need to be alert to the possibility that young carers and their families may have a negative and fearful view of children's services because of the Social Services Departments' child protection duties. It may have to be explained to families that children's divisions of Social Services Departments provide a wide range of services to help families.

18   **Parents of disabled children**

18.1   Under the provision of the Carers Act, parents who provide substantial and regular care for disabled children will be able to request an assessment. The main legislative framework for the provision of services to families with disabled children is Part III of the Children Act 1989. Volume 6 of Regulations and Guidance is essential reading for those providing services for disabled children and their families.

18.2   Clearly all parents, especially those with young children, provide substantial and regular care. With non-disabled children, the degree of care usually diminishes as the children grow older and become more independent. Parents of disabled children may well be providing a substantial and regular level of care beyond that which would usually be expected for a child of a similar age. Local authorities will also wish to consider the impact of a child's disability on siblings in the family.

18.3 This section is necessarily short as much of the preceding guidance which applies to carers of adults applies equally to parents of disabled children. This should be read with guidance on the Children Act 1989.

18.4 Volume 6 of Children Act 1989 Regulations and Guidance underlines the importance of

- providing early information to parents
- ascertaining the wishes and feelings of parents and children
- making an assessment of needs of the child and family leading to a plan which is regularly reviewed
- working in partnership with parents
- providing short periods of accommodation as a family support service to strengthen the ability of a family to care for their child and to promote the child's welfare
- co-ordinating services with education, health and the voluntary sector
- planning for a smooth transition to adulthood

An awareness of these themes will shape any assessment requested under the Act.

## Annex 1
## Carers (Recognition and Services) Act 1995
## Practice Guidance

### Types of carer

1 This annex provides a brief summary of research, which is described in much more detail elsewhere. A secondary analysis of the 1985 General Household Survey undertaken by the Social Policy Research Unit at the University of York identified two different sorts of caring activity;

— those carers who are heavily involved and providing a great deal of personal and/or physical care;

— those who might be more accurately described as 'helpers' who provide practical help for friends, neighbours and relatives and who do not usually live in the same household.

2 It is from this analysis a figure of 1.6 million heavily involved carers is derived. An analysis of the 1990 General Household Survey broadly confirmed these figures and indicated that those carers who were heavily involved were now even more so.

3 Parker and Lawton developed a typology of caring activities based on the eight tasks defined in the GHS survey.

— Help with personal care eg dressing, bathing, toileting.

— Physical help eg with walking, getting in and out of bed or up and down stairs.

— Help with paperwork and financial matters.

— Other practical help eg preparing meals, doing shopping, housework or household repairs.

— Keeping the helped person company.

— Taking the helped person out.

— Giving medicine, including injections, changing dressings.

— Keeping an eye on the helped person to see that s/he is all right.

4 The analysis also documents a wide range of involvement in caring, from people providing under two hours of help a week to those providing a hundred or more. People providing substantial hours of help, tended to undertake a greater range of

tasks; personal and/or physical care were highly associated with long hours of care. Of people providing 20-49 hours a week, 58% were providing personal and/or physical care. Of those caring for 50-99 hours, the figure is 75% and for over a hundred hours it is 85%. The analysis also found that typically such carers were more likely to be sole carers, receiving little help from others, were living in the same household and were caring for someone with a mental impairment.

5    The 'heavily involved carer' is likely to be someone who
  — provides long hours of help;
  — carries out a range of helping activities;
  — is likely to provide both personal and physical assistance;
  — is more likely to be looking after someone in the same household;
  — is more likely to be caring for someone with a mental impairment;
  — is more likely to be caring without any help from others.

6    This analysis can be criticised for potentially excluding carers of people with chronic mental health problems eg, Schizophrenia, because of its emphasis on tasks. The provision of personal care is not a major feature of caring for someone diagnosed as mentally ill. Responsibility and supervision can be a prominent feature. Other factors, for example, being the sole carer; caring for someone in the same household are likely to be common with other carers. The circumstances of carers of people who misuse drugs and alcohol may be similar.

7    Carers of people with dementia often provide both personal care and supervision.

8    The analysis also shows that apart from those supporting people aged over 85, those caring for children (whether young or adult) and spouses in the same household are the most likely to be heavily involved and that almost the same proportion of male carers as female carers are heavily involved.

## (2)  CARERS (RECOGNITION AND SERVICES) ACT 1995
## POLICY GUIDANCE

### Purpose

1    The aim of this policy guidance (which is issued under Section 7(1) of the Local Authority Social Services Act 1970) is to set out the Government's view of *what* local authorities should be doing to implement the Carers (Recognition and Services) Act 1995. The Act is concerned with carers' assessment. Detailed policy and practice guidance already exists on assessment and care management. This guidance is intended to supplement that, insofar as is relevant to the implementation of the Act.

2    The accompanying practice guide gives advice on *how* the Act might be implemented. Rather than repeat information which is contained in other reports, the practice guide, where relevant, cross refers readers to existing material.

### Context—policy aims and objectives

3    The Carers (Recognition and Services) Act 1995 is consistent with the Government's policy aims for both community care and disabled children. The White Paper, 'Caring for People' has as its second key objective 'to ensure that service providers make practical support for carers a high priority' and that 'assessment of care needs should also take account of the needs of caring family, friends

and neighbours'. The Children Act 1989 Guidance (Volume 6) emphasises that Social Services Departments should carry out assessments of children in a manner which takes account of the child's and parent's circumstances and preferences.

4   The Act is concerned with carers who are either providing or intending to provide a substantial amount of care on a regular basis. Under the Act, a carer is entitled, on request, to an assessment when a local authority carries out an assessment of the person cared for in respect of community care services (under Section 47(1)(*a*) of NHSCCA 1990) or services for children (for the purposes of the Children Act 1989 or Section 2 of the CSDPA 1970). The results of the carer's assessment should be taken into account when the local authority is making decisions about services to be provided to the user.

5   However, the Act is only one, albeit very important, aspect of a range of ways in which local authorities can assist carers:

(*a*)   by continuing to use their powers in paragraph 2(1) of Schedule 8 of the NHS Act 1977 supplemented by Section 111 of the Local Government Act 1972 to provide or support services such as carer support groups and information. Such services should be available to all carers without requiring an assessment

(*b*)   by acting on their continuing responsibility to involve carers who are not covered by the scope of the Act in a user's assessment. Section 8 of the Disabled Persons (Services, Consultation and Representation) Act 1986 requires the local authority to have regard to the ability of a carer to provide or continue to provide care when deciding what services to provide to the disabled person.

(*c*)   Where a carer is requesting help, but the user refuses an assessment local authorities are reminded of their responsibilities arising from Section 47 of the NHS and Community Care Act 1990, Schedule 8 of the NHS Act 1977 and Section 17 of the Children Act 1989. (See paragraph 11.2 of the Practice Guidance.)

## Scope of the Act

6   The provisions of the Act cover

(*a*)   Adults (people aged 18 and over) who provide or intend to provide a substantial amount of care on a regular basis.

(*b*)   Children and young people (under 18) who provide or intend to provide a substantial amount of care on a regular basis.

(*c*)   Parents who provide or intend to provide a substantial amount of care on a regular basis for disabled children. (For a definition of disability refer to Section 17(11) of Children Act 1989.)

7   For the purposes of the Act the term carer includes people who may or may not be a relative and who may not be living with the person for whom they are caring.

The Act excludes from the definition of carer volunteers who provide care as part of their work for a voluntary organisation and anyone who is providing care by virtue of a contract of employment or any other contract. This would exclude anyone who is providing personal assistance for payment, either in cash or kind.

8   It is important to recognise that the effects of the Act will be gradual. As many authorities already offer carers an assessment, the legislation in effect enshrines good practice into statute. The Act provides that those carers who are providing a substantial amount of care on a regular basis have a right to request an assessment at the time of the user's assessment. The provisions of the Act will affect carers

where the person for whom they care is in the process of being assessed. Or, where a re-assessment of the user is taking place, either as part of a review or because of a change in circumstances of either the user or the carer arising for example, from a deterioration in the health of the user or a change in the carer's ability to continue to provide care.

9 The Act links the results of a carer's assessment to the local authority's decision about services for the user. The aim is to encourage an approach which considers support already available from family, friends or neighbours, the type of assistance needed by the person being assessed and how and whether the current arrangements for care can sustain the user in the community. Many of the services which assist carers are provided to the user. Views and circumstances of users and carers may be distinct but the nature of caring requires that they are considered together and reflected in the services to be provided to the user.

10 The Department considers that the terms 'regular' and 'substantial' in the expression, 'a substantial amount of care on a regular basis', should be interpreted in their everyday sense since Parliament has not provided otherwise in the Act.

11 The reference to a 'substantial amount of care on a regular basis' means that not all carers will be eligible for an assessment under the Act. It will be for local authorities to form their own judgment about what amounts to 'regular' and 'substantial' and to make their views known. In so doing, they may need to make decisions about the relative needs of carers in their area to ensure that those with regular and substantial caring responsibilities can receive, where requested, an assessment under this Act. The Act reinforces existing good practice; over bureaucratic responses or procedures should be avoided.

12 Local authorities should ensure any eligibility criteria (or other statements) which describe levels of need which they will meet under current community care legislation also reflect their responsibilities under this Act and allow the consideration of a carer's ability to provide and continue to provide care.

## Young carers and parents of disabled children

13 Where the carer is either under 18 or the parent of a disabled child, local authorities should consider whether the Children Act 1989 applies. It provides a framework for all services for children in need, including disabled children, and those young carers, who because of the extent and effect of their caring responsibilities, are children in need. It emphasises certain principles, such as the need to ascertain and give due weight to the wishes and feelings of children and to promote the upbringing of children by their families. These principles should inform a local authority's assessment of either a parent of a disabled child or of a young carer.

14 It is important to provide integrated services through clearly identified links between community care and children's legislation so that adequate support is available for the family via community care services for the adult and children's services for the child. It will be up to local authorities to make the relevant management arrangements according to local structure and organisation.

They should ensure that staff have sufficient knowledge of the range of the Social Services Department's responsibilities and provision so that they can make appropriate arrangements to support families where children have assumed a caring role. The authority should be aware of its responsibilities under Section 17(1) of the Children Act 1989 for 'children in need' particularly where a child may be either considerably affected by a parent's illness or disability, or caring for a parent but not on a regular or substantial basis.

## When to do a carer's assessment under the Carers (Recognition and Services) Act

15 (a) Local authorities should carry out a carer's assessment when requested by a carer at the time of a user's assessment and the carer is:
- a carer as defined in paragraphs 6 and 7
- and either providing a substantial amount of care on a regular basis
- or intending to provide a substantial amount of care on a regular basis.

(b) When requested by a carer either as part of a review of the circumstances of the user or when because of change in circumstances of either the user or carer a user is being reassessed and the carer is otherwise eligible.

16 By including carers both providing or intending to provide care, the Act covers those carers who are about to take on substantial and regular caring tasks for someone who has just become, or is becoming, disabled either through accident or severe physical or mental ill health. Local and health authorities will need to ensure that hospital discharge procedures take account of the provisions of the Act and that carers are involved once planning for discharge starts.

## Carers with community care needs

17 Carers may have community care needs in their own right by reason of their old age, physical or mental ill health or physical or learning disability. Where it appears to the local authority that a carer who is over the age of 18 may have a need for community care services, then the local authority should carry out an assessment under Section 47(1)(a) of the NHS and Community Care Act.

## Carers who either do not want or do not qualify for a carer's assessment

18 It should not be assumed that all qualifying carers will want their own assessment. Local authorities should continue to follow current policy and practice guidance on involving carers when either a regular or substantial carer does not want their own assessment or when a carer is providing care on less than a substantial and regular basis.

## Information

19 Local authorities should ensure that their published information about community care tells carers about their right under this Act: describes which carers will be eligible for an assessment and how the authority's assessment procedures work.
20 Many carers with substantial caring responsibilities may not know about their right under the Act. Local authorities should ensure that it becomes part of routine assessment practice to inform any carer who appears to be eligible under this Act of their right to request an assessment.

## The assessment

21 The focus of the carer's assessment for the purposes of this Act should be on the carer's ability to care and to continue caring. The assessment should take account of the carer's circumstances, their age, views and preferences, the amount of support available to them. It should not automatically assume a willingness by the carer to continue caring, or to continue providing the same level of support.

22   Where the carer is a child the impact of caring may be different as it may affect the child's health and development by the restrictions that providing regular and substantial care might place on the child's educational and leisure opportunities. This should be carefully considered as part of the assessment. It is equally important that the assessment focuses on how best to enable an ill or disabled parent (or other family member) to live independently so that the parent's ability to parent is supported rather than undermined. Consideration should be given as to whether the child is a 'child in need' under the Children Act 1989.

23   When doing an assessment of a parent of a disabled child the considerations in paragraph 17 above apply. The assessment should take account of the extent to which parents of disabled children provide a substantial level of care on a regular basis beyond that which parents would provide for a non-disabled child of a similar age.

24   Many local authorities already offer carers an assessment. Recent studies have shown that carers are not always aware either that they have been offered or that they have had an assessment. Authorities should ensure that good practice and adequate recording are developed so that both carers and professional staff share the same understanding of the process which has taken place. It should not be necessary to create elaborate systems and procedures to achieve this.

25   It should not be assumed that any request by a qualifying carer for an assessment under this Act can only be met by a separate assessment. In some cases it may be appropriate to carry out the carer's assessment at the same time as the user's assessment, whereas in others carers and/or users may want the opportunity for private discussion with the care manager. Authorities should discuss how the assessment is to be done with the carer and ascertain whether a separate assessment or joint assessment with the user is appropriate.

## Equal opportunities

26   Existing guidance emphasises the importance of ensuring that assessment is equally available to all members of the community and that

(a)   assessment procedures should be readily accessible to all potential users and carers

(b)   where individuals have communication difficulties arising from disability and/or sensory impairment, authorities should take active steps to make suitable arrangements to ensure that, in this case, the carer, can fully participate in the assessment

(c)   authorities should also ensure that carers from black and ethnic minority backgrounds, whose first language is not English, can participate fully in any assessment.

Authorities will need to respond sensitively to the particular circumstances of carers from all backgrounds, ethnic origins and different lifestyles.

## Inter-agency working

27   Section 47(3) of the NHS and Community Care Act 1990 requires Social Services Departments to bring apparent housing and health care needs to the attention of the appropriate authority and invite them to assist in an assessment of a person's need for community care services. The Children Act 1989 Section 27 places a qualified duty on local education, health and housing authorities to co-operate with local authorities in relation to functions under Part III of the Children Act. Authorities should, therefore, already have collaborative arrangements in place for

obtaining the input of health or housing, when appropriate. A carer's assessment may alert the SSD to either health, education or housing needs. Social services authorities and all other agencies will need to ensure that existing inter-agency arrangements are appropriate for referrals resulting from a carer's assessment.

### NHS involvement

28   Increased patient involvement in purchasing is a specific objective in the 1996/97 NHS Priorities and Planning Guidance which states:

> Give greater voice and influence to users of NHS services and their carers in their own care, the development and definition of standards set for NHS services locally and the development of NHS policy both locally and nationally (p 9)

Collaboration with local authorities in the implementation of the Carers (Recognition and Services) Act is, therefore, part of the achievement of existing NHS priorities.

29   The Continuing Care guidance, 'NHS Responsibilities for Meeting Continuing Health Needs' HSG(95)8, LAC (95)5 and the more recently published arrangements for monitoring implementation, (EL/95/88, CI/95/37) provide a good opportunity for local authorities to review with NHS commissioning agencies and NHS providers how they might best be involved in carers' assessment.

30   Primary care staff, including GPs and community nurses through their contact with users and carers, are in a good position to notice signs of stress, difficulty or rapidly deteriorating health particularly in carers. The provision of the Act will help primary care staff to meet the medical and nursing needs of their patients who are carers. When making a referral for a user's assessment they should be able to inform the carer that they may also have a right to request an assessment and will be well-placed to encourage patients whom they consider will benefit most to take up the opportunity. Social Services Departments should make sure that primary care staff have relevant information about social services criteria and know who to contact to make a referral. GPs, nurses and other members of multi-disciplinary teams, may be able to assist in an assessment of a carer's ability to provide and to continue to provide care.

### Education departments

31   Social services departments should work closely with local education authorities when carrying out assessments of young carers and parents of disabled children. Section 166 of the Education Act 1993 places a qualified duty on social services departments to assist local education authorities in their work with children with special educational needs. Detailed guidance is contained in the Code of Practice on the Identification of Special Educational Needs and in the Pupils with Problems Guidance (Circulars 8/94 to 13/94).

### The decision

32   The Act requires the local authority to take the results of any carer's assessment into account when making decisions about services to be provided to the user.

33   The decision about services to be provided should be informed by the assessment of carer and user taken together. Both user and carer should be fully involved

in any discussion about the results of the assessment and proposed care plan. This should describe needs to be met by the local authority, services to be provided to the user, how they will assist the user and where relevant, how services provided to the user will assist the carer. Where the user is a disabled child, the relevant services will be those which may be provided under Part III of the Children Act 1989 and/or Section 2 of the Chronically Sick and Disabled Persons Act 1970. Where the user is an adult, the relevant services will be those referred to in Section 46(3) of the NHS and Community Care Act 1990. Young carers may be entitled to receive services described in Part III of the Children Act 1989.

34    The care plan and results of assessment should be confirmed in writing or in a format which is accessible to both user and carer. It is important that local authorities record the results of the assessments and that users and carers are informed of complaints procedures.

## (3)  C1(95)12—LETTER FROM HERBERT LAMING TO DIRECTORS OF SOCIAL SERVICES DATED 28 APRIL 1995

To: Directors of Social Services

Dear Director

### YOUNG CARERS

The Department of Health shares the growing concern that the difficulties facing young carers and their families have been hidden and have received too little attention. Many young people are having to take on levels of caring responsibilities for disabled, sick or mentally ill parents which disrupt their education and deny them usual opportunities for social development.

\*    \*    \*    \*    \*

The Children Act 1989 and the NHS and Community Care Act 1990 together provide the necessary powers and duties for local authorities to respond to the needs of young carers. Where the disabled person is a parent, it is essential that the community care assessment focuses on the family and considers how to support the parent and recognise the needs of any young carers. Services for the family can be provided under children's or adult legislation. It is clear for local authorities to decide how to prevent integrated services through clearly identified links between community care and children's provision. Annex A provides details of legislation and the development programme, as well as discussing some key principles.

\*    \*    \*    \*    \*

### ANNEX A

#### SSI
#### Young Carers

### 1   The legislation

*1.1   The Children Act 1989 and family support*
The Children Act 1989 reiterates the principle in law that the **welfare of the child** is paramount. The Act also emphasises the **importance of family support services for**

**children in need.** The definition of children in need includes children who are 'unlikely to achieve or maintain, or to have the opportunity of achieving or maintaining a reasonable standard of health or development without the provision of services . . .' (Section 17(10)). Research has demonstrated that many young people carry out a level of caring responsibilities which prevents them from enjoying normal social opportunities and from achieving full school attendance. Many young carers with significant caring responsibilities should therefore be seen as children in need.

Local authorities are required to provide a range and level of family support services appropriate to the children's needs. Volume 2 of Children Act Regulations and Guidance explains the concepts of family support. For example, paragraph 2.14 reads, '(Families) may look to social services for support and assistance. If they do this, they should receive a positive response which reduces any fears they may have of stigma or loss of parental responsibilities.'

### 1.2 NHS and Community Care Act 1990 and assessments
Section 47 of the NHS and Community Care Act 1990 requires a local authority to carry out an assessment 'where it appears to a local authority that any person for whom they may provide or arrange for the provision of community care services may be in need of any such services' and to ensure, at the same time, that the requirements of Section 4 of the Disabled Persons (Services, Consultation and Representation) Act 1986 are applied.

Community care has placed considerable emphasis on the development of assessment and care management to achieve more flexible support for users and carers. Where the user is also a parent assessment should focus on the whole family. It should take account of the support needs of parents both to maintain their independence and to fulfil their parenting role. The assessment should also consider the impact of the disability or illness on family members including any children in the family who are assuming caring responsibilities.

## 2 Guiding principles for the development of practice

### 2.1 Definition
At this stage of development, we are using the following working definition—young carer means a child or young person who is carrying out significant caring tasks and assuming a level of responsibility for another person, which would usually be taken by an adult. The term refers to children or young people under 18 years caring for adults (usually their parents) or occasionally siblings. It does not refer to young people under 18 years caring for their own children. Nor does the term refer to those children who accept an age appropriate role in taking increasing responsibility for household tasks in homes with a disabled, sick or mentally ill parent.

### 2.2 Mainstream services
A key principle is to ensure that young carers' needs and those of the disabled person for whom they care, receive proper attention from mainstream services. In the longer term the aim is to ensure that children are not expected to undertake caring responsibilities to the extent that they themselves become in need of services.

### 2.3 Staff awareness
If staff carrying out assessments do not expect to find children carrying out heavy and sometimes, intimate, caring tasks for an adult, they may fail to notice it or to

ask the right questions to gather the information. Health and social services managers need to ensure that staff are aware of this possibility and adjust their practice accordingly.

2.4  *Management arrangements*

Staff from a range of different agencies are likely to have contact with families where children are assuming a significant caring responsibility. These include teachers, GPs, district nurses, out patient clinic and home care staff. Both health and educational staff have a key role in identifying young carers, and may refer the family to social services. Social Services Departments should ensure that they have procedures in place so that, whatever route is used to gain access to services, an assessment of the whole family is offered which identifies both parents' and children's needs. Some assessments will involve inter-agency collaboration. Families may well have needs which require services from different parts of SSDs. Coordination of practice and policy across services for children and adults will be necessary. Both Children's Services Plans and Community Care Plans should recognise the needs of young carers with cross-referencing between plans to ensure good coordination.

*    *    *    *    *

# Materials 5

# Department of Health Guidance Letters on Implementation

*Contents*

## A. EL(92)13/CI(92)10—'Implementing Caring for People' from Andrew Foster and Herbert Laming, Social Services Inspectorate

We have identified eight key tasks on which local authorities, working closely with other agencies, including health authorities need to concentrate in 1992-3 in order to meet these requirements.

They are:

— agreeing the basis for required assessment systems for individuals;
— clarifying and agreeing arrangements for continuing care for new clients in residential and nursing homes including arrangements for respite care;
— ensuring the robustness and mutual acceptability of discharge arrangements;
— clarifying roles of GPs and primary healthcare teams;
— ensuring that adequate purchasing and charging arrangements are in

place of originals who will be receiving residential and nursing home care;

— ensuring that financial and other management systems can meet the new demands likely after 1 April 1993;

— ensuring that staff are suitably trained, wherever appropriate on a joint basis;

— informing the public of the arrangements made by the authority for assessment and the provision of care.

(*Letter cancelled on 1 April 1994.*)

## B. EL(92)65/CI(92)30—'Implementing Caring for People' from Andrew Foster and Herbert Laming dated 21 September 1992

4 We consider it essential all authorities reach agreements by 31 December on:

— agreed strategies governing health and local authority responsibilities for placing people in nursing homes, and the numbers likely to be involved during 1993/94;

— how hospital discharge arrangements will be integrated with assessment arrangements.

### Changes in services

5 In our March letter we made clear that health and social services authorities should not make unilateral withdrawals from service and financial commitments. Changes to the existing pattern of service should only be made by mutual consent. Health authorities should not adjust the level of their continuing care provision except as part of an agreed strategy with the relevant local authority.

\* \* \* \* \*

## C. CI(92)34—'Implementing Caring for People: Assessment' from Herbert Laming (the 'Laming Letter') dated 14 December 1992

5 The principal duty relating to assessment is Section 47 of the 1990 Act, which states:

47(1) . . . where it appears to a local authority that any person for whom they may provide or arrange for the provision of community care services may be in need of such services, the authority—

(a) shall carry out an assessment of his needs for those services

(b) having regard to the results of that assessment, shall then decide whether his needs call for the provision by them of any such services'

Two important points should be noted about this:

• first, authorities do not have a duty to assess on request, but only where they think that the person may be in need of services they provide;

• second, the assessment of need and decisions about the services to be provided are separate stages in the process.

## Information

6   In advance of April 1993, authorities should publish readily understandable information about:
   — the services currently available;
   — how to access assessment;
   — the care management and assessment procedures;
   — criteria for determining the type or level of assessment;
   — criteria for accessing resources and services;
   — any standards against which the assessment arrangements will be measured, including the estimated length of time between referral and the completion of an assessment;
   — the complaints procedure and how to gain access to it.

7   The publication of this material will enable front-line staff, relevant independent organisations and members of the public to have a clear understanding of the type of circumstances in which individuals are likely to be helped and the priority that will be afforded to them. This will help to ensure that unrealistic expectations are not placed on the new arrangements.

8   This information should also assist both users and carers to participate more effectively in the assessment process and thereby to influence the outcome.

## Level of assessment

9   The type and level of assessment that is offered to an individual should relate to the level and complexity of need that is being presented, the aim being to keep the process as simple and efficient as possible. Most assessments are likely to be simple and straightforward. Staffing arrangements and documentation should reflect this. Comprehensive multi-agency assessments are both time consuming and expensive. They should normally be reserved for the minority of users with the most complex needs. A full scale assessment of all needs for community care services should be offered to individuals appearing to be disabled, as prescribed by Section 47(2) of the NHS and CC Act.

10   Authorities should, therefore have:
   a.   a procedure for screening or filtering referrals according to agreed criteria.
   b.   published criteria for:
      i.    identifying disabled persons under the terms of the legislation;
      ii.   determining the appropriate type and level of assessment;
      iii.  involving other agencies (see paragraph 19).
   c.   staff with designated responsibility for operating these criteria.

*     *     *     *     *

## Assessment and service provision

12   The assessment should focus on the difficulties for which individuals are seeking assistance, but it should take account of all circumstances relevant to those individuals:
   — their capacities and incapacities;
   — their preferences and aspirations;
   — their living situation;
   — the support available from relatives and friends;
   — any other sources of help.

This information then provides the context for subsequent decisions about what services (if any) will be provided.

13   An authority may take into account the resources available when deciding how to respond to an individual's assessment. However, once the authority has indicated that a service should be provided to meet an individual's needs and the authority is under a legal obligation to provide it or arrange for its provision then the service must be provided. It will not be possible for an authority to use budgeting difficulties as a basis for refusing to provide the service.

14   Authorities can be helped in this process by defining eligibility criteria, ie: a system of banding which assigns individuals to particular categories, depending on the extent of the difficulties they encounter in carrying out every day tasks and relating the level of response to the degree of such difficulties. Any 'banding' should not, however, be rigidly applied, as account needs to be taken of individual circumstances. Such eligibility criteria should be phrased in terms of the factors identified in the assessment process. (The Community Care Support Force has circulated examples of how a number of authorities have tackled this task.) Authorities should ensure that all staff undertaking assessments understand and apply these criteria consistently.

15   As far as individual users are concerned, their care plans (of which they should receive a copy) should spell out the extent to which their needs qualify for assistance under the terms of the eligibility criteria. Care plans should also define the contribution to be made by each agency and professional towards the meeting of those individuals' needs.

\*    \*    \*    \*    \*

**Urgent needs and unusual assessments**

22   In urgent cases of need, authorities do not have to undertake an assessment before providing services if they are required as a matter of urgency. However, once temporary arrangements have been made an assessment must be undertaken as soon as practicable thereafter (Section 47(5) and (6) of the NHS and CC Act).

23   Authorities' arrangements must also be flexible enough for them to undertake assessments of their residents when they are not in the locality. This will be particularly relevant for those people without a settled way of life or where a user has been placed some distance from the local authority. Flexibility would include taking advice for example from voluntary agencies or the probation service or making reciprocal arrangements with other Social Services Departments. Decisions to commit resources after the assessment remain with the paying authority.

\*    \*    \*    \*    \*

**Monitoring and review**

27   Authorities should establish systems for the regular monitoring and review of:
   (*a*)   eligibility criteria for resources and services;
   (*b*)   the current pattern of available services in the light of user-expressed preferences;
   (*c*)   inter-agency joint working arrangements;
   (*d*)   the standards of performance achieved in the care management and assessment arrangements;
   (*e*)   the individual care plans.

\*    \*    \*    \*    \*

31 The care plans of all users should be subject to regular review. For frail people in the community, frequent reviews and adjustments of their care plans are likely to be needed. Before any changes in services are made for existing users, they should be re-assessed. In those cases, where assessments have been undertaken, particularly under Section 2(1) of the CSDP Act 1970, authorities must satisfy themselves, before any reduction in service provision takes place that the user does not have a continuing need for it. So long as there is a continuing need, a service must be provided although, following review, it is possible that an assessed need might be met in a different way.

(*Letter cancelled on 1 April 1994.*)

## D. EL(93)18/CI(93)12—'Implementing Caring for People' from Alan Langlands and Herbert Laming dated 15 March 1993

5 We also expect authorities to make progress during 1993/4 on:
— the development of assessment and care management systems, including progress on management and information systems;
— increasing the involvement of service users and carers in the planning and delivery of community care services;
— beginning to shift the balance of resources towards non-residential care, and the provision of more respite care and support for carers;
— improving collaboration with housing authorities and agencies.

(*Letter cancelled on 31 March 1994.*)

## E. EL(93)119/CI(93)35—'Community Care' from Alan Langlands and Herbert Laming dated 23 December 1993

Incorporates the SSI/RHA community care monitoring for September 1993 (national summary).

## F. EL(94)57/CI(94)20—'Community Care Monitoring for 1994/95' from Herbert Laming and Alasdair Liddell

(*Letter cancelled on 31 December 1995.*)

## G. CI(95)12—'Young Carers' from Herbert Laming to Directors of Social Services dated 28 April 1995 (see Materials 4, section M(3) above in Carers section)

(*Various other letters regarding monitoring of community care are not reproduced in this edition*)

# Appendices

# Contents

# Appendix 1

# Checklist and Guides

*Contents*

## A.  Practitioner Checklist

### Introduction

The checklists that follow are intended to provide a practical summary of some of the themes touched on in the main text so as to guide applicant and authority advisors in the event that legal problems arise in respect of assessment, service provision, reassessment (or review) or complaints procedures. A list of requirements for both parties in respect of an application for judicial review is also included.

Every advisor intending to carry out work in this particular field will need to obtain the following information:

- Local authority's Community Care Plan for current and past years.
- Copies of authority's policies on community care provision and eligibility criteria.
- Details of the authority's complaints procedure and identity of Complaints Officer.
- Copies of any collaborative policies with the local health authority/NHS trust, eg regarding hospital discharge.
- Any joint agreements between the social services and housing departments (or County Council and District Council).
- A thorough knowledge of the types of community care services referred to in the relevant statutes, directions, guidance and circulars (see Materials).

---

### The first interview with the client

*1   Funding*

Ascertain whether the client is eligible for advice and assistance under the Legal Aid 'Green Form' scheme and advise accordingly. In clearly urgent cases, consider asking the client to complete full Legal Aid forms at this stage as well. Alternatively, the forms may be signed at a later stage, if appropriate. Advise client regarding operation of Legal Aid, the Statutory Charge and likely level of costs over course of case.

## 2 The client

In many cases, the client who is first referred may be a carer of a disabled person, or there may be other members of the household who may be affected. Consider issues of conflict, especially where there are financial implications of any decision regarding service provision, or obvious differences of opinion between potential clients. It may be recommended to take instructions from all individuals affected, and if a conflict arises, referrals to other solicitors may need to be made. Where decisions affect a person who is potentially incapable of managing and administering their property and affairs, verify instructions personally if possible to ascertain the level of legal capacity. If legal proceedings are contemplated, consideration will need to be given to the potential identity of any next friend, including the possible involvement of the Official Solicitor if no other appropriate next friend is available.

## 3 Instructions

Take full instructions from the client, including, but not necessarily limited to, the following:

- Basic details, such as names of persons affected, relationship to client, addresses, dates of birth, National Insurance numbers, financial means, GP's and consultant's names and addresses, local social services and housing offices, hospital.
- Full details of any disabilities, including a brief chronological history, details of treatment/medication, likelihood of deterioration and/or improvement.
- Details of difficulties with mobility, shopping, washing, cleaning, feeding, accessing amenities and educational opportunities, etc.
- Details of services (if any) being provided, and whether the client is satisfied with these. If not, discuss with client the level and types of services that are required.
- Full chronological history of involvement with social services/housing departments and health services, using any documents produced by client to assist in memory recall, including any meetings, reviews, decisions and/or promises made. Try to ascertain identity of individuals if possible.
- Clarify with client what the client ultimately wants. This will be crucial to the issue of appropriate remedy. For example, if the client wants an apology for delay or maladministration, the complaints procedure or a complaint to the Ombudsman may be the most appropriate course of action. If, however, the issue is one of lack of action on the part of the authority concerning services which are required urgently, these remedies will not be useful in obtaining relief and, ultimately, an application for judicial review may be necessary.
- Advise client initially on available remedies, likely timescales, and costs of case.
- Obtain all relevant documentation from client, and ask client to sign forms authorising access to social services/housing/health files.
- Agree with client the course of action to be taken, and confirm this in writing. Stress the importance of keeping the advisor fully informed of any developments at all times.

## Types of problem/remedies

This will need to be reviewed throughout the lifetime of a case, and the client fully consulted concerning any developments. In almost all cases, a letter before action will need to be written to the authority setting out in full the following:

- The relevant details gleaned from the client in interview.
- The client's *prima facie* need for community care services which the authority is empowered to provide/arrange for the provision of.
- A request that the authority takes appropriate action (eg, carries out an assessment, or provides urgent services prior to an assessment).
- A request that the authority responds with confirmation as to the above within a set time period, failing which further (specified) action will be taken. This will be appropriate in serious/urgent cases, depending on the history of the matter.

### (a) Refusal to assess

If an authority has refused to assess need, consider whether this decision is lawful. If, after a letter before action (see below), the refusal is still maintained, consider either application for leave for judicial review, or asking the Secretary of State to exercise his default powers.

NB: The latter will only be appropriate where an authority is simply refusing to carry out assessment at all. In practice, judicial review is the means of challenge where an authority has misunderstood/misapplied the threshold of eligibility for an assessment.

### (b) Failure to assess

Often, no response is forthcoming from the authority within the time period specified in the letter before action. It may be appropriate to make an immediate application for leave to move for judicial review (see below), or to make further attempts to elicit a response. In cases involving serious/urgent need, or delay, matters should not be left to drift. Cases which are not serious may nevertheless justify an immediate complaint to the authority's Complaints Officer.

### (c) The assessment

Monitor the assessment process carefully, and keep in close contact with the client. If there are any complaints as to how it is being carried out, record these in writing to the authority so as to avoid any suggestion that any breach of the rules of natural justice is being waived.

If the assessment process is so inadequate or manifestly unfair as to render it unlawful, consider writing a further letter before action setting out full details before making a potential application for judicial review to stop the process continuing. In practice, however, the court would probably regard any such application as premature, save in the most serious/urgent cases. Cases which involve a clear lack of action on the part of the authority may render the authority open to challenge, if the assessment process is not completed.

Remember that an authority should assess a person's needs for services that it is empowered to provide, even for such services that the particular authority does not in practice provide. For example, this might include certain types of accommodation traditionally thought to be the remit of housing departments (or District Councils).

### (d) The decision

If no decision is reached within a reasonable time (which is likely to depend on the particular facts of the case), judicial review may be appropriate. The authority should be kept fully informed of any proposed action, with reasonable time limits imposed prior to issue of proceedings.

Alternatively, and probably more appropriately in non-urgent cases, the authority's complaints procedure should be invoked to try to achieve a resolution. In exceptional cases (where the authority is simply refusing to provide a decision at all) the default powers of the Secretary of State may be sought.

If a decision is not reasoned the authority should be asked, in writing, to provide such reasons within a specified time period. Judicial review should be sought if reasons are clearly neither adequate nor intelligible, particularly in serious cases.

Once a decision is made its legality or fairness may be challenged by judicial review. However, consideration should always be given to invoking the authority's complaints procedure. If the matter is urgent, practitioners may usually legitimately seek judicial review due to the need for interim provision of services unless the authority agrees to provide services pending the outcome of the complaints procedure.

For both a potential applicant and authority, it is sensible to try to clarify the matters at issue in order to decide on the choice of remedy, and so that valuable time is not wasted in canvassing those matters over which there is essentially no conflict.

If there is real uncertainty as to whether an application for judicial review or the complaints procedure should be used, proceedings for judicial review may be issued, but the application for leave may be adjourned pending the outcome of the complaints procedure. This avoids delay problems with the court and preserves an applicant's option to continue with the judicial review at the appropriate time if the complaints regime is not producing results. Proceedings can also be continued in the event that the statutory time periods for the complaints procedure are not adhered to.

## Tactical considerations

In general, cases can be separated into four categories:
  (1)  Urgent/serious, where prompt action and services are required.
  (2)  Non-urgent cases, which can wait for a three to six month period, but where ultimately services may be required.
  (3)  Cases where issues of poor practice, lack of communication/consultation, lack of provision of services in the past have occurred, but where a care package is now satisfactory. Also cases where compensation for past failings is sought.
  (4)  Cases where the authority has refused to assess or reach a decision.

For those cases falling into category 1, the main tension will be between whether to invoke the authority's complaints procedure or to seek judicial review. Tactically, judicial review will often produce results, but the High Court will not lightly see the statutory complaints procedure ignored. However, as a rough guide, if resolution cannot wait for the procedure to be finalised, judicial review should be used. Do bear in mind that often the time limits in the complaints procedure are not adhered to, delaying the process still further.

Cases falling into category (2) are more uncertain. Unless the matter becomes urgent, then usually the complaints procedure should be used, but bear in mind that situations change, and a case may become urgent over time. If an important point of law is at issue, however, judicial review should be sought.

For complaints regarding past practice, where an explanation, apology or compensation is sought, or improvements in working practices are the aim, the choice will be between the complaints procedure or a complaint to the Ombudsman. Although in general the Ombudsman requires the complaints procedure to be exhausted first, this is often not appropriate, especially where the possibility of a compensation awarded for maladministration or delay is the aim. Remember that although complaints to the Ombudsman may be resolved more quickly, the average time for completion of the whole process can take 18 months, and compensation awards are low.

For those cases falling into category (4), a request to the Secretary of State for the exercise of his default powers may sometimes be the most appropriate course of action (in cases of total breakdown). In most cases, judicial review will be appropriate.

## B.  Complaints Procedure Guide

1   Complainant is dissatisfied with the outcome of the informal resolution process.

2   Authority provides full details as to formal complaints procedure and invites a written formal complaint, offering assistance and support.

3   Complainant sets out written complaint in full, and sends to authority's Complaints Officer requesting that the formal complaints procedure is applied.

4   The complaint is registered.

5   The Complaints Officer sends the complaint to the manager or member responsible for the original decision for action/comment. If this cannot be agreed, senior management may become involved and a response sent to the CO. An investigator may be appointed to produce a report.

6   The response (including the investigator's report) is forwarded to the complainant within 28 days. If this is not possible, a written explanation must be given, and a response must be provided within 3 months in any event. The authority must provide full details to the complainant of how to take the matter further.

7   The authority records when the written response is provided.

8   If dissatisfied, the complainant sends notification to the CO within 28 days of receipt of the response.

9   A review panel must be convened within 28 days of the request from the complainant. The authority must notify the complainant at least 10 days before the hearing of the date, time and venue and that they can be accompanied by a representative.

10   The authority should ensure that all relevant persons are notified of the review, given that they may be required to attend to make representations.

11   After the review, the panel makes its findings and recommendations in writing within 24 hours. Any differences in opinion should be recorded.

12   A copy of the recommendations and findings is sent to the authority, complainant and any other person with sufficient interest in the case.

13    The authority considers the findings of the panel and decides within 28 days whether to accept the recommendations. If not accepted, full reasons should be given and the possibility of a judicial review of non-acceptance should be carefully considered.

14    The authority records all representations, the findings and whether all time limits have been complied with.

15    The complainant considers the panel's findings/authority's position and considers whether a complaint to the Ombudsman should be made, or whether an application for judicial review may be appropriate.

## C.   Judicial Review Guide

### The applicant

1    Consider whether appropriate to apply for Emergency Legal Aid—at this stage or at stage 4 below.

2    Send letter before action to authority, setting out full details and requesting response within specified time period.

3    If no response received, start to prepare JR application. If request for extra time to respond made by authority, decide whether this is reasonable and whether to agree. If unsatisfactory response received, write to authority explaining why, and requesting full response within new time period.

4    If not already obtained, apply for Emergency Legal Aid (telephone application in very urgent cases, but in most cases a written application will need to be made). Send statement in support to Legal Aid Board, setting out full history, authority's obligations, and matters complained of. Also send copy of letter before action if application made at this stage. As many Area Offices will be unused to dealing with community care cases, as full and detailed an application as possible may need to be made.

5    If Legal Aid certificate granted, check limitations. These will usually be a costs limit up to £4,000 (including Counsel's fees), and proceedings up to the post leave stage. It is important to obtain regular updates on work in progress figures and Counsel's fee notes to ensure that applications to increase the costs limitation are made in good time.

6    Choose appropriate Counsel and check availability with clerk.

7    Check finally with client as to any further contact with local authority before drafting instructions.

8    Draft affidavit in support of application. It is best that this is done by the solicitor, who will have full knowledge of the client's instructions, rather than Counsel. Consider whether the Form 86A should also be drafted (in most community care cases, this will be done by Counsel, but it is a matter for the individual solicitor). The affidavit should exhibit all relevant correspondence and papers, including the letter before action.

9    Instruct Counsel, enclosing draft affidavit, all client's papers, correspondence and copy Legal Aid certificate.

10   Once draft affidavit is approved by Counsel, swear it. Check Form 86A once received and engross.

11   Paginate the Form 86A, followed by the affidavit and exhibits. Prepare index to paginated bundle, marking essential reading with an asterisk, and putting explanatory note at bottom of index as to this. Prepare five copies of the paginated bundle:
  •   two (one original) for the Crown Office
  •   one for Counsel
  •   one for file
  •   one for service on Respondent authority (prior to leave application if *inter partes*).

12   Prepare Notice of Acting and Notice of Issue of Legal Aid and obtain issue fee cheque of £20.

13   Issue application for leave at Crown Office of the High Court:
  •   pay fee of £20 on Form 86A
  •   lodge original bundle and copy, Notice of Acting and Legal Aid certificate
  •   inform Crown Office of whether oral hearing is sought, or application on the papers
  •   provide Counsel's details.

14   Crown Office will allocate a case number, and if an oral hearing is sought, liaise with Counsel's clerk as to listing.

15   If *inter partes*, inform Respondent authority of listing and serve bundle as soon as possible.

16   Leave application takes place. If on the papers, and leave is refused, consider renewing application by way of oral hearing on Form 86B (provided by Crown Office).

17   After grant of leave, obtain copy of order from Crown Office Associates as soon as possible and check. Diarise time limit for the filing of the Respondent's affidavit.

18   Within 14 days of the grant of leave:
  •   draft Form 86
  •   serve copy of Form 86, order, bundle, Notice of Acting and Issue on Respondent authority
  •   telephone to check above received
  •   draft and swear short affidavit of service (the Crown Office does not require the bundle to be exhibited)
  •   pay £100 fee on Form 86 and lodge original plus copy, together with affidavit of service (plus copy) at Crown Office.

19   Check that any order for interim relief complied with.

20   Write to Respondent authority requesting clarification as to whether an affidavit in response will be filed.

21   Keep in constant contact with client to check any changes in position.

22   On receipt of Respondent's affidavit, send to Counsel and client and review position. Arrange conference if appropriate, and apply for amendment to Legal Aid certificate if so advised to cover final hearing.

23 Consider filing further affidavit prior to final hearing to update Court of current position and serve.

24 Final hearing will either be fixed by Crown Office in consultation with Counsel's clerks, or 'warned'. If warned letter received, serve on Counsel's clerk and Respondent.

25 Paginate and index final bundle, comprising Form 86A, order granting leave and all affidavits, lodge and serve at least five working days before final hearing.

26 Counsel will prepare skeleton arguments and serve on each other. For Applicant's Counsel, this must be done five full days before any final hearing, and for Respondent Counsel this must be at least two days before the hearing. Counsel will lodge these with the Crown Office directly.

27 Final hearing takes place. Ensure question of costs dealt with and an order for Legal Aid Taxation obtained in any event.

28 Serve copy of order on Respondent once received and ensure compliance with terms.

29 Consider whether order should be appealed to the Court of Appeal.

30 Report fully to client and deal with the issue of costs, including discharge of client's Legal Aid certificate if appropriate.

31 Note that if settlement is reached prior to final hearing, Consent Order plus details of why agreement reached should be filed with Crown Office. Check order received and any hearing date is vacated.

*The local authority*

1 As soon as letter before action received, if not addressed to Legal Department, forward immediately.

2 Legal Department takes urgent instructions from client department and if necessary, writes to Applicant's solicitor to request extra time. Respond as fully as possible to Applicant in order to avoid proceedings, and consider suggesting (in appropriate cases) that the complaints procedure be utilised and/or that proceedings are adjourned pending outcome of complaints procedure.

3 If Applicant's solicitor is of the opinion that the complaints procedure is not appropriate, consider position carefully to avoid proceedings. Instruct Counsel at an early stage.

4 Ask Applicant's solicitor whether interim relief will be sought and in most cases, seek to be served as soon as possible with the papers, in order to decide whether to attend any oral leave hearing to oppose the grant of leave or interim relief. Inform Applicant's solicitor of any intention to oppose leave and provide Counsel's details. Also inform Crown Office.

5 Attend oral leave hearing and if leave granted, reconsider position.

6 If order granting leave on the papers (no oral hearing) is received, consider whether to apply for leave to be set aside on the basis of material non-disclosure or if the case is plainly unarguable. However, this procedure should be used sparingly, and if unsuccessful, may incur further costs for the authority.

7   Check Form 86 and bundle served by Applicant within time limits and diarise time for filing Respondent's affidavit. Ensure any order for interim relief complied with.

8   Take full instructions from client department and consider arranging conference with Counsel. Decide whether to file affidavit in response and notify Applicant and Crown Office of intention to do so.

9   If it is decided to file affidavit evidence, then this must be within the prescribed time limits. Any application to extend this must be made before the expiry of the time period, as otherwise the affidavit may be excluded.

10   File and serve affidavit. Consider any further affidavit filed by Applicant and check that time limits for filing and service of final trial bundles are complied with. Keep Counsel and client department informed at all stages and consider settlement at all times.

11   On receipt of final hearing date, ensure Counsel and client department informed, and check that Counsel produces skeleton argument within time limits.

12   Attend final hearing, and ensure final order deals with costs issue. Obtain copy order and consider appealing any adverse decision.

13   If proceedings settled prior to final hearing, ensure that Applicant served signed Consent Order with Crown Office. Reasons will have to be given for settlement and Respondents should ensure that these do not create precedent for the future.

## Costs

As with most actions, costs will usually follow the event. However, in community care actions for judicial review it is sometimes difficult to decide whether an Applicant or Respondent has been successful, particularly in those cases where the case has settled post leave or even pre leave but post issue.

*Before issue*
There is currently no authority for the proposition that a costs application may be made prior to the issue of proceedings, although this may result in the privately funded Applicant suffering a loss, or the Legal Aid Board put to expense. If the current proposals as to reform of the Legal Aid Board are enacted, more legally aided Applicants will be required to make contributions towards their certificates, and for a longer period, and it will therefore be necessary for Applicant solicitors to issue proceedings at the first opportunity.

*Post issue, before leave*
In cases where proceedings have been issued, but the application for leave has not yet taken place, if the Respondent authority has had notice of the proceedings and has taken steps to provide the relief sought, thus rendering the proceedings academic, there may be an argument that the costs of the proceedings to date should be paid to the Applicant. If not agreed, then the leave application may be used for a specific costs application. Applicants' solicitors should exercise caution in uncertain cases, especially as the question of leave will not yet have been adjudicated.

*Post leave, prior to final hearing*

This is the stage at which most community care cases settle. Although the grant of leave is by no means a guarantee that the final hearing will result in a judgment in the Applicant's favour, if the Respondent has taken steps to satisfy the relief sought, the Applicant should in most cases be able to mount a strong argument that the costs to date should be paid. If agreement cannot be reached, the courts will entertain a costs application on the date of the final hearing, although this will be limited to short argument and will not be a complete run of all the issues.

*Public bodies*

It has been argued that in community care cases, where the Applicant is legally aided, and the Respondent is a public body, no order for costs should be made. However, the Legal Aid Board has made it clear that an assisted person is entitled to an order for costs in the same way as a privately funded Applicant would be. Indeed, it is certainly in the Board's interest to ensure that in all appropriate cases the costs of litigation are recouped. Just because two different public bodies are involved in litigation does not mean that they are not accountable for their budgets.

As far as a Respondent is concerned, careful consideration needs to be given to the issue of costs from the outset. Failure to respond adequately (or at all) to a letter before action can be costly and result in litigation which might otherwise have been avoided. However, there are cases where a Respondent might successfully argue that proceedings should not have been brought, or where the Applicant has prevented a reasonable settlement from being agreed. In some cases, therefore, a costs application may be resisted, although the chances of this being successful are diminished where the Respondent has had full notice of the leave application.

Although it is possible in theory to obtain a costs order against a legally aided Applicant, such cases are extremely rare and little will be achieved by a Respondent in obtaining such an order if it is not to be enforced without leave of the court due to the Applicant's lack of means.

## Conclusion

From the perspective of both sides, judicial review is a remedy that creates a precedent for the future.

There is, from either side's point of view, little point in fighting a judicial review case which is likely to create such a precedent unless the merits are perceived to lie in one direction. Whilst judicial review is, undoubtedly, concerned with legality rather than merits, the facts of a case (particularly concerning community care issues) not infrequently influence the court. From either side, therefore, careful consideration should be given at all stages as to whether proceeding to a final hearing will produce an unfortunate (and costly) result for the future.

# Appendix 2

# Judicial Review Case Study

*Contents*

## A.  The Facts

Christine Dalston, aged 35, lives alone with her 10 year old son James in a 2 bed-room flat owned by the London Borough of Doombridge. She is severely disabled suffering from severe epilepsy. Despite medication she suffers up to 3 'grand mal' fits each week which render her unconscious. James is a young carer and he is, both as a child and young carer, affected by his mother's condition. The Dalston's solic-itor sends a letter before action requesting a community care assessment of Ms Dalston under the National Health Service and Community Care Act 1990 and of James Dalston under the Children Act 1989 and the Carers (Recognition and Services) Act 1995 . . .

## B.  Letter Requesting Community Care Assessment

The Manager
Department of Social Services
Chepney Area (West)
London Borough of Doombridge
15 Queen's Road
London W25

2 February 1996

Dear Sir/Madam

Re: Christine Dalston and James Dalston, 3 The Falls, Wentworth Drive, W21

We have been instructed by Christine Dalston on behalf of herself and her 10 year old son in relation to their urgent need for community care services. Ms Dalston is 35 years old and lives alone with her son at 3 The Falls, Wentworth Drive. The tenancy was granted when she was approximately 18/19 years old and is in her sole name.

In 1987, Ms Dalston was diagnosed as suffering from severe epilepsy. She is prescribed the strongest medication for her condition, but nevertheless suffers from between two and three 'grand mal' fits each week. There is no warning of when she may fit, and she has suffered from the fits in the street, cooking her dinner, in the bath, in a lift or on a flight of stairs, or late at night when in bed. The frequency of the fits increases with stress. When she has suffered a fit on the stairs, or in the street, she has suffered bruising and other injuries.

When Ms Dalston suffers a fit at home, it is her son who bears the main caring role. For example, when Ms Dalston fits in the bath, her son has to lift her (with difficulty) out of the bath and ensure that she is placed in the recovery position. Although she has a 'care phone', which her son uses, this is only to provide supportive advice.

On occasion, Ms Dalston's condition has required hospitalisation. For example, in November 1995, as a result of stress caused by the frustration at her condition and the lack of assistance provided to her, she collapsed at the Council offices. She was then admitted to the Royal Doombridge Hospital. On occasions when she does require hospitalisation, there is nowhere for her son to stay and on occasion he has had to remain at the hospital all night with her.

Ms Dalston's son, James, has had to bear the brunt of his mother's condition on his own from a very young age. The caring role has affected him greatly as he is extremely worried about his mother and this has affected his ability to experience life as a normal child. He does not go out to activities save for cubs on a Wednesday evening because he is concerned that Ms Dalston may fit without him being present.

The family's problems have been exacerbated by harassment of them by other tenants on the estate which started a few years ago. James was playing downstairs and some children on the estate assaulted him with a cricket bat. Ms Dalston tried to intervene, and suffered a fit, after which she woke up in hospital. After this incident, the mother of the children has been threatening to kill her, and James has been threatened on numerous occasions. In 1994, the mother assaulted Ms Dalston, which brought on another epileptic fit. The threats are still continuing.

Ms Dalston made an application for a housing transfer some five or six years ago, due to the harassment and the increasing severity of the fits. Her current flat is on the second floor, and although it is accessible by stairs and a lift, Ms Dalston is frightened to go out due to the fact that she has suffered panic attacks whilst in the lift, epileptic fits, and also fits on the stairs which has resulted in injury to her. She desperately requires a transfer to a ground floor flat away from the estate, both due to the harassment by neighbours and the severity of her medical condition, which affects both her and her son.

For the last 10 years or so, Ms Dalston has had contact with Social Services, but her Social Worker, Linda Smith, has been off sick for over one year. Although Ms Dalston received a letter from David Moss, Team Manager of your office on 21 March 1995 that a fully community care assessment would be carried out, no duty Social Worker attended. To our knowledge, a comprehensive community care assessment has not been carried out of Ms Dalston's needs for Community Care

Services, nor has an assessment been carried out of James Dalston's needs as a child in need and child carer.

Around Easter 1995, Ms Dalston was offered an alternative property at 15 Chievely House, Park Estate, London, W21. This also was a second floor property on a much quieter estate. Ms Dalston felt she had to refuse the offer as it did not properly address the issue of her medical condition, being on the same level as her current property. In our view, her medical condition was not adequately taken into account by the Housing Department.

Her management priority was therefore withdrawn as she was deemed to have refused a reasonable offer. She has been told that her current medical priority is 'C' and her application for transfer currently attracts 35 points and falls within the GENERAL target group. We request that the comprehensive community care assessment urgently readdresses the issue of Ms Dalston's medical priority and need for a ground floor property. James is due to start school in September in the Southwark area, and Ms Dalston would be willing to accept properties in the Grove and Chepney area to increase the chances of her being transferred.

We are enclosing a copy of a letter dated 13 March 1995 which was sent to Peter Jones, Housing Allocations Officer, for your information. A copy of this letter was sent to Linda Smith of Social Services, the Director of Social Services, and three Councillors. Despite the letter from your office in March 1995, Ms Dalston's need for Community Care Services and James's needs have not been assessed or addressed in any way.

We therefore request that you carry out an urgent comprehensive assessment of our client's needs for community care services under the NHS and Community Care Act 1990 and the Chronically Sick and Disabled Persons Act 1970, and liaise with the Health and Housing Departments regarding our client's priority for a housing transfer. We also request that you carry out an urgent assessment of James Dalston's needs as a child under the Children Act 1989 and as a child carer without delay.

If we do not hear from you with a satisfactory response within seven days of the date of this letter, we shall advise our client to apply for Legal Aid in order to make an application for leave for Judicial Review and Interlocutory Injunction without further notice to you.

Yours faithfully


MARX, TROTSKY & LUXEMBOURG
Encl


## C.  The Notice of Application (Form 86A) for Leave to Move

IN THE HIGH COURT OF JUSTICE                    *CO/    /1996*

QUEEN'S BENCH DIVISION

CROWN OFFICE LIST


In the matter of an application by Christine Dalston, & James Dalston (a minor by his Mother and next friend the aforementioned Christine Dalston) for leave to apply for Judicial Review (Ord 53, r 3)

And in the matter of the National Health Service and Community Care Act 1990, ss 46, 47, the Chronically Sick and Disabled Persons Act 1970, s 2 and the Children Act 1989, s 17, and the Carers (Recognition and Services) Act 1995, s 1.

| Applicant's Ref No | Notice of Application for leave to apply for Judicial Review (Ord 53, r 3) | Crown Office Ref No |
|---|---|---|
| | | |

This form must be read together with Notes for Guidance obtainable from the Crown Office

To the Master of the Crown Office, Royal Courts of Justice, Strand, London WC2A 2LL

| Name, address and description of applicant | Christine Dalston and James Dalston (by his mother and next friend Christine Dalston) both of: 3 The Falls, Wentworth Drive, London W21 |
|---|---|
| Judgment, order, decision or other proceeding in respect of which relief is sought | Failure and/or refusal of the London Borough of Doombridge ('the Council') to make a service provision decision (or even to commence the assessment and decision-making process) in respect of each of the Applicants under (as appropriate), the National Health Service and Community Care Act 1990, s 47 and/or the Chronically Sick and Disabled Persons Act 1970, s 2 and/or the Children Act 1989, s 17 and/or the Carers (Recognition and Services) Act 1995, s 1 and to provide services pursuant to such decision or by way of emergency provision. |

## Relief sought

(1)   Mandamus to compel the Council to make a service provision decision in respect of each of the Applicants under (as appropriate), s 47 of the National Health Service and Community Care Act 1990 ('NHSCCA'), and/or s 2 of the Chronically Sick and Disabled Persons Act 1970 ('CSDPA'), and/or s 17 of the Children Act 1989 and to provide services pursuant to such decision(s). Further or alternatively.

(2)   A declaration that no social services authority, acting reasonably, could fail to make a service provision decision in respect of each of the Applicants. Further or alternatively,

(3) A declaration that any service provision decision in respect of Christine Dalston should be made in the light of an assessment of the needs and capabilities of James Dalston as her carer.

(4) A mandatory interlocutory injunction requiring the Council to undertake an immediate assessment of each of the Applicant's needs.

(5) Further or other relief as appropriate.

(6) An expedited hearing. In the event that an expedited hearing is ordered, the applicant seeks an Order abridging time for service of the Respondent's evidence to 14 days after service of notice of the grant of leave.

(7) The applicant seeks an oral hearing of the application for leave.

(8) Costs.

| Name and address of the applicant's solicitors or, if no solicitors acting, the address for service of the applicant | Jane Marx Marx, Trotsky & Luxembourg Garden House, 39 Falcon Court London W25 |
|---|---|
| Signed .............................................. | Dated                                  1996 |

## Grounds on which relief is sought

*Essential background*

1  The factual background is set out in detail in the affidavit of Jane Marx in support of this application ('the affidavit').

2  Each Applicant is in apparent need of community care services and/or services under the Children Act 1989, s 17, which the Council is empowered or required to provide.

3  Christine Dalston suffers from a severe epileptic condition which was first diagnosed in 1987. She is 35 years old. She lives at 3 The Falls, Wentworth Drive, London W21 with her only son, James. The flat is on the second floor of the building. This is of course far from suitable for someone subject to frequent fits, since the stairs and lift in particular pose a daily hazard to Ms Dalston. Having a fit in the lift or on the stairs, which happens from time to time, is highly dangerous and has in the past caused her injury.

4  Ms Dalston has previously asked the Council for a housing transfer. She was offered a tenancy of a property at 15 Chievely House, Park Estate, London W21, but that was also on the second floor and was therefore eventually deemed to be unsuitable by Ms Dalston because it did not address the medical problems mentioned above.

5  As aforesaid, Ms Dalston suffers frequent epileptic attacks, often two or three times a week. The attacks occur suddenly and without warning. When a fit occurs, very frequently the only person available to assist Ms Dalston to ease her distress is her son, James. A Senior Registrar in Neurology has written of Ms Dalston that:

> [she] suffers from an epileptic disorder and is prone to have repeated falls. These may happen suddenly and without warning, and may result in serious

injury if they occur in unprotected surroundings . . . she has to use the stairs regularly, which puts her at an increased risk of serious injury . . .

6   Moreover, Ms Dalston's GP has referred to her suspicion that Ms Dalston 'has a learning disability' although, as she says 'I do not think this has ever formally been looked into'. Ms Dalston's medical records are exhibited to the affidavit of Jane Marx at JM1.

7   James Dalston is 10 years old. As a result of his mother's medical condition, James is not able to live the normal active life of a 10 year old boy. Often he has to stay in to look after his mother, whose condition can suddenly deteriorate if she suffers a fit, when his friends are enjoying their leisure time.

8   This challenge centres on the failure by the Council to assess the needs of either applicant for community care services. It is submitted that the Council has a duty so to assess and, having made such an assessment, a further duty to decide, in the light of the assessment, what services to make available to those assessed. The Council therefore has to perform a two stage task, involving:

(a)   the assessment of need, and

(b)   the making of a 'service provision decision'.

9   The Council did suggest in a letter to the first applicant dated 21 March 1995 that steps were being taken to arrange for a 'full assessment' of her community care needs to be carried out 'in the next week or so'. However, no such assessment took place at that time, or since.

10   The Applicant's solicitor made a final request for an assessment of community care needs of the Applicants by letter dated 2 February 1996. There has been no response to that request.

*The law of community care*

11   Under section 46(3) of the National Health Service and Community Care Act 1990, 'community care services' are defined as follows:

services which a local authority may provide or arrange to be provided under any of the following provisions—

(a)   Part III of the National Assistance Act 1948;

(b)   section 45 of the Health Services and Public Health Act 1968;

(c)   section 21 of and Schedule 8 to the National Health Service Act 1977; and

(d)   section 117 of the Mental Health Act 1983.

12   Section 47 of the National Health Service and Community Care Act 1990 ('NHSCCA') provides:

(1)   Subject to subsections (5) and (6) below, where it appears to a local authority that any person for whom they may provide or arrange for the provision of community care services may be in need of any such services, the authority—

(a)   shall carry out an assessment of his needs for those services; and

(b)   having regard to the results of that assessment, shall then decide whether his needs call for the provision by them of any such services.

(2)   If at any time during the assessment of the needs of any person under subsection (1)(a) above it appears to the local authority that he is a disabled person, the authority—

(a) shall proceed to make such a decision as to the services he requires as is mentioned in section 4 of the Disabled Persons (Services, Consultation and Representation) Act 1986 without his requesting them to do so under that section; and

(b) shall inform him that they will be doing so and of his rights under that Act.

(3) If at any time during the assessment of the needs of any person under subsection 1(a) above, it appears to a local authority—

(a) that there may be a need for the provision to that person by such District Health Authority as may be determined in accordance with regulations of any services under the National Health Service Act 1977, or

(b) that there may be a need for the provision to him of any services which fall within the functions of a local housing authority (within the meaning of the Housing Act 1985) which is not the local authority carrying out the assessment,

the local authority shall notify that District Health Authority or local housing authority and invite them to assist, to such extent as is reasonable in the circumstances, in the making of the assessment; and, in making their decision as to the provision of the services needed for the person in question, the local authority shall take into account any services which are likely to be made available for him by that District Health Authority or local housing authority.

\* \* \* \* \*

(5) Nothing in this section shall prevent a local authority from temporarily providing or arranging for the provision of community care services for any person without carrying out a prior assessment of his needs in accordance with the preceding provisions of this section if, in the opinion of the authority, the condition of that person is such that he requires those services as a matter of urgency.

13 Section 4 of the Disabled Persons (Services, Consultation and Representation) Act 1986 provides:

(4) When requested to do so by—
(a) a disabled person,
(b) his authorised representative, or
(c) any person who provides care for him in the circumstances mentioned in section 8,

a local authority shall decide whether the needs of the disabled person call for the provision by the authority of any services in accordance with section 2(1) of the 1970 [Chronically Sick and Disabled Persons'] Act (provision of welfare services).

14 Section 2(1) of the Chronically Sick and Disabled Persons Act 1970 states:

Where a local authority having functions under section 29 of the National Assistance Act 1948 are satisfied in the case of any person to whom that section applies who is ordinarily resident in their area that it is necessary in order to meet the needs of that person for that authority to make arrangements for all or any of the following matters, namely—

(a) the provision of practical assistance for that person in his home;

\* \* \* \* \*

(*e*)  the provision of assistance for that person in arranging for the carrying out of any works of adaptation in his home or the provision of any additional facilities designed to secure his greater safety, comfort or convenience;

\* \* \* \* \*

then subject to the provisions of section 7(1) of the Local Authority Social Services Act 1970 (which requires local authorities, in the exercise of certain functions, including functions under the said section 29, to act under the general guidance of the Secretary of State) it shall be the duty of that authority to make those arrangements in the exercise of their functions under the said section 29.

15  Section 29(1) of the National Assistance Act 1948 provides:

A local authority may, with the approval of the Secretary of State and to such extent as he may direct in relation to persons ordinarily resident in the area of the local authority shall make arrangements for promoting the welfare of persons to whom this section applies, that is to say persons aged 18 or over who are blind, deaf or dumb or who suffer from mental disorder of any description, and other persons aged 18 or over who are substantially and permanently handicapped by illness, injury, or congenital deformity or such other disabilities as may be prescribed by the Minister.

16  The Children Act 1989 section 17 provides, in so far as is material:

(1)  It shall be the general duty of every local authority (in addition to the other duties imposed upon them by this part)—
 (*a*)  to safeguard and promote the welfare of children within their area who are in need; and
 (*b*)  so far as is consistent with that duty, to promote the upbringing of such children by their families
by providing a range and level of services appropriate to those children's needs.
(2)  For the purpose principally of facilitating the discharge of their general duty under this section, every local authority shall have the specific duties and powers set out in Part I of Schedule 2.
(3)  Any service provided by an authority in the exercise of functions conferred on them by this section may be provided for the family of a particular child in need or for any member of his family, if it is provided with a view to safeguarding or promoting the child's welfare.

\* \* \* \* \*

(10)  For the purposes of this Part a child shall be taken to be in need if—
 (*a*)  he is unlikely to achieve or maintain, or to have the opportunity of achieving or maintaining, a reasonable standard of health or development without the provision for him of services by a local authority under this Part;
 (*b*)  his health or development is likely to be significantly impaired, or further impaired, without the provision for him of such services. . . .

17  Part I of Schedule 2 of the Children Act 1989 provides, *inter alia*:

3.—Where it appears to a local authority that a child within their area is in need, the authority may assess his needs for the purposes of this Act at the same time as any assessment of his needs is made under—

(*a*) the Chronically Sick and Disabled Persons Act 1970;

\* \* \* \* \*

(*c*) the Disabled Persons (Services, Consultation and Representation Act) 1986; or
(*d*) any other enactment.

\* \* \* \* \*

**8.**—Every local authority shall make such provision as they consider appropriate for the following services to be available with respect to children in need within their area while they are living with their families—

(*a*) ...

\* \* \* \* \*

(*c*) home help. . . .

18 By Schedule 13, paragraph 27 of the Children Act 1989, the 1970 Chronically Sick and Disabled Persons' Act is applied to children.

19 Section 1 of the Carers (Recognition and Services) Act 1995 provides, materially, that:

(1) ... in any case where—
(*a*) a local authority carry out an assessment under s 47(1)(*a*) of the National Health Service and Community Care Act 1990 of the needs of a person . . . for community care services, and
(*b*) an individual ('the carer') provides or intends to provide a substantial amount of care on a regular basis for the relevant person,
the carer may request the local authority, before they make their decision as to whether the needs of the relevant person call for the provision of any services, to carry out an assessment of his ability to provide and to continue to provide care for the relevant person, and if he makes such a request, the local authority shall carry out such an assessment and shall take into account the results of that assessment in making that decision.

20 Section 7 of the Local Authority Social Services Act 1970 provides:

Local authorities shall, in the exercise of their social services functions, including the exercise of any discretion conferred by any relevant enactment, act under the general guidance of the Secretary of State.

*Submissions*

21 The Council is required to undertake an assessment of need under s 47(1)(*a*) NHSCCA where it appears to a local authority that 'any person for whom they may provide or arrange for the provision of community care services may be in need of any such services.'

22 The apparent need of the present Applicants for services which the Council is empowered or under a duty to provide places the Council under a statutory duty to assess the Applicants and to reach a service provision decision. By failing to respond in any way to the Applicants' ostensible need the Council is in breach of its said duty and has, thereby, acted unlawfully.

23 In any event, faced with the apparent need of the present Applicants no local authority, acting reasonably, could have failed to reach a service provision decision

with the utmost expedition and to provide services in accordance with that decision and/or to provide emergency services *ad interim*. Section 47(5) of the NHSCCA 1990 is particularly relevant in this context.

24   Under the NHSCCA an assessment of need is usually the first step towards a service provision decision. Materially, s 47(1)(*b*) NHSCCA requires the local authority to 'decide whether his needs call for the provision by them of any such services.' However, services may be provided on an emergency basis without assessment (see NHSCCA, s 47(5)—see above). However, no services will or can be provided in circumstances where (as here) a Council simply fails to respond to a proposed service user's plea for help. The Council has failed to make any service provision decision or to provide services in accordance with such decision or to provide emergency services or to respond at all to the Applicants' urgent request for their case to be heard and determined.

25   It is, further, material to note that the duty to reach a service provision under s 47 NHSCCA is triggered not by a request from the service user (as is the position under, say, the Housing Act 1985) but merely by the existence of apparent need.

26   A separate service provision decision is required under s 47(2) NHSCCA in the case of a person who appears to the assessing authority to be 'a disabled person.' The first named Applicant falls within the definition of a 'disabled person' in section 29 of the National Assistance Act 1948 in that she is ordinarily resident in the Council's area, is over 18 and is substantially and permanently handicapped by illness and or disability. In such a case the disabled person is required to be told that the assessing authority is proceeding to make a decision under s 2 CSDPA and of his rights under DPSCRA (see NHSCCA, s 47(2)(*b*)).

27   Therefore Christine Dalston is entitled to an assessment of her needs under section 47(1) and (2) NHSCCA and to a service provision decision under each of those two subsections. The Council has failed to perform any of this analysis of her community care needs.

28   The Council's performance in relation to James Dalston is no better. James Dalston is a child 'in need' within the meaning of the Children Act 1989 not least because of the extent and effect on him of his role as a young carer for his disabled mother. His health and development are suffering as a result of his undertaking the substantial caring burden. As a child 'in need' within the meaning of section 17(10) of the Children Act 1989, the Council has a duty to provide him with services pursuant to section 17(1) and or (3) of that Act. The Council has failed to do so. Section 17, referring as it does to the concepts of need and provision of services therefore mirrors in the context of children precisely that two stage process established by the NHSCCA 1990.

29   Section 7 of the Local Authority Social Services Act 1970 ('LASSA') requires local authorities to 'act under' guidance issued by the Secretary of State in the exercise of his social services functions. The Government White Paper which set out the new philosophy of Community Care, entitled 'Caring for People' is itself section 7 LASSA guidance. It has as its second key objective:

> 'to ensure that service providers make practical support for carers and high priority'
> and also states that
> 'assessment of care needs should also take account of the needs of caring family, friends and neighbours.'

30   Further, a request has been made to the Council for an assessment of James Dalston as a young carer under the Carers (Recognition and Services) Act 1995. Notwithstanding this request no assessment under the 1995 Act has been undertaken.

31   Therefore, the assessment of Christine Dalston must take into account the needs of James Dalston.

32   Accordingly, it is submitted that each of the Applicants has a right to a decision as to what services are to be provided to them and to the family as a whole in view of their interrelated needs.

33   It is, further, submitted that the Council's failure to act in any way is unlawful and/or *Wednesbury* irrational.

JACOB SAMUELSON

## D.   Applicant's Affidavit in Support

DEPONENT: J. MARX
FILED ON BEHALF OF: The Applicants
NUMBER OF AFFIDAVIT: 1st
DATE SWORN:
DATE FILED:

IN THE HIGH COURT OF JUSTICE                 CASE NO: CO/        1996

QUEEN'S BENCH DIVISION

CROWN OFFICE LIST

BETWEEN                                    R

—and—

THE MAYOR AND BURGESSES OF THE          Respondents
LONDON BOROUGH OF DOOMBRIDGE

ex parte
CHRISTINE DALSTON                 Applicants
JAMES DALSTON
(A minor by his Mother and Next Friend Christine Dalston)

AFFIDAVIT OF JANE MARX

I, JANE MARX, Solicitor and Partner at Messrs. Marx, Trotsky & Luxembourg solicitors of Garden House, 39 Falcon Court, London W25, HEREBY MAKE OATH and say as follows:

1   I am a Solicitor and partner at Messrs Marx, Trotsky & Luxembourg of Garden House, 39 Falcon Court, London W25 and have conduct of this matter on behalf of the firm. I make this Affidavit in support of an application by Christine Dalston and James Dalston for leave to apply for judicial review, together with interim relief,

of the failure and/or refusal of the London Borough of Doombridge to make a service provision decision (or even to commence the assessment and decision making progress) of the Applicants' needs for community care services.

2 I am authorised to make this Affidavit on behalf of the Applicants due to the urgency of the situation, and due to the First Applicant's disability. Save where is stated otherwise, the information contained within this Affidavit and the Form 86A accompanying this application is true to the best of my knowledge and belief.

3 The First Applicant, Christine Dalston, is aged 35 years old. She lives alone with her son, James Dalston, who is aged 10 years. The family live in a two bedroom flat owned by the Respondents, the London Borough of Doombridge which is situated on the second floor of a block.

4 The First Applicant is severely disabled. In 1987, after the birth of her son, she was diagnosed as suffering from severe epilepsy. She has been unable to return to work since. She is prescribed the strongest medication for her condition, but nevertheless suffers between two and three 'grand mal' fits each week. These fits involve major seizures, spasms of her limbs, and periods of unconsciousness followed by periods of chronic weakness and dizziness, sometimes lasting several days. She also suffers from other, less serious seizures on a frequent basis. There is no warning of when she may suffer a seizure, and she has suffered from fits in the street, cooking her dinner, in the bath, in the lift or on the flights of stairs, or even late at night when in bed. The frequency of the fits increases with stress and doing physical activity, such as housework. There is now shown and produced to me marked exhibit 'JM.1' copies of letters and extracts from her medical records confirming her condition and the urgency of the situation.

5 On several occasions Ms Dalston's seizures have resulted in injury. For example, she has suffered from fits in the street, causing her to fall, resulting in severe bruising. She has also suffered from fits on the stairs to the property, and in the lift and it is only a matter of time before more permanent injury is caused.

6 On occasion, Ms Dalston's condition has required hospitalisation. For example, in November 1995, as a result of stress caused by the frustration at her condition and the lack of assistance provided by the Respondent local authority, she collapsed at the offices of the local authority. She was then admitted to the Royal Freely Hospital.

7 When Ms Dalston suffers a fit at home, it is her son James who bears the main caring role. For example, when Ms Dalston fits in the bath, her son has to lift her (with difficulty) out of the bath and ensure that she is made comfortable whilst she regains consciousness. The last fit in the bath occurred on the 14 February 1996. James is very frightened by the fits and his inability to understand what is happening.

8 Ms Dalston has been provided with a 'care phone'. This is a telephone linked to a care organisation who can be telephoned if she is in difficulty. However, as Ms Dalston does not have warning of when the fits might occur, she is unable to summon assistance herself. When her son, James telephones for assistance, sometimes the care organisation takes several hours to attend the property, and on occasion, nobody attends at all. This means that James must care for his mother alone until she regains consciousness. James often spends all night caring for his mother, which means that he is exhausted for school the next day.

9    On the occasions when Ms Dalston has required hospitalisation, James Dalston has to stay with her in hospital as there is nowhere else for him to go. He has had to remain at the hospital all night with his mother and as a result, Ms Dalston has been forced to discharge herself from hospital earlier than she might otherwise have done.

10    From a very young age, James Dalston has had to bear the brunt of his mother's condition on his own. The caring role has affected him greatly as he is extremely worried about his mother and this has limited his ability to experience life as a normal child. He sometimes blames himself for his mother's condition. He does not go out to activities or to friends save for 'Cubs' on Wednesday evening due to his concern that Ms Dalston may fit without him being present. James Dalston also suffers from asthma and has had frequent attacks. The fact that the family live on the second floor of the block increases the likelihood of an attack, and he sometimes finds it difficult to go up and down stairs. Ms Dalston also finds it difficult to mount the stairs, not only due to her fear of suffering a fit and falling, but also due to the chronic weakness which follows a fit for some days afterwards.

11    The family's problems have been exacerbated by harassment by other tenants on the estate which started a few years ago. James Dalston has been assaulted and when Ms Dalston tried to intervene, she suffered a fit, after which she woke up in hospital. After this incident, the family threatened to kill Ms Dalston. She has also been assaulted, which brought on another epileptic fit. The threats are still continuing.

12    Ms Dalston made an application for a housing transfer some five or six years ago, due to the harassment and the increasing severity of the fits. There is now shown and produced to me marked exhibit 'JM.2' a copy of her application for housing and medical self assessment. I am informed by Ms Dalston that she has completed over five sets of these forms over the years. The family desperately requires a transfer to a ground floor flat away from the estate, both due to the harassment by neighbours and the severity of her medical condition, which affects both her and her son. Unfortunately, although Ms Dalston was offered an alternative property at 15 Chievely House, Park Estate, London W21, this was also on the second floor and as it did not properly address the issue of her medical condition Ms Dalston was reluctantly forced to refuse the offer. She has now been told that her current medical priority has been deemed to be level 'C' which means that she falls within the general Housing List. She has been informed that it is very unlikely that she will be offered a property on the ground floor and that the housing department will be unable to transfer her for the foreseeable future. There is now shown and produced to me marked exhibit 'JM.3' a copy of a memo from Peter Jones, Lettings Manager of the Respondents' housing department to Ms Dalston's councillor.

13    From 1985 to 1995, Ms Dalston has had contact with social services. However, since the beginning of 1995, her social worker, Linda Smith, has been absent from work due to illness. Ms Dalston wrote a lengthy letter detailing the family's needs for community care services on the 13 March 1995, a copy of which was sent to Linda Smith and the Director of Legal Services. She requested ground floor accommodation, information relating to epilepsy for herself and her son, counselling, advice as to how she could assist her son with the extra stimulation that he needs, and someone who would visit or telephone at least once a week to make sure that the family were safe.

14    She received a response from David Moss, Team Manager of the social services office by a letter dated 21 March 1995. Mr Moss stated in the letter 'to try to resolve some of the issues mentioned in your letter, I am asking a Duty Social Worker to visit in the next week or so, to carry out a full community care assessment. From that, we should be in a position to offer you some of the help that you require and have subsequently requested'. Ms Dalston then received a further letter from John Green, Duty Manager at social services dated 23 March 1995. Mr Green informed Ms Dalston in the letter that he would forward her information regarding epilepsy and stated that in Ms Smith's absence, her cases were being dealt with by the duty system. He stated 'it would not be possible to identify someone who could contact you weekly. I would suggest that if you feel James needs extra stimulation then it would be sensible to discuss this with his school'. I am informed by Ms Dalston and believe that despite the assurance from social services that a full Community Care Assessment of the family's needs for community care services would be carried out, no further action was taken and no Duty Social Worker visited the family. There is now shown and produced to me marked exhibit 'JM.4' copies of these letters.

15    I am informed and believe that Ms Dalston subsequently contacted social services and the housing department by telephone and in person at their offices at 15 Queen's Road, W25 requesting assistance. Ms Dalston informs me that she made over twenty visits in the last year to try to get help. She was told that as her Social Worker was absent due to illness, she would not be allocated another Social Worker.

16    Accordingly, Ms Dalston instructed me to assist her with her need for community care services. I wrote a letter before action dated 2 February 1996 to the Manager of social services detailing the family's needs and requesting an assurance within seven days that an assessment would be carried out of the family's needs for community care services. There is now shown and produced to me marked exhibit 'JM.5' a copy of this letter. Unfortunately, to date, I have not received any response from the local authority's social services department and I am informed by Ms Dalston that she has heard nothing either. A copy of the letter was sent to the housing department and I received a response dated 13 February 1996 stating that the letter had been passed to the Allocations Department to respond. I have heard nothing further.

17    Due to Ms Dalston's severe medical condition, she is at serious risk of permanent injury. This has a serious effect on both Ms Dalston, and her son as a child carer. The family have requested assistance and have been assured that this will be provided, although no action has been taken by the Respondents to date. In the circumstances, I humbly request that the court grants the relief sought in the Form 86A, including an interim injunction requiring the local authority social services department to assess the family's needs for community care services without further delay.

Sworn by JANE MARX          )
this 1 March 1996            )
at 52 The Lodge,             )
Blue Street,                 )
London W21                   )

## E. Leave to Issue a Motion for Judicial Review

CO/96
Dated the 4th day of March 1996

IN THE HIGH COURT OF JUSTICE

QUEEN'S BENCH DIVISION

CROWN OFFICE LIST

BEFORE THE HONOURABLE MR JUSTICE SCRATCH

IN THE MATTER of an application for leave to apply for Judicial Review

R

v

LONDON BOROUGH OF DOOMBRIDGE

ex parte

(1) CHRISTINE DALSTON

(2) JAMES DALSTON (A minor by his Mother and Next Friend)

UPON HEARING Mr J Samuelson of Counsel on behalf of the above-named Applicants for leave to issue a Notice of Motion for Judicial Review of the failure and/or refusal of the Respondent to make a service provision decision (or even to commence the assessment and decision-making process) in respect of each of the Applicants under (as appropriate), the National Health Service and Community Care Act 1990, s 47 and/or the Chronically Sick and Disabled Persons Act 1989, s 17 and to provide services pursuant to such decision or by way of emergency provision

AND UPON READING the statement lodged pursuant to Order 53 Rule 3(2) of the Rule of the Supreme Court

AND UPON READING the affidavit of Jane Marx sworn the 1st day of March 1996 together with the exhibits referred to therein filed on behalf of the Applicants in support of this application

AND UPON an Undertaking by the Respondent to carry out a Community Care and Children Act 1989 Assessment

IT IS ORDERED that this application be allowed and that the said Applicants do have leave to issue a Notice of Motion for Judicial Review as aforesaid

IT IS FURTHER ORDERED that this matter be expedited and that the time for filing of the Respondent's affidavits by abridged to 28 days

AND IT IS ORDERED that the cost of the Applicants be taxed in accordance with Regulation 107 of the Civil Legal Aid (General) Regulations 1989

*[This matter occupied the time of the Court from 2.15pm to 2.35pm]*

By the Court

## F. Outline Submissions of Applicants

### R v LB OF DOOMBRIDGE, ex p DALSTON AND DALSTON

#### Outline Submission of Applicants

*1 Introduction*

1.01   This is an application for judicial review of the failure of the social services and children and families division of the LB of Doombridge ('the Council') to make a service provision decision in respect of each applicant, namely Christine Dalston (aged 35) and her son James (aged 10). Interim relief was sought at the leave stage in the form of an injunction requiring the Council to undertake an immediate assessment of each of the Applicants' needs. In the event the Council provided undertakings to carry out the appropriate assessments.

1.02   The application is brought by a family of 2 applicants who live in a 2 bedroom flat owned by the Council's housing department. The first applicant Christine Dalston is severely disabled and has to be cared for by her 10 year old son, the second applicant who brings this application by his mother and next friend.

1.03   In law, the position is entirely straightforward. If any or all of a family have apparent need for services which a Council is empowered by statute to provide, the Council must carry out an assessment of the person or persons evincing such need and in the light of the assessment it must make a service provision decision (ie a decision as to what, if any, services to provide). The assessments to which the Applicants are entitled are (in the case of Christine Dalston) an assessment under s 47(1)(*a*) of the National Health Service and Community Care Act 1990 and an assessment of her needs for services under s 2 of the Chronically Sick and Disabled Persons Act 1970 (as required by s 47(2) of the 1990 Act). James Dalston is entitled to assessments for his needs for services both under s 47(1)(*a*) of the 1990 Act and under the Children Act 1989, and s 1 of the Carers (Recognition and Services) Act 1995.

1.04   A summary of the Applicants' 'apparent needs' appears in the affidavit in support of this application.

1.05   Currently, the Applicants enjoy no social services support whatever from the relevant Departments of the Council.

1.06   It is against this background that a letter before action were sent to the Council on February 2 1996 seeking some form of proposal within 7 days. No response whatever was received and this application was, therefore, lodged with the Crown Office. The current position is that the Council is, pursuant to its undertakings granted at the leave stage, proposing to carry out assessments of the applicants but no such assessments have, as yet, been concluded.

*2 The Law*

2.01   There must be an assessment of need under s 47(1)(*a*) NHSCCA where it appears to a local authority that 'any person for whom they may provide or arrange for the provision of community care services may be in need of any such services.' Community care services are defined in s 46(3) NHSCCA and include, materially, Part III NAA services, and services under s 45 of the Health Services and Public Health Act 1968 and s 21 of and schedule 8 to the National Health Service Act 1977.

The duty to assess arises independently of any request made by the service user and is contingent solely upon the existence of apparent need.

2.02    The duty to reach a service provision decision arises 'in the light of the assessment' (NHSCCA, s 47(1)(*b*)). Thus without an assessment the duty to reach a service provision decision cannot crystallise although services may be provided on an emergency basis (s 47(5) NHSCCA).

2.03    A seperate duty to reach a service provision decision arises under NHSCCA s 47(2) in the case of a person, such as Mrs. Dalston, who appears to the assessing authority to be a 'disabled person' (see: NHSCCA s 47(8), DPSCRA s 16, NAA s 29). As a matter of law an apparently disabled person must be told that the assessing authority is proceeding to make a decision under s 2 CSDPA and of his or her rights under DPSCRA (NHSCCA s 47(2)(*b*)).

2.04    S 17 of the Children Act 1989 is also highly material because it requires a local authority to act 'to safeguard and promote the welfare of children within their area who are in need'.

2.05    As a 'young carer' James Dalston is entitled to an assessment of his needs, in any event, as part of the s 47 assessment process (see s 1 of the Carers (Recognition and Services) Act 1995).

2.06    Finally, note s 7 LASSA and the relevant Guidance which emphasises the importance of assessing the carers' needs and involving the carer during the course of a s 47 NHSCCA assessment.

## 3    Submissions of Law

3.01    On any view each of the Applicants is and was entitled to a service provision decision: this flows from their right to be assessed for community care services since each of them evinced an apparent need for community care services in general and domiciliary support under Part III NAA and/or s 2 CSDPA in particular.

3.02    The statutory underpinning of such assessment is clear (see above).

3.03    It is also clear that each applicant is and was entitled to the earliest of service provision decisions not merely as a consequence of a statutory assessment but *ad interim* (NHSCCA s 47(5)).

3.04    No reasonable authority faced with a request for a service provision could have failed to respond.

3.05    This is not an alternative remedy case because:
  (1)    If the Council denies that it owes a social services function to the Applicants then the complaints regime is automatically excluded (NHSCCA s 50 inserting a news s 7B into LASSA). See, also, *Policy Guidance*.
  (2)    If the Council accepts that it does have a social services function to discharge there can be no sensible point in requiring the Applicants to proceed through a complaints regime which admits of no interim relief whatever. Judicial review permits (and did permit) clear interim relief in an urgent case such as the present.
  (3)    In any event the timing and content of the service provision decision and assessment processes raise genuine points of principle.

JACOB SAMUELSON

## G.  Respondent's Affidavit

Respondent<br>
1st<br>
Sworn On:<br>
Filed on:

IN THE HIGH COURT

QUEEN'S BENCH DIVISION

CROWN OFFICE LIST

Case No: CO/ 96

BETWEEN                                         R

—and—

THE MAYOR AND BURGESSES OF THE LONDON
BOROUGH OF DOOMBRIDGE            Respondent

ex parte
CHRISTINE DALSTON
JAMES DALSTON
(A minor by his Mother and Next Friend Christine Dalston)   Applicants

---

AFFIDAVIT OF MORTON JOBSWORTH

---

I, MORTON JOBSWORTH, Local Government Officer at The Town Hall, Acacia Place, Doombridge, London W25 MAKE OATH and say as follows:—

1   I am employed by the Respondent within its Social Services Directorate as Assistant Director, Childcare, and I am duly authorised to make this Affidavit. I make this Affidavit relying on facts within my own knowledge, information provided by the Applicants and files and records kept by the Respondent which I believe to be true.

2   I have been employed by the Respondents as a Senior Social Services Manager since 1992 and I have 10 years experience as a Social Services Manager. I have been qualified as a Social Worker since 1975.

3   I am the Senior Officer within the Childcare Division; responsible for all services for children and carers in the Borough. I am also a member of the Directorate Management Team and have delegated responsibility for other aspects of social work provision.

4   I make this Affidavit to assist the court in determining whether the relief sought by the Applicants in their Application for Judicial Review should be granted and I am familiar with the background to the case. I have read the Applicants' Bundle of Documents comprising Form 86A and the Affidavit of Jane Marx (referred to hereafter as 'JM1'). There is now produced and shown to me marked 'MJ' a bundle of documents relevant to the case before the Court.

5   I am familiar with the statutory framework for providing child care and the Government Guidance issued and contained within relevant circulars. The Respondent Council has also developed its own policies including procedures for assessing children in need (MJ pages 1 to 11).

6   The Respondent Council has also developed policies for providing community care and according priority for those requiring for services (MJ pages 12 to 15).

7   I am aware of the Order of the Court made on Monday 4th March 1996 and the undertaking given by the Respondent to carry out a Community Care and Child Care Assessment. These assessments were completed by 20th March 1996 and copies provided to the Applicants' solicitor are exhibited to my Affidavit (MJ pages 16 to 43).

8   I have read the Affidavit of Jane Marx and the Social Services file and it is clear that assessment of the needs of the Applicants should have been undertaken from at the very latest, March 1995, when the Respondent's Team Manager wrote to Ms Dalston and said that he would be requesting a full community care assessment (JM1 page 39). By March 1995 MS Dalston's social worker, Linda Smith, was on long term sick leave and did not subsequently return to work during the remainder of 1995.

9   The response of the Manager to whom this request was made (Peter Jones) of 23rd March 1995 (JM1 page 40) indicates, without stating explicitly, that no formal community care assessment would be made. I am strengthened in my opinion by the fact that he marked the file 'NFA' (No Further Action) in August 1995. As such, the case had no allocated social worker and any issues which arose would be dealt with on an ad-hoc basis by the duty team.

10   The Applicant's solicitors also wrote a letter before action dated 2nd February 1996 requesting an assessment. The letter was received in the correct office, it having moved the week previously, by 8th February 1996 and entered on the Respondent's computer databases. Whoever made the entry should then have drawn to the Team Manager's attention that a response was needed the following day. No response was made; the letter has not been found and there is no recollection of it from the officers concerned.

11   The circumstances in which this letter was lost do, however, need to be understood. In the week that the letter was sent to the local office, 6 Social Services bases were amalgamated to create new local offices. Due to building work, the relevant office is currently working from 3 split sites. Combined with this physical move, all the local Social Services teams in this area were re-organised into new child care and community care local teams. There was, therefore, very considerable disruption of staff, case papers and working arrangements. Although the loss is very regrettable it has to be understood in the context of this dislocation.

12   I have investigated, at length, these shortcomings and have concluded that no assessment was initiated in February 1996 because the Respondent's Team Manager was not aware that a request had been received from the Applicant's solicitor.

13   Assessments have now been completed by social workers within the Assessment and Care Managements (Community Care) and Assessment and Family Support (Child Care) Teams. The social workers were provided with copies of the Applicants' Solicitors' Affidavit and Form 86A, and had access to the Social Services file. The family were interviewed on a number of occasions and information obtained from others who have contact with the family, including: family doctor, school teacher, school nurse and the health authority.

14 The assessment contained within the Care Plan completed by the Care Manager, Gordon Richards, dated 19th March 1996 (MJ pages 16 to 20) states that Ms Dalston is severely disabled with epilepsy and suffers 2 to 3 fits each week. These fits leave her weak and tired. During these fits and until she is sufficiently recovered, her son James (D.O.B. 30/7/85) is her sole carer. Ms Dalston also referred to harassment she and James suffer from residents on the estate. Christine reports her needs as: (1) to move to a ground floor property; (2) assistance with housework and shopping; and (3) James to be relieved of the burden of worry.

15 The family currently occupy 3 The Falls, Wentworth Drive, London W21. This is a 2 bedroomed, 2nd floor flat, in a 4 storey block serviced by 2 lifts and an entry phone system.

16 Various services were offered by the Care Manager, Gordon Richards, to Ms Dalston. These were:
- (a) Payment of telephone rental charges;
- (b) Information on Epilepsy;
- (c) An escort to accompany Ms Dalston to the Post Office and the supermarket every Monday;
- (d) A homehelp to visit twice a week to undertake housework and check Ms Dalston is okay;
- (e) Meals on Wheels (this was declined);
- (f) Attendance at Doomsbridge Day Centre.

The Care Manager has also stated that he will make representations to the Housing Department regarding the Applicant's request for rehousing and has requested that the Occupational Therapy Department provide an urgent assessment of Ms Dalston's housing needs. A care plan was completed and discussed with Ms Dalston (MJ pages 16 to 20).

17 A child in need assessment of James Dalston has also been completed by the Assessment Family Support Team Social Worker, Simone Ibrahim (MJ pages 37 to 43). The Social Worker stated that 'James presents as very mature and sensible and certainly appears to cope well with assisting his mother practically . . . however he said that when his mother has a seizure he is "terrified" and feels "panicky" about what to do'. James clearly bears a lot of responsibility for supporting his mother and it is to his immense credit that he appears to be coping, in the main, well at home and at school.

18 The social worker report says that Ms Dalston feels guilty about the responsibilities she places on James and is concerned that he doesn't 'get out enough'. Part of the reason for the latter being previous harassment from neighbours. The social worker recommends that:—
- (a) the School be made more aware of James's home circumstances;
- (b) Home Care services be provided for Christine to alleviate James of some of his responsibilities;
- (c) counselling be provided for James;
- (d) information be provided for after school activities;
- (e) information be provided to James to help him better understand his mother's illness;
- (f) Advice be provided to Christine and James on the use of the Carephone Service (Telehelp); and that,
- (g) the family be transferred to a ground floor property.

The assessment was discussed and approved by Christine.

19    Having read and considered these assessments, the Social Services file and the matters raised by the Applicants' solicitor I have asked that the Social Worker also consider the following:

    (*a*)    provision for James when his mother is hospitalised; in particular, whether a foster carer might be appropriate, or financial assistance for placement with a family friend;

    (*b*)    advice on use of Telehelp if Christine has a fit in the bath.

20    Although the Applicants' request for rehousing will be supported by Social Services, the speed with which and likelihood of accommodation being provided is determined by the Respondent's housing policies.

21    The Respondent Council faces great demands on its scarce housing stock. Ground floor properties being particularly sought after and limited in availability. Applications for rehousing are awarded priority in accordance with the Council's allocations policy (MJ pages 44 to 55). Ms Dalston's case was reviewed by the Council's Medical Advisor on 13 February 1996 and awarded a 'C' priority (MJ pages 56 and 57). This is a low priority and as such Christine has no foreseeable prospect of rehousing (MJ page 60).

22    The relevant Housing Manager has, none the less, indicated (MJ pages 58 and 59) that he will be awarding Ms Dalston an urgent management priority. This will increase the number of points Ms Dalston has for rehousing, but due to the shortage of ground floor properties and the number of applicants with a higher priority it does not significantly increase the likelihood of an offer being made.

23    I am satisfied the assessments undertaken have addressed the needs of these Applicants and the services that are, and will be provided, will alleviate much of their difficulties. Their needs will be subject to regular review and a social worker, Gordon Richards, has been allocated to the family.

Sworn by Morton Jobsworth
at 69 Cheapside, Doombridge, London W25
in
this 2nd June, 1996

Before me,
A Solicitor empowered to accept Oaths

This Affidavit is filed on behalf of the Respondent

## H.   Consent Order

IN THE HIGH COURT OF JUSTICE                         Case No. CO/ 96
QUEEN'S BENCH DIVISION
CROWN OFFICE LIST

BETWEEN                             R

—and—

THE MAYOR AND BURGESSES OF THE
LONDON BOROUGH OF DOOMBRIDGE    Respondents

ex parte
CHRISTINE DALSTON
JAMES DALSTON
(A minor by his Mother and Next Friend Christine Dalston)    Applicants

---

## CONSENT ORDER

---

UPON the Respondents undertaking to carry out an assessment of the Applicants' need for accommodation under Part III of the National Assistance Act 1948, and thereafter reaching a service provision decision in accordance with Section 47(1)(*b*) of the NHS and Communtiy Care Act 1990 within a reasonable time, it is hereby ordered by consent that:

1 The proceedings number CO/713/96 be withdrawn, on the basis that the Respondents do pay the Applicants' costs, to be taxed if not agreed.

2 The final hearing of this matter which has been fixed for 20 June be vacated.

3 Legal Aid Taxation of the Applicants' costs.

4 The reasons for the making of this order are that:
   (*a*) The Respondent Council has complied with its undertaking to the Court dated 4 March 1996 by carrying out adequate assessments of need for both Applicants and reaching service provision decisions thereafter which are acceptable to the Applicants.
   (*b*) The Respondent Council has agreed to pay the Applicants' costs, to be taxed if not agreed.

DATED this                    day of                    1996


........................................    ........................................
Solicitor to the Council                    Messrs Marx, Trotsky & Luxembourg
Legal Services                              Garden House,
London Borough of Doombridge                39 Falcon Court
Town Hall, Acacia Place,                    London W25
Doombridge
London W25

Ref:                                        Ref:

Solicitors for the Respondents              Solicitors for the Applicant

## I. Final Order

IN THE HIGH COURT OF JUSTICE                                    CO/ 96

QUEEN'S BENCH DIVISION                    Dated the 25th day of June 1996

CROWN OFFICE LIST

BEFORE MASTER QUILLS QC MASTER OF THE CROWN OFFICE IN CHAMBERS

IN THE MATTER of an application for Judicial Review

R

—and—

THE MAYOR AND BURGESSES OF THE
LONDON BOROUGH OF DOOMBRIDGE

ex parte
CHRISTINE DALSTON
JAMES DALSTON
(A minor by his Mother and Next Friend Christine Dalston)

UPON READING the form of consent dated the 18th day of June 1996 signed by solicitors on behalf of all parties and

UPON the Respondents undertaking to carry out an assessment of the Applicants' need for accommodation under Part III of the National Assistance Act 1948, and thereafter reaching a service provision decision in accordance with Section 47(1)(b) of the NHS and Community Care Act 1990 within a reasonable time

AND the Applicant having withdrawn the Notice of Motion herein dated the 11th day of March 1996

BY CONSENT

IT IS ORDERED that the costs of this application be taxed by a Taxing Master if not agreed and paid by the Respondents to the Applicants' Solicitors

AND IT IS ORDERED the final hearing of this matter which has been fixed for 20 June be vacated

AND IT IS FURTHER ORDERED that the costs of the Applicant be taxed on the standard basis in accordance with Regulation 107 of the Civil Legal Aid (General) Regulations 1989

By the Court

# Index

437